SOURCES

Notable Selections in *Early Childhood Education*

About the Editors

KAREN MENKE PACIOREK is an associate professor of early childhood education at Eastern Michigan University. She received a B.A. in early childhood education from the University of Pittsburgh, an M.A. in early childhood education from George Washington University, and a Ph.D. in early childhood education from Peabody College of Vanderbilt University. She is the coeditor, with Joyce Huth Munro, of *Annual Editions: Early Childhood Education* (Dushkin Publishing Group/Brown & Benchmark Publishers). She is the president of the 4,500-member Michigan Association for the Education of Young Children. Her presentations at local, state, and national conferences center around curriculum planning, guiding behavior, and preparing the learning environment. She also does consulting work with child-care centers and public schools in the Ypsilanti, Michigan, area.

JOYCE HUTH MUNRO is the director of Teacher Education at Centenary College. She received her Ph.D. in early childhood education from Peabody College of Vanderbilt University and her M.Ed. from the University of South Carolina. She is the coordinator of the Case Researchnet for the National Association of Early Childhood Teacher Educators and a case editor for Allyn & Bacon's Case Series in Education. Her interests in research and writing have focused on the use of teaching cases in the preparation of preservice teachers and on in-service professional development. Currently, she is studying the use of technology in student-teacher conferencing.

SOURCES

Notable Selections
in *Early Childhood*
Education

Edited by

KAREN MENKE PACIOREK

Eastern Michigan University

JOYCE HUTH MUNRO

Centenary College

Dushkin Publishing Group / Brown & Benchmark Publishers

A TIMES MIRROR HIGHER EDUCATION GROUP COMPANY

We dedicate this book to our major professor, mentor, and friend Earline Doak Kendall. Thank you for all you have done for us, the profession, and especially for young children and their families.

Manufactured in the United States of America

First Edition

10 9 8 7 6 5 4 3 2 1

Library of Congress Cataloging-in-Publication Data
  Main entry under title:
    Sources: notable selections in early childhood education/edited by Karen Menke Paciorek and Joyce Huth Munro.
    Includes bibliographical references and index.
    1. Education, Preschool. 2. Education, Elementary. 3. Child development.
    I. Paciorek, Karen Menke, *comp.* II. Munro, Joyce Huth, *comp.*
                                                                            372.21
  1-56134-321-8   95-74675

 Printed on Recycled Paper

1.1   From Erik H. Erikson, "Erik H. Erikson's 'A Healthy Personality for Every Child,' " in Robert H. Anderson and Harold G. Shane, eds., *As the Twig Is Bent* (Houghton Mifflin, 1971). Copyright © 1971 by Robert H. Anderson and Harold G. Shane. Reprinted by permission.

Acknowledgments and copyrights are continued at the back of the book on pages 371–373, which constitute an extension of the copyright page.

Preface

*A*lthough it has been shaped by psychology, sociology, and other related fields, the study of early childhood education has matured through the years and has produced its own theories, methods, and philosophies. New theories have revolutionized how we view the intelligence of children. What we have learned has had great impact on programs for children. Research informs our view of family structures and provides better ways of communication. As a formal discipline, early childhood education is fascinating and dynamic.

The field of early childhood education is all about establishing good early childhood programs: planning effective curricula; arranging appropriate facilities, equipment, and materials; and communicating with parents, staff, and administration. And at its core, early childhood education is all about working with young children. These are the critical topics discussed in the 43 selections contained in this book, culled from the works of distinguished educators and theorists. The authors' views have all shaped contemporary understanding of early childhood experiences and learning settings, and they are worth encountering firsthand.

Sources: Notable Selections in Early Childhood Education takes a unique approach in providing an overview of the field. First, this book brings together classic articles, book excerpts, speeches, and U.S. government bulletins representing the work of predominant scholars. Such a variety of primary sources provides instructors and students with a wide range of fresh and important information on early childhood education.

Second, each selection is preceded by an introductory headnote that establishes the relevance of the selection and provides biographical information on the author. The authors whose works were chosen for inclusion in this anthology are not all educators. Some are theorists, psychologists, philosophers, social activists, medical doctors, and industrialists. Yet when they write about young children, insights from these related disciplines blend and converge. From one selection to another, a strong interdisciplinary dimension is obvious.

The third unique feature of *Sources* is an amazing continuity of philosophy and perspective over time. Through many decades, the central tenets of practice that are suitable for young children have been highly consistent, although the authors' terminology has changed. So a particular theme—for example, play as children's work—introduced by a kindergarten pioneer long ago in a series of scholarly letters sounds remarkably the same today discussed by a prominent theorist in an article from a professional journal. It is obvious from the original sources included in this book that cutting-edge knowledge of today and landmark studies of yesterday are based on steady, consistent thought and belief about young children. To highlight similarities of philosophy over time, the selections in each chapter are in chronological order.

Finally, we have included several selections that are at variance with the continuity and consistency found throughout this anthology. Some of these articles were startling when they first appeared in print, and several still are today. They may have shaped our understanding of early childhood education or they may have been discredited. Nevertheless, they have been included here because they have historical significance.

Selection procedure Choosing selections for *Sources* required us to sift through over 400 years of classic writings about young children by the leaders in the field. We initially worked chronologically but quickly discovered patterns emerging: much of what authors in the late 1800s or early 1900s said were the best practices for young children are the same views being proposed today. The history of this profession is deeply rooted in practices that have proved successful over time and are still working today. We chose 15 broad topics related to the care and education of young children and grouped older writings together with more recent, related selections. The reader is now able to see similarities over 100 years. This approach allows the reader to enjoy what we call classic classics and contemporary classics.

Professionals in early childhood education have changed very little in their fundamental thinking over the past 100 years. Some educators may have jumped on bandwagons, but for the most part there has been little philosophical change in how major theorists believe children learn best. What we show in this collection of notable selections is a strong continuity in the field of early childhood education. Over time, most of what educators have been saying are the best practices for children are still what educators today believe to be the most developmentally appropriate ways to care for and educate young children.

Just as it would be very difficult to choose one Picasso painting or one Mozart piece for inclusion in a collection, it was difficult to choose only one selection from among the many publications of certain authors. Which selection should we choose? We turned to many individuals who gave us suggestions and advice. We appreciate all of their assistance.

A word to the instructor An *Instructor's Manual With Test Questions* (multiple-choice and essay) is available through the publisher for instructors using *Sources: Notable Selections in Early Childhood Education* in the classroom.

We welcome comments about the choices made for this first edition of *Sources* and encourage readers to submit selections for consideration for future editions. Send your input to us in care of SOURCES, Dushkin Publishing Group/Brown & Benchmark Publishers, Sluice Dock, Guilford, CT 06437 or on-line at: ted_paciorek@emuvax.emich.edu or jhmunro@aol.com.

Acknowledgments We have maintained an ongoing relationship with the outstanding professionals at Dushkin Publishing Group/Brown & Benchmark Publishers for the past 10 years. We are grateful to Mimi Egan, publisher for

iii

*Notable
Selections in
Early
Childhood
Education*

the Sources series, for her advice and support from the very beginning. We are also grateful to Rick Connelly, vice president and general manager, and Ian A. Nielsen, publisher of Annual Editions, who have generously agreed to our requests and have supported us and our work on *Sources* and *Annual Editions: Early Childhood Education.*

We have benefited from the support and interest of many professionals who assisted with early drafts of the table of contents for this book. We are deeply indebted to Dorothy Hewes, who gave her time and valuable expertise to the selection process. She is truly the historical expert in the field and the one person who has kept the history of this profession alive while sparking an interest in others to explore its roots. We were also fortunate to have the insightful suggestions of Linda Edwards, Blythe Hinitz, George Morrison, Edna Ranck, and Carol Seefeldt. Janalen Riccinto, a graduate assistant at Eastern Michigan University, and Vicki Silfies, a library assistant at Centenary College, deserve special recognition for their dedicated and thorough work. And we are grateful to Marilyn Smith, executive director of the National Association for the Education of Young Children, for her contributions of historical facts.

Finally, we owe much to our families for putting up with the endless piles of articles all over the floors in our homes and the hours we spent in front of the computer. To Michael, Clark, and Clay Paciorek and to Jamie Munro, many thanks. We love you.

Karen Menke Paciorek
Eastern Michigan University

Joyce Huth Munro
Centenary College

SOURCES

Contents

Preface i

PART ONE   *Development of Young Children 1*

CHAPTER 1   Growth and Learning 3

1.1   **ERIK H. ERIKSON,** from "Erik H. Erikson's 'A Healthy Personality for Every Child,' " in Robert H. Anderson and Harold G. Shane, eds., *As the Twig Is Bent* 3

"In each stage of child development . . . there is a central problem that has to be solved . . . if the child is to proceed with vigor and confidence to the next stage."

1.2   **JEAN-CLAUDE BRINGUIER,** from *Conversations With Jean Piaget* 14

"A test is related to performance, to results. We're interested in how the child reasons and how he discovers new tools, so we use direct conversation, informal conversation."

1.3   **DAVID ELKIND,** from "The Hurried Child: Is Our Impatient Society Depriving Kids of Their Right to Be Children?" *Instructor & Teacher* 23

"We must see childhood as a stage of life, not just the anteroom to life."

CHAPTER 2   Children in Crisis 29

2.1   **ANNA FREUD AND DOROTHY T. BURLINGHAM,** from *War and Children* 29

"An individual is afraid quite naturally and sensibly when there is some real danger present in the outside world which threatens either his safety or his whole existence."

2.2 **ROBERT COLES,** from *The South Goes North: Volume III of Children of Crisis* 37

"It is about time the lives of ghetto children were seen as something more than a tangle of psychopathology and flawed performances in school."

2.3 **MARIAN WRIGHT EDELMAN,** from *The Measure of Our Success: A Letter to My Children and Yours* 42

"Family and community values and supports are disintegrating among all races and income groups, reflecting the spiritual as well as economic poverty of our nation."

PART TWO *Programs for Young Children* 51

CHAPTER 3 Day Nurseries/Nursery Schools 53

3.1 **ABIGAIL ADAMS ELIOT,** from "Report of the Ruggles Street Nursery School and Training Center," in Samuel J. Braun and Esther P. Edwards, eds., *History and Theory of Early Childhood Education* 53

"With a little wise guidance perhaps, each child selects what he wants from a special closet containing a variety of material.... In this work he is guided as little as possible and is limited only in two ways: he must make a genuine attempt to use what he has taken, and he must put away one thing before taking another."

3.2 **KATHERINE H. READ,** from *The Nursery School: A Human Relationships Laboratory* 56

"Time is required to build as well as understand relationships, but during the process these 'rules' will give clues to appropriate action."

3.3 **ALICE STERLING HONIG,** from "Quality Infant/Toddler Caregiving: Are There Magic Recipes?" *Young Children* 71

"Metamorphosed through adult sensibilities, skills, and creativity, daily care situations can be turned into prime opportunities to further the early learning careers of infants and toddlers."

CHAPTER 4 Kindergarten 78

4.1 **ELIZABETH P. PEABODY,** from *Guide to the Kindergarten and Intermediate Class*, rev. ed. 78

"Let a child himself hammer out some substance with a mallet, and he will never forget the meaning of malleable."

vii

*Notable
Selections
in Early
Childhood
Education*

4.2 **PATTY SMITH HILL,** from "Kindergarten," in *The American Educator Encyclopedia* 82

"The unification in training, supervision and organization of teachers of early childhood has produced whole-hearted cooperation and good will on the part of kindergarten and primary teachers, creating curricula so closely integrated that the child passes from one to the other undisturbed by the normal differences which legitimately survive as the child matures."

4.3 **BERNARD SPODEK,** from "The Kindergarten: A Retrospective and Contemporary View," in Lilian G. Katz, ed., *Current Topics in Early Childhood Education, vol. 4* 92

"The difference between the concerns of kindergartens of 30 years ago and those of today is with the intensity of academic instruction in the kindergarten."

PART THREE *Practice With Young Children* 105

CHAPTER 5 Play 107

5.1 **FRIEDRICH FROEBEL,** from *The Education of Man* 107

"[T]o learn a thing in life and through doing is much more developing, cultivating, and strengthening, than to learn it merely through the verbal communication of ideas."

5.2 **MILDRED B. PARTEN,** from "Social Participation Among Pre-School Children," *The Journal of Abnormal and Social Psychology* 114

"One child suggests that they are all making supper. Soon the various family roles are assigned or adopted and the children speak about their shares in preparing the meal."

5.3 **LUCY SPRAGUE MITCHELL,** from *Our Children and Our Schools: A Picture and Analysis of How Today's Public School Teachers Are Meeting the Challenge of New Knowledge and New Cultural Needs* 120

"With adults as well as with children, interests and attitudes are not built up through words but through direct experiences. . . . So we philosophized little in the beginning but began to work actively with individual teachers in what they called 'demonstration teaching.' "

CHAPTER 6   Learning Environments   130

6.1   **MARIA MONTESSORI,** from *The Montessori Method: Scientific Pedagogy as Applied to Child Education in "The Children's Houses"*   130

"The lessons, then, are individual, and *brevity* must be one of the chief characteristics."

6.2   **HARRIET M. JOHNSON,** from *Children in the Nursery School*   135

"An urban situation must be faced as an urban situation and attacked and developed for what it is worth, not as a poor substitute for the country. The country environment must be treated in the same way."

6.3   **SYBIL KRITCHEVSKY, ELIZABETH PRESCOTT, AND LEE WALLING,** from *Planning Environments for Young Children: Physical Space*   144

"Just as adults behave in one way at a table set for a formal dinner, and in a very different way at the same table set for a poker game, children tend to behave in ways suggested by spatial contents and arrangements."

CHAPTER 7   Sound Practice   150

7.1   **JOHN DEWEY,** from "Three Years of the University Elementary School," Stenographic Report of a Speech Prepared for a Meeting of the Parents' Association of the University Elementary School   150

"The various kinds of work, carpentry, cooking, sewing, and weaving, are selected as involving different kinds of skill, and demanding different types of intellectual attitude on the part of the child, and because they represent some of the most important activities of the everyday outside world."

7.2   **SAMUEL CHESTER PARKER AND ALICE TEMPLE,** from *Unified Kindergarten and First-Grade Teaching*   156

"Strange to say, arithmetic, in the form of counting and measuring, has been more highly developed in some kindergartens than in many first grades."

7.3   **ELIZABETH JONES AND LOUISE DERMAN-SPARKS,** from "Meeting the Challenge of Diversity," *Young Children*   160

"Early childhood educators committed to developmentally appropriate practice . . . have a solid foundation for meeting the challenges of diversity."

7.4   **NATIONAL ASSOCIATION FOR THE EDUCATION OF YOUNG CHILDREN,** from *Developmentally Appropriate Practice in Early*

"The challenge for curriculum planners and teachers is to ensure that the content of the curriculum is taught so as to take optimum advantage of the child's natural abilities, interests, and enthusiasm for learning."

PART FOUR   *Teaching Young Children   183*

CHAPTER 8   Teacher Preparation and Development   185

8.1   SUSAN E. BLOW, from "Kindergarten Education," in Nicholas Murray Butler, ed., *Education in the United States*   185

"The power of kindergarten over the minds of its students arises from the fact that it connects the ideal of self-culture with the ideal of child-nurture."

8.2   MARGARET McMILLAN, from *The Nursery School*   191

"The teacher of little children is not merely giving lessons. She is helping to make a brain and nervous system, and this work which is going to determine all that comes after, requires a finer perception and a wider training and outlook than is needed by any other kind of teacher."

8.3   ROBERT ROSENTHAL AND LENORE JACOBSON, from *Pygmalion in the Classroom: Teacher Expectation and Pupils' Intellectual Development*   193

"[C]hildren defined as disadvantaged are expected by their teachers to be unable to learn."

8.4   LILIAN G. KATZ, from "Developmental Stages of Preschool Teachers," *The Elementary School Journal*   205

"It is useful to think of the growth of teachers as occuring in stages, linked very generally to experience gained over time."

CHAPTER 9   Observation and Assessment   211

9.1   DOROTHY H. COHEN AND VIRGINIA STERN, from *Observing and Recording the Behavior of Young Children*   211

"If we tend to see play materials as a means of keeping idle hands busy, or if we evaluate their use in terms of work, we are likely to miss the special role they do play."

9.2   **ARNOLD GESELL,** from "Early Mental Growth," in Arnold Gesell et al., *The First Five Years of Life: A Guide to the Study of the Preschool Child* 224

"[T]he demands of society and the findings of science are compelling us to see a new significance in the preschool years."

9.3   **SAMUEL J. MEISELS,** from "Uses and Abuses of Developmental Screening and School Readiness Testing," *Young Children* 233

"The use of exlusionary tests suggests that children should conform to school programs, rather than schools adjusting to the needs of children."

CHAPTER 10   Parenting 246

10.1   **BETTYE M. CALDWELL,** from "What Is the Optimal Learning Environment for the Young Child?" *American Journal of Orthopsychiatry* 246

"[T]he optimal environment for the young child is one in which the child is cared for in his own home in the context of a warm, continuous emotional relationship with his own mother under conditions of varied sensory input."

10.2   **MARGARET O'BRIEN STEINFELS,** from *Who's Minding the Children? The History and Politics of Day Care in America* 259

"We cling to that catchword—family-centered—because it permits us to ignore the responsibilities and reordering of priorities that would go along with a social and economic system that would make the raising of children, the 'making of human beings human' an important task."

10.3   **IRA J. GORDON,** from "Parent Education and Parent Involvement: Retrospect and Prospect," *Childhood Education* 266

"We need to tie, where possible, parent education efforts to work, family income, and housing and zoning programs, medicare and medicaid, teacher education, professional education of social workers, psychologists, etc."

PART FIVE   *Educational Systems for Young Children* 277

CHAPTER 11   Employer-Sponsored 279

11.1   **ROBERT OWEN,** from *The Life of Robert Owen* 279

"These children, to be well trained and educated, should never hear from their teacher an angry word, or see a cross or threatening expression of countenance."

11.2   JAMES L. HYMES, from "Industrial Day Care's Roots in America," *Proceedings of the Conference on Industry and Day Care*   283

"I am taken with how costly good servies to children and families have to be. I am taken with how costly bad services always are."

CHAPTER 12   Federal Involvement in Early Childhood   289

12.1   DOAK S. CAMPBELL, FREDERICK H. BAIR, AND OSWALD L. HARVEY, from *Educational Activities of the Works Progress Administration*   289

"The emergency nursery school is not intended as a convenience for the relief of parents; it is not a crèche but an educational institution."

12.2   KEITH OSBORN, from "Project Head Start: An Assessment," *Educational Leadership*   297

"[F]or me—as well as many teachers, physicians, social workers and others who worked actively in the program—the day to day, here and now experience which the children received made the program a success."

12.3   ROCHELLE BECK, from "The White House Conferences on Children: An Historical Perspective," *Harvard Educational Review*   303

"In the sweep of seven decades, the image conveyed is one of children, smaller than anyone else, lighter in physical weight and political clout, easily picked up and blown wherever the winds of economic, political, and social movements were heading."

CHAPTER 13   Research   317

13.1   G. STANLEY HALL, from "The Contents of Children's Minds on Entering School," in Theodate L. Smith, ed., *Aspects of Child Life and Education by G. Stanley Hall and Some of His Pupils*   317

"Many children half believe the doll feels cold or blows, that it pains flowers to tear or burn them, or that in summer when the tree is alive it makes it ache to pound or chop it."

13.2   GRETA G. FEIN AND ALISON CLARKE-STEWART, from *Day Care in Context*   329

"Day care that focuses on the child becomes unavoidably future-oriented, for within a developmental framework the present and the future are interlocked."

xii

*Notable
Selections
in Early
Childhood
Education*

13.3 LAWRENCE J. SCHWEINHART AND DAVID P. WEIKART, from
"Changed Lives, Significant Benefits: The High/Scope Perry Preschool
Project to Date," *High/Scope Resource* 337

"The results are in. High-quality, active learning preschool programs can
help young children in poverty . . . to become economically self-sufficient,
socially responsible adults."

CHAPTER 14 Reform/Policy 350

14.1 DOROTHY W. BARUCH, from "When the Need for Wartime
Services for Children Is Past—What of the Future?" *Journal of
Consulting Psychology* 350

"[The child care centers] have shown themselves worthy of continuing to
serve children and parents in the postwar world . . . as a well-integrated
and cohesive part of what all the schools of the nation must eventually
undertake."

14.2 MARVIN LAZERSON, from "Social Reform and Early-Childhood
Education: Some Historical Perspectives," *Urban Education* 358

"I am terribly pessimistic about the possibilities of substantive social
change through preschooling."

14.3 SHARON LYNN KAGAN, from "The New Advocacy in Early
Childhood Education," *Teachers College Record* 366

"We must put ambivalence aside, muster our energy, and stay informed
and active. The profession needs all its members, practitioners and advocates, now as never before."

Index 374

PART ONE

Development of Young Children

Chapter 1 Growth and Learning 3

Chapter 2 Children in Crisis 29

CHAPTER 1 Growth and Learning

1.1 ERIK H. ERIKSON

A Healthy Personality for Every Child

Erik Erikson's stages of psychosocial development have been the corner-stone of our knowledge base in viewing the complex area of personality. As a follower of Sigmund Freud, he emphasized the connections between the ego and social forces that influence it during one's lifetime. His thesis is that for optimal development to occur, the ego must adjust to society's needs and changes. The following selection is from *A Healthy Personality for Every Child: A Digest of the Fact Finding Report to the Midcentury White House Conference on Children and Youth* (1951). In that report, Erikson expanded on his eight life-span stages of psychosocial development. Included here are the first three stages, which apply to personality development of the young child. The focus on trust, autonomy, and initiative all are accompanied with specific examples of how adults in the life of a young child can shape the development of a healthy personality through their interactions with the child.

Erikson (1902–1994) was a psychoanalyst at the Austin Riggs Center and a professor of human development at Harvard University. Throughout his career, he presented numerous lectures based on research in which he participated at Harvard, Yale University, and the University of California. His experiences in clinical practice provided early childhood educators with a specific framework for healthy development of the child's personality. He believed children's development is based on their interactions with others, including parents and peers, and on their experiences in school and at play.

Many attempts have been made to describe the attributes of healthy personality. They have been put succinctly as the ability to love and the ability to work. A recent review of the literature suggests that the individual with a healthy personality is one who actively masters his environment, shows a unity of personality, and is able to perceive the world and himself correctly. Clearly, none of these criteria applies to a child. It seems to us best, then, to present . . . an outline that has the merit of indicating at one and the same time the main course of personality development and the attributes of a healthy personality.

This developmental outline was worked out by Erik H. Erikson, a psychologist and practicing psychoanalyst who has made anthropological field studies and has had much experience with children. It is an analysis that derives from psychological theory, to which is added knowledge from the fields of child development and cultural anthropology. The whole is infused with the author's insight and personal philosophy.

In each stage of child development, the author says, there is a central problem that has to be solved, temporarily at least, if the child is to proceed with vigor and confidence to the next stage. These problems, these conflicts of feeling and desire, are never solved in entirety. Each shift in experience and environment presents them in a new form. It is held, however, that each type of conflict appears in its purest, most unequivocal form at a particular stage of child development, and that if the problem is well solved at the time the basis for progress to the next stage is well laid.

In a sense personality development follows biological principles. Biologists have found that everything that grows has a groundplan that is laid out at its start. Out of this groundplan the parts arise, each part having its time of special ascendancy. Together these parts form a functioning whole. If a part does not arise at its appointed time, it will never be able to form fully since the moment for the rapid outgrowth of some other part will have arrived. Moreover, a part that misses its time of ascendancy or is severely damaged during its formative period is apt to doom, in turn, the whole hierarchy of organs. Proper rate and normal sequence is necessary if functional harmony is to be secured.

Personality represents the most complicated functioning of the human organism and does not consist of parts in the organic sense. Instead of the development of organs, there is the development of locomotor, sensory, and social capacities and the development of individual modes of dealing with experience. Nevertheless, proper rate and proper sequence are as important here as in physical growth, and functional harmony is achieved only if development proceeds according to the groundplan.

In all this it is encouraging for parents and others who have children in charge to realize that in the sequence of his most personal experiences, just as in the sequence of organ formation, the child can be trusted to follow inner laws of development, and needs from adults chiefly love, encouragement, and guidance.

The operation of biological laws is seen, also, in the fact that there is constant interplay between organism and environment and that problems of personality functioning are never solved once and for all. Each of the components of the healthy personality to be described below is present in some form from the beginning, and the struggle to maintain it continues throughout life.

For example, a baby may show something like "autonomy" or a will of his own in the way he angrily tries to free his head when he is tightly held. Nevertheless, it is not until the second year of life that he begins to experience the whole conflict between being an autonomous creature and a dependent one. It is not until then that he is ready for a decisive encounter with the people around him, and it is not until then that they feel called upon to train him or otherwise curb his free-questing spirit. The struggle goes on for months and finally, under favorable circumstances, some compromise between dependence and independence is reached that gives the child a sense of well-being.

The sense of autonomy thus achieved is not a permanent possession, however. There will be other challenges to that sense and other solutions more in keeping with later stages of development. Nevertheless, once established at two or three years of age, this early sense of autonomy will be a bulwark against later frustrations and will permit the emergence of the next developmental problem at a time that is most favorable for its solution.

So it is with all the personality components to be described. They appear in miniature early in life. The struggle to secure them against tendencies to act otherwise comes to a climax at a time determined by emergence of the necessary physical and mental abilities. There are, throughout life, other challenges and other responses but they are seldom so serious and seldom so decisive as those of the critical years.

In all this, it must be noted in addition, there is not the strict dichotomy that the analysis given below suggests. With each of the personality components to be described, it is not all or nothing: trust *or* mistrust, autonomy *or* doubt, and so on. Instead, each individual has some of each. His health of personality is determined by the preponderance of the favorable over the unfavorable, as well as by what manner of compensations he develops to cope with his disabilities.

THE SENSE OF TRUST

The component of the healthy personality that is the first to develop is the sense of trust. The crucial time for its emergence is the first year of life. As with the other personality components to be described, the sense of trust is not something that develops independent of other manifestations of growth. It is not that the infant learns how to use his body for purposeful movement, learns to recognize people and objects around him, and also develops a sense of trust. Rather, the concept "sense of trust" is a short-cut expression intended to convey the characteristic flavor of all the child's satisfying experiences at this early age. Or, to say it another way, this psychological formulation serves to condense, summarize, and synthesize the most important underlying changes that give meaning to the infant's concrete and diversified experience.

Trust can exist only in relation to something. Consequently a sense of trust cannot develop until the infant is old enough to be aware of objects and persons and to have some feeling that he is a separate individual. At about three months of age a baby is likely to smile if somebody comes close and talks to him. This shows that he is aware of the approach of the other person, that pleasurable sensations are aroused. If, however, the person moves too quickly or speaks too sharply the baby may look apprehensive or cry. We will not "trust" the unusual situation but will have a feeling of uneasiness, of mistrust, instead.

Experiences connected with feeding are a prime source for the development of trust. At around four months of age a hungry baby will grow quiet and show signs of pleasure at the sound of an approaching footstep, anticipating (trusting) that he will be held and fed. This repeated experience of being hungry, seeing food, receiving food, and feeling relieved and comforted assures the baby that the world is a dependable place.

Later experiences, starting at around five months of age, add another dimension to the sense of trust. Through endless repetitions of attempts to grasp for and hold objects, the baby is finally successful in controlling and adapting his movements in such a way as to reach his goal. Through these and other feats of muscular coordination the baby is gradually able to trust his own body to do his bidding.

The baby's trust-mistrust problem is symbolized in the game of peek-a-boo. In this game, which babies begin to like at about four months of age, an object disappears and then reappears. There is a slightly tense expression on the baby's face when the object goes away; its reappearance is greeted by wriggles and smiles. Only gradually does a baby learn that things continue to exist even though he does not see them, that there is order and stability in his universe. Peek-a-boo proves the point by playful repetition.

Studies of mentally ill individuals and observations of infants who have been grossly deprived of affection suggest that trust is an early-formed and important element in the healthy personality. Psychiatrists find again and again that the most serious illnesses occur in patients who have been sorely neglected or abused or otherwise deprived of love in infancy. Similarly, it is a common finding of psychological and social investigators that individuals diagnosed as a "psychopathic personality" were so unloved in infancy that they have no reason to trust the human race and, therefore, no sense of responsibility toward their fellow men.

Observations of infants brought up in emotionally unfavorable institutions or removed to hospitals with inadequate facilities for psychological care support these findings. A recent report says: "Infants under six months of age who have been in an institution for some time present a well-defined picture.

The outstanding features are listlessness, emaciation and pallor, relative immobility, quietness, unresponsiveness to stimuli like a smile or a coo, indifferent appetite, failure to gain weight properly despite ingestion of diets which are entirely adequate, frequent stools, poor sleep, an appearance of unhappiness, proneness to febrile episodes, absence of sucking habits."[1]

Another investigation of children separated from their mothers at six to twelve months and not provided with an adequate substitute comes to much the same conclusion: "The emotional tone is one of apprehension and sadness, there is withdrawal from the environment amounting to rejection of it, there is no attempt to contact a stranger and no brightening if a stranger contacts him. Activities are retarded and the child often sits or lies inert in a dazed stupor. Insomnia is common and lack of appetite universal. Weight is lost, and the child becomes prone to current infections."[2]

Most significant for our present point, these reactions are most likely to occur in children who up to the time of separation at six to nine months of age had a happy relation with their mothers, while those whose relations were unhappy are relatively unaffected. It is at about this age that the struggle between trusting and mistrusting the world comes to a climax, for it is then that the child first perceives clearly that he and his environment are things apart. That at this time formerly happy infants should react so badly to separation suggests, indeed, that they had a faith which now was shattered. Happily, there is usually spectacular change for the better when the maternal presence and love are restored.

It is probably unnecessary to describe the numerous ways in which stimuli from without and from within may cause an infant distress. Birth is believed by some experts to be a painful experience for the baby. Until fairly recently doctors were likely to advise that babies be fed on schedule and that little attention be paid to their cries of hunger at other times. Many infants spent many of the waking hours of the first four months doubled up with colic. All of them had to be bathed and dressed at stated times, whether they liked it or not. Add to these usual discomforts the fact that some infants are handled rather roughly by their parents, that others hear angry words and loud voices, and that a few are really mistreated, and it will not be difficult to understand why some infants may feel the world is a place that cannot be trusted.

In most primitive societies and in some sections of our own society the attention accorded infants is more in line with natural processes. In such societies separation from the mother is less abrupt, in that for some time after birth the baby is kept close to the warmth and comfort of its mother's body and at its least cry the breast is produced. Throughout infancy the baby is surrounded by people who are ready to feed it, fondle it, otherwise comfort it at a moment's notice. Moreover, these ministrations are given spontaneously, wholeheartedly, and without that element of nervous concern that may characterize the efforts of young mothers made self-conscious and insecure by our scientific age.

We must not exaggerate, however. Most infants in our society, too, find smiles and the comfort of mother's soft, warm body accompanying their intake of food, whether from breast or bottle. Coldness, wetness, pain, and boredom—for each misfortune there is prompt and comforting relief. As their own bodies come to be more dependable, there is added to the pleasures of increasing sensory response and motor control the pleasure of the mother's encouragement.

Moreover, babies are rather hardy creatures and are not to be discouraged by inexperienced mothers' mistakes. Even a mother cat has to learn, and the kittens endure gracefully her first clumsy efforts to carry them away from danger. Then, too, psychologists tell us that mothers create a sense of trust in their children not by the particular techniques they employ but by the sensitiveness with which they respond to the children's needs and by their over-all attitude.

For most infants, then, a sense of trust is not difficult to come by. It is the most important element in the personality. It emerges at the most vulnerable period of a child's life. Yet it is the least likely to suffer harm, perhaps because both nature and culture work toward making mothers most maternal at that time.

THE SENSE OF AUTONOMY

The sense of trust once firmly established, the struggle for the next component of the healthy personality begins. The child is now twelve to fifteen months old. Much of his energy for the next two years will center around asserting that he is a human being with a mind and will of his own. A list of some of the items discussed by Spock under the heading, "The One Year Old," will serve to remind us of the characteristics of that age and the problems they create for parents. "Feeling his oats." "The passion to explore." "He gets more dependent and more independent at the same time." "Arranging the house for the wandering baby." "Avoiding accidents." "How do you make him leave certain things alone?" "Dropping and throwing things." "Biting humans." "The small child who won't stay in bed at night."

What is at stake throughout the struggle of these years is the child's sense of autonomy, the sense that he is an independent human being and yet one who is able to use the help and guidance of others in important matters. This stage of development becomes decisive for the ratio between love and hate, between cooperation and wilfulness, for freedom of self-expression and its renunciation in the make-up of the individual. The favorable outcome is self-control without loss of self-esteem. The unfavorable outcome is doubt and shame.

Before the sense of autonomy can develop, the sense of trust must be reasonably well-established and must continue to pervade the child's feeling about himself and his world. Only so dare he respond with confidence to his new-felt desire to assert himself boldly, to appropriate demandingly, and to hurl away without let or hindrance.

As with the previous stage, there is a physiological basis for this characteristic behavior. This is the period of muscle-system maturation and the consequent ability (and doubly felt inability) to coordinate a number of highly conflicting action patterns, such as those of holding on and letting go, walking, talking, and manipulating objects in ever more complicated ways. With these abilities come pressing needs to use them: to handle, to explore, to seize and to drop, to withhold and to expel. And, with all, there is the dominant will, the insistent "Me do" that defies help and yet is so easily frustrated by the inabilities of the hands and feet.

For a child to develop this sense of self-reliance and adequacy that Erikson calls autonomy, it is necessary that he experience over and over again that he is a person who is permitted to make choices. He has to have the right to choose, for example, whether to sit or whether to stand, whether to approach a visitor or to lean against his mother's knee, whether to accept offered food or whether to reject it, whether to use the toilet or to wet his pants. At the same time he must learn some of the boundaries of self-determination. He inevitably finds that there are walls he cannot climb, that there are objects out of reach, that, above all, there are innumerable commands enforced by powerful adults. His experience is much too small to enable him to know what he can and cannot do with respect to the physical environment, and it will take him years to discover the boundaries that mark off what is approved, what is tolerated, and what is forbidden by his elders whom he finds so hard to understand.

As problems of this period, some psychologists have concentrated particularly on bladder and bowel control. Emphasis is put upon the need for care in both timing and mode of training children in the performance of these functions. If parental control is too rigid or if training is started too early, the child is robbed of his opportunity to develop, by his own free choice, gradual control of the contradictory impulses of retention and elimination.

To others who study child development, this matter of toilet training is but a prototype of all the problems of this age range. The sphincters are only part of the whole muscle system, with its general ambiguity of rigidity and relaxation, of flexion and extension. To hold and to relinquish refer to much more than the bowels. As the child acquires the ability to stand on his two feet and move around, he delineates his world as me and you. He can be astonishingly pliable once he has decided that he wants to do what he is supposed to do, but there is no reliable formula for assuring that he will relinquish when he wants to hold on.

The matter of mutual regulation between parent and child (for fathers have now entered the picture to an extent that was rare in the earlier stage) now faces its severest task. The task is indeed one to challenge the most resourceful and the most calm adult. Firmness is necessary, for the child must be protected against the potential anarchy of his as yet untrained sense of discrimination. Yet the adult must back him up in his wish to "stand on his own feet," lest he be overcome by shame that he has exposed himself foolishly and by doubt in his self-worth. Perhaps the most constructive rule a parent can follow is to forbid only what "really matters" and, in such forbidding, to be clear and consistent.

Shame and doubt are emotions that many primitive peoples and some of the less sophisticated individuals in our own society utilize in training children. Shaming exploits the child's sense of being small. Used to excess it misses its objective and may result in open shamelessness, or, at least, in the child's secret determination to do as he pleases when not observed. Such defiance is a normal, even healthy response to demands that a child consider himself, his body, his needs, or his wishes evil and dirty and that he regard those who pass judgment as infallible. Young delinquents may be produced by this means, and others who are oblivious to the opinion of society.

Those who would guide the growing child wisely, then, will avoid shaming him and avoid causing him to doubt that he is a person of worth. They will be firm and tolerant with him so that he can rejoice in being a person of independence and can grant independence to others. As to detailed procedures, it is impossible to prescribe, not only because we do not know and because every situation is different but also because the kind and degree of autonomy that parents are able to grant their small children depends on feelings about themselves that they derive from society. Just as the child's sense of trust is a reflection of the mother's sturdy and realistic faith, so the child's sense of autonomy is a reflection of the parents' personal dignity. Such appears to be the teaching of the comparative study of cultures.

Personal autonomy, independence of the individual, is an especially outstanding feature of the American way of life. American parents, accordingly, are in a particularly favorable position to transmit the sense of autonomy to their children. They themselves resent being bossed, being pushed around; they maintain that everybody has the right to express his opinion and to be in control of his affairs. More easily than people who live according to an authoritarian pattern, they can appreciate a little child's vigorous desire to assert his independence and they can give him the leeway he needs in order to grow up into the upstanding, look-you-in-the-eye kind of individual that Americans admire.

It is not only in early childhood, however, that this attitude toward growing children must be maintained. As was said at the outset, these components of the healthy personality cannot be established once and for all. The period of life in which they first come into being is the most crucial, it is true. But threats to their maintenance occur throughout life. Not only parents, then, but everybody who has significant contact with children and young people must respect their desire for self-assertion, help them hold it within bounds, and avoid treating them in ways that arouse shame or doubt.

This attitude toward children, toward all people, must be maintained in institutional arrangements as well. Great differences in educational and economic opportunity and in access to the law, discrimination of all kinds are threats to this ingredient of mental health. So, too, may be the over-mechanization of our society, the depersonalization of human relations that is likely to accompany large-scale endeavor of all kinds.

Parents, as well as children, are affected by these matters. In fact, parents' ability to grant children the kind of autonomy Americans think desirable depends in part on the way they are treated as employees and citizens. Throughout, the relation must be such as affirms personal dignity. Much of the shame and doubt aroused in children result from the indignity and uncertainty that are an expression of parents' frustrations in love and work. Special attention must be paid to all these matters, then, if we are to avoid destroying the autonomy that Americans have always set store by.

Having become sure, for the time being, that he is a person in his own right and having enjoyed that feeling for a year or so, the child of four or five wants to find out what kind of person he can be. To be any particular kind of person, he sees clearly, involves being able to do particular kinds of things. So he observes with keen attention what all manner of interesting adults do (his parents, the milkman, the truck driver, and so on), tries to imitate their behavior, and yearns for a share in their activities.

This is the period of enterprise and imagination, an ebullient, creative period when phantasy substitutes for literal execution of desires and the meagerest equipment provides material for high imaginings. It is a period of intrusive, vigorous learning, learning that leads away from the child's own limitations into future possibilities. There is intrusion into other people's bodies by physical attack, into other people's ears and minds by loud and aggressive talking. There is intrusion into space by vigorous locomotion and intrusion into the unknown by consuming curiosity.

By this age, too, conscience has developed. The child is no longer guided only by outsiders; there is installed within him a voice that comments on his deeds, and warns and threatens. Close attention to the remarks of any child of this age will confirm this statement. Less obvious, however, are experts' observations that children now begin to feel guilty for mere thoughts, for deeds that have been imagined but never executed. This, they say, is the explanation for the characteristic nightmares of this age period and for the over-reaction to slight punishment.

The problem to be worked out in this stage of development, accordingly, is how to will without too great a sense of guilt. The fortunate outcome of the struggle is a sense of initiative. Failure to win through to that outcome leaves the personality overburdened, and possibly over-restricted by guilt.

It is easy to see how the child's developing sense of initiative may be discouraged. So many of the projects dreamed up at this age are of a kind which cannot be permitted that the child may come to feel he is faced by a universal "No." In addition he finds that many of the projects are impossible of execution and others, even if not forbidden, fail to win the approval of the adults whom he has come to love. Moreover, since he does not always distinguish clearly between actuality and phantasy, his over-zealous conscience may disapprove of even imaginary deeds.

It is very important, therefore, for healthy personality development that much leeway and encouragement be given to the child's show of enterprise and imagination and that punishment be kept at a minimum. Boys and girls at this stage are extraordinarily appreciative of any convincing promise that someday they will be able to do things as well, or maybe better, than father and mother. They enjoy competition (especially if they can win) and insistence on goal; they get great pleasure from conquest. They need numerous examples of the kinds of roles adults assume, and they need a chance to try them out in play.

The ability that is in the making is that of selecting social goals and persevering in the attempt to reach them.

If enterprise and imagination are too greatly curbed, if severe rebukes accompany the frequently necessary denial of permission to carry out desires, a personality may result that is over-constricted. Such a personality cannot live up to its inner capacities for imagination, feeling, or performance, though it may over-compensate by immense activity and find relaxation impossible.

Constriction of personality is a self-imposed constriction, an act of the child's over-zealous conscience. "If I may not do this, I will not even think it," says conscience, "for even thinking it is dangerous." Resentment and bitterness and a vindictive attitude toward the world that forces the restriction may accompany this decision, however, and become unconscious but functioning parts of the personality. Such, at least, is the warning of psychiatrists who have learned to know the inmost feelings of emotionally handicapped children and adults.

This developmental stage has great assets as well as great dangers. At no time in life is the individual more ready to learn avidly and quickly, to become big in the sense of sharing obligation and performance. If during this preschool period the child can get some sense of the various roles and functions that he can perform as an adult, he will be ready to progress joyfully to the next stage, in which he will find pleasurable accomplishment in activities less fraught with phantasy and fear.

There is a lesson in this for later periods of personality development as well. As has been said before, these conflicts that come to a head at particular periods of a child's life are not settled once and for all. The sense of initiative, then, is one that must be continually fostered, and great care must be taken that youngsters and young people do not have to feel guilty for having dared to dream.

Just as we Americans prize autonomy, so too do we prize initiative; in fact, we regard it as the cornerstone of our economic system. There is much in the present industrial and political mode of life that may discourage initiative, that may make a young person think he had best pull in his horns. What these tendencies are and what they may do to youngsters and to their parents, who too must feel free if they are to cultivate the sense of initiative in their children, is a subject that warrants much serious discussion.

THE SENSE OF ACCOMPLISHMENT

The three stages so far described probably are the most important for personality development. With a sense of trust, a sense of autonomy, and a sense of initiative achieved, progress through the later stages is pretty well assured. Whether this is because children who have a good environment in their early years are likely to continue to be so favored, or whether it is because they have attained such strength of personality that they can successfully handle later difficulties, research has not yet made clear. We do know that nearly all children who get a good start continue to develop very well, and we know that some of those who start off poorly continue to be handicapped. Observations of this sort seem to support psychological theory in the conclusion that personality is pretty well set by about six years of age. Since, however, some children develop into psychologically healthy adults in spite of a bad start, and since some who start well run into difficulties later, it is clear that much research is needed before this conclusion can be accepted as wholly correct.

REFERENCES

1. Harry Bakwin, "Emotional Deprivation in Infants," *Journal of Pediatrics*, 35 (October 1949), pp. 512–529.
2. John Bowlby, M.D., Summary of Dr. René Spitz's observations, unpublished manuscript.

Experiments With Children: The Discovery of Developmental Stages

Jean-Claude Bringuier chose a conversation with Jean Piaget (1896–1980) as a good way to present a very small sampling of Piaget's work with young children. Bringuier, a French journalist and television interviewer, captures an insightful collection of thoughts by the renowned Swiss psychologist/educator in the following selection from *Conversations With Jean Piaget* (University of Chicago Press, 1980). The conversation with Bringuier, Piaget's fourth in a series that spanned six years, was conducted in 1969. Bringuier extracts Piaget's thoughts on a variety of topics related to his observations of young children on their development. The interview includes some conversations an associate of Piaget's had with three young children at the International Center for Genetic Epistemology in Geneva, Switzerland. Piaget provides insight on the children's responses.

Piaget, who published his first paper on mollusks at the age of 10, has provided a wealth of information on the development of young children. His writing spans 76 years and includes over 20 million words written on children and their development. He initially became interested in the incorrect answers children gave to I.Q. tests, and he kept daily logs containing observations of his own three children and others. After years of hearing similar responses from children, Piaget began to see patterns emerging. He documented the patterns or stages of development he observed.

A *bottle half full of colored liquid is placed on a table. A child is asked to draw what he sees. He does so.*

Then the bottle is tilted, so that it stands at an angle to the table. The child is asked to make another drawing, again "by copying what he sees." The child draws the table and the tilted bottle; the line indicating the level of the liquid inside is drawn at right angles to the bottle, as in the original position.

15

Jean-Claude Bringuier

Every time the experiment is run, the same "error" is made.

Bringuier: Let's go back to your actual work, to your methods. How do you work? What happens?

Piaget: Ah! I have some fine collaborators. At the beginning of the year I suggest a program of experiments, and it is often further developed by the team members, who add new ideas to it. The students help too, which gives them some training. The experiments are coordinated and complement one another.

Bringuier: The raw material that comes to you is a set of conversations?

Piaget: A series of informal conversations with the children, on topics we've chosen; from them we derive protocols that are the written results of the conversations.

Bringuier: How long does a study last?

Piaget: Usually a year.

Bringuier: How can you tell when it's finished?

Piaget: I have only one criterion. I consider an investigation finished when we no longer find out anything new, that's all. When the new protocols we collect repeat what we already know, we take up a new subject.

Bringuier: So from this raw material you write books?

Piaget: Yes, alas.

Bringuier: Why alas?

Piaget: I mean alas for the reader.

Bringuier: Let's go back to the content of these conversations. Are they a kind of test?

Piaget: No. A test is related to performance, to results. We're interested in how the child reasons and how he discovers new tools, so we use direct conversation, informal conversation.

Bringuier: Is a test always a kind of examination?

Piaget: An examination, yes, and especially a standardization. You ask, you select, you fix the questions in advance. How can we, with our adult minds, know what will be interesting? If you follow the child wherever his answers lead spontaneously, instead of guiding him with preplanned questions, you can find out something new . . . Of course, there are three or four questions we always ask, but beyond that we can explore the whole area instead of sticking to fixed questions.

Bringuier: But surely, some questions have to be included in order to produce statistics. (*Piaget wrinkles his nose.*) Just to have a coherent body of information.

Piaget: Exactly. Once the work of clearing away, of groundbreaking, has been done, which consists of discovering new things and finding things that hadn't been anticipated, you can begin to standardize—at least if you like that sort of thing—and to produce accurate statistics. But I find it more interesting to do the work of groundbreaking.

Bringuier: And you're not afraid the individual cases will be too individual?

Piaget: Why, no. What's so remarkable is that the answers show an unbelievable convergence. While you were preparing this interview, I was classifying the new documents that just came. Twenty-five kids I don't know, and they all say the same thing! At the same age!

Bringuier: Because they're from the same social class and the same city?

Piaget: I don't think so.

Bringuier: Because they're at the same level of evolution?

Piaget: Yes.

Bringuier: I think this brings us to one of your main ideas: that children, regardless of their society and their historical period, go through a series of stages in the evolution of intelligence that is always the same.

Piaget: It's the same because each stage is necessary to the following one. It's called a "sequential order."

Bringuier: Each stage allows the next stage to occur?

Piaget: That's right. It becomes probable, whereas at the beginning it wasn't. Now that can be verified easily enough anywhere, though there will be cases of delay or acceleration.

Bringuier: The order stays the same?

Piaget: Yes.

Bringuier: Now, what is the order? What are the major stages?

Piaget: Well, there are different levels. Sensory-motor intelligence, before language. Then you have . . .

Bringuier: That's in the infant?

Piaget: Yes, the infant. Then the semiotic function appears—language, symbolic play, mental images, and so forth, up until about the age of seven—which permits the representation of thought, but it is a preoperational thought. There are as yet no operations in the sense I'll define later. The operations I call "concrete" begin at around age seven; they apply directly to objects and are defined as being internalized or internalizable and reversible; that is, they can go in either direction. Addition and subtraction are examples of this. Then come formal operations, which no longer relate directly to objects . . .

Everything began for Jean Piaget when he was watching a ten-month-old baby at play:

I watched him playing with a ball. It was before my own children were born. The ball rolled under an armchair; he went looking for it and found it. He threw it again. It disappeared under a deep sofa with a fringe. He couldn't find the ball. Then he went back to the armchair, where he had found it before.

For him the object isn't completely localizable. It's still part of the action that was successful. It isn't yet a body moving independently, which, being under the couch, couldn't be under the armchair. Later it becomes a body moving independently, and the child looks for it in terms of its localizations. Then you can speak of the permanence of the object—what we mentioned the other day.

A ball that wasn't where it "should" have been. From this banal occurrence, this incident of daily life, Jean Piaget went on to derive his fundamental intuitions regarding the psychology of intelligence. An adult finds "absurd" the behavior of the baby—the baby who, however, prefigures in a certain way the man he will become. Where is the threshold . . . where are the thresholds?

At this point the scholar and his collaborators are engaged in various experiments. They are in a room at the International Center for Genetic Epistemology. A young woman,[1] and a little blonde girl sit facing each other.

Nadine, aged five

—When's your birthday?

—I don't know.

—Have you been five a long time?

—Yes.

—Look, we're going to play games. Tell me what this is. What is it? I know you've used them before—they're little checkers. What color are they?

—Some are green and some are red.

—Green and red. Which are prettier?

—The red ones.

—The red ones. So I'll be green. Watch what I'm going to do. I'm putting my green checkers like this. There. You see? I'm lining them up. Now you take the little red checkers and put them below mine. Like I did.[2] There, very good. Now, tell me, what do you think? Are there just as many red pieces as green ones? Are they the same? Or maybe there are more green ones? What do you think? More red ones? (*Nadine hesitates.*) If you look at the greens and then at the reds, are there more greens or more reds?

—They're both the same.

—All right. They're the same. How did you know?

—There aren't more greens or reds.

—There aren't more greens or reds! Fine. Now watch what I'm going to do. (*She spreads out the red checkers.*) Now, tell me if there's the same number of greens and reds. No? Which has more?

—The reds.

—There are more reds. Why?

—Because you changed them.

—I changed them, yes. But how do you know there are more reds?

—Because the greens are closer together.

—But Nadine, suppose we counted them. If we counted them with a finger, how many would there be? Would there be the same number of reds and greens, or would they be different?

—They'd be the same!

—Let's put them back the way they were before. (*She does so.*) How are they now?

—They're the same.

—And if you count them, what do you get?

—There's the same number.

—That's good. Now we're going to change the greens. What have we got now?

—The reds are closer together than the greens.

—Yes. And if we counted them, would there be more reds? Or more greens? Or would they be the same?

—No.

—What would we get?

—Because the greens are spread out more and the reds are closer together.

—Yes. So, what do we have? More greens, or more reds, or the same of each?

—More greens.

—More greens this time. What do we have to do to make them the same again?

—Have to put them like they were before.

—Have to put them like they were before. Like that, they're alike now? Okay, now we'll play with something else.

Taïma, aged six

—Do you know when your birthday is?

—I already had it. May first.

—Mine's in June, I told you a few minutes ago. Do you see these two balls? Do you know what they're made of?

—Modeling clay.

—Modeling clay, yes. And what color are they?

—Red.

—And the other one?

—White.

—It's white. Now look at the two balls of modeling clay and tell me if they're both the same size. Do they both have the same amount of clay in them?

—Yes.

—They're the same?

—Yes.

—Are you sure, or are you not very sure?

—No.

—You're not very sure? Do you think one of them is bigger than the other? Is there more clay in one of them? (*Taïma hesitates, then makes up her mind.*)

—No.

—So they're both the same? Now do you know what we're going to do? We're going to say it's cake—not really, but just pretend. You take the red cake, and I'll take the white. If we eat them, we'll both eat the same amount?

—Yes.

—Yes. Okay, now watch. I'm going to take my cake and do something with it. Tell me what I'm doing. Look. What is it?

—It's a stick.

—A stick. Now, what do you think? If I eat this stick, and you eat your clay ball, will we both eat the same amount, or does one of us have more to eat than the other?

—You have more to eat than I do.

—Yes? Why?

—Because that's longer than this.

—Okay. And suppose I make it longer—you see, even longer—you see, like this?

—You'll have more.

—I still have more to eat than you do?

—Yes.

—If I take it again and make it into a ball, like I had a minute ago—like it was at the beginning—how much will we each have to eat?

—The same.

—The same?

—Yes.

—All right. Now we'll take your ball. Look, I'm going to flatten it out like this. What shall we call this, what I just made?

—A steak.

—A steak? Well, okay. It's a funny color for a steak. Not cooked yet, right?

—Yes.

—Now, you eat your steak and I'll eat my ball. Do we both have the same amount to eat? Or does one of us have more?

—Yes. (*Taïma smiles and points to herself.*)

—You have more? Why?

—Because mine's fatter than yours.

—Fatter. But yours is so thin. Look.

—It's bigger.

—Bigger. So you really have more, do you?

—Yes.

—Is that right? Is it right? Are you sure?

—Yes.

—But when yours was a ball too—when it was a ball like this one—how much did we have, each of us?

—The same.

—The same? So now it's changed?

—Yes.

—And to make them the same again, what do we have to do?

—Have to make it into a ball again.

—Your clay?

—Yes.

Sophie, aged six

—Tell me, Sophie, would you like to play with the scales?

—Yes.

—Okay. Now look: do these two balls weigh the same?

—No.

—I don't think so either. Which is heavier?

—This one.

—This one. I want them to be exactly the same. Look now.

—This is lower than that.

—I'm going to take off another little piece. Is that it, now?

—Yes.

—Yes. How can you tell they weigh the same?

—Because I saw it there.

—You watched the pointer?

—Yes.

—That means they weigh the same? We'll take them off the scales. We'll make a long stick with the red one, and we'll leave your ball like it is. If I weigh them now—if I put them back on the scales—what would we see?

—This one would be heavier.

—Why?

—Because—because it's lighter when you make it like that.

—Are you sure? Like this?

—Yes.

—Why is it lighter when you roll it out like this? Because we didn't try it, did we?

—Because this one's thin and this one's fat.

—Now I see. And suppose I rolled this one back into a ball, how would it be?

—It would be heavier.

—Suppose I made two balls and weighed them, how would they be?

—The same.

—The same? Are you sure?

—Yes.

—How do you know?

—Because they are the same balls.

Resumption of our conversation at the home of Jean Piaget. We begin to talk about these experiments.

Piaget: Yes, for the little ones there is more clay than before because it is longer.

Bringuier: Or shorter!

Piaget: Or less because it's thinner. Never both at once. When they see one dimension, they don't see the other. Whereas, at a certain level, they see both and see the compensation: it's longer, therefore thinner, so it's the same. But this presupposes reversibility.

Bringuier: Then they understand that matter is conserved.

Piaget: First, matter; then, a year or two later, with the same arguments, weight; and finally, volume. Volume measured by the level of water displaced if you drop a pellet or clay sausage into a glass of water.

Bringuier: But it's funny they start with matter.

Piaget: Yes, it's quite something, because matter without weight or volume can't be perceived.

Bringuier: A pure concept.

Piaget: Required by the principle of conservation. Yes, a pure concept. As Poincaré used to say, "Something has to be conserved, or reasoning is not possible," but we don't know ahead of time what it is.

Bringuier: Before we go on, I want to say something about the experiments. Your collaborators have told me that a reversal occurs if the stick of modeling clay is made even longer.

Piaget: That's right. The child says, "There's more because it's longer"; but suddenly that doesn't work any more, and he says, "It's too thin, there's less than before!"

Bringuier: But he can see perfectly well that it's the same operation, continued.

Piaget: Of course!

Bringuier: It isn't logical.

Piaget: No, not at all. That's all prelogical.[3] And then, too, there's something in the conversations that I find very interesting. The argument often goes like this: It's the same amount; it hasn't changed, because you haven't taken anything away. The little ones knew very well you hadn't taken any of it away! But that was no argument for them. Whereas it becomes an argument. There you have a transformation of structure. It becomes necessary. It's the Kantian a priori—but at the end, not at the beginning. Necessity at the end and not at the beginning. (*A silence.*)

Bringuier: That's enough about the experiments. As regards these structures, do you think the child—whom you've been studying for a good many years now—is universal, over time and also geographically? Because, in fact, you've worked primarily with Swiss children, and mostly with children from Geneva.

Piaget: That's a big problem, which presupposes some very difficult research, because comparative child psychology requires you to go to remote societies and master their languages—that's the domain of ethnographers and anthropologists; but at the same time, you have to know the interview technique. The technique takes months to learn. The interviewer must have an ethnographer's training in order to go into a different society, and he must have a psychologist's technique in order to know how to interview. So far, we've seen, on the one hand, anthropologists who thought they were reproducing experiments, for instance, but it was done very superficially, and, on the other hand, well-trained people in psychology who didn't know the children's language and had to conduct the interviews through interpreters. So, broadly speaking, what we've found up until now is remarkable agreement, but with accelerations and delays, as I've mentioned before. To give an example of a delay, I had a student who worked in Teheran. The children of Teheran are at about the same level, at the same ages, as children in Geneva, but the ones in the rural areas, who are illiterate, show two, three, or four years' delay in passing through the same stages; that's the main thing.

Bringuier: In the same order?

Piaget: Yes, of course. The stages are an order of succession. It isn't the average age. But much comparative work has been done. Miss Churchill did some experiments. I just saw a psychologist from Canberra who did conversation experiments with the Aruntas of Australia—you know, the tribe in the middle of Australia. Well, she found the same things, but with a *décalage* [phase difference]. Then there are the Canadians—Laurendeau, Pinard, and Boisclair—who did experiments in Martinique. Children in Martinique are in the French school system until they earn their elementary-school certificate. They do get through, but in my studies of operations and conversations they are four years behind.

Bringuier: What causes that?

Piaget: Their society, which is lazy. The father of one of these children had just built a house. When it was finished, he realized he had forgotten to put in the stairs.

Bringuier: And your impression is that the surroundings become more important as the child gets older?

Piaget: Certainly![4]

Bringuier: But, if that is so, how true is the current theory—which comes from psychoanalysis—that says that everything is completed in the first three years?

Piaget: No! Cognitively, it isn't so. No, no! They're exaggerating. Oh, no! New constructions occur during adolescence.

NOTES

1. The questioner is Catherine Dami, assistant at the Center.
2. It is part of the "conversation" technique to follow, and imitate if necessary, the child's way of speaking so that he will feel the distance from the adult as little as possible.
3. This remark of Piaget's, coming, after all, at the end of the discussion, left me with the impression that a door had been opened. The very tranquillity of his comment, its matter-of-fact tone, were probably what brought me face to face with what it meant—brought it home to me. Clearly, the child's reasoning did not rest on an inarticulate or poorly formulated logic; it wasn't a clumsy attempt at adult logic. It owed nothing to that logic. It rested instead on something else, another world—a world that Piaget had been exploring for a long time. From what he said, I sensed the dimensions, the true perspective, of his research—or at least believed that I did.
4. Since then, a number of comparative research studies have been done in Africa by five or six psychologists from Geneva, under the direction of B. Inhelder.

1.3 DAVID ELKIND

The Hurried Child: Is Our Impatient Society Depriving Kids of Their Right to Be Children?

David Elkind's work observing and writing about young children spans 30 years. Elkind was born in 1931 in Detroit, Michigan, and is currently a professor of child study at Tufts University in Medford, Massachusetts. Early in his professional career, he worked as a postdoctoral fellow at Jean Piaget's International Center for Genetic Epistemology in Geneva, Switzerland. It was there that his observations of young children led him to investigate their thinking at a variety of levels. In the 1980s Elkind wrote three influential books entitled *The Hurried Child: Growing Up Too Fast Too Soon* (Addison-Wesley, 1988), *All Grown Up and No Place to Go: Teenagers in Crisis* (Addison-Wesley, 1984), and *Miseducation: Preschoolers at Risk* (Alfred A. Knopf, 1987). Elkind wrote *The Hurried Child* while serving as president of the National Association for the Education of Young Children (1986–1988).

The following selection from "The Hurried Child: Is Our Impatient Society Depriving Kids of Their Right to Be Children?" *Instructor & Teacher* (May 1982) presents Elkind's view of how young children in America are being raised. Our fast-paced society has led many parents to put their children's development on high speed, often bypassing the once-in-a-lifetime opportunities only available in childhood. Elkind attempts to put the brakes on society's rush to get children from childhood to adulthood so quickly. He advocates play as one effective way to counterbalance the hectic lifestyles many children lead.

*P*ressure to succeed at all costs, pressure to cope, pressure to survive—Sound like the beginning of a list of adult stressors? It probably is, but add to it pressure to achieve before one is ready to achieve, pressure to grow up and quit acting like a child when one still *is* a child, and pressure to struggle to the top when one is only four, six, or eight years old. Combine those pressures and others, and you have the stressors we are placing on our children as we hurry them into premature adulthood.

We even want them to *look* like adults. Take, for example, the mid-teens sex symbol who sensually gyrates her hips as she models the designer jeans that are so appealing to the young. As a matter of fact, today even preschoolers wear miniature versions of adult clothing. From LaCoste shirts to scaled-down designer fashions, a whole range of adult costumes is available to children.

Three or four decades ago, boys wore short pants and knickers until they began to shave; getting a pair of long pants was a true rite of passage. Girls were not permitted to wear makeup or sheer stockings until they were in their teens. Children's clothing signaled adults that children were to be treated differently, perhaps indulgently, and children could more easily act like children; but no longer. Clothing is just one of the more obvious examples of how we hurry today's children into adulthood, pushing them toward many different types of achievement and exposing them to experiences that tax their adaptive capacity.

Look at the media, for example. Music, books, films, and television increasingly portray young people as precocious and present them in more or less explicit sexual or manipulative situations, reinforcing the pressure on children to grow up fast in their language, thinking, and behavior. Can children be hurried into growing up fast emotionally, as well? The answer is no. Feelings and emotions have their own timing and rhythm and cannot be hurried. Young teenagers may look and behave like adults, but they usually don't feel like adults. Growing up emotionally is complicated and difficult under any circumstances but may be especially so when children's behavior and appearance say "adult" while their feelings cry "child."

Academic achievement is another example of the many pressures adults place on children to grow up fast, to succeed at all costs. Society has no room for the "late bloomers," the children who come into their own later in life rather than earlier. Children have to be successful early or they are regarded as flops. This pressure to succeed has gone so far that many parents refuse to allow their children to be retained in kindergarten—despite all of the evidence that this is the best possible time to retain a child. "But," the parents say, "how can we tell our friends that our son failed kindergarten?"

A recent study of children who have been held back in kindergarten found that almost all of the parents involved were pleased with the result. They thought that repeating kindergarten had given their children, who were socially or intellectually below the norm at that time, a chance to catch up at their own speed. Many of these children were able to join their own age group later and, far from being handicapped, were helped by the opportunity to move at their own pace.

AT WHAT AGE SHOULD A CHILD KNOW HOW TO READ?

As teachers know all too well, parents hurry children when they insist that the children acquire academic skills, such as reading, at an early age (indeed, some programs now promise parents that they can teach their children to read as infants and toddlers). This pressure by parents reflects the parent's desires, not the children's needs or inclinations. Although some children gravitate to reading early, seeking out books and adults to read to them, such children seem to learn to read on their own and with little fuss or bother; but they are in the minority. Only 1 to 3 children in 100 are estimated to read proficiently (at second grade level) on entrance to kindergarten. If learning to read were as easy as learning to talk, as some people claim, many more children would learn to read on their own. The fact that they do not, despite being surrounded by print, suggests that learning to read is not a spontaneous or simple skill. The majority of children can, however, learn to read with ease if they are not hurried into it.

Children confronted with the task of learning to read before they have the requisite mental abilities may develop long-term learning difficulties. In one high school, for example, we informally compared the grades of students who had fall birthdays (September, October, November, and December) and had entered kindergarten before they were five years old with the grades of students who have spring or summer birthdays (April, May, June, and July) and had entered school after they were five years old. Boys in particular who entered kindergarten after age five rather than before had an advantage, in terms of grades.

Children should be challenged intellectually, but the challenge should be constructive, not debilitating. Forcing a child to read early, just like forcing an adolescent to take algebra when simple arithmetic is still a problem, can be a devastating experience for a young person who is not intellectually prepared for the task.

THE ABUSE OF THE FACTORY SYSTEM

Schools today hurry children because administrators are pressured to produce better "products." This pressure leads administrators to treat children like empty bottles on an assembly line, getting a little fuller at each grade level. When the bottles don't get full enough, management puts pressure on the operator (the teacher, who is held accountable for filling her or his share of the bottles) and on quality control (making sure that the information is valid and the bottle is not defective). This factory approach causes schools to hurry children because it ignores individual differences in mental abilities and learning rates. The child who cannot keep up in this system, even if only temporarily, is often regarded as a defective vessel and is labeled "learning disabled" or "minimally brain damaged" or "hyperactive."

The factory mentality of our schools has been reinforced by machine-scored group testing probably more than any other single factor. Dependence on such testing has grown dramatically over the past 10 years, as parents and legislators have more vocally expressed their dissatisfaction with the schools and with children's attainments. Whether blame is placed on television, single-parent homes, working mothers, or the decline of authority, academic performance has been declining, and efforts to remedy the situation rely heavily on testing and teacher accountability. The problem with this system is that it pushes children too much, forcing them into a uniform mold. Children are being pressured to produce for the sake of teachers and administrators.

Management programs, accountability, and test scores are what schools are all about today, and children know it. Children have to produce—or else. This pressure may be good for many children, but it is bound to be bad for those who can't keep up. Their failure is more public and therefore more humiliating than ever before. Even worse, society convinces children who fail to achieve that they are letting down their parents, their peers, their teachers, the principal, the superintendent, and the school board. This is a heavy burden for many children to bear; therefore, they become much more concerned with grades than with what they know. Not surprisingly when these young people go out into the work world, they are less concerned with the job than with the pay and the perquisites of the job. What schools have to—and parents ought to—realize is that the attitudes they inculcate in young people are carried over into the occupational world.

Schooling and education are thought of in narrow terms; the focus is on attaining basic concepts and skills. But education—true education—is coincident with life and is not limited to special skills or concepts and particularly not to test scores. Education should not come packaged or sequenced. Much of it is spontaneous, an outgrowth of openness and curiosity that must be imparted to children. Pressuring children to get certain marks on tests that, at best, measure rote knowledge is hardly the way to improve children's education. What good is education if children can read but not understand what they read or if they know how to compute but not where, when, or what to compute?

CHILDREN ARE HURRIED BECAUSE WE ARE HURRIED

What is the first expensive, utilitarian gift that we usually give our children? A watch! We hurry our children basically because we hurry ourselves. For all of our technological finesse and sophisticated systems, we are a people who cannot—will not—wait. We are, in short, a hurried people, and only in the context of a society that is hell-bent on doing jobs more quickly and better and is impatient with waiting and inefficiency can we understand the phenomenon of hurried children and hope to help them. First we must recognize what we cannot do. We cannot change the basic thrust of American society, for which hurrying is the accepted and valued way of life. When hurrying reflects cultural values like being punctual, then urging children to be on time has social justification. But the *abuse of hurrying* harms children—that is, when hurrying 27

David Elkind

justification. But the *abuse of hurrying* harms children—that is, when hurrying serves parental or institutional needs at the children's expense without imbuing them with redeeming social values.

Young children two to eight years old tend to perceive hurrying as a rejection, as evidence that their parents do not really care about them. Children are emotionally astute in this regard and tune in to what is a partial truth. To a certain extent, hurrying children from one caregiver to another each day, or into academic achievement, or into making decisions they are not really able to make is a rejection. It is a rejection of children as they see themselves, of what they are capable of coping with and doing. Children find such rejection very threatening and often develop stress symptoms as a result.

Accordingly, when parents have to hurry young children, when they have to take the children to a child care center or to a babysitter, they need to appreciate children's feelings about the matter. Giving children a rational explanation—"I have to work so we can eat and buy clothes" and so on—helps, but it isn't enough to deal with the child's implicit thought—"If they really loved me, they wouldn't go off and leave me." We need to respond to the child's feelings more than to her intellect. One might say, for instance, "I'm really going to miss you today. I wish you could be with me." The exact words are less important than the message that the separation is painful but necessary for the parents, too.

School-age children are more independent and more self-reliant than are younger children. Consequently, school-age children often seem to welcome hurrying because they are eager to take on adult chores and responsibilities, particularly in single-parent homes, in which they may try intuitively to fill the role of the absent parent. The danger with this age group is that too often parents interpret this display of maturity as true maturity rather than what it is—a kind of game. The image to keep in mind for this age group is Peter Pan, who wanted to assume adult responsibilities but did not want to grow up and accept some of the negative qualities that children perceive as characteristic of adults. Children want to play at being grown up, but they don't want adults to take them too seriously.

WE CAN COUNTERACT THE EFFECTS OF HURRYING

One effective tool against the onslaught of hurrying is play. Unfortunately, the value and the meaning of play are poorly understood in our hurried society. Indeed, what happened to adults in U.S. society has now happened to children—play has been transformed into work. What was once recreational—such as sports and summer camp musical training—is now professionalized and competitive. In schools, when budgets are tight the first areas to be cut are art, music, and drama. Television and other media, suffused with the new realism, offer little in the way of truly imaginative fantasy. Perhaps the best evidence of the extent to which children are hurried is the lack of opportunities for genuine play available to them.

Children need to do more than play, of course. At every turn they are learning social rules—how to behave in a restaurant, on a plane, and at a friend's house; how to put on clothes and take them off; how to eat with utensils; how to wash behind their ears; how to dry themselves with a towel, and so on. Children can also learn basic concepts about space, time, number, color, and so on. But they need to be given an opportunity for pure play as well as for work. If adults believe that each spontaneous interest of a child is an opportunity for a lesson, they foreclose the child's opportunities for pure play.

Play is nature's way of enabling us to deal with stress, for children as well as for adults. Parents can help by investing in toys and playthings that give the greatest scope to a child's imagination—for example, a good set of blocks that give children leeway to create and that can be used for years; crayons; paints; clay; and chalk. These are all creative play materials because they allow for a child's personal expression.

Along the way, all of us—parents, teachers, and citizens—must assert the value of the arts in the schools. Overemphasizing the basics in contemporary education without a balancing emphasis on personal expression through the arts hurries children by destroying the necessary balance between work and play. The need for employees to have modes of personal expression at work is just beginning to be realized and appreciated by American industry. Schools must recognize that children also work better, learn better, and, yes, grow better if the time they spend in social adaptation—learning the basics—is alternated with healthy periods devoted to avenues for self-expression. Far from being a luxury, time and money spent on the arts enhance learning and development by reducing the stress of personal adaptation and giving children an aesthetic perspective to balance the workday perspective.

We must see childhood as a stage of life, not just the anteroom to life. Hurrying children into adulthood violates the sanctity of life by giving one period priority over another. If we value human life, we will value each period equally and give unto each stage of life what is appropriate to that stage.

We should appreciate the value of childhood with its special joys, sorrows, worries, and concerns. Valuing childhood does not mean seeing it as a happy, innocent period but rather as an important period of life to which children are entitled. They have a right to be children, to enjoy the pleasures and to suffer the trials of childhood that are infringed upon by hurrying. Childhood is the most basic human right of children.

CHAPTER 2 Children in Crisis

2.1 ANNA FREUD AND
DOROTHY T. BURLINGHAM

Survey of Psychological Reactions

The effects of World War II on the children of Europe were most traumatic partly because they were forced to endure nightly air raids. From 1942 to 1945, psychoanalysts Anna Freud and Dorothy T. Burlingham focused their energies on the Hampstead War Nursery for children in London. The nursery was a residential center for 80 children, operating under the premise that young children would suffer serious lifelong consequences if essential food, medical care, nurturing, and educational opportunities were restricted. Research at the nursery, which later became the Hampstead Child Therapy Clinic, was the basis of three books by Freud and Burlingham.

Anna Freud (1895–1982), the daughter of neurologist Sigmund Freud, who was a pioneer in psychoanalysis, carried on her father's work as it applied to the emotional and social development of young children. She wrote and lectured extensively, and for a number of years she worked closely with the Foster Parents Plan for War Children, Inc., in New York City, an organization that provided humanitarian aid to the families and communities of children affected by warfare. Her "Kinderseminar" series was a significant influence on psychoanalyst Erik Erikson.

War and Children (Medical War Books, 1943), from which the following selection is taken, is considered the first psychological study of the effects of war on children. In it, Freud and Burlingham describe vivid life experiences of children of war. This selection is significant not only for its insights on war's effects but also for implications that can be drawn today. Many children are being raised in a war-like environment in America's communities, as well as in other countries. The sounds of assault weapons in the streets are not all that different from the sounds of German bombers flying overhead. The fear of abandonment by fathers sent off to war and mothers working long hours is similar to the fear children experience when the only parent they know is incarcerated for drug involvement. Many children today exhibit some of the same behaviors Freud and Burlingham observed in young children over 50 years ago.

*A*ll our bigger children have had their fair share of war experiences. All of them have witnessed the air raids either in London or in the provinces. A large percentage of them has seen their houses destroyed or damaged. All of them have seen their family life dissolved, whether by separation from or by death of the father. All of them are separated from their mothers and have entered community life at an age which is not usually considered ripe for it. The questions arise which part these experiences play in the psychological life of the individual child, how far the child acquires understanding of what is going on around it, how it reacts emotionally, how far its anxiety is aroused, and what normal or abnormal outlets it will find to deal with these experiences which are thrust on it.

It can be safely said that all the children who were over two years at the time of the London "blitz" have acquired knowledge of the significance of air raids. They all recognise the noise of flying aeroplanes; they distinguish vaguely between the sounds of falling bombs and anti-aircraft guns. They realize that the house will fall down when bombed and that people are often killed or get hurt in falling houses. They know that fires can be started by incendiaries and that roads are often blocked as a result of bombing. They fully understand the significance of taking shelter. Some children who have lived in deep shelters will even judge the safety of a shelter according to its depth under the earth. The necessity to make them familiar with their gas masks may give them some ideas about a gas attack, though we have never met a child for whom this particular danger had any real meaning.

The children seem to have no difficulty in understanding what it means when their fathers join the Forces. We even overhear talk among the children where they compare their fathers' military ranks and duties. A child, for instance, with its father in the navy or air force, will be offended if somebody by mistake refers to the father as being "in the army." As far as the reasoning processes of the child are concerned, the absence of the father seems to be accounted for in this manner.

Children are similarly ready to take in knowledge about the various occupations of their mothers, though the constant change of occupation makes this slightly more difficult. Mothers of three-year-olds will change backwards and forwards between the occupations of railway porter, factory worker, bus conductor, milk cart driver, etc. They will visit their children in their varying uniforms and will proudly tell them about their new war work until the children are completely confused. Though the children seem proud of their fathers' uniforms, they often seem to resent it and feel very much estranged when their mothers appear in such unexpected guises.

It is still more difficult for all children to get any understanding of the reason why they are being evacuated and cannot stay in the place where their mothers are. In the case of our children, as in the case of many others, this is further aggravated by the fact that they actually did live in London with their mothers during the worst dangers and were sent to the country afterwards when London seemed quite peaceful. They reason with some justification that they can live wherever their mothers do and that if "home" is as much in danger as all that, their mothers should not be there either. This, of course, concerns the bigger children of five or more.

The understanding of catastrophes, like the death of father, has little to do with reasoning. In these cases children meet the usual psychological difficulties of grasping the significance of death at such an early age. Their attitude to the happening is completely a matter of emotion.

We may, of course, be often wrong in assuming that children "understand" the happenings around them. In talking, they only use the proper words for them but without the meaning attached. Words like "army", "navy", "air force", may mean to them strange countries to which their fathers have gone. America, for the children, the place where all the good things, especially the parcels come from, was discovered the other day to mean to one child at least "a merry car". The word "bombing" is often used indiscriminately for all manners of destruction of unwanted objects. "London" is the word used for the children's former homes, irrespective of the fact whether the child now lives in Essex or still in Hampstead.

Several of our children in Wedderburn Road used to say in talking: "When I was still in London . . ."

And one boy of four once explained in a London shop, to the shop assistant's great astonishment: "I used to live in London, but London is all bombed and gone, and all the houses have fallen down".

He was unable to realise the fact that the comparatively unbombed street in which he now lived with us was still the same city. "Home" is the place to which all children are determined to return, irrespective of the fact that in most cases they are aware of its destruction. "War", above everything else, signifies the period of time for which children have to be separated from their parents.

A striking example of such "misunderstanding" was Pamela, a girl of four and a half years, who as we thought, had perfectly grasped the meaning of evacuation. She was a thrice bombed child, lived in Wedderburn Road, and like all others waited for the opening of our country house. We had carefully explained to all the children that they were being transferred to the country and the reason for it.

But when at last, after weeks of expectation—because the lease of the country house did not materialise—she stood in our front hall, all dressed and ready, waiting for the American ambulance car to take her out, she exclaimed joyfully; "The war is over and we are going to the country. It has lasted a long time!"

The longing for the Country House, which had been the centre of interest for the Nursery children for some weeks, had suddenly got confused in her mind with the more general longing for the end of the war, which would as all the children firmly believed, take them all back to their former homes and to their parents.

REACTION TO DESTRUCTION

In this war, more than in former ones, children are frequently to be found directly on the scenes of battle. Though, here in England, they are spared the actual horror of seeing people fight around them, they are not spared sights of destruction, death, and injury from air raids. Even when removed from the places of the worst danger there is no certainty, as some of our cases show, that they will not meet new bombing incidents at places to which they were sent for safety. General sympathy has been aroused by the idea that little children, all innocently, should thus come into close contact with the horrors of the war. It is this situation which led many people to expect that children would receive traumatic shocks from air raids and would develop abnormal reactions very similar to the traumatic or war neuroses of soldiers in the last war.

We can only describe our observation on the basis of our own case material, which excludes children who have received severe bodily injuries in air raids though, as mentioned before, it does not exclude children who have been bombed repeatedly and partly buried in debris. So far as we can notice, there were no signs of traumatic shock to be observed in these children. If these bombing incidents occur when small children are in the care either of their own mothers or a familiar mother substitute, they do not seem to be particularly affected by them. Their experience remains an accident, in line with other accidents of childhood. This observation is borne out by the reports of nurses or social workers in London County Council Rest Centres where children used to arrive, usually in the middle of the night, straight from their bombed houses. They also found that children who arrived together with their own families showed little excitement and no undue disturbance. They slept and ate normally and played with whatever toys they had rescued or which might be provided. It is a widely different matter when children, during an experience of this kind, are separated from or even lose their parents.

It is a common misunderstanding of the child's nature which leads people to suppose that children will be saddened by the sight of destruction and aggression. Children between the ages of one and two years, when put together in a play-pen will bite each other, pull each other's hair and steal each other's toys without regard for the other child's unhappiness. They are passing through a stage of development where destruction and aggression play one of the leading parts. If we observe young children at play, we notice that they will destroy their toys, pull off the arm and legs of their dolls or soldiers, puncture their balls, smash whatever is breakable, and will only mind the result because complete destruction of the toy blocks further play. The more their strength and independence are growing the more they will have to be watched so as not to create too much damage, not to hurt each other or those weaker than themselves. We often say, half jokingly, that there is continual war raging in a nursery. We mean by this, that at this time of life destructive and aggressive impulses are still at work in children in a manner in which they only recur in grown-up life when they are let loose for the purposes of war.

It is one of the recognised aims of education to deal with the aggressiveness of the child's nature, i.e. in the course of the first four of five years to change the child's own attitude towards these impulses in himself. The wish to hurt people, and later the wish to destroy objects, undergo all sorts of changes. They are usually first restricted, then suppressed by commands and prohibitions; a little later they are repressed, which means that they disappear from the child's consciousness. The child does not dare any more to have knowledge of these wishes. There is always the danger that they might return from the unconscious; therefore, all sorts of protections are built up against them—the cruel child develops pity, the destructive child will become hesitant and over careful. If education is handled intelligently the main part of these aggressive impulses will be directed away from their primitive aim of doing harm to somebody or something, and will be used to fight the difficulties of the outer world—to accomplish tasks of all kinds, to measure one's strength in competition and to use it generally to "do good" instead of "being bad" as the original impulse demanded.

In the light of these considerations it is easier to determine what the present war conditions, with their incidents of wholesale destruction may do to a child. Instead of turning away from them in instinctive horror, as people seem to expect, the child may turn towards them with primitive excitement. The real danger is not that the child, caught up all innocently in the whirlpool of the war, will be shocked into illness. The danger lies in the fact that the destruction raging in the outer world may meet the very real aggressiveness which rages in the inside of the child. At the age when education should start to deal with these impulses confirmation should not be given from the outside world that the same impulses are uppermost in other people. Children will play joyfully on bombed sites and around bomb craters, they will play with blasted bits of furniture and throw bricks from crumbled walls at each other. But it becomes impossible to educate them towards a repression of, a reaction against destruction while they are doing so. After their first years of life they fight against their own wishes to do away with people of whom they are jealous, who disturb or disappoint them, or who offend their childish feelings in some other way. It must be very difficult for them to accomplish this task of fighting their own death wishes when, at the same time, people are killed and hurt every day around them. Children have to be safeguarded against the primitive horrors of the war, not because horrors and atrocities are so strange to them, but because we want them at this decisive stage of their development to overcome and estrange themselves from the primitive and atrocious wishes of their own infantile nature.

FIVE TYPES OF AIR RAID ANXIETY

What is true about the child's attitude to destruction applies in a certain measure to the subject of anxiety. Children are, of course, afraid of air raids, but their fear is neither as universal nor as overwhelming as has been expected. An explanation is required as to why it is present in some cases, absent in others, comparatively mild in most and rather violent in certain types of children.

It will be easier to answer these practical questions if we draw on our theoretical knowledge about the motives for fear and anxiety reactions in human beings. We have learned that there are three main reasons for the development of fear reactions:

An individual is afraid quite naturally and sensibly when there is some real danger present in the outside world which threatens either his safety or his whole existence. His fear will be all the greater the more he knows about the seriousness of the danger. His fear will urge him to adopt precautionary measures. Under its influence he will either fight it or if that is impossible, try to escape from it. Only when the danger is of overwhelming extent and suddenness will he be shocked and paralysed into inaction. This so-called "real anxiety" plays its part in the way in which children are afraid of air raids. They fear them as far as they can understand what is happening. As described above they have, in spite of their youth, acquired a certain degree of knowledge of this new danger. But it would be a mistake to over-rate this understanding, and consequently, to over-rate the amount or the permanency of this real fear of air raids. Knowledge and reason only play a limited part in a child's life. Its interest quickly turns away from the real things in the outer world, especially when they are unpleasant, and reverts back to its own childish interests, to its toys, its games and to its phantasies. The danger in the outer world which it recognises at one moment and to which it answers with its fear, is put aside in another moment. Precautions are not kept up, and the fear gives way to an attitude of utter disregard.

There is the observation made by one of our colleagues during a day-light air raid in a surface shelter into which a mother had shepherded her little son of school age. For a while they both listened to the dropping of the bombs; then the boy lost interest and became engrossed in a story book which he had brought with him. The mother tried to interrupt his reading several times with anxious exclamations.

He always returned to his book after a second, until she at last said in an angry and scolding tone: "Drop your book and attend to the air raid".

We made exactly the same observations in the Children's Centre at the time of the December, March, and May raids. When our unexploded bomb lay in the neighbouring garden, the children began by being mildly interested and afraid. They learned to keep away from glass windows and to avoid the entrance into the garden. By keeping up continual talk about the possible explosion we could have frightened them into continuation of that attitude. When-ever we let the subject alone their interest flagged. They forgot about the men-ace from the glass whenever they returned to their accustomed games; when the threat from outside lasted more than a week they began to get cross with it and denied its presence.

In spite of the bomb still being unremoved they suddenly declared: "The bomb is gone and we shall go into the garden!"

There is nothing outstanding in this behaviour of children towards the presence of real danger and real fear. It is only one example of the way in which, at this age, they deal with the facts of reality whenever they become unpleasant. They drop their contact with reality, they deny the facts, get rid of their fear in this manner and return, apparently undisturbed, to the pursuits and interests of their own childish world.

The second reason for anxiety can best be understood by reverting to the child's attitude towards destruction and aggression which we have described before. After the first years of life the individual learns to criticise and over-come in himself certain instinctive wishes, or rather he learns to refuse them conscious expression. He learns that it is bad to kill, to hurt and to destroy, and would like to believe that he has no further wish to do any of these things. But he can only keep up this attitude when the people in the outer world do likewise. When he sees killing and destruction going on outside it arouses his fear that the impulses which he has only a short while ago buried in himself will be awakened again.

We have described above how the small child in whom these inhibitions against aggression have not yet been established is free of the abhorrence of air raids. The slightly older child who has just been through this fight with itself will, on the other hand, be particularly sensitive to their menace. When it has only just learned to curb its own aggressive impulses, it will have real out-breaks of anxiety when bombs come down and do damage around it.

This type of anxiety we have only seen in one girl of another age group, ten years old, who ardently wished to leave England altogether and to return to Canada, where she had been born, where everything was peaceful and "no horrid things to see".

The third type of anxiety is of a completely different nature. There is no education without fear. Children are afraid of disobeying the commands and prohibitions of their elders either because they fear punishments or because they fear losing their parents' love whenever they are naughty. This fear of authority develops a little later into a fear of the child's own conscience. We regard it as progress in the child's education when commands and prohibitions from outside become more and more unnecessary, and the child knows what to do and what not to do under the direction of his own conscience. At the time when this nucleus of inner ideas which we call conscience, is formed, it turns back continually to the figures of the outside world on the one hand, to the imaginations of his own phantasy on the other, and borrows strength from both to reinforce the inner commandments.

The child of four or five who is afraid in the evening before sleep because it thinks it has done wrong or thought forbidden thoughts, will not only have a "bad conscience" or be afraid what father and mother would say if they knew about its wickedness. It will also be afraid of ghosts and bogeymen as reinforcements of the real parent figures and of the inner voice.

Children have a large list of dangers which serve as convenient symbols for their conscience—they are afraid of policemen who will come and arrest them, gypsies and robbers who will steal them, chimney sweeps or coal carriers who will put them in their bags, dustmen who will put them in their bins, lions and tigers who will come and eat them, earthquakes which will shake their houses, and thunderstorms which will threaten them. When they receive religious teaching they may leave all else aside and be afraid of the devil and of hell. There are many children who cannot go to sleep in the evening because they are afraid that God will look in on them and punish them for their sins. There are others who receive no religious teaching who transfer the same fear to the moon. They cannot fall asleep if the moon looks at them through the window; there are even children who cannot fall asleep because their fears are busy with expectations of the end of the world.

For children in this stage of development of their inner conscience air raids are simply a new symbol for old fears. They are as afraid of sirens and of bombs as they are afraid of thunder and lightning. Hitler and German planes take the place of the devil, of the lions again in the morning.

In the Children's Centre, for instance, Charlie, four and a half years old, called from his bed in the evening that the shelter was not safe enough, and that the house would fall down on him. He would certainly have called out in the same way in peace time to say that he had a fear of earthquakes or of thunderstorms. Roger, four years old, demanded that his mother come every evening and stand arched over his bed until he fell asleep. It is well known that there are many children of that same age, who, at all times, refuse to go to sleep unless their mothers stand by to hold their hands and safeguard them against forbidden actions. There is another boy of the same age whom the nursery superintendent has to assure with endless repetitions that if she leaves him at night he will surely find her and the tigers.

This fear also only disguises itself as a fear of air attack at night. When we inquire into it more closely we realise that he is afraid that he has done wrong somehow, and that for punishment his teacher and protector will be spirited away at night. We can convince ourselves of the truth of this explanation when we have the chance to remove these children from the danger and put them in surroundings where there is no talk of air raids. They will slowly revert to their former forms of anxiety. We shall know that peace has returned when nothing is left for the children to be afraid of except their own former ghosts and bogeymen.

2.2 ROBERT COLES

Vitality in Ghetto Children

For years Robert Coles has been travelling the backcountry roads, cities, and small towns of America, interacting with and observing children. Often his tattered box of crayons and pad of paper were the only introduction needed. Any child who wanted to participate became a subject. In his books, he demonstrates his young subjects' struggle for life through his words and their crayon drawings. In *The South Goes North: Volume III of Children in Crisis* (Little, Brown, 1971), from which the following selection is taken, Coles discusses his observations of children in crisis with a focus on children in the cities of the North.

Coles was born in Boston in 1929. His career in psychiatry began at hospitals in and around Boston in the 1950s and 1960s. He holds degrees from Harvard University and Columbia University. At the request of the United States Commission on Civil Rights, Coles travelled extensively to gather data for *Children of Crisis: A Study of Courage and Fear* (Little, Brown, 1977). That project was followed by over 40 more books and numerous articles.

Coles has received five national awards, including the Pulitzer Prize, for his *Children of Crisis* series. He has been recognized by many education and social service agencies and organizations for his contributions in bringing attention to the problems of young children in crisis in America. Coles continues to lecture and write at Harvard University, where he has been a faculty member since 1966.

When I read about ghetto children in psychiatric journals and educational reviews—not to mention the public press—I do not recognize the boys and girls I meet and observe every day. From the psychiatric quarter I hear about the mental illness that plagues the poor (though none of us has noticed psychiatrists—or any other kind of doctors—rushing in large numbers to practice in Harlem, Watts, or Chicago's South Side). I read about how apathetic or unruly ghetto children are: the "culturally disadvantaged," the blacks and Puerto Ricans, the surly, suspicious, "deprived" whites who come from Appalachia to northern cities, or the older southern immigrants who still live in the slums. One report mentions the "poor impulse controls" of lower-class black children; another, the "personality defects" of slum boys who, at five or six, are destined to be "sociopaths," delinquents, or worse. The picture is bleak: untended or brutalized children threaten teachers, assault one another, violate school regulations or city ordinances, and in general show themselves bound for a life of crime, indolence, or madness.

Educators confirm what their brother social scientists have noted: ghetto children do not take to school; they are nasty—or plain lazy. I wish they at least were frankly described that way. Instead one has to wrestle with the impossible jargon of educational psychologists who talk about "motivational deficits" or "lowered achievement goals" or "self-esteem impairment." We are told that slum schools must be "enriched" with programs to suit children who live in a vast cultural wasteland. Machines, books, audiovisual equipment, special "curricula," smaller classes, trips to museums, contacts with suburban children, with trees and hillsides—the ghetto child needs all of that and more. He needs personal "guidance." He could benefit from knowing a VISTA [Volunteers in Service to America] volunteer or a college student who wants to be a tutor or a housewife from the other side of town who wants to give poor children the things her own children take for granted.

Though some of those assertions are obviously correct, their cumulative implication is misleading and unfair. It is about time the lives of ghetto children were seen as something more than a tangle of psychopathology and flawed performances in school. Children in the ghetto do need help, but not the kind that stems from an endless, condescending recital of their troubles and failures—and often ignores or caricatures the strength, intelligence, and considerable ingenuity they do possess.

As I have already indicated, for a long time I, too, looked only for the harm inflicted on the boys and girls who grow up on the wrong side of the tracks. I found plenty to point to. Yet, while I was busy documenting such conditions I failed to see the other side of the picture. Determined to record every bit of pathology I could find, I failed to ask myself what makes for survival in the poor; indeed, sometimes for more than that—for a resourcefulness and vitality that some of us in the therapy-prone suburbs might at least want to ponder, if not envy.

My dilemma was not too different from the one that many civil-rights workers—particularly the white middle-class kind—have come to recognize. In 1964, when by the hundreds we went south to Mississippi, the emphasis was on setting free a cruelly oppressed people. Again and again the black man's plight was analyzed, his suffering emphasized. We had come to put an end to it all, to fight with the weak against the strong. At that time a writer like Ralph Ellison—who for years has insisted upon the rich culture that Negroes have created for themselves—was summarily dismissed by "liberators" who could not imagine they had a lot to learn from the victimized rural blacks of the South.

However, one by one we had to face the ironies in our apparently clear-cut situation. "It's not so easy, the longer you stay down here," said one northern student who had been living with a black family for a few months. "They're poor and beaten down. They can't talk right, and they can't write at all. There aren't any pictures on their walls, and the cabins they live in—you wouldn't even use them for a summer hideaway. They're scared out of their minds when a cop comes near them, like in a police state. But something starts happening to the way you think, because you like the people, the poor, down-trodden Negro, and the more time you spend with him the more you begin to admire him, and even wish your own family were more like his."

"If I talk like that up in Cambridge," he went on, "they'll tell me how romantic I am, how naïve. They'll say it's fine for me to talk—with my white skin and my father's bank account and my ability to leave any minute I want. I know, because a few months ago if I heard someone like me talking about 'the dignity' and 'real character' and 'integrity' of the people down here, I would tell them to get their kicks some other way, not by going native with the people who live the way they do because they have no other choice. And most of all, I would tell them to go ask the sharecropper in the Delta if he wants to stay the way he is, with his 'dignity' and 'integrity', or get what the rest of us have, the cars and clothes and washing machines and everything else.

"It's a fact that a lot of the people we've met down here are stronger than we ever assumed. And a lot of them really do treat their children in a different way than we do—and sometimes it's for the better. The kids are close. They sleep together and help one another. They don't go off by themselves, the way we do. They're respectful to their parents, and to grown-ups, and very good to one another. They have a real warmth and humor and a natural kind of direct-ness or honesty—I don't know what to call it, but I see every one of us noticing it, and I hear them all trying to describe it, even the hard-nosed social science types. They're ashamed at what they see; they don't want to be troubled by finding anything 'good' in people they came to save from everything 'bad.' "

The longer we talked in our all-night "soul sessions," the more we found ourselves in agreement. We had shared similar experiences and found them surprising and worth considering. I think more than anything else we felt chastened by the sight of our own arrogance.[1] Late one night, a black man who lived nearby spoke up, confirming our feelings. "The people who help us, we're grateful to them," he said, "but I wish they wouldn't keep on telling us how sorry they are for us, how bad we have it. And I with their eyes wouldn't pop out every time they stay with us and see we're not crying all day long and running wild or something. The other day a white fellow, he said how wonder-ful my home is, and how good we eat and get along together, and how im-pressed he was by it all. And I was sure glad, but I wanted to take him aside and say, 'Ain't you nice, but don't be giving us that kind of compliment, because it shows on you what you don't know about us.' "

Of course people under stress can develop special strengths, while secu-rity tends to make one soft, though no one in his right mind can *recommend* hardship or suffering as a way of life, nor justify slavery, segregation, or pov-erty because they sometimes produce strong, stubborn people. The issue is one of justice—and not only to the black man. The black man deserves to be seen for who he is and what he has become. If giving him his due—as a citizen and longtime victim of all sorts of exploitation—requires first calling him de-stroyed, "sick," a psychological cripple, or a moral menace, then perhaps we should recognize our own political bankruptcy. If psychological or sociological labels are to be pinned on the black man, then those who do so might at least be careful to mention the enormous, perplexing issues that plague the white suburban middle class: a high divorce rate, juvenile crime, political indifference or inertia to match any rural black man's, psychiatric clinics and child-guidance centers filled to the brim and with waiting lists so long that some are called only after two or three years, greed and competitiveness that worried teachers see in the youngest boys and girls and accept wearily as a manifestation of the "system."

There are, to be fair, some observers who have consistently remarked on the considerable energy and "life" they see in slum children. They have seen openness, humor, real and winning vitality. Many ghetto children I know have a flesh and blood loyalty to one another, a disarming code of honor, a sharp, critical eye for the fake and pretentious, a delightful capacity to laugh, yell, shout, sing, congratulate themselves, and tickle others. Their language is often strong and expressive, their drawings full of action, feeling, and even searing social criticism.

One thing is certain, though: ghetto childhood tends to be short and swift. Those fast-moving animated children quickly grow old rather than grow up, and begin to show signs of the resignation accurately described by writer after writer. At twelve or thirteen these children feel that schools lead nowhere, that there will be jobs for only a few, that ahead lies only the prospect of an increasingly futile and bitter struggle to hang on to such health, possessions, and shelter as they have.

"They are alive, and you bet they are, and then they go off and quit," said one mother, summing it up for me. "I can tell it by their walk and how they look. They slow down and get so tired in their face, real tired. And they get all full of hate, and they look cross at you, as if I cheated them when I brought them into the world. I have seven, and two of them have gone that way, and to be honest, I expect my every child to have it happen—like it did to me. I just gave up when I was about fourteen or so. And what brings us back to life is having the kids and keeping them with us for a while, away from the outside and everything bad. But there comes a day when they ask you why it's like it is for us, and all you can do is shrug your shoulders, or sometimes you scream. But they know already, and they're just asking for the record. And it doesn't take but a few months to see that they're no longer kids, and they've lost all the hope and the life you tried to give them."

The vitality of each new child restores at least the possibility of hope in a parent, and so life in the ghetto persists in seeking after purpose and coherence. Mothers tell their children to do this or not to do that—even as they hold their breath in fear and doubt. Meanwhile, many of us comfortably on the outside hide our shame by listing the reasons we can't change things in our society, or by making the people who need those changes utterly dull and deteriorated.

Though we may console ourselves with some of the programs we offer the poor, others are not only condescending and self-defeating, but they overlook the very real assets and interests of ghetto children. It has never occurred to some of the welfare workers, educators, Head Start teachers I have met that "their" programs and policies bore, amuse, or enrage children from the slums.

Consider, for example, one ghetto family I visit twice a week. They are on welfare. Two children were in a Head Start program for a summer. An older son took part in an "enrichment" program. A teen-aged cousin has been in the Job Corps. At school the children are told by their teachers what they already know, that their school is "inadequate." The building is old, the corridors are packed with many more students than they were intended for, and the teachers are disciplinarians at most. The head of this family is a woman not much over thirty who regularly calls herself "old." Once she added that she was also "sick," and I immediately took notice, expecting to hear about an ache or pain I could diagnose. But she went on to say that she was "tired of everything they try to do to help us. They send us those welfare checks, and with them comes that lady who peeks around every corner here and gives me those long lectures on how I should do everything—like her, of course. I want to tell her to go charge around and become a spy, or one of those preachers who can find sin in a clean handkerchief.

"Then they take my kids to the Head Start thing, and the first thing I hear is the boys' fingernails are dirty, and they don't eat the proper food, and they don't use the right words, and the words they do use, no one can make them out. It's just like that with the other kids. They try to take them to those museums and places, and tell them how sorry life is here at home and in the neighborhood, and how they are no good, and something has to be done to make them better—make them like the rich ones, I guess.

"But the worst is that they just make you feel no good at all. They tell you they want to help you, but if you ask me they want to make you into *them* and leave you without a cent of yourself left to hang on to. I keep on asking them, why don't they fix the country up so that people can work, instead of patching up with this and that and giving us a few dollars—to keep us from starving right to death? Why don't they get out of here and let us be, and have our lives?"

I can think of many things that could be done to take advantage of what that mother already has. The city might help her take part in a school she felt was hers, was sensitive to her feelings, her experiences, her desires—as indeed schools are in many other communities. There is work in her neighborhood, in her building, that she and her family might want to do, might be paid to do. Her children might be encouraged to use the strong and familiar idiom they know. Why should they learn the stilted talk of people who continue to scorn them? They might be appreciated for their own dress, their own customs, their own interests and energies—their *style*. They might read books that picture them, their lives and their adventures. Perhaps, then, some perennial "observers" would be surprised. With work, with money, with self-respect that is not slyly thwarted or denied outright by every "public" agency, the poor might eventually turn out to be very much like—us.

NOTE

1. I have tried to document our experience and our dilemmas in the first volume of *Children of Crisis* and especially in its sequel, *Migrants, Sharecroppers, Mountaineers*.

If the Child Is Safe: A Struggle for America's Conscience and Future

In her search for the perfect birthday gift for her first-born son's 21st birthday, Marian Wright Edelman, a noted civil rights lawyer and champion for children, wrote a letter to her three sons. The letter became the best-selling book *The Measure of Our Success: A Letter to My Children and Yours* (Beacon Press, 1992), from which the following selection is taken. In the book, Edelman, through humor and with keen insight, describes her upbringing and the valuable lessons she learned from her family. She talks about the mix that her black Southern Baptist heritage and her husband's white Jewish culture brought to their sons. She offers 25 lessons for life, which transcend time and can apply to every child in America.

Edelman, founder and president of the Children's Defense Fund, was the first black woman to be admitted to the bar in Mississippi. Born in 1939, she is a graduate of Spelman College and Yale Law School. Her professional career began during the civil rights movement in the South in the 1960s. Through the years she has remained a steadfast advocate for children and families. The Children's Defense Fund, founded in 1973, provides a constant reminder to U.S. citizens that the state of children in America is fragile.

> If the child is safe everyone is safe.
> —G. Campbell Morgan, "The Children's Playground in the City of God,"
> The Westminster Pulpit (circa 1908)

> There is no finer investment for any country than putting milk into babies.
> —Winston Churchill

*T*he 1990s' struggle is for America's conscience and future—a future that is being determined right now in the bodies and minds and spirits of *every* American child—white, African American, Latino, Asian American, Native American, rich, middle class, and poor. Many of the battles for this future will not be as dramatic as Gettysburg or Vietnam or Desert Storm, but they will shape our place in the twenty-first century no less.

Ironically, as Communism is collapsing all around the world, the American Dream is collapsing all around America for millions of children, youths, and families in all racial and income groups. American is pitted against American as economic uncertainty and downturn increase our fears, our business failures, our poverty rates, our racial divisions, and the dangers of political demagoguery.

Family and community values and supports are disintegrating among all races and income groups, reflecting the spiritual as well as economic poverty of our nation. All our children are growing up today in an ethically polluted nation where instant sex without responsibility, instant gratification without effort, instant solutions without sacrifice, getting rather than giving, and hoarding rather than sharing are the too-frequent signals of our mass media, business, and political life.

All our children are threatened by pesticides and toxic wastes and chemicals polluting the air, water, and earth. No parent can shut out completely the pollution of our airwaves and popular culture, which glorify excessive violence, profligate consumption, easy sex and greed, and depict deadly alcohol and tobacco products as fun, glamorous, and macho.

All our children are affected by the absence of enough heroines and heroes in public and daily life, as the standard for success for too many Americans has become personal greed rather than common good, and as it has become enough to just get by rather than do one's best.

All our children are affected by escalating violence fueled by unbridled trafficking in guns and in the drugs that are pervasive in suburb, rural area, and inner city alike.

Young families of all races, on whom we count to raise healthy children for America's future, are in extraordinary trouble. They have suffered since the early 1970s a frightening cycle of plummeting earnings, a near doubling of birth rates among unmarried women, increasing numbers of single-parent families, falling income—the median income of young families with children fell by 26 percent between 1973 and 1989—and skyrocketing poverty rates. Forty percent of all children in families with a household head under thirty are poor. While many middle-class youths and young families see the future as a choice between a house and a child, many undereducated, jobless, poor youths and young adults trapped in inner-city war zones see the future as a choice between prison or death at the hands of gangs and drug dealers.

More and more Americans feel their children are being left behind. But poor children suffer most, and their numbers are growing—841,000 in 1990 alone. They are the small, faceless victims who have no one to speak and fight for them. We were mesmerized by the 1987 death of Lisa Steinberg, a child whose adoption was never completed or abuse detected by our overburdened, inadequate child welfare system. We cheered when Jessica McClure was rescued from an open well shaft in the yard of an unregulated family day care center run by a relative, a danger she should not have come close to in the first place. But when eight-month-old Shamal Jackson died in New York City from low birth-weight, poor nutrition, and viral infection—from poverty and homelessness—we didn't hear much about him. During his short life, he slept in shelters with strangers, in hospitals, in welfare hotels, in the welfare office, and in the subways he and his mother rode late at night when there was no place else to go. In the richest nation on earth, he never slept in an apartment or house. Nor have we heard about two-pound "Jason" fighting for his life at Children's Hospital in Washington, D.C., or about thousands of other babies in similar neonatal intensive care wards all over America. At birth—three months before he was due—Jason weighed just over one pound. He lives because tubes connect his lungs and every available vein to the many machines that are needed to feed him and keep him warm and enable him to take his next breath. He has a heart problem and has already suffered seizures because of damage to his nervous system caused by bleeding into his head—damage that, if he lives, will probably be permanent.

What exactly led to Jason's premature birth will never be known. We do know, however, that unless a mother receives early and ongoing prenatal care, conditions that lead to prematurity cannot be detected or treated. A third of our mothers do not receive the care they need because our health care system, unlike that of every other major industrialized nation, does not provide universal basic coverage for mothers and children.

Remember these children behind the statistics. All over America, they are the small human tragedies who will determine the quality and safety and economic security of America's future as much as your and my children will. The decision you and I and our leaders must make is whether we are going to invest in every American child or continue to produce thousands of school dropouts, teen parents, welfare recipients, criminals—many of whom are alienated from a society that turns a deaf ear to the basic human needs and longings of every child.

If recent trends continue, by the end of the century poverty will overtake one in every four children, and the share of children living with single parents will also rise. One in every five births and more than one in three black births in the year 2000 will be to a mother who did not receive cost-effective early prenatal care. One of every five twenty-year-old women will be a mother, and more than four out of five of those young mothers will not be married. And the social security system that all of us count on to support us in our old age will depend on the contributions of fewer children—children we are failing today.

If we do not act immediately to protect America's children and change the misguided national choices that leave too many of them unhealthy, unhoused, ill-fed, and undereducated, during the next four years

1,080,000	American babies will be born at low birth-weight, multiplying their risk of death or disability,
143,619	babies will die before their first birthday,
4,400,000	babies will be born to unmarried women,
2,000,000	babies will be born to teen mothers,

15,856	children 19 or younger will die by firearms,
2,784	children younger than 5 will die by homicide,
9,208	children 19 or younger will commit suicide,
1,620,000	young people ages 16 to 24 will fail to complete high school,
3,780,000	young people will finish high school but not enroll in college,
599,076	children younger than 18 will be arrested for alcohol-related offenses, 359,600 for drug offenses, and 338,292 for violent crimes,
7,911,532	public school students will be suspended, and
3,600,000	infants will be born into poverty.

It is a spiritually impoverished nation that permits infants and children to be the poorest Americans. Over 13 million children in our rich land go without the basic amenities of life—more than the total population of Illinois, Pennsylvania, or Florida. If every citizen in the state of Florida became poor, the president would declare a national disaster. Yet he and Congress have yet to recognize child and family poverty and financial insecurity as the national disaster it is and to attack it with a fraction of the zeal and shared commitment we now apply to digging out after a devastating hurricane or earthquake or fire. We moved more than 1.7 million elderly persons out of poverty in the three years following the 1972 revisions to the Social Security Act that indexed senior citizens' benefits to inflation. Surely we can provide families with children equitable treatment.

It is a morally lost nation that is unable and unwilling to disarm our children and those who kill our children in their school buses, strollers, yards, and schools, in movie theaters, and in McDonald's. Death stalks America's playgrounds and streets without a declaration of war—or even a sustained declaration of concern by our president, Congress, governors, state and local elected officials, and citizens.

Every day, 135,000 children bring a gun to school. In 1987, 415,000 violent crimes occurred in and around schools. Some inner-city children are exposed to violence so routinely that they exhibit post-traumatic stress symptoms similar to those that plague many Vietnam combat veterans. Still, our country is unwilling to take semiautomatic machine guns out of the hands of its citizens. Where are the moral guerrillas and protesters crying out that life at home is as precious as life abroad? Isn't it time for a critical mass of Americans to join our law enforcement agencies and force our political leaders to halt the proliferation of guns? Every day twenty-three teens and young adults are killed by firearms in America.

In response to a distant tyrant, we sent hundreds of thousands of American mothers and fathers, sons and daughters, husbands and wives, sisters and brothers to the Persian Gulf. According to Secretary of State James Baker, the Gulf War was fought to protect our "life style" and standard of living and the rights of the Kuwaiti people. No deficit or recession was allowed to stand in the way. How, then, can we reconcile our failure to engage equally the enemies of poverty and violence and family disintegration within our own nation? When are we going to mobilize and send troops to fight for the "life style" of the 100,000 American children who are homeless each night, to fight for the standard of living of thousands of young families whose earning capacity is eroding and who are struggling to buy homes, pay off college loans, and find and afford child care? Where are the leaders coming to the rescue of millions of poor working- and middle-class families fighting to hold together their fragile households on declining wages and jobs? Why are they not acting to help the one in six families with children headed by a working single mother—29 percent of whom are poor? Isn't it time to tell our leaders to bail out our young families with the same zeal as they bailed out failed thrift and banking institutions to the tune of an estimated $115 billion by 1992?

What do we *really* value as Americans when the president's 1992 budget proposed only $100 million to increase Head Start for *one year* and no addition for child care for working families, but $500 million *each day* for Desert Storm, $90 million *each day* to bail out profligate savings and loan institutions, and hundreds of millions more to give capital gains tax breaks to the rich? Between 1979 and 1989, the average income (adjusted for inflation) of the bottom fifth of families dropped by 6 percent while that of the top fifth surged upward by 17 percent. The poorest fifth of American families with children lost 21 percent of their income.

Why were we able to put hundreds of thousands of troops and support personnel in Saudi Arabia within a few months to fight Saddam Hussein when we are unable to mobilize hundreds of teachers or doctors and nurses and social workers for desperately underserved inner cities and rural areas to fight the tyranny of poverty and ignorance and child neglect and abuse?

Isn't it time for the president and Congress and all of us to redefine our national security and invest as much time and leadership and energy to solving our problems at home as we do to our problems abroad?

It is an ethically confused nation that has allowed truth-telling and moral example to become devalued commodities. Too many of us hold to the philosophy that "government is not the solution to our problems, government is the problem." If government is seen as an illegitimate enterprise, if the public purposes of one's job are not considered a high calling, and if government has no purpose other than its own destruction, the restraints against unethical behavior in both the public and private sectors quickly erode. As a result, for every Michael Deaver and for every Elliot Abrams, from the public sector, there is an Ivan Boesky or a Reverend Jim Bakker in the private sector. If the only principle our society adheres to is economist Adam Smith's "Invisible Hand," it leaves little or no room for the human hand, or the hand of God, whom the prophet Micah said enjoined us "to be fair and just and merciful." There is a hollowness at the core of a society if its members share no common purpose, no mutual goals, no joint vision—nothing to believe in except self-aggrandizement.

Isn't it time for us to hold our political leaders to their professed beliefs and promises about getting children ready for school and providing them health care and education?

It is a dangerously short-sighted nation that fantasizes absolute self-sufficiency as the only correct way of life. Throughout our history, we have given government help to our people and then have forgotten that fact when it came time to celebrate our people's achievements. Two hundred years ago, Congress granted federal lands to the states to help maintain public schools. In 1862, President Lincoln signed the Morrill Land-Grant Act, granting land for colleges. The first food voucher and energy assistance programs came, not during the New Deal or the War on Poverty, but at the end of the Civil War, when Congress and President Lincoln created the Freedman's Bureau. Federal help for vaccinations, vocational education, and maternal health began, not with Kennedy, Johnson, and Carter, but under Madison, Wilson, and Harding, respectively.

Our parents, grandparents, and great-grandparents benefited from this government help just as we all do today. Only the most blind of economists could doubt that American prosperity, like Japan's, is built on the synergistic relations between government and private initiative. But it is some of the most blind economists, political scientists, and "moral philosophers" who have the ear of many of our leaders or are themselves political leaders. Too many of them suffer from the peculiarly American amnesia or hypocrisy that wants us to think that poor and middle-class families must fend entirely for themselves; that makes us forget how government helps us all, regardless of class; and that makes us believe that the government is simply wasting its billions supporting a wholly dependent, self-perpetuating class of poor people, while doing nothing but taxing the rest of us.

Chrysler and Lee Iacocca didn't do it alone. Defense contractors don't do it alone. Welfare queens can't hold a candle to corporate kings in raiding the public purse. Most wealthy and middle-class families don't do it alone. Yet some begrudge the same security for low- and moderate-income families with children who must grow up healthy, educated, and productive to support our aging population.

The president and Congress and public must take the time and have the courage to make specific choices and not wield an indiscriminate budget ax or hide behind uniform but unjust freezes of current inequalities. They must also take time to distinguish between programs that work (like immunization, preventive health care, and Head Start) and programs that don't (like the B2 stealth bomber). They must apply the same standards of accountability for programs benefiting the rich and poor and middle class alike. They must hold the Pentagon to the same standards of efficiency as social programs. And isn't it time for the president and Congress to invest more in preventing rather than trying to mop up problems after the fact? Isn't it time to reassess national investment priorities in light of changing national and world needs? Does it make sense for our federal government to spend each hour this fiscal year $33.7 million on national defense, $23.6 million on the national debt, $8.7 million on the savings and loan bailout, $2.9 million on education, and $1.8 million on children's health?

Making hard choices and investing in our own people may help restore the confidence of citizens in government. The overarching task of leadership today in every segment of American society is to give our youths, and all Americans, a sense that we can be engaged in enterprises that lend meaning to life, that we can regain control over our families and our national destiny, and that we can make a positive difference individually and collectively in building a decent, safe nation and world.

America cannot afford to waste resources by failing to prevent and curb the national human deficit, which cripples our children's welfare today and costs billions in later remedial and custodial dollars. Every dollar we invest in preventive health care for mothers and children saves more than $3 later. Every dollar put into quality preschool education like Head Start saves $4.75 later. It costs more than twice as much to place a child in foster care as to provide family preservation services. The question is not whether we can afford to invest in every child; it is whether we can afford not to. At a time when future demographic trends guarantee a shortage of young adults who will be workers, soldiers, leaders, and parents, America cannot afford to waste a single child. With unprecedented economic competition from abroad and changing patterns of production at home that demand higher basic educational skills, America cannot wait another minute to do whatever is needed to ensure that today's and tomorrow's workers are well prepared rather than useless and alienated—whatever their color.

We cannot go back and change the last decade's birth rates. But we can prevent and reduce the damages to our children and families and ensure every child a healthy start, a head start, and a fair start right now. In the waning years of the twentieth century, doing what is right for children and doing what is necessary to save our national economic skin have converged.

When the new century dawns with new global economic and military challenges, America will be ready to compete economically and lead morally only if we

1. stop cheating and neglecting our children for selfish, short-sighted, personal, and political gain;
2. stop clinging to our racial past and recognize that America's ideals, future, and fate are as inextricably intertwined with the fate of its poor and nonwhite children as with its privileged and white ones;
3. love our children more than we fear each other and our perceived or real external enemies;
4. acquire the discipline to invest preventively and systematically in all of our children *now* in order to reap a better trained work force and more stable future *tomorrow;*
5. curb the desires of the overprivileged so that the survival needs of the less privileged may be met, and spend less on weapons of death and more on lifelines of constructive development for our citizens;
6. set clear, national, state, city, community, and personal goals for child survival and development, and invest whatever leadership, commitment, time, money, and sustained effort are needed to achieve them;
7. struggle to begin to live our lives in less selfish and more purposeful ways, redefining success by national and individual character and service rather than by national consumption and the superficial barriers of race and class.

The mounting crisis of our children and families is a rebuke to everything America professes to be. While the cost of repairing our crumbling national foundation will be expensive in more ways than one, the cost of not repairing it, or of patching cosmetically, may be fatal.

The place to begin is with ourselves. Care. As you read about or meet some of the children and families in this country who need your help, put yourself in their places as fellow Americans. Imagine you or your spouse being pregnant, and not being able to get enough to eat or see a doctor or know that you have a hospital for delivery. Imagine your child hungry or injured, and you cannot pay for food or find health care. Imagine losing your job and having no income, having your unemployment compensation run out, not being able to pay your note or rent, having no place to sleep with your children, having nothing. Imagine having to stand in a soup line at a church or Salvation Army station after you've worked all your life, or having to sleep in a shelter with strangers and get up and out early each morning, find some place to go with your children, and not know if you can sleep there again that night. If you take the time to imagine this, perhaps you can also take the time to do for them what you would want a fellow citizen to do for you. Volunteer in a homeless shelter or soup kitchen or an afterschool tutoring or mentoring program. Vote. Help to organize your community to speak out for the children who need you. Visit a hospital neonatal intensive care nursery or AIDS and boarder baby ward and spend time rocking and caring for an individual child. Adopt as a pen pal a lonely child who never gets a letter from anyone. Give a youth a summer job. Teach your child tolerance and empathy by your example.

Essential individual service and private charity are not substitutes for public justice, or enough alone to right what's wrong in America. Collective mobilization and political action are also necessary to move our nation forward in the quest for fairness and opportunity for every American.

PART TWO

Programs for Young Children

Chapter 3   Day Nurseries/Nursery Schools   53

Chapter 4   Kindergarten   78

CHAPTER 3 Day Nurseries/Nursery Schools

3.1 ABIGAIL ADAMS ELIOT

Report of the Ruggles Street Nursery School and Training Center

A great deal of what we know about how early programs for young children operated has been gleaned from reading observations, teachers' diaries, and letters. One such program is described in the following selection from "Report of the Ruggles Street Nursery School and Training Center," in Samuel J. Braun and Esther P. Edwards, eds., *History and Theory of Early Childhood Education* (Wadsworth, 1972). In it, Abigail Adams Eliot presents a detailed view of a classroom in the Ruggles Street Nursery School. The school operated in a lower socioeconomic area of Boston. Prior to Eliot's influence, it was a day nursery offering basic custodial care, with a major emphasis on maintaining a clean and neat environment. The goal was discipline, and children had little opportunity to engage in activities specifically designed for their enjoyment or development.

After graduating from Radcliffe College in 1914, Eliot became a social worker in Boston. In 1921 she went to England for six months to study with Margaret McMillan, who, along with her sister Rachel, operated open-air nursery school programs for children from the slums of London.

When Eliot returned to Boston in January 1922, she began a new type of nursery school housed at 147 Ruggles Street. It broke away from the traditional day nursery by offering planned experiences for young children and involving their parents.

In 1930 Eliot became one of the first women to receive a doctoral degree from Harvard University's Graduate School of Education and the first at Harvard to focus on young children in a nursery school setting as a subject for a doctoral dissertation. Eliot worked at the Ruggles Street Nursery School and Nursery Training School for 30 years. By 1951 the training school had evolved into the Eliot-Pearson Child Study Center at Tufts University. To help develop nursery training on the west coast, Eliot moved to California and assisted in the establishment of Pacific Oaks College.

*T*he main playroom contained low tables and chairs, blackboards, blossoming plants on low window sills, an aquarium containing goldfish, a sand box, packing box, boxes of "mighty blocks," piano and low shelves. In the toilet rooms beyond low sinks containing basins with low faucets and low soap containers; the mirrors are low, and so are the hooks for towels, combs, cups, tooth brushes, each marked with a child's name and a small distinguishing picture. Upstairs two large sleeping rooms are full of little beds, mostly of the folding variety for use out-of-doors in good weather; each child has his own bed and blanket sleeping bag. [The yard is complete with flower garden, pool and sandbox.]

What do they do all day? During the hour when they are arriving, there is in attendance every day a nurse from the Community Health Association who inspects each child for symptoms of contagious disease. She also talks with the mothers about health problems, and the mothers in turn consult her; she helps teach the children health habits. The steadily growing group of children plays about, each as he chooses, until the nurse is ready to wind up with a unanimous gargle of salt and water—a fascinating noise truly! The next half hour is spent partly in the kindergarten "circle," but chiefly in music, rhythm work, songs, dramatic games, and "the band." Preparations follow for the mid-morning lunch,—preparations all quite in the children's charge, from hand-washing to placing of tables and chairs, passing the cups and napkins, pouring milk and handing round crackers. Clearing up afterwards is also done by the children, in turn day by day: they wash and wipe the cups, clear the table, sweep the floor.

Next follows a period of "quiet" occupations at tables or on the floor. With a little wise guidance perhaps, each child selects what he wants from a special closet containing a variety of material—certain of the kindergarten gifts, some of the Montessori apparatus, and some of Miss McMillan's; also chalk, scissors, paste, plasticine, hammers and nails, and several kinds of blocks.

In this work he is guided as little as possible and is limited only in two ways: he must make a genuine attempt to use what he has taken, and he must put away one thing before taking another. Sometimes a child will remain busily engaged with one occupation for as much as three-quarters of an hour; another may in the same length of time try his hand at three different things. Often the older children like to be gathered in a group to work out some simple "project." In due season, everyone is seen putting away his occupation and, if it is an out-of-doors day, lugging his chair within and perhaps replacing it by some of the big playthings shown in the pictures, for this is the period of active play recorded in some of the best illustrations.

Dinner hour is approaching. The company swarms again into the toilet rooms and with immense pride and zest prepares itself, with an elaborate washing of faces and hands, combing of hair, drinking of water, and tying on of bibs. Even more than the luncheon, dinner gives scope for amazing baby achievements—patience in waiting, skill in passing, courtesy in giving and receiving—and all with perfect decorum yet perfect content.

Dinner over, they brush their teeth and clamber gaily upstairs, or trot out under the trees, take off their shoes, crawl into their bags, and sleep. After nearly two hours of sleep or quiet resting, they get up happy and fresh and are ready for a drink of orange juice and a romp or stories or games before going home.

Initial Support Through Guides to Speech and Action

Katherine H. Read was a professor in the School of Home Economics at Oregon State University when she wrote *The Nursery School: A Human Relationships Laboratory* (W. B. Saunders, 1950), one of the earliest texts in the field of early childhood education and the source of the following selection. The book's subtitle is a clue to the evolution of early childhood education.

During the 1920s and 1930s, many nursery schools were established, providing a setting for the new field of child study. The nursery school became a laboratory for observing young children. In the early years of early childhood education, nursery school teachers studied children's physical growth and development. By the late 1940s, when Read was completing her text, the focus of study had turned to the emotional-social development of children. From Read's perspective, the teachers of nursery schools were to learn from children through constant observation, interpretation, and evaluation. Their goal was to understand behavior, both the children's and their own as adults.

Read's book was reprinted several times and translated into six languages. Due to its widespread use in teacher education programs, it has been a valuable source of information for many people working in the field. Almost 50 years later, although some teaching practices have changed, Read's guidelines are still viewed as appropriate for teachers when interacting with young children.

WE ARE LIKELY TO FEEL INADEQUATE AT FIRST

Before we can follow any "guides," we must first accept the feeling of being new and strange in a situation. We must feel comfortable about being inadequate. In any new experience we are sure to be uncertain about what to do, to feel somewhat inadequate and thus uncomfortable. When we stop to think about this, we realize that feelings like these are to be expected. They form an almost inevitable part of any learning and do not need to be concealed or denied. In making a good adjustment in any new situation we must first accept the reality of our feelings and respond to them in a positive way.

Too frequently we only increase our feelings of inadequacy by struggling against them, making it more difficult to develop constructive ways of acting— as a person who fears drowning makes help difficult because of his struggles. Sometimes we try to defend ourselves against feeling inadequate in a new situation by plunging into action as though to take our minds off the way we feel. In the nursery school we may do unnecessary things like talking to children when talking serves no useful purpose for the child. We may offer help which is not needed or try to start activities which have no real place at the moment in the child's pattern of play. Sometimes we my defend ourselves against feeling inadequate by withdrawing and taking no action at all. Sometimes we may fight against the necessity for direction at first by being very critical of the direction given; and at other times we may seek reassurance by trying to be completely dependent on instructions, insisting that these be specific and detailed so that there is no room for uncertainty.

These adjustments or defenses are part of a resistance to change which we all feel and which is sometimes a protection and often a limitation on growth. All of us have established certain patterns of reacting in new situations. These patterns are probably made up of more and less constructive adaptations. It is important for us to identify these adaptations and to select and add to the more useful ones. It is not always useful to reject an experience just because we are uncomfortable in it. Growth is often an uncomfortable process. Probably no growth takes place without some struggle. But growth is rewarding and satisfying when we have mobilized our resources and reduced the conflicts which interfere with our growth. Instead of spending energy trying to deny feelings, we can make constructive use of them.

GUIDES OR SIMPLE RULES GIVE SUPPORT

When one feels inadequate, one needs support of some kind. What are the supports available in the situation? In the nursery school, for example, what help can one get from the experienced teacher? What help can one find in one's own past experiences in related situations, in books or from discussion? In any new experience we begin to gain confidence when we assemble the useful, appropriate supports and build a framework in which to operate.

. . . [We] will list some technics and principles which can be depended on at first as guides to action in the nursery school. These can be applied in an increasingly individual way with added experience. The success of some of these technics depends in part on the relationship built up with individual children. Time is required to build as well as understand relationships, but during the process these "rules" will give clues to appropriate action. In time, with experience and increasing insight, each one of us will make her own generalizations and add new interpretations.

Set down alone, these statements may seem somewhat like letters in an alphabet. Only when they are combined by experience into larger units will they have much meaning. At this point they must be accepted as part of the alphabet which goes to make a "language" of human behavior.

Here they are.

GUIDES

In Speech
1. State suggestions or directions in a positive rather than a negative form.
2. Give the child a choice only when you intend to leave the situation up to him.
3. Use only words and a tone of voice which will help the child feel confident and reassured, not afraid or guilty or ashamed.
4. Avoid motivating a child by making comparisons between one child and another or encouraging competition.
5. Use your voice as a teaching tool.
6. Redirection is likely to be most effective when it is consistent with the child's own motives or interests.

In Action
7. Avoid making models in any art medium for the children to copy.
8. Give the child the minimum of help in order that he may have the maximum chance to grow in independence.
9. Make your suggestions effective by reinforcing them when necessary.
10. The timing of a suggestion may be as important as the suggestion itself.
11. When limits are necessary, they should be clearly defined and consistently maintained.
12. Be alert to the total situation. Use the most strategic positions for supervising.
13. The health and safety of the children are a primary concern at all times.
14. Observe and take notes!

GUIDES IN SPEECH

1. State Suggestions or Directions in a Positive Form.

A positive suggestion is one which tells a child what to do instead of pointing out what he is not to do. If a child has already done what he shouldn't do or we estimate that he is about to do this,, he needs help in getting another, better, idea. We give him this kind of help when we direct his attention to what we want him to do.

It has been demonstrated experimentally that directions stated in a positive way are more effective than the same directions given negatively. This can be subjected to proof informally in many situations. For example, a teacher in nursery school demonstrated it in this situation. She was finding it difficult to weigh the children because almost every child reached for support when he felt the unsteadiness of the scale platform. When the teacher asked them not to touch anything, she had very little success. She changed her negative direction to a positive one. "Keep your hands down at your sides," and the children did just that. Telling them what to do, instead of what not to do, brought results.

A positive direction is less likely to rouse resistance than a negative one. It makes help seem constructive rather than limiting and interfering. Perhaps the child is doing the thing because he thinks it annoys us. By emphasizing the positive we reduce the attention and thus the importance of the negative aspect of his behavior. We usually help rather than hinder when we make a positive suggestion.

In addition, when we make suggestions in a positive way we are giving the child a sound pattern to imitate when he himself directs his friends. He is likely to be more successful, to meet with less resistance, if he puts his suggestions in a positive form. We give him a good social tool to use. One can tell something about the kind of direction that a child has received as one listens to the kind of direction that he gives in play.

More important still, having clearly in mind what we want the child to do, we can steer him toward this behavior with more confidence and assurance—with more chance of success. Our goal is clear to us and to him. We are more likely to feel adequate and to act effectively when we put a statement positively.

To put directions positively represents a step in developing a more positive attitude toward children's behavior inside ourselves. Our annoyance often increases as we dwell on what the child shouldn't be doing, but our feelings may be different when we turn our attention to what the child should be doing in the situation. We may have more sympathy for the child's problem as we try to figure out just what he could do under the circumstances. It helps us appreciate the difficulties he may be having in figuring out a better solution.

At first it is wise to allow oneself no exceptions to this rule, to discard negative suggestions entirely. It is too easy to slip into old habits and rely on the negative. Making only positive suggestions is a hard exercise because most of us have depended heavily on negative suggestions in the past and have had them used on us. We tend to resist the effort it takes to discover different words and different patterns of thinking. But it is worth correcting oneself whenever one makes a negative statement in order to hasten the learning of this basic technic. Every direction should be given in a positive form.

Here are some examples:

1. "Ride your tricycle around the bench," instead of "Don't bump the bench."
2. "Throw your ball over here," instead of "Don't hit the window."
3. "Leave the heavy blocks on the ground," instead of "Don't put the heavy blocks on that high board."
4. "Give me the ball to hold while you're climbing," instead of "Don't climb with that ball in your hand."
5. "Take a bite of your dinner now," instead of "Don't play at the table."
6. "Take little bites and then it will all go in your mouth," instead of "Don't take such big bites and then you won't spill."
7. "Pull the plug now and dry your hands," instead of "Don't spend any more time washing."

Here Is an Exercise. Observe and record ten positive statements and contrast each with the corresponding negative statement. Estimate the effectiveness of the statements you recorded.

2. Give the Child a Choice Only When You Intend to Leave the Situation Up to Him.

Choices are legitimate. With increasing maturity one makes an increasing number of choices. We accept the fact that being able to make decisions helps develop maturity. But there are decisions which a child is not ready to make because of his limited capacities and experience. We must be careful to avoid offering him a choice when we are not really willing to let him decide the question. Sometimes one hears a mother say to her child, "Do you want to go home now?" and when he replies, "No," she acts as though he were being disobedient because he did not answer the question in the way she wanted him to answer it. What she really meant to say was, "It's time to go home now."

Questions such as the one above are more likely to be used when a person feels uncertain or wishes to avoid raising an issue which he is not sure that he can handle. Sometimes using a question is only a habit of speaking. But it is confusing to the child to be asked a question when what is wanted is not information but only confirmation. It is important to guard against the tendency to use a question unless the circumstances make a question legitimate.

Circumstances differ, but usually the nursery school child is not free to choose such things as the time to go home or the time to eat or rest. He is not free to hurt others or to damage property. On the other hand, he is free to decide such things as whether he wants to play outside or inside, or what play materials he wants, or whether he needs to go to the toilet (except in the case of a very young child).

Sometimes a child may be offered a choice to clarify a situation for him. For example, he may be interfering with someone's sand pies and the teacher may ask, "Do you want to stay in the sandbox?" A response of "Yes" is defined further as, "Then you will need to play at this end of the box out of Bobby's way."

It is important to be clear in one's mind as to whether one is really offering the child a choice before one asks a question. Be sure that your questions are legitimate ones.

Here Is an Exercise. Observe and record ten situations in which a child was asked a question. Classify the reasons for using a question as

1. to get information about a fact
2. to discover an opinion or preference
3. to define a situation
4. some other purpose

Did the questions serve legitimate purposes? Did they clarify or confuse the situations in which they were used? Discuss briefly.

3. Use Only Words and Tone of Voice Which Will Help the Child Feel Confident and Reassured.

The words that one uses are important as well as how one uses them. The wise parent or teacher will never use words which are calculated to make a child feel afraid or guilty or ashamed. This means that words like "bad boy" or "naughty girl" will never appear in the vocabulary of understanding parents and teachers.

I can hear someone saying helplessly, "But aren't there things that a child can't be allowed to do? Doesn't one have to show a child sometimes that he's been naughty?" Of course there are things which a child cannot be allowed to do, but making a child ashamed or guilty is not the only way to change his behavior. In fact, building feelings like these in him may make it more difficult for him to be "good." Feeling afraid or ashamed or guilty are such damaging feelings that they often prevent learning and create problems greater than the old ones. It is dangerous to rely on creating such feelings as a method of control.

One of the reasons why we study behavior is to gain understanding and skills so that we will not have to fall back on crude methods. We need to learn constructive ways of influencing behavior if we are to promote sound personality growth. Neither children nor adults are likely to develop desirable behavior patterns as the result of fear or shame or guilt. Improvement will be more apparent than real, and any change is likely to be accompanied by resentment and an underlying rejection of the behavior involved when these methods of control are used.

Perhaps the adult observes a child annoying a group of children in the doll corner. She may recognize the child's behavior as a clumsy attempt to find a place in the group. Rather than reprove him, she may suggest "You might ask them if you can be the daddy for them." If this brings success, he gains confidence and his behavior improves. Labeling his first approach as "bad" discourages his friendliness and gives him no help.

It takes time to learn constructive ways of guiding behavior. The first step is to eliminate the destructive patterns in use. We must discard the gestures, the expressions, the tones of voice as well as the words that convey the impression that we disapprove and want the other person to feel ashamed of himself. . . .

Here Is an Exercise. Observe and record a situation in which the adult changed a child's behavior pattern and added to his feeling of confidence at the same time.

4. Avoid Comparisons and Competition Among Children.

Comparing one child to another is a dangerous way to try to influence behavior. We may get results in changed behavior, but these changes may not all be improvements. Some of these results are sure to be damaging to the child's feeling of adequacy and his friendliness.

Competitive schemes for getting children to dress more quickly or to eat more of anything else may have some effects that are not what we want.

Children who are encouraged to be competitive are very likely to quarrel more with one another. In any competition someone always loses and he's likely to feel hurt and resentful. Even the winner may be afraid of failing next time, or he may feel an unjustified superiority if the contest was an unequal one. Competition does not build friendly, social feelings.

Competition not only handicaps smooth social relationships but creates problems within the child himself. We live in a highly competitive society, it is true, but the young child is not ready to enter into much competition until his concept of himself as an adequate person has developed enough so that he can stand the strains and the inevitable failures that are part of competition. On the one hand, constant success is not a realistic experience, and does not prepare a child well for what he will meet later. Too many failures, on the other hand, may make him feel weak and helpless. Both are poor preparation for a competitive world. For sound growth it is important to protect children from competitive situations until they are more mature. It is important to avoid competitive kinds of motivation.

It is important, too, to keep children from placing an undue value on success and failure. Children should not feel that their chances for getting attention and approval depend on being "first" or "beating" someone or being the "best." They should feel sure of acceptance whether they succeed or fail.

This raises a question about what is sound motivation, anyway. Do we really get dressed in order to set a speed record or to surpass someone else? Motivation like this could logically lead to such useless activities as flagpole sitting. Isn't it true, rather, that the reason for getting dressed is to keep warm and comfortable? Isn't it also true that we dress ourselves because there is satisfaction in being independent and that we complete dressing quickly in order to go on to another activity? There may be a point in spending time enjoying the process of dressing if there happens to be nothing of any greater importance coming next. We may be better off when we get pleasure out of the doing of a thing, not just in getting the thing done. It is wise to be sure that we are motivating children in a sound way even though we may move more slowly. We ensure a sounder growth for them, and give them a better preparation for the years ahead.

One has only to listen to children on a playground to realize how disturbing highly competitive feelings are to them. Statements like "You can't beat me," or "I'm bigger than you," or "Mine is better than yours" increase the friction and prevent children from getting along well together.

Here Is an Exercise. Observe situations in which the teacher attempts to influence a child's behavior by giving him a motive for changing. List the motives used and analyze their value for the child. Was the motive sound? Was it related to the situation? Was it one that the child could use again in other situations?

5. Use Your Voice As a Teaching Tool.

All of us have known parents and teachers who seem to feel that the louder they speak, the greater their chances of controlling behavior. We may also have observed that these same people often have more problems than the parents and teachers who speak more quietly but are listened to.

It may be necessary to speak firmly, but it is never necessary to raise one's voice. The most effective speech is simple and direct and slow. Decreasing speed is more effective than raising pitch.

It is a good rule never to call or shout across any play area, inside or outside. It is always better to move nearer the person to whom you are speaking. Children as well as adults grow irritated when shouted at. Your words will get a better reception if they are spoken quietly, face to face.

Speech conveys feelings as well as ideas. Children are probably very sensitive to the tone quality, the tightness in a voice, for example, which reveals annoyance or unfriendliness or fear—no matter what the words may be. One can try for a pleasant tone of voice and one may find one's feelings improving along with one's voice.

The teacher sets a pattern, too, in her speech as she does in other ways. Children are more likely to use their voices in loud harsh ways if the teacher uses her voice in these ways. Voice quality can be improved with training, and every one of us could probably profit from speech work to improve our voice. A well-modulated voice is an asset worth cultivating.

Here Is an Exercise. Listen to the quality of the voices around you. What feeling do the tones express when one pays no attention to the words spoken? Note the differences in pitch, in rate, and in volume in the voices of the teachers. Report a situation in which you feel that the tone of voice was more important than the words in influencing the child's behavior.

6. Redirection Is Most Effective When Consistent With the Child's Motives or Interests.

What does this mean? It simply means that we'll be more successful in changing the child's behavior if we attempt to turn his attention to an act which has equal value as an interest or outlet for him. If he's throwing a ball dangerously near a window, for example, we can suggest a safer place to throw it. If he's throwing something dangerous because he's angry, we can suggest an acceptable way of draining off angry feelings—like throwing against a backstop or using a punching bag or pounding at the workbench. In the first case his interest is in throwing and in the second case it's in expressing his anger. Our suggestions for acting differently will take into account the different meaning in his behavior. We will always try to suggest something which meets the needs he is expressing in his behavior.

If a group is running around wildly after a long period of quiet play, its members may need a suggestion about engaging in some vigorous and constructive play like raking leaves outside. Their needs will not be met by a suggestion about sitting quietly and listening to a story. The meaning of their behavior lies in a need for activity. The teacher's part is to help them find some acceptable expression for this need. If they are running around wildly, on the other hand, because they are fatigued by too much activity and stimulation, a suggestion about listening to a story meets their need for rest.

To redirect wisely requires some understanding of why the child is acting as he does. Insight will increase with experience and thought and contacts with the individual child. There can be no rules. If we could say that when children are noisy, one should do this or that, it would be simple. We can only say that it depends on why the child is behaving as he is.

Redirection will be most successful when the individual interests of the child are considered. One child enjoys music, another books. A suggestion for quiet play, for example, will take different forms depending on the interests of the child. Some children enjoy certain companions more than others. Some are satisfied by having some time alone with an adult while others are restless without companions of their own age. As one knows the child, one can direct more effectively in terms of motive and individual interests.

Effective redirection faces the situation and does not avoid or divert. The teacher who sees a child going outdoors on a cold day without his coat does not give him help when she stops him by saying, "Stay inside and listen to the story now." She is avoiding the question of the need for a coat. She helps him by saying, "You'll be ready to go out as soon as you put on your coat." On the other hand, suggesting a substitute activity may help the child face a situation as in the case of two children wanting the same piece of equipment. The teacher helps when she says to one, "No, it's Bill's turn now. You might rake these leaves while you're waiting for your turn." By her redirection she helps him face his problem. Redirection should help the child face his problem by showing him how it can be met, not by diverting him.

GUIDES IN ACTION

7. Avoid Making Models in Any Art Medium for the Children to Copy.

This may seem like an arbitrary rule. We hope that it will seem justified later. Of course it takes away the fun of drawing a man or making little dogs or Santa Clauses out of clay for an admiring crowd of preschoolers. All this may seem like innocent fun, but we must remember that art is valuable because it is a means of self-expression. It is a language to express feelings—to drain off tension or to express wellbeing. The young child needs avenues of expression. His speech is limited. His feelings are strong. In clay or sand or mud, at the easel, through finger paints, he expresses feelings for which he has little other language. If he has models before him, he may be blocked in using art as a means of *self*-expression. He will be less likely to be creative and more likely to be limited to trying to copy. Art then becomes only another area where he strives to imitate the adult who can do things much better than he can.

Notice what happens to a group at the clay table when the adult makes something. The children watch and then ask, "Make one for me." It isn't much use to say, "You make one for yourself." They can't do it as well and they feel that the adult is uncooperative. Most of them drift away from the table, the meaning gone out of the experience. It is no longer art or self-expression.

You may see children cramped over a paper with a crayon trying to make a car like the one the adult made, or children who will not touch the paints because they are afraid that they can't "make something." They may well envy the joy of the freer child who splashes color at the easel, delighting in its lines and masses, and is well content with what he's done. He has had no patterns to follow.

The need for help with technics comes much later after the child has explored the possibilities in different art media and feels that these can be used as avenues of self-expression. Then the child will want to learn how to use the material to express better what *he* wants to express, but not to imitate better.

The skillful teacher will avoid getting entangled in "pattern making" under any guise. She may sit at the clay table, for example, feeling the clay, patting it and enjoying it as the children do, but she will not "make" anything. It is possible, of course, for children to watch adults who have found in art a means of self-expression as they work in their favorite medium, and for this to be a valuable experience for the children. Being with an adult who is expressing himself through an art medium is valuable for any child, but it is a very different experience from having an adult draw a man or a dog to amuse one. Avoid patterns!

Here Is an Exercise. Which statements may have the effect of patterning the child's expression and reducing his creativeness?

1. What are you painting?
2. What lovely colors!
3. Your picture would be nicer if it were neater.
4. See what a nice house you can make.
5. It's fun to paint, isn't it?
6. You're not through yet. You're supposed to cover all the paper.
7. That doesn't look much like a car, does it?

8. Give the Child the Minimum of Help in Order That He May Have the Maximum Chance to Grow in Independence.

There are all kinds of ways to help a child help himself if we take time to think about them, such as letting him help to turn the door knob with us, so that he will get the feel of how to handle a door knob and may be able to do it alone some day, or such as putting on his rubbers while he sits beside us instead of picking him up and holding him on our laps, a position which will make it hard for him ever to do the job himself someday. Too many times the child has to climb down from the adult's lap when he might have started in a more advantageous position in the first place on his trip to independence.

Giving the minimum of help may mean showing a child how to get a block or box to climb on when he wants to reach something rather than reaching it for him. It may mean giving him time enough to work out a problem rather than stepping in and solving it for him. Children like to solve problems, and it is hard to estimate how much their self-confidence is increased by independent solving of problems. To go out and gather a child into one's arms to bring him in for lunch may be an effective way of seeing that he gets there, but it deprives him of the chance to take any responsibility in getting himself inside. It is important to give a child the minimum of help in order to allow him to grow himself as much as possible.

Here Is an Exercise. Observe and record five situations in which the adult gave only the minimum of help needed by the child for success. Estimate the value of the situation for the child.

9. Make Your Suggestions Effective by Reinforcing Them When Necessary.

Sometimes it is necessary to add several technics together in order to be effective. A verbal suggestion, even though given positively, may not be enough in itself. "It's time to come in for lunch," may need to be reinforced by another suggestion as, "I'll help you park your wagon," if the child is reluctant to leave his play, and then reinforced by actual help in parking. A glance at the right moment, moving nearer a child, a verbal suggestion, actual physical help are all technics, and one must judge when they are to be used. Give only the minimum help necessary but give as much help as may be necessary.

One teacher says quietly, "It's time to go inside now" and moves toward the house. The child moves with her. Another teacher says, "It's time to go inside" and stands as though waiting to see what the child will do. He stays where he is for her behavior does not reinforce her words. Her behavior suggests something different.

When several children are playing together, some will accept suggestion more readily than others for different reasons. Success with one child will reinforce one's chances of success with others. It's wise to consider which child to approach first when one wishes to influence a group.

One of the most common faults of parents and teachers is that of using too many words, of giving two or three directions when one would have been sufficient. Anxiety and insecurity often take the form of over-verbalizing, showering the child with directions. Children will develop a protective "deafness" to too many words. It is important to have confidence in the child's ability to hear and respond to one suggestion, given only once. It is better to add different technics together until one is successful rather than to depend solely on words.

Here Is an Exercise. Observe and record five situations in which the adult appeared to be successful because she used several technics.

10. The Timing of a Suggestion May Be As Important As the Suggestion Itself.

Through experience and insight one can increase one's skill in giving a suggestion at the moment when it will do the most good. When a suggestion fails to get the desired results, it may be due to the "timing."

Advice given too soon deprives the child of a chance to try to work a thing out for himself. It deprives him of the satisfaction of solving his own problem. It may very well be resented. A suggestion made too late may have lost any chance of being successful. The child may be too discouraged or irritated to be able to act on it.

Help at the right moment may mean a supporting hand *before* the child loses his balance and falls, or arbitration *before* two boys come to blows over a wagon, or the suggestion of a new activity *before* the group grows tired and disorganized. Under a skillful teacher a group functions more smoothly because of all the things that never happen. Effective guidance depends on knowing how to forestall and prevent trouble by the proper timing of help as much as on knowing what to do when trouble occurs.

Here Is an Exercise. Report a situation in which the suggestion or help was well timed. Why?

Report a situation where the suggestion of help given failed apparently because of poor timing. Why?

11. When Limits Are Necessary, They Should Be Clearly Defined and Consistently Maintained.

There are some things which must not be done. There are limits beyond which a child cannot be allowed to go. The important thing is to be sure that the limits set are necessary limits and that they are clearly defined. Much of the difficulty between adults and children which is labeled "discipline" exists because of confusion about what the limits are. In a well-planned environment there will not be many "no's" but these "no's" will be clearly defined and the child will understand them.

We are very likely to overestimate the child's capacity to grasp the point of what we say. Our experience is much more extensive than his. Without realizing it we take many things for granted. The child lacks experience. If he is to understand what the limits are, these limits must be clearly and simply defined for him.

When we are sure that a limit is necessary and that the child understands it, we can maintain it with confidence. It is easy to feel unsure or even guilty about maintaining limits. Our own feelings bother us here. We may be afraid to maintain limits because we were over-controlled, and we turn away from the resentment and hostility that limits arouse in us. Because of our past experiences we may not want to take any responsibility for controlling behavior. Gradually we should learn to untangle our feelings and handle situations on their own merits with confidence and without hesitation.

The adult must be the one who is responsible for limiting children so that they do not come to harm or do not harm others or destroy property. Children will feel more secure with adults who can take this responsibility. They will feel freer because they can depend on the adult to stop them before they do things that they would be sorry about later.

It's necessary, of course, to interpret behavior from the child's point of view. A child may be disturbed after he has thrown a block and hurt a playmate, but he won't be disturbed over having shouted a few insults—unless the adult tries to make him feel disturbed. The adult is responsible for limiting the block throwing but not necessarily the word throwing.

Here Is an Exercise. Observe and report one situation in which a limit was set for the child's behavior. Why? How did the adult define the limit for the child. How did the adult maintain it? What was the child's response? What were the positive values for the child in the situation? What were the negative values, if any?

12. Use the Most Strategic Positions for Supervising.

Sometimes one will observe an inexperienced teacher with her back to most of the children as she watches one child. On the other hand, the experienced teacher, even when she is working with one child, will be in a position to observe at a glance what the other children are doing. She is always alert to the total situation.

Turning one's back on the group may represent, consciously or unconsciously, an attempt to limit one's experience to a simple situation. It is quite natural that one should feel like withdrawing from the more complex situations at first, or that one should take an interest in one particular child because other children seem more difficult to understand. It is a natural tendency but one should guard against it. It is important to develop skill in extending one's horizons. Observation of the total situation is essential to effective guidance. It is essential if the children are to be safe.

It is important to develop skill in being aware of all that is happening in a situation instead of only one part of it if one is to make the most of the opportunities for helping children. Safety requires teachers who are alert to see that all areas are supervised and not just one area. Enrichment of experience also will come when a teacher is observing all the children and their interests, not just one child. The teacher who is reading to children, for example, may encourage a shy child to join the reading group by a smile or she may forestall trouble by noticing a child who is ready for a change in activity and by encouraging him to join the group before his lack of interest disrupts the play of others.

Sitting rather than standing is another technic for improving the effectiveness of one's supervision. One is often in a better position to help a child when one is at the child's level, and children may feel freer to approach the adult who is sitting. It also makes possible more unobtrusive observation.

In the laboratory nursery school where there may be many adults, it is important that the adults avoid gathering in groups, such as near the entrance or in the locker room or around the sandbox. Grouping calls attention to the number of adults present. It may limit the children's feeling of freedom and may increase any tendency they have to feel self-conscious or to play for attention. Too many adults in one place may also mean that other areas are being left unsupervised.

Where one stands or sits is important in forestalling or preventing difficulties. A teacher standing between two groups engaged in different activities can make sure that one group does not interfere with the other and so can forestall trouble.

"Remote control" is ineffective control in the nursery school. Stepping between two children who are growing irritated at each other may prevent an attack, but it cannot be done if one is on the other side of the playroom. Trouble in the doll corner, for example, may be avoided by a teacher moving quietly near as tension mounts in the "family" and suggesting some solution. Her suggestion is more likely to be acceptable if her presence reinforces it. Trouble is seldom avoided by a suggestion given at a distance.

Depending on the physical plan of the school, certain spots will be more strategic for supervision than others. If the teacher is standing near the entrance of the coat room, it will be easy for her to see that the child hangs up his coat before he goes on to play. If she is standing on the far side of the room, she is not in a position to act effectively if he chooses to disregard her reminder. Some places are favorable because it is possible to observe many corners and others are "blind spots" as far as much observation goes.

Choose the position for standing or sitting which will best serve your purposes.

Here Is an Exercise. Make a diagram of the plan of your school and put a check mark on the spots which are strategically good for supervision. List places where close supervision is needed for safety, such as at the workbench.

At a particular time indicate on a chart where the adults are placed and the positions of the children. Criticize the position and distribution of adults from the standpoint of teaching effectiveness.

13. The Health and Safety of the Children Are a Primary Concern.

The good teacher must be constantly alert to the things which affect health such as seeing that drinking cups are not used in common, that towels are kept separate, that toys which have been in a child's mouth are washed, that the window is closed if there is a draft, that wraps are adjusted to changes in temperature or activity.

The good teacher must also be alert to things which concern the safety of children. Being alert to safety means observing and removing sources of danger such as protruding nails, unsteady ladders or boards not properly supported. It means giving close supervision to children who are playing together on high places, or to children who are using potentially dangerous things as hammers, saws and shovels. The point is familiar but clearcut and important. The skillful teacher never relaxes her watchfulness.

Here Is an Exercise. List ways in which you have observed a teacher protecting the health and safety of the children in the nursery school.

14. Observe and Take Notes.

Underlying all these guides is the assumption that teaching is based on ability to observe behavior objectively and to evaluate its meaning. As in any science, conclusions are based on accurate observations. Jot down notes frequently, statements of what happens, the exact words that a child uses, the exact sequence of events. Make the note at the time or as soon after the event as possible, always dating each note. Reread these notes later and make interpretations. Skill in observing and recording is essential in building understanding. Improve your ability to select significant incidents and make meaningful records.

3.3 ALICE STERLING HONIG

Quality Infant/Toddler Caregiving: Are There Magic Recipes?

Much discussion on quality child care focuses on the needs of three- and four-year-olds. The terms *infants* and *toddlers* are often left out of the conversation. Early childhood educators believe that child care for children through age two is necessary, but they seem to be unable to prescribe the necessary ingredients for providing that care. In the following selection from "Quality Infant/Toddler Cargiving: Are There Magic Recipes?" *Young Children* (May 1989), Alice Sterling Honig details what she believes are the necessary components of a quality child care program, focusing on the knowledge of child development that staff bring to the setting. She believes that the adults who provide care are the key element of a quality program. According to Honig, their job is to individualize the routines of care, such as feeding, diapering, and dressing, to match the child's tempo. From the adult's responsive caregiving routine comes the infant-toddler curriculum.

Honig (b. 1929) has devoted her career to observing and working with young children. She is most noted for her work with J. Ronald Lally in developing and researching programs of enrichment for families of infants and toddlers. From their collaboration has come *Infant Caregiving: A Design for Training* (Syracuse University Press, 1972). Dr. Honig is a professor of child development at Syracuse University. She has directed the Children's Center at the university, which is the oldest federally funded infant-toddler child care center in the country.

A magic elixir for helping infants and toddlers grow into successful school achievers, socially adept with parents, peers, and teachers, would fetch a high price from today's parents and other caregivers. Busy with professional commitments, parents hope that child care professionals will know of the programmatic package, the right toys, the exact exercises, and other "cookbook" ingredients to produce that well-adjusted, eager young learner so devoutly desired.

A survey of research findings on environmental and personal variables that can support dreams for children's success provides clues to many of the ingredients required for a high-quality infant/toddler program (Honig, 1985a). Yet most of these ingredients are not specifically or routinely taught in schools; neither can they be easily bought or prescribed uniformly in identical doses as panaceas for childrearing.

INDIVIDUALIZED, ATTENTIVE LOVING

The primary ingredient to help young children flourish consists of *loving, responsive* caregivers, generously committing *energy, body-loving,* and *tuned-in attentiveness* to their child's well-being. And every ingredient counts! Since infants come into the world with different temperaments and styles of adjusting, this commitment requires much patience and much flexibility as new parents and caregivers tune into and learn about their child's unique qualities. Getting to know a baby takes time and committed interest. The new baby may be impulsive or reflective; adaptable, irritable, or slow to warm up (Thomas, Chess, & Birch, 1968). Adults have to be aware of differences in temperament, lest, for example, they respond to the intense baby's irritability with negative or exasperated tensions. Such responses can create miseries for an infant who already has troubles (Wittmer & Honig, 1988). Perhaps she finds it hard to get a thumb to her mouth to suck for self-comfort and lacks the easy adaptability of a temperamentally calmer child. Each baby needs a caregiver who recognizes and validates his or her special self. Dancing an Eriksonian duet of "giving and getting" in infant nurturing requires the commitment of both partners (Honig, 1987), but the caregivers need to be the skillful initiators. Adults are the driving force in the spiral growth of baby loving and cooperating. It is the adult "expert" partner who imbues the early relationship with somatic certainty (the security babies build through physical closeness) and the predictability of daily rhythms.

Because of the need to create a meaningful harmony in personal interchanges with infants, selecting caregivers of infants poses a different problem from selecting preschoolers' caregivers. Furman (1986), in her perceptive book for nursery teachers, advises that preschool teachers should leave sensuous and intimate relations to parents. But for babies, such relations are integral to their care. The quality infant/toddler caregiver *must* be involved and, of course, needs to be relaxed and to accept the sensuous nature of intimate ministrations such as feeding, burping, cuddling, and diapering.

RESPECTING TEMPOS AND EXPLORATION NEEDS

Research has clarified specific qualities caregivers should have that nurture the roots of intellectual competence, cooperative interactions, and resilience in coping with stresses (Honig, 1986). Some of these adult qualities are: tender, careful holding in arms; feedings that respect individual tempos; accurate interpretation of and prompt, comforting attention to distress signals; giving opportunities and freedom to explore toys on floor; and giving babies control over social interactions (Martin, 1981). Feedings should be as lengthy or short as the nursing baby desires. Holding and cuddling on hips and shoulders and laps should be leisurely. The toddler who needs to confirm your presence by piling toys into your lap after brief trips away from you needs to know that you will accept these tokens, these demands for attention. Toddlers often see-saw dramatically between needs for securing adult involvement and needs to defy adults with indifference or disobedience.

Adult generosity promotes babies' cognitive alertness and secure trusting attachment to caregivers (Ainsworth, 1982; Stern, 1985). Such gifts set foundations for an inner sense of safety and of high self-esteem (Honig, 1982a): All is right with the world; grown-ups are predictable and kind; people can be counted on to care for baby and to fix and soothe troubles, whether a scraped knee, a fearful feeling, or a hunger crankiness. Tender, tuned-in caregiving energizes toddlers' joyous and courageous explorations of strange environments. Courage to cope flows from adult caring and, significantly, also leads to increased compliance and cooperation with caregivers (Honig, 1985b; 1985c).

LANGUAGE MASTERY EXPERIENCES

Rich language interchanges and lengthy sequences of turn-taking talk are further critical ingredients to promote optimal development (Honig, 1984). Caregivers need to read books in a leisurely, involved fashion on a daily basis with young children. This frequent reading correlates with later intellectual zestfulness, rich language skills, and child success at school entry (Swan & Stavros, 1973). Research in family day care and center care as well as in families confirms the importance of language mastery in boosting cognitive competence of infants and toddlers (Clarke-Stewart, 1973; Carew, 1980; Tizard, 1981).

SHARED ACTIVITIES

Colorful toys and environments can indeed aid early learning. Yet provision of graded materials needs genuine, insightful thoughtfulness from caregivers using the equipment. Adults need to *understand infant developmental levels and sensorimotor stages* when providing toys to promote understandings of space and causality. Adults need to engage in joint activities as grist for child learnings. Roll a ball back and forth. Watch what interests a baby, and *talk* about what she is pointing to, jabbering at, or exploring with eyes or hands. Otherwise, too many toys in a center may simply result in babies crawling and toddlers wandering aimlessly among scattered playthings or engaging in chaotic, even destructive, behaviors with materials.

The too-difficult toy or learning game urged by a pushy parent or caregiver can turn off a child's interest in learning. Toddlers often show us that we have chosen just the right toy by enthusiastically tackling that activity (such as stacking cups or pushing poker chips through a coffee can slot) over and over again. Thus, young children need both ingredients:

1. responsive adults who ensure children's well-being through innumerable small interchanges of mutually pleasurable caregiving, language-permeated playfulness, and bodily cherishing and
2. a variety of learning opportunities and challenges tailored to children's capabilities and interests.

Such a "prescription" is most likely to lead to young children with ego-resilience, self-control, and the internal motivation to persist positively at difficult problem-solving tasks (Matas, Arend, & Sroufe, 1978).

FEEDING FINESSE AND HEALTH CARE

Optimal nutrition and preventive health care measures to boost wellness are important ingredients sometimes given insufficient attention as promoters of intellectual motivation and achievement. For example, iron deficiency, even without anemia, is associated with infant irritability, shortened attention span, solemnity, and lowered IQ. Fortunately, administration of intramuscular iron to such infants produces higher IQ scores and more infant responsive smiling for a caregiving adult within a week (Honig & Oski, 1986). Scrupulously careful handwashing procedures can reduce the frequency of infectious illness, particularly diarrhea, in centers (Lee & Yeager, 1986).

PROMOTING BABY ALTRUISM

Another domain sometimes neglected in setting up infant/toddler programs has to do with the nurturing of prosocial, altruistic behaviors. Adults need to be aware of how important they are as early rule-givers and role models for caring, sharing, and helping. Yarrow and colleagues (Pines, 1979) found that when mothers categorically rejected aggression and hurting as a way for their toddlers to resolve social problems, *and* consistently displayed empathic comfort for the toddlers' own hurts and frights, then well before 2 years of age these children showed concern for others' distress. Toddlers offered comforts (such as their own bottle or blanket!) to upset peers and tired family members. Such "baby altruism" was quite stable when the children were studied through teachers' reports 5 years later.

Caregiver expectations about children can lead to self-fulfilling prophecies. Baumrind (1977) describes "authoritative parenting" where families with high involvement and commitment to their young ones *and* high expectations and firm rules with reasons have children most likely to be good learners and reasonable with preschool teachers and peers. Adults who expect toddlers to be terrors may very well see their fears fulfilled. Calm caregivers with a sense of humor and extra supplies of patience and admiration will find toddlers brave (though unsteady) adventurers on the rough trails toward independent, self-actualized functioning. Adjusting one's will and wishes to those of peers and teachers is bound to be a struggle. Adult empathy can ease the toddler's inevitable trials. The no-saying toddler who insists he wants to take a bath with his new shoes on can be exasperating—but also a remarkable little person in stretching a caregiver's coping ingenuity. The hungry, yet defiant, toddler who gleefully runs away calling "No no no" when called for lunchtime will cheerfully charge back to the lunch area if lured with comments such as "Yummy hamburgers, good carrots!"

CONTINUITY OF CARE AND COGNITIVE FACILITATION

One of the concerns child development specialists have is whether "inoculations" such as high-quality, enriched out-of-home care can provide a supplemental boost for infants and toddlers who have otherwise had insufficient loving and language experiences. A further question is whether such enrichment for young children will have lasting effects. Will family and school need to continue to provide optimal supports for children over many years? Longitudinal research suggests that long-range effects of early stimulation do depend crucially on the *stability* and *continuity* of care. For example, early optimal home stimulation scores are more likely to correlate with positive outcomes for children when *later* home scores also show parental facilitation of cognitive development. On the other hand, remedially enriching early education programs as a supplement for disadvantaged infants and preschoolers do indeed seem to prevent a typical downward slide in intelligence test scores for children from low-education families (Honig & Lally, 1982; Ramey & Gowen, 1986). Quality infant/toddler programs have even been found to decrease social delinquency in later adolescent years (Berrueta-Clement, Schweinhart, Barnett, Epstein, & Weikart, 1985; Lally, Mangione, Wittmer, & Honig, 1986).

CONCLUSIONS

Lest these various prescriptions for an optimal infant/toddler rearing environment seem too difficult to expect from adults who may not have much training initially in child development knowledge and skills, it is important and cheering to note how many easy-to-read materials are currently available for caregivers. Many journals, such as *Young Children* or *Day Care and Early Education* frequently provide special articles for infant/toddler teachers with creative curricular ideas and special insights about aspects of early development. Books with homey, easy-to-carry-out learning games with toddlers are available (Honig, 1982b; Miller, 1985).

Directors and trainers of infant/toddler caregivers will also find materials to enhance their continuous in-service efforts to ensure high-quality care (Willis & Ricciuti, 1975; Honig & Lally, 1981; Cataldo, 1983; Greenberg, 1987a, 1987b; Godwin & Schrag, 1988). Such resources can especially help the busy caregiver to restructure daily routines into enriching experiences. Metamorphosed through adult sensibilities, skills, and creativity, daily care situations can be turned into prime opportunities to further the early learning careers of infants and toddlers.

REFERENCES

Ainsworth, M. D. S. (1982). Early caregiving and later patterns of attachment. In M. H. Klaus & M. O. Robertson (Eds.), *Birth, interaction and attachment.* Skilman, NJ: Johnson & Johnson.

Baumrind, D. (1977). Some thoughts about child rearing. In S. Cohen & T. J. Comiskey (Eds.), *Child development: Contemporary perspective* (pp. 248–258). Itasca, IL: Peacock.

Berrueta-Clement, J., Schweinhart, D. J., Barnett, W. S., Epstein, A. S., & Weikart, D. P. (1985). *Changed lives: The effects of the Perry Preschool Program on youths through age 19.* Ypsilanti, MI: High/Scope Press.

Carew, J. V. (1980). Experience and the development of intelligence in young children at home and in day care. *Monographs of the Society for Research in Child Development, 45*(6–7, Serial No. 187).

Cataldo, C. Z. (1983). *Infant and toddler programs: A guide to very early childhood education.* Reading, MA: Addison-Wesley.

Clarke-Stewart, K. A. (1973). Interactions between mothers and their young children: Characteristics and consequences. *Monographs of the Society for Research in Child Development, 38*(6–7, Serial No. 153).

Furman, E. (Ed.). (1986). *What nursery school teachers ask us about.* Madison, CT: International Universities Press.

Godwin, A., & Schrag, L. (Eds.). (1988). *Setting up for infant care: Guidelines for centers and family day care homes.* Washington, DC: NAEYC.

Greenberg, P. (1987a). Ideas that work with young children: Infants and toddlers away from their mothers? *Young Children, 42*(4), 40–42.

Greenberg, P. (1987b). Ideas that work with young children: What is curriculum for infants in family day care (or elsewhere)? *Young Children, 42*(5), 58–62.

Honig, A. S. (1982a). The gifts of families: Caring, courage, and competence. In N. Stinnett, J. Defrain, K. King, H. Lingren, G. Fowe, S. Van Zandt, & R. Williams (Eds.), *Family strengths 4: Positive support systems* (pp. 331–349). Lincoln, NE: University of Nebraska Press.

Honig, A. S. (1982b). *Playtime learning games for young children.* Syracuse, NY: Syracuse University Press.

Honig, A. S. (1984, Winter). Why talk to babies? *Beginnings,* 3–6.

Honig, A. S. (1985a). High quality infant/toddler care: Issues and dilemmas. *Young Children, 41*(1), 40–46.

Honig, A. S. (1985b). Research in review: Compliance, control and discipline (Part 1). *Young Children, 40*(2), 50–68.

Honig, A. S. (1985c). Research in review: Compliance, control, and discipline (Part 2). *Young Children, 40*(3), 47–52.

Honig, A. S. (1986). Research in review: Stress and coping in children. In J. B. McCracken (Ed.), *Reducing stress in young children's lives* (pp. 142–167). Washington, DC: NAEYC.

Honig, A. S. (1987). The Eriksonian approach: Infant-toddler education. In J. Roopnarine & J. Johnson (Eds.), *Approaches to early childhood education* (pp. 49–69). Columbus, OH: Merrill.

Honig, A. S., & Lally, J. R. (1981). *Infant caregiving: A design for training.* Syracuse, NY: Syracuse University Press.

Honig, A. S., & Lally, J. R. (1982). The family development research program: Retrospective review. *Early Child Development and Care, 10,* 41–62.

Honig, A. S., & Oski, F. A. (1986). Solemnity: A clinical risk index for iron deficient infants. In A. S. Honig (Ed.), *Risk factors in infancy* (pp. 6–84). New York: Gordon & Breach.

Lally, J. R., Mangione, P., Wittmer, D., & Honig, A. S. (1986, November). *An early intervention program 10 years later: What happened to high risk infants who received quality early childhood education? The Syracuse University study.* Seminar presented at the annual conference of the National Association for the Education of Young Children, Washington, DC.

Lee, C., & Yeager, A. (1986). Infections in day care. *Current Problems in Pediatrics, 16,* 129–184.

Martin, J. A. (1981). A longitudinal study of the consequences of early mother-infant interaction: A microanalytic approach. *Monographs of the Society for Research in Child Development, 46*(3, Serial No. 190).

Matas, L., Arend, R. A., & Sroufe, L. A. (1978). Continuity of adaptation in the second year: The relationship between quality of attachment and later competence. *Child Development, 49,* 547–556.

Miller, K. (1985). *Things to do with toddlers and twos.* Marshfield, MA: Telshare Publishing Co.

Pines, M. (1979). Good samaritans at age two? *Psychology Today, 13*(1), 66–77.

Ramey, C. T., & Gowen, J. W. (1986). A general systems approach to modifying risk for retarded development. In A. S. Honig (Ed.), *Risk factors in infancy* (pp. 9–26). New York: Gordon & Breach.

Stern, D. (1985). *The interpersonal world of the infant: A view from psychoanalysis and developmental psychology.* New York: Basic.

Swan, R. W., & Stavros, H. (1973). Child-rearing practices associated with the development of cognitive skills of children in low socioeconomic areas. *Early Child Development and Care, 2,* 22–38.

Thomas, A. S., Chess, S., & Birch, H. G. (1968). *Temperament and behavior disorders in children.* New York: New York University Press.

Tizard, B. (1981). Language at home and at school. In C. B. Cazden (Ed.), *Language in early childhood education* (rev. ed., pp. 17–27). Washington, DC: NAEYC.

Willis, A., & Ricciuti, H. A. (1975). *A good beginning for babies: Guidelines for group care.* Washington, DC: NAEYC.

Wittmer, D. S., & Honig, A. S. (1988). Teacher recreation of negative interactions with toddlers. In A. S. Honig (Ed.), Optimizing early child care and education [Special issue]. *Early Child Development and Care, 31,* 77–88.

CHAPTER 4 Kindergarten

4.1 ELIZABETH P. PEABODY

Object Lessons

Early in their careers, sisters Elizabeth Peabody (1804–1894) and Mary Peabody (1806–1887) operated a dame school—a school in which the basics of reading and writing are taught by a woman in her own home—for a short time. As young women teaching and tutoring in and around Boston, they became acquainted with many influential educational leaders of the day, including Horace Mann, whom Mary later married. Both women were involved in many educational, literary, and teaching ventures intended to better society.

When Elizabeth heard about kindergarten, which was founded by German educator Friedrich Froebel, she was prompted, at age 56, to start the first English-speaking, American kindergarten. Prior to that, the few kindergartens that existed were conducted in German for the children of German immigrants. Shortly after establishing her own program, Elizabeth travelled to Germany to study Froebelian kindergartens and returned as a self-appointed authority on kindergartens. In 1877 Elizabeth became the first president of the American Froebel Union. She and Mary worked for many years to promote the value of kindergartens. They wrote, lectured, and met with influential leaders, including Presidents Abraham Lincoln and Grover Cleveland.

Elizabeth Peabody is best known for her tireless efforts to promote the kindergarten and educational experiences for children who were affected by the Civil War, including displaced southern slave children and Native American children. In the Commissioner of Education's Annual Report of 1870, she urged that kindergartens be expanded into public school systems across the nation and begged for the establishment of a free national school of kindergarten education to supply teachers to public schools in southern states and American territories. Nine years later, kindergarten education was instituted in Baltimore, Maryland.

The following selection is from Elizabeth Peabody's *Guide to the Kindergarten and Intermediate Class* (E. Steiger, 1877), which was published with Mary Mann's *Moral Culture of Infancy* as one volume.

I now come to Object Lessons. . . . The brain is not to be overstrained in childhood, but it is to be used. Where it is left to itself, and remains uncultivated, it shrinks, and that is disease. A child is not able to direct its own attention; it needs the help of the adult in the unfolding of the mind, no less than in the care of its body. Lower orders of animals can educate themselves, that is, develop in themselves their one power. As the animals rise in the scale of being, they are related more or less to their progenitors and posterity, and require social aid. But the human being, whose beatitude is "the communion of the just," is so universally related, that he cannot go alone at all. He is entirely dependent at first, and never becomes independent of those around him, any further than he has been so educated and trained by his relations with them, as to rise into union with God. And this restores him again to communion with his fellow-beings, as a beneficent Power among its peers.

The new method of education gives a gradual series of exercises, continuing the method of Nature. It cultivates the senses, by giving them the work of discriminating colors, sounds, etc.; sharpens perception by leading children to describe accurately the objects immediately around them.

Objects themselves, rather than the verbal descriptions of objects, are presented to them. The only way to make words expressive and intelligible, is to associate them sensibly with the objects to which they relate. Children must be taught to translate things into words, before they can translate words into things. Words are secondary in nature; yet much teaching seems to proceed on the principle that these are primary, and so they become mere counters, and children are brought to hating study, and the discourse of teachers, instead of thirsting for them. To look at objects of nature and art, and state their colors, forms, and properties of various kinds, is no painful strain upon the mind. It is just what children spontaneously do when they are first learning to talk. It is a continuation of learning to talk. The object-teacher confines the child's attention to one thing, till all that is obvious about it is described; and then asks questions, bringing out much that children, left to themselves, would overlook, suggesting words when necessary, to enable them to give an account of what they see. It is the action of the mind upon real things, together with clothing perceptions in words, which really cultivates; while it is not the painful strain upon the brain which the study of a book is. To translate things into words, is a more agreeable and a very different process from translating words into things, and the former exercise should precede the latter. If the mind is thoroughly exercised in wording its perceptions, words will in their turn suggest the things, without painful effort, and memory have the clearness and accuracy of perception. On the other hand words will never be used without feeling and intelligence. Then, to read a book will be to know all of reality that is in it.

I am desirous to make a strong impression on this point, because, to many persons, I find object-teaching seems the opposite of teaching! They say that to play with things, does not give habits of study. They think that to commit to memory a page of description about a wild duck, for instance, is better than to have the wild duck to look at, leading the child to talk about it, describe it, and inquire into its ways and haunts! They do not see that this study of the things themselves exercises the perception, and picturesque memory, which is probably immortal, certainly perennial, while the written description only exercises the verbal memory. Verbal memory is not to be despised; but it is a consequence, and should never be the substitute for picturesque memory. It is the picturesque memory only which is creative. . . .

Object-teaching should precede as well as accompany the process of learning to read. In Germany, even outside of Kindergarten, *thinking schools* have long preceded *reading schools,* and yet learning to read German, in which every sound is represented by a different letter, and every letter has one sound, cultivates the classifying powers, as learning to read English cannot. With children whose vernacular is English, it is absolutely injurious to the mind to be taught to read the first thing. I must speak of the reasons of this in another place, my purpose here being to show that object-teaching is necessary, in order to make word-teaching, whether by teacher's discourse, or by the reading of books, a means of culture at any period.

Every child should have the object to examine, and in turn each should say what is spontaneous. Out of their answers series of questions will be suggested to the teacher, who should also be prepared with her own series of questions,—questions full of answers.

The first generalization to which children should be led is into the animate and inanimate,—what lives and what exists without manifestation of life. The next generalization will be into mineral, vegetable, animal, and personal.

But you can begin with chairs, tables, paper, cloth, etc., coming as soon as possible to natural objects. . . . Sea anemones, star-fishes, clams, and oysters are easily procured. If sea anemones, taken into a bottle of salt water, clinging to stones, look like mere mosses at first, on the second day it is pretty certain, that in their desire for food they will spread themselves out, displaying their inward parts in the most beautiful manner. Every child in the class should have his turn at the object, if there are not objects enough for each,—should tell what he sees, and be helped to words to express himself. This, I must repeat, is the true way of learning the meaning of words; and leaves impressions, which no dictionary, with its periphrases and mere approximations to synonymes can give. Let a child himself hammer out some substance with a mallet, and he will never forget the meaning of malleable; and so of other words. . . .

The greatest difficulty about object-teaching is that it requires personal training, and wide-awake attention in teachers, of a character much more thorough than they commonly have. When it shall become general, as it certainly must, it will no longer be supposed that any ordinary person who can read and write, and is obliged to do something for a living, will be thought fit to keep a school for small children! The present order of things will be reversed. Ordinary persons, with limited acquirements, will be obliged to confine themselves to older pupils, who are able to study books and only need to have some one to set their lessons and hear them recited; while persons of originality and rich culture will be reserved to discover and bring out the various genius and faculty which God has sown broadcast in the field of the race, and which now so often runs into the rank vegetation of vice, or wastes into deserts of concentrated mediocrity. Then this season of education will command the largest remuneration, as it will secure the finest powers to the work; and because such work cannot be pursued by any one person for many years, nor even for a short time without assistance, relieving from the ceaseless attention that a company of small children requires, for little children cannot be wound up to go like watches; but to keep them in order, the teacher must constantly meet their outbursting life with her own magnetic forces; while their employments must be continually interchanged, and mingled with their recreations.

Children ought to continue these Kindergarten exercises from the age of three to nine; and if faithfully taught, they could then go into what is called scholastic training, in a state of mind to receive from it the highest advantages it is capable of giving; free from the disadvantages which are now so obvious as to have raised, in our practical country, a party prejudiced against classical education altogether.

Kindergarten

The name Patty Smith Hill (1868–1946) is synonymous with kindergarten education in the United States. Her career began in 1889 in Louisville, Kentucky, where she was the director of an experimental demonstration kindergarten. She went on to teach and direct several kindergartens. In 1905 Hill was invited to go to Teachers College, Columbia University, where she was a faculty member until her retirement in 1935. There she furthered the kindergarten movement by introducing new courses into the college curriculum. Shortly after becoming a professor, Hill became the president of the International Kindergarten Union (1908–1910). This organization later combined with the Primary Council to form the Association of Childhood Education International. The new association was the first to align the goals and concerns of kindergarten and primary-grade teachers.

As director of the Louisville Free Kindergarten Association, Hill wrote a program manual in 1898 to be used in the kindergartens under her supervision. She urged teachers to focus on the economic conditions, environment, and mental ability of children when planning learning activities. Influenced by a summer of study with G. Stanley Hall, a founder of modern American child psychology, Hill wanted to do away with kindergarten curriculum guides that prescribed rigid methods using the Froebel gifts. (Friedrich Froebel was the German educator known for his introduction of the kindergarten—or "child's garden"—the objective of which was the cultivation of the child's self-development, self-activity, and socialization.) Hill's manual was an early attempt at systematic, developmentally appropriate practice.

The following selection from "Kindergarten," published in *The American Educator Encyclopedia* (American Educator, 1941), provides a look at the history of the early kindergartens in the United States. "Kindergarten" is a full account of the early beginnings from one who helped to chart the course. It provides an opportunity to develop an understanding of the many different roles kindergarten teachers served in earlier years.

When the kindergarten was first introduced into the United States it survived as a philanthropy long before it was accepted as an organic member of the educational system. During this long probation period it was eagerly sought by missions, institutional churches and philanthropic organizations as the most hopeful form of social regeneration.

This was a period of national social awakening and religious disillusionment in America. As a nation the people were then gradually awakening to the new social problems resulting from enormous increases in foreign populations. The tides of immigration brought to American shores peoples difficult to assimilate and slow to accept American ideals and standards of living. Slums were in process of formation. They became sources of disease, crime, delinquency and industrial disorders, breeding centers of problems which America was unprepared to meet.

Religious disillusionment followed the efforts of churches to locate missions in the city slums, for the purpose of converting the dwellers therein. Thoughtful religious leaders with a new consciousness of the fact that an "overnight conversion," however sincere, might be only of temporary value, had to cope with the habits of character due to years of wrong living. The spirit might be willing, but the flesh was weak, and little could be accomplished through efforts to reconstruct adult society.

The kindergarten appeared on the horizon at the right moment for philanthropy, but at the wrong time for public education. Society turned to the young child as the one great hope, and kindergartens opened rapidly under religious and philanthropic influences all over America. They were located in the worst slums of the cities, and highly cultured and intelligent young women prepared themselves in normal schools supported by philanthropists. These young women entered upon the work with rare enthusiasm and consecration to the cause. No neighborhood was too criminal, no family too degenerate, no child too bad. Into Little Italy, Little Russia, Little Egypt and the Ghettos they went, offering daily care to humanity in its early years.

Both kindergartners and philanthropic boards soon saw the need of the ministrations of the physician, the nurse, the social worker or the visiting teacher. Funds were so low that the kindergartner taught in the morning and spent her afternoons as a social-welfare worker, eagerly seeking work for the unemployed parents, space in hospitals for ill mothers, sisters or brothers, searching for physicians who would remove adenoids and tonsils or dentists who would extract diseased teeth, free of charge. This was the most important contribution of the pioneer kindergartners, as at this period the kindergarten was frequently the only social agency offering a helping hand in the rapidly-increasing slums.

Education and philanthropy were widely removed in those days. Schools accepted no responsibility for the physical condition of the child, or for the home which sent the child to school ill-nourished and diseased in body and mind. Thus the kindergartner of that day came into daily contact with family life at its lowest ebb. She was trained by necessity to see the child she attempted to teach handicapped in his learning by the social conditions of the home and slum in which he lived.

Philanthropic boards, with financial problems which they could not solve, then turned to the public schools asking them to adopt the kindergarten as the foundation grade in the public-school system. As an entering wedge, these philanthropic boards requested the use of vacant rooms in public-school buildings—for there were such in those days—and the kindergartner was allowed to enter, although somewhat as a stepchild. The least attractive room, left unused for this reason, was turned over for her use rent free. Salaries and running expenses were still being defrayed by the philanthropic agencies, which were convinced through experience of the educational as well as the philanthropic value of the kindergarten. The next step was to persuade boards of education to accept full financial responsibility, and the kindergarten soon became an accepted member of the public-school system.

Troubles soon followed, however, as the kindergarten was something of a misfit in the public schools at this period and for many years afterwards. In the first place, the long experience under philanthropic influences greatly increased the inherent tendency of the kindergarten to include in education responsibility for all those conditions in the home which hindered the learning and general welfare of the child. When the kindergartner entered the public schools she found no opportunities to continue this welfare work. There was no medical inspection, no school nurse, no school luncheon, no school psychologist, no social case-worker, no visiting teacher. The kindergartner's previous training, which included such ministrations as these, struck a strange chord in a public-school system.

Soon after the public schools were induced to adopt these philanthropic kindergartens, assuming financial as well as administrative responsibility, the proportion of children to teacher was heavily increased, to the detriment of child and teacher. In order to reduce costs per capita and to reach large numbers of children, the double session was introduced, with different groups of children for each session. This plan of necessity eliminated all welfare work formerly done by the kindergartner in the afternoons, such as home visiting, medical and clinical coöperation and various other forms of parental guidance and assistance.

The Froebelian philosophy as interpreted by the kindergarten included the all-round care of the child—in the home as well as the school. Even as early as 1840, we are told that a noted visitor to Froebel's first kindergarten in Blankenburg found the room empty and was directed to the fountain on the village green, where he discovered Middendorf, one of Froebel's first co-workers, teaching the boys to wash their feet and the little girls to mend their clothes. Such social welfare and community work as this was the heritage of the kindergarten from its earliest establishment, and it is unfortunate that this birthright was relinquished and temporarily lost when the kindergarten, under public-school administration, had to conform to the traditional procedure of the school in order to survive.

Adjustment to public-school conditions came slowly, but as educators became more familiar with and more reconciled to the self-active playing, singing, dancing and talking kindergarten child, there grew up a consciousness on the part of both kindergarten and primary teachers that there were but slight differences in the nature and needs of the six-year-old primary child and the joyously-working kindergarten child as promoted into the primary grade the day or week before.

Until this happy adjustment took place, the promotion of the self-active kindergarten children into the grades had made it possible for the poorest and most formal first-grade teacher to criticize and condemn the work of the best kindergarten teacher as well as the kindergarten cause, because of the wide gap that existed between kindergarten and primary ideals at that time. . . .

Patty Smith Hill

MODERN IMPROVEMENTS IN THEORY AND PRACTICE IN NURSERY SCHOOL, KINDERGARTEN AND PRIMARY GRADES

If an intelligent observer who had not visited the kindergarten for half a century entered one today, like old Rip Van Winkle he would rub his eyes with surprise at the marked improvements which have been substituted since his last visit. Such an observer would see the same Froebelian theories of self-activity and development used as guiding principles, but he would discover them applied through far better methods of teaching and with new improved materials and equipment substituted.

These improvements may be listed under the following headings:

1. Larger and more artistic play materials and equipment;
2. Improved methods of teaching through utilization of the laws of learning, as opposed to traditional methods;
3. Emphasis upon sanitation and health in the new curriculum, and demands for sanitary rooms, equipment and modes of cleaning;
4. Improved standards of literature and art in the types of stories, songs and dramatization used;
5. Increasing opportunities for first-hand experience in nature study and elementary science;
6. Emphasis on guidance through increasing utilization of self-expression and social coöperation in the social organization of the class;
7. Improved methods of parental guidance, using individual and group conferences with teachers and parents in coördinating home and school;
8. Unified curricula and coöperation between the nursery school, kindergarten and primary grades.

Larger and More Artistic Play Materials and Equipment

If our imaginary Rip Van Winkle returned to observe a modern kindergarten after a lapse of years, he would search in vain for even a remnant of the original Froebelian materials, so small and light as to strain the immature muscles of eye and hand now known to be weak and poorly coördinated in early life. The tiny cubes, circles, squares and triangles inherited from Froebel's day are poor materials for construction at this stage of child life, as one slip of immature fingers, or even a deep breath, may annihilate the child's production in the twinkling of an eye.

Former so-called "occupations" with paper to be sewed, folded, cut, pasted or woven into abstract geometric figures have likewise disappeared. These materials are easily torn and disfigured in the process of folding, cutting and weaving, and they lead to products of slight interest to the little worker dependent upon teacher dictation or direction. These activities also have given place to occupations of absorbing interest, such as sewing with large needles and stitches in making doll clothes which are of necessity exceedingly simple. With hammer and saw, furniture is constructed for the doll house. Instead of paper strips for weaving, the children are given large, soft twine and yarn with which to weave their own rugs on self-made looms, or to braid their harness for driving horses.

The new blocks are much larger, some being a yard in length, and are made of heavier wood, in order to call into use the large fundamental muscles of the child's whole body, which must be exercised as an immediate requirement of health.

While it is possible for the child to work alone with these larger construction materials, sooner or later, as he transfers his construction from table to floor, building bridges, tall houses and ships large enough to enter, and as he climbs, fetches and carries alone, he inevitably discovers his need for another child to coöperate with him. When he mounts a safe, low stepladder provided for the purpose, to place a roof on his house or bridge, he discovers the economy of effort in social coöperation. Here we have the true origin of genuine social coöperation; namely, the need of one person for another person in creating social projects. The child also finds that social coöperation requires modifications of his original plan which, as it grows, demands the use of the suggestions offered by another individual or the group.

Manufacturers have responded to the demand for these larger materials, providing slides, "jungle-gyms" for climbing, swings, see-saws, teeter boards and merry-go-rounds, adapted to the size and maturity of the children. Kindergartners have also introduced many home-made materials of their own invention, such as loaded kegs for rolling, and large, hollow blocks for reaching, stretching, lifting, pulling and pushing. These are all normal modes of exercise essential to growth. Through such innovations as these the sedentary habits developed by chair and table, which the former small materials cultivated, have now been excluded.

Geometric drawing, introduced by Froebel partly because of his passion for mathematics, surveying and architecture, has also disappeared from the curriculum. Instead, children now use charcoal, gay crayons, large brushes and pails of bright-colored paint, while standing at large easels illustrating their own conceptions of the world they are trying to understand through genuine self-expression.

Large, soft balls stimulating vigorous rolling and tossing on the floor or in the playground are now substituted for the tiny ones formerly used for table play. Soft wood has been introduced with strong tools, so that with saws, hammers and nails, children may safely learn to make their own toys. Dolls play a large role in dramatizations of home and community life, and also serve as motives for construction.

All these substitutes have come to stay, but in improved form as kinder-gartners and manufacturers learn by experience the more specific interests and abilities of children.

Improved Methods of Teaching Through Utilization of the Laws of Learning

Traditional methods of teacher-dictated products, formerly called "forms of life," and balanced symmetrical figures, called "forms of beauty," were more emphasized by early disciples of Froebel than by Froebel himself. Today, these have practically gone out of use and given way to self-expression in painting, drawing, modeling, carpentering and so on. The new methods and materials provide wider scope for the child's innate interest in manipulation as he discovers for himself the qualities and possibilities of new materials; or they serve as raw materials through which the child can work toward an end or purpose which he has in his mind and desires to attain. A wise teacher allows the child to experiment and discover his own ways and means for arriving at goals. The same educational principles are applied as the child learns to create his own dramatic plays, displacing the former teacher-dictated games.

Discussion of children's own ideas is now substituted for what was formerly called the "morning talk." In the previous method, the morning talk was largely given over to the teacher, who addressed a self-active, wriggling, inattentive group of children endeavoring to keep still while their teacher imposed her ideas on a group disciplined to assume, at least, an appearance of attention in order to avoid correction.

Differences of opinion, which naturally arise among children in work and play and which easily lead to quarrels and fighting, the teacher now endeavors to handle not by scolding, punishment or other such corrective means. Instead, she tries to compromise differences by building up public opinion of right and wrong through discussion and exchange of ideas between the children themselves and the teacher as leader of the group. . . .

Importance of Guidance

Corrective work in kindergarten has always been gentle and humane, and on the whole enlightened, for by 1826 Froebel, in his best known work, *The Education of Man,* clearly stated his guiding principles in matters of discipline and control as follows: "Education in instruction and training, originally and in its first principles, should necessarily be passive, following (only guarding and protecting), not prescriptive, categorical, interfering . . . for the undisturbed operation of the Divine Unity is necessarily good, cannot be otherwise than good . . . thus the duckling hastens to the pond and into the water, while the young chick scratches the ground, and the young swallow catches its food upon the wing and scarcely ever touches the ground."

But for fear this might be interpreted as a purely laissez-faire policy, Froebel with equal conviction, taking another lesson from nature and the gardener, added: "The grapevine must indeed be pruned; but the pruning as such does not insure wine. On the other hand, pruning, although done with the best intention, may wholly destroy the vine, or at least impair its fertility and productiveness, if the gardener fails in his work passively and attentively to follow the nature of the plant."

These guiding principles expressed by Froebel in no uncertain terms throw several heavy responsibilities on the gardener (or educator):

1. The gardener must know the laws which he must obey in order to secure normal growth and wholesome development.
2. The gardener must be sympathetic, but must also be well acquainted with manifestations of abnormalities and those unbalanced forms of growth which may obstruct and reduce productivity;
3. The gardener must acquire skill in the art of eradicating obstructions without undue disturbances of the growth processes.

Self-expression thus becomes a means to a higher end, requiring the mature insight and guidance of parent or teacher working with and through the children toward the goals of self-reliance and ability to coöperate with other people.

It requires little intelligence to "let children go" in unrestricted activity, and still less for an adult with a threatening scowl or rod to cower children into submission to authority. On the other hand, ability to guide so that children may gain an understanding of the ethical ends toward which they are working, the teacher meanwhile winning their coöperation in discovering the best means to this end, demands intelligence of the highest order in the art of teaching.

Guidance is indeed a difficult art for the teacher to master, and is easily misunderstood by untrained or unintelligent observers. Such misunderstandings grow somewhat naturally out of the fact that the teacher, endeavoring to keep herself more or less in the background, may appear as an ideal onlooker, although at the very moment she may be concentrating on and carefully scrutinizing each child's progress. The teacher herself must possess a goodly store of knowledge and the techniques which the children must gradually acquire, while holding herself in readiness to offer criticism, information, suggestion or redirection in order to prevent waste of time and effort.

Guidance is no free and easy method of steering children's spontaneous activities toward worthy ends. It still leaves ample scope for the wise use of authority or command whenever danger threatens the progress or safety of the individual or the group. Many illustrations of prompt, unquestioning obedience to commands or signals easily come to mind, such as fire drills in the schools and traffic signals in the streets.

A study of the respective functions of (1) teacher, (2) children and the (3) materials of the curriculum as they react upon one another in the processes of teaching and learning in school life may throw light upon the social organization of the school.

These three constituent forces acting and reacting upon each other are as follows:

1. The *materials* of the curriculum serve two functions:
   a. They provide the media for experimentation or for the expression of the child's ideas in process of formation or clarification;
   b. Or again, some materials, such as literature, may be used as a means of summing up or clarifying individual or group ideas.
2. *Children*, as the chief learners in the school group, stimulate and check one another as they learn through social contacts the necessity for compromise and adjustment. In so doing they spontaneously offer criticism and information in the exchange of experiences and ideas required in coöperative projects.
3. Last but not least, guidance as the most subtle art of teaching depends upon a well-trained *teacher* skilled in fruitful observation, that she may record, advise and redirect the activities of the children in order to keep them moving in directions of worth to the child and to society.

The sum and substance of the art of guidance, deep and wide in its ramifications, means the wise interaction of these three—materials, children and teacher—in the social life of the school. When skillfully achieved this is the real test of good teaching.

Parental Guidance and Coöperation

Froebel was greatly indebted to both Comenius and Pestalozzi for the emphasis he laid upon the mother and the father in the education of the child. As a result all kindergartners of all schools of philosophy included parental participation even in the pioneer period.

We must acknowledge that these early attempts at parental guidance were frequently poorly planned and carried out, for advice and counsel were offered to groups of tired mothers and fathers at the end of an exhausting day in the home or the shop. But however poorly done, the good will manifested by all persons concerned indicated the worthiness of the attempt, and often produced surprisingly good results. The very fact that the kindergarten child, in the majority of cases, had to be accompanied to school by a parent or a mature member of the household gave the kindergartner an opportunity to become acquainted with the older members of the child's family—a contact usually denied the teacher in the grades. Mutual concern regarding the welfare of the youngest children invariably served as an entering wedge into the hearts and minds of the parents, inspiring their good will and their desire to coöperate with teachers.

Great progress has been made in this parental movement, especially in the well-equipped nursery-school clinics in universities which are sufficiently endowed to enjoy the coöperation of authorities in many fields of child welfare. Consequently, many progressive public and private schools today are including in their offerings to parents and teachers medical inspection and psychological and psychiatric clinical services where all the findings from varied sources of information are coördinated, giving parents and teachers a fairly dependable picture of the child as a whole. These coördinated records of each child furnish data for individual conferences with the mother or the father, or better still with both. Individual conferences are a vast improvement over the old group method, which fell back upon the teacher as a means of getting information and advice to the group. However, the lecture method is still in use where parental groups are sufficiently mature to coöperate in making their own programs, and in sharing in the selection of expert speakers on child welfare.

Parents are provided today with help and guidance never before offered in the history of education. On the whole, parents are responding with astonishing good will, joining forces with teachers in their war against the prevalent neglect of early childhood. It has been said by a judge in courts for children, that, if the thorough-going coördinated case-studies now provided only in the courts for child criminals, unfortunately all too late, could be introduced for school use at the nursery school and kindergarten period, criminality could be tremendously reduced.

Unified Curricula for the Nursery School, Kindergarten and Primary Grades

One of the movements most productive of good in early childhood education occurred (1930–31) when the former International Kindergarten Union and the Primary Council decided to unite their forces in a new organization called the Association for Childhood Education. This new organization includes nursery-school, kindergarten and primary teachers. Such merging of interests, with sections adapted to the requirements of teachers of different age-level groups, has reduced the frequent objectionable requests for teacher-absence at many conferences. This merger of two separate organizations—one for kindergartners, another for primary teachers—was epoch-making. It is resulting today in common aims, purposes and curricula built upon knowledge drawn from each field.

When this reorganization took place, the National Association for Nursery Education was urged to become an integral part of the larger organization. The nursery-school teachers decided against this proposition at the time, and still hold their national conferences at dates and places different from those of the Association for Childhood Education. However, the desire to learn from each other is still so strong that all three groups of teachers attend annual conferences of both groups when school finances and grants of leaves of absence make it possible, In time, the larger unification will undoubtedly take place for the good of all three organizations.

The valuable results which flowed from the unification of kindergarten and primary interests may best be appreciated when we take into account the fact that, formerly, kindergarten and primary teachers were not only trained in separate normal schools but were supervised after graduation by leaders from the two groups. This lack of coöperation between kindergarten and primary teachers caused a break in the child's life, with undue consciousness of the differences in ideals and in achievements required as the pupil was promoted from the kindergarten to the first grade.

The unification in training, supervision and organization of teachers of early childhood has produced whole-hearted coöperation and good will on the part of kindergarten and primary teachers, creating curricula so closely integrated that the child passes from one to the other undisturbed by the normal differences which legitimately survive as the child matures.

As the school and home agree on the common attitudes, ideals and objectives which must be disseminated in their efforts to protect and develop all the children of all the people, whether princes or paupers, we may hope for a better day, when society shall adopt and apply the appeal Froebel made to his own generation: "Come, let us live with our children." With his deep reverence for all childhood and the rights of all life to grow, Froebel cast aside man's artificial distinctions between weeds and flowers, appealing to parents and teachers in these words: "Take care of my flowers, but don't forget my weeds."

The Kindergarten: A Retrospective and Contemporary View

Bernard Spodek (b. 1931) has been involved in early childhood education for the past 35 years, first as a teacher of preschool, kindergarten, and primary grades, and more recently as a teacher educator. He received his doctoral degree from Teachers College, Columbia University, in 1962. Since 1965 Spodek has been a professor of early childhood education at the University of Illinois. He has written numerous articles on a variety of topics related to the education of young children, and he has coauthored such books as *New Directions in the Kindergarten, Early Childhood Education Today, Preparing Teachers of Disadvantaged Young Children*, and *Teaching in the Early Years*. Spodek was elected president of the National Association for the Education of Young Children in 1976.

Spodek's experience and scholarship make him well suited to chronicle the history of kindergarten in the United States. The following selection is from his article "The Kindergarten: A Retrospective and Contemporary View," in Lilian G. Katz, ed., *Current Topics in Early Childhood Education, vol. 4* (Ablex, 1982). His account provides background information on the foundation, evaluation, teacher preparation, and curriculum of kindergarten. Spodek particularly focuses on the 1970s, showing how primary education extended downward into kindergarten. The result was a shift from developmental continuity to achievement in kindergartens, with test-oriented instruction taking priority. Spodek links several factors together that have altered kindergarten: curriculum based on specific learning outcomes; developmental theories emphasizing early learning; social pressure for teaching academic skills; and standardized tests to evaluate achievement.

CONTEMPORARY KINDERGARTEN PRACTICES

During the past decade or so, we have seen another major shift in kindergarten practices. The concern for young children's development and for the creation of programs reflecting their needs and interests seems to be lessening. In its place can be found a concern for the achievement of specific learning goals. It seems as though the kindergarten is again being reconstituted, this time essentially as a downward extension of primary education. Thus, the change is from a concern for continuity of development to a concern for continuity of achievement.

A number of strategies have been used to alter the kindergarten to make it more responsive to primary education. One is to adopt prescribed, commercially prepared educational programs, often extensions of textbook series in academic areas. Such adoptions, it is suggested, ensure the continuity of learning through the elementary school. Prescriptive programs have also been suggested and adopted; these have been designed to provide children with the prerequisites for success in later school learning. Many such programs are based upon "nationally validated" early childhood curricula originally created for handicapped or potentially handicapped young children (Fallon, 1973; Far West Laboratory, 1976). While a range of program alternatives are suggested, in many cases the activities prescribed are tied to a screening or evaluation instrument, so that success or failure on a specific test item determines the child's sequence of learning activities. In both cases, once programs are selected, teachers function less as decision-makers and more as technicians who implement predetermined activities.

A number of influences seem to have led to the present situation. Among these are the following:

1. Kindergarten attendance has become the rule rather than the exception.
2. Major shifts in the orientations of early childhood curricula have taken place.
3. Parallel shifts in developmental theories used to justify early childhood curriculum have occurred.
4. Social pressures to offer academic instruction at an early age have been exerted.
5. The use of standardized achievement tests in evaluating the education progress of young children has increased.
6. Many kindergarten teachers are inadequately prepared to be effective early childhood curriculum makers.

Kindergarten the Rule

Kindergartens were first introduced in the public schools in 1873, with kindergarten children representing only slightly over 1% of the elementary school student population (K–8) at the turn of the century (42% of these attended private schools). It was estimated that, in 1922, only about 12% of 5-year-olds attended kindergartens. Even by 1964, less than half of the 5-year-olds attended kindergartens, while in 1978 the numbers exceeded 80%. Enrollment seems to have become stabilized at slightly over 82% in 1977 and 1978 (Grant & Eiden, 1980). . . .

Only in recent years could elementary program designers expect that children entering the primary grades would first have been in kindergarten. Once attendance became the norm, kindergartens received much more attention from those who develop elementary programs and educational materials. Kindergarten education then became the expected beginning point for children in schools and thus a focus for building educational continuity into school programs.

Shift in Curriculum Orientation

During the past 145 years that kindergartens have been in existence, they have been used to achieve a range of different goals, including teaching philosophical idealism, Americanizing children, building proper habits, providing emotional prophylaxis [measures designed to preserve health] for children, serving as a vestibule for the primary grades, presenting the content of school subjects to young children, and helping to develop learning-to-learn skills (Spodek, 1973). This period of curriculum development can be characterized by both its continuities and discontinuities. The continuities can be seen in the persistent concern for two types of goals for young children: the support or stimulation of growth or development, and the achievement of specific learning (Spodek, 1977). Concern for growth can be found in the original Froebelian kindergarten. This same concern was articulated in a different way in the progressive kindergarten, as well as in the development of nursery education.

The alliance of the reform kindergarten with the progressive primary school was supported by a mutual concern for the growth of the child. The idea of "development as the aim of education" (Kohlberg & Mayer, 1972), a basic progressive education concept, provided the connection between early childhood educators and developmental psychologists. "Growth" or "development," used in a metaphorical sense by progressive educators, seemed to take on a literal meaning in early childhood education. As the progressive education movement waned, there was a general lessening of concern for development and an increase in the concern for achieving specific learning outcomes. This concern for learning was imposed upon the kindergarten as well, with the kindergarten conceived of as preparing children for the learning they will achieve in later school years. Gans, Stendler, and Almy (1952) characterized this "readiness" view of the kindergarten as the *3Rs Curriculum* some 30 years ago:

> The 3Rs approach has not only prevailed in the primary grades, but it has reached down into the five-year-old kindergarten. Counting, some writing and reading readiness activities chiefly in the form of workbook exercises have been typical

experiences in kindergarten where this curriculum has been in operation. Under such a setup the kindergarten is seen as a year of settling down for children, of adjusting to sitting still and following directions, so that they will be better prepared for a more rigorous attack on the 3Rs during first grade. (p. 80–81)

The difference between the concerns of kindergartens of 30 years ago and those of today is with the intensity of academic instruction in the kindergarten. Instead of being concerned with using the kindergarten year to get children prepared for the organization of the primary grades, both the organization and the content of these grades seem to have been introduced into the kindergarten.

Shifting Developmental Theories

The advent of the Head Start Program has been characterized as resulting from the joining of new views of human development with new concerns for social justice. At the time that educators seemed to be increasing their concerns for the problems of educating disadvantaged children, new ideas relating to cognitive development—and especially to the importance of the early years on this development—seemed to be coming to the fore. The work of Jean Piaget, which had been accumulating for decades, began to receive the attention of American psychologists and educators. Piaget's theories described children's cognitive development as moving through a series of stages with achievement at later stages dependent upon successful progress through earlier stages. The early experiences of the child were seen as having significant impact on total intellectual development, even though direct instruction was not viewed as effective in moving children through these stages. Hunt, in his classic formulation *Intelligence and Experience* (1961), brought together a wealth of theory and research from many sources in support of the idea that these early experiences could have a major impact on the developing intellect. Bloom's (1964) analysis of test data on intelligence suggested that a great deal of the variance in later tests of intelligence could be accounted for by the variance in tests taken by children before 5 years of age. Thus, it was demonstrated that what children learn early in life could affect their continued learning.

In addition to this awareness, behavioral psychologists were demonstrating that by manipulating the motivational sets of children, and by analyzing complex tasks in terms of simpler components to be taught separately and later integrated, many specific skills could be learned by children at an early age. Behavioral principles were used to understand development and to provide the basis for systematic programs to teach young children (Bijou & Baer, 1961).

While each of the developmental theories briefly described above is different from the others, and none of the theories directly translates into the kindergarten program, all have been used to support the notion that intellectual development begins early in life and that what one learns in the early childhood years can have serious consequences for later learning. Growing out of the empirical research and the theory generation that took place in child development during this period, a number of educational programs arose for young children a the kindergarten and pre-kindergarten level. While these programs were originally designed for poor children, and many became the bases of the planned variations of Head Start and Follow-Through, a number of these programs or their variants have been broadly generalized to other early childhood populations.

While the evidence accumulated that there was much that young children could learn prior to first grade, there was no unanimity on the issues of what young children ought to learn during that period—what priorities ought to be given to the different learnings that are possible—and what the long-term consequences of particular learnings are. As kindergartens moved under the influences of the elementary school, it was felt in many cases that those learnings most consistent with what is taught later in school, or which seemed to be preparatory to later school learning, ought to be supported in the kindergarten. Yet there is no evidence that there are greater long-term payoffs for these kinds of learning activities than there are for activities more consistent with the growth ideology of the progressive kindergarten.

Early Instruction in Academic Skills

The introduction of reading and writing into the kindergarten is certainly not a new phenomenon. An exhibit at the 1876 Philadelphia Centennial Exposition labeled "The American Kindergarten" was criticized for encouraging such activities as reading and writing. This intrusion of academics into the Froebelian kindergarten was defended by citing a need to "Americanize the kindergarten idea" (Ross, 1976). Formal reading instruction was never considered a part of the Froebelian kindergarten, nor did the progressive kindergarten offer more than informal activities related to basic academic skills.

A number of pressures have led to the increased concern for teaching academic skills in the kindergarten. On the one hand, there seem always to have been parents who wished their children to be involved in academic instruction as early as possible. Many of these parents have gifted children, or at least view their children as gifted. Montessori preschool programs have been attractive to these parents because of the promise made that their children would learn the three R's significantly earlier than they would have traditionally. Books have been made similarly available, detailing instructions for parents to engage in activities which promise to give their young children superior minds, or at least early access to school learning. These parents may strive to enroll their children early in school and/or to influence the school to make academics available to their children at the earliest possible moment. Wagner (1977) describes Alice Beck, an exemplary kindergarten teacher whose classroom is characterized as providing child-centered education through individualization and project learning. She deals with parental pressure to teach academics in kindergarten by meeting with parents early in the year to find out what they want for their children from kindergarten. She explains her goals to parents, encourages classroom visits, solicits help on projects, and informs the parents regularly and honestly about their child's activities.

A greater pressure to offer early instruction in academic skills, however, has resulted from the concern that the public schools may not be adequately preparing all children in the area of basic academic skills. The perceived failure of the public school system to provide adequate basic skills instruction has led to a number of suggested solutions, including the use of minimum competency tests and instruction in the academic skills at the earliest possible moment. The logic of this latter position seems inviolate. When the teaching of academic skills has begun in first grade, there have been failures. Some of these failures could be overcome by providing additional instructional time well before the initial assessment of success.

A number of concerns might be raised with this approach. To add instructional time for academic skills within the kindergarten requires that the time be taken from some other activities, activities which are also educational. Thus, there are no absolute gains in learning, but rather there are trade-offs; at best, achievement is gained in one area at the expense of achievement in other areas. With the addition of instruction in academics in the kindergarten, losses have been those activities that traditionally have been highly prized: art, music, science (including nature study), as well as opportunities for expression and play. These were the very activities kindergartens were applauded for having introduced into the elementary school in years past.

While articles on kindergarten cooking (Placek, 1976), block building (Liedke, 1975), art (Warfield, 1973), environmental values (Bryant & Hungerford, 1977) and science (David, 1977) can still be found in the professional literature, often the justification for their inclusion in the kindergarten is related to the academic outcomes that can be derived. The use of blocks, for example, is advocated for teaching mathematical concepts of grouping, comparing, one-to-one correspondence, and ordering, as well as for familiarizing children with numbers and number names (Liedke, 1975). Thus, the academic values are used to justify the inclusion of these program activities. In addition, one can question what is actually taught in kindergartens in relation to academics. Durkin (1978) has criticized current kindergarten reading practices for sometimes being offered prematurely to children; when offered, the programs may themselves be poor.

In moving academics downwards into the kindergarten, too often the focus has been on mechanical learning. While mechanics are not the most critical aspects of academic learning, they are the ones that are most often assessed by standardized tests.

Increased Use of Standardized Tests

Directly related to the concern for instruction in the basic skills has been the call for the increased use of standardized achievement tests to periodically and regularly assess the achievement of these skills in children. While in the past educators often advocated postponing administration of standardized achievement tests, assessment instruments are now being presented to children at earlier and earlier ages. These tests also influence what is taught.

A number of states have developed their own testing programs, while others have used commercially available standardized tests. Brickon and Roeber (1978) describe the development of a state kindergarten assessment program in Michigan. Teachers were able to use the formal instruments developed by the state education agency, other standardized tests, or other informal assessment techniques in their pilot program. Interestingly, most assessment was done in the area of cognitive and psychomotor skills, areas most easily assessed using the state-developed instruments. When the areas of music and art were assessed, evaluation was most often done through teacher observation.

An example of the relationship of testing to the teaching of basic skills can be found in *The National Conference on Achievement Testing and Basic Skills* (National Institute for Education of the Department of Health, Education and Welfare, 1978). The call at the conference, by educators and politicians alike, was for the improvement of instruction in basic academic skills and, beginning early, for the regular and continued administration of standardized achievement tests as a way of improving instruction in basic academic skills.

Since the content of most standardized achievement tests in the early grades is on the mechanics of reading, language, and arithmetic, and since programs at these grades are assessed by children's achievement on these tests, the focus on instruction more often leans toward teaching letter-sound associations, computation skills, spelling, punctuation, and the like, rather than toward higher-order academic processes such as comprehension, problem solving, and the application of principles to real problems.

One of the issues raised in the recent evaluation of the program models in Follow-Through was that the instruments used to evaluate achievement were more appropriate for some areas than for others. Since most tests used focused on achievement in the mechanics of reading, language, and arithmetic, those models that emphasized instruction in these skills were strongly favored in the evaluation (House, Glass, McLean, & Walker, 1977). Because program elements that are evaluated tend to receive greater attention from school personnel, especially when schools are being criticized, program goals such as social competence, for which there are no adequate standardized measures, tend to receive lower priorities.

The view that standardized test are best for evaluating kindergarten programs becomes an issue in that academic goals alone, rather than a broad range of educational/developmental goals, become the basis for judging the program. Kindergarten programs can become totally academically oriented if they only seek to achieve those goals that can be assessed through standardized achievement tests. Lesiak and Wait (1974) describe how a traditional kindergarten program was modified into a "diagnostically oriented" program through the intervention of school psychologists. Prescriptive activities were provided to children in three program domains, based upon a profile developed for each child using objective assessment techniques (tests).

Hutchins (1981) found that the adoption of a preschool screening program contributed to the valuing of more measurable education objectives and the use of more direct instructional methods in a kindergarten. In addition, the pace, sequence, and quantity of learning offered each child was often governed by the screening test, and the program itself was legitimated in the community in relation to that test. Thus, a cyclical pattern was established whereby a set of tests not only determined a child's educational experiences but also legitimated those experiences.

99

Bernard Spodek

Inadequate Preparation of Kindergarten Teachers

Within the early childhood tradition, the teacher is seen as the individual responsible for the development and modification of the curriculum. Teachers must know a great deal in order to create and choose appropriate educational activities for young children. This knowledge is provided in programs of teacher preparation and is attested to by state teacher certification. The area of teacher preparation and certification in early childhood education has recently been surveyed (Spodek & Saracho, 1982). Generally, programs require that teachers have knowledge of principles of learning and of child growth and development, as well as of foundations and general education. Most important is the knowledge of curriculum and teaching methods appropriate to the age level of the children to be taught. Opportunities to practice this knowledge are provided in practicum situations.

The last survey of teacher certification programs related to early childhood education in the United States indicated that even though kindergarten teachers may have completed teacher education programs and become certified, they might not necessarily know a great deal about early childhood education. Of the 44 states responding to a survey and requiring that kindergarten teachers be certified, 35 required certification in elementary education. In only 8 of these was a kindergarten or early childhood endorsement available. Thus, in the majority of states, anyone prepared to be an elementary school teacher has been considered competent to teach kindergarten (Education Commission of the States, 1975). Another recent study of college programs preparing early childhood teachers revealed that a majority of students in most of the programs take a double major and/or prepare for dual certification. The other certificate in most instances was in elementary teaching (Spodek & Davis, 1981).

In some states, kindergarten teachers are certified in early childhood education. In other cases, they receive a kindergarten endorsement on an elementary certificate. In still other cases (Illinois, for example), an elementary teaching certificate is all that is required for teaching in the kindergarten as well as in the elementary grades. Thus, while some teachers may have been provided with an in-depth program in early childhood education, others will have a course or two in addition to their elementary curriculum and methods courses, and many will have no preparation specifically related to kindergarten teaching. Yet all will be considered prepared to teach kindergarten.

Given this range of preparation for teaching kindergarten, it is reasonable to assume that many teachers responsible for making educational decisions in the kindergarten will not have been adequately prepared to make those decisions. These teachers will have knowledge of elementary education methods and curriculum, but not necessarily of early childhood methods and curriculum. It would be reasonable to expect those teachers to view the inclusion of elementary programs in the kindergarten as appropriate.

Even those teachers prepared in an early childhood tradition may not be adequately prepared to cope with program decisions for the kindergarten. The child development point of view in the latter tradition more often than not reflects a "growth" mentality and avoids a concern for achievement. This orientation may be inadequate for assimilating the demands of teaching academic subjects. Teachers trained in this tradition might only have their own experience in elementary school to rely on as the basis for decisions, and thus may be ignorant of developmentally appropriate methods of approaching academics.

CONCLUSIONS

The field of early childhood education has changed dramatically during the past two decades. Much of the change is related to increases in the field—greater numbers of children served, more programs in existence, and more practitioners employed. Much of the focus of the field has been determined by changes at the prekindergarten level—the development of Head Start and other similar federally funded educational programs, increases in the number of children in day care centers as well as changes in the sponsorship of these centers, and the availability of programs for preschool handicapped children. Such changes reflect new federal policies which have channelled increasing amounts of federal money into the field. These policies have an impact on the kindergarten as well, even though kindergartens are primarily supported by state and local funds. A spill-over effect has occurred, leading to increased acceptance for kindergartens (Tanner, 1973).

Because kindergartens are within the states' domains, they have been shaped by different influences than have prekindergarten programs. Political influences at the state level have led to dramatic increases in the availability of kindergartens and the parallel increases in kindergarten attendance already described. Prior early childhood initiatives have served to provide a base for kindergarten initiatives. In addition, state budget surpluses and new federal revenue sharing funds in the 1970s have allowed state legislatures to establish such new services as public school kindergartens (Forgione, 1975).

In any one community, a number of influences in addition to the six discussed here may affect decisions about what to offer children in the kindergarten. With the demands for teaching academic skills early, with greater reliance on standardized tests for assessing instruction, and with the unsureness that kindergarten teachers might feel about the nature of the programs they have been offering, decisions are often delegated to others. Packaged programs coupled with assessment procedures or integrated into a total textbook adoption package may be difficult to resist. The process of program development at the school level may be giving way in many communities to more general district-wide program adoptions. The idea of tailoring programs to meet individual children's needs and interests may be giving way to providing proably with later instructional offerings.

Sadly, early childhood educators have had relatively little impact on re-cent early childhood policies. Consensus does not exist within the field as to the value of different kinds of programs or even as to the value of any early childhood program. Available research is equivocal and tends to be used by policy makers to support predetermined positions (Forgione, 1975).

Most often, the policy concerns of early childhood educators have been to increase the availability of early childhood programs for children. Perhaps it is time now to look beyond the quantitative aspect of early childhood education to its qualitative aspects. As things now stand, most children will attend kin-dergarten at age 5. But what kind of kindergarten will it be? Will the program be broadly developmental? Will it be designed to achieve objectively measur-able academic outcomes? Will teachers be adequately prepared to provide ap-propriate educational experiences for young children? Will the program reflect a commitment to developmental as well as to academic continuity?

As we attempt to influence the directions that kindergartens take, we need to develop an understanding of the factors that have shaped and contin-ued to shape kindergarten practices, including influences within individual teachers, within the profession, within school systems, and within communi-ties. We need also to learn how to use that knowledge to influence practice. This might require that we become politically as well as pedagogically astute.

REFERENCES

Bijou, S.W., & Baer, D. M. *Child development I: A systematic and empirical theory.* New York: Appleton-Century-Croft, 1961.

Bloom, B. *Stability and change in human characteristics.* New York: Wiley, 1964.

Blow, S. E. (First report). In Committee of Nineteen, *The kindergarten.* Boston, MA: Houghton Mifflin Company, 1923.

Brickon, P. T., & Roeber, E. D. The role of the state agency in local assessment programs. Paper presented at the Annual Meeting of the National Council on Measurement in Education, Toronto, Canada, March 1978.

Bryant, C. K., & Hungerford, H. R. An analysis of strategies for teaching environmental concepts and values clarification in kindergarten. *Journal of Environmental Educa-tion,* 1977, *9,* 44–49.

Committee of Nineteen. *The kindergarten.* Boston: Houghton Mifflin Company, 1913.

David, A. R. Science for fives. *Childhood Education,* 1977, *53,* 206–210.

DeLima, A. *Our enemy, the child.* New York: New Republic, 1925.

Dewey, J. Froebel's educational principles. *Elementary School Record,* 1900, *1*(5), 143–151.

Durkin, D. Pre-first grade starts in reading: Where do we stand? *Educational Leadership,* 1978, *36,* 174–177.

Education Commission of the States. *Early childhood programs*: A state survey, 1974–75. Denver, CO: Education Commission of the States, 1975.

Fallon, B. J. *Forty innovative programs in early childhood education.* Belmont, CA: Fearon, 1973.

Far West Laboratory. *Educational programs that work*. San Francisco, CA: Far West Laboratory for Educational Research and Development, 1976.

Forgione, P. D., Jr. Rationales for early childhood policy making: The role of five SEA's in early childhood education policy making. Paper presented at the Annual Meeting of the American Educational Research Association, Washington, DC, March 1975.

Froebel, F. (W. H. Hartmann, trans.) *The education of man*. New York: Appleton, 1887.

Foster, G., & Headley, M. *Education in the kindergarten*. New York: American Book Co., 1948.

Gans, R., Stendler, C. B., & Almy, M. *Teaching young children in nursery school, kindergarten and the primary grades*. Yonkers-on-Hudson, NY: World Book Co., 1952.

Garrison, C. G., Sheehy, E. D., & Dalgliesh, A. *The Horace Mann Kindergarten for five-year-old children*. New York: Columbia University Teachers College, Bureau of Publications, 1937.

Grant, W. V., & Eiden, L. J. *Digest of educational statistics*, 1980. Washington, DC: National Center for Education Statistics, 1980.

Gregory, B. C. The necessity of continuity between the kindergarten and the elementary school: The present status, illogical and unFroebelian. In B. C. Gregory, J. B. Merrill, B. Payne, & M. Giddings (Eds.), *The coordination of the kindergarten and the elementary school*. 7th Yearbook of the National Society for the Scientific Study of Education, Pt. 2. Chicago: University of Chicago Press, 1908.

Hall G. S. The ideal school as based on child study. *Journal of Proceedings and Addresses of the National Education Association*. 1901, 474–490.

House, E. R., Glass, G. V., McLean, L. D., & Walker, D. F., *No simple answer: Critique of the "Follow Through" evaluation*. Urbana, IL: University of Illinois, 1977.

Hunt, J. M. *Intelligence and experience*. New York: Ronald Press, 1961.

Hutchins, E. J. A preschool screening examination and a public school. Paper presented at the Annual Meeting of the American Educational Research Association, Los Angeles, CA, April 1981.

Kohlberg, L., & Mayer, R. Development as the aim of education. *Harvard Educational Review*, 1972, 42, 449–496.

Lesiak, W. J., & Wait, J. A. The diagnostic kindergarten: Initial step in the identification and programming of children with learning problems. *Psychology in the Schools*, 1974, 11, 282–289.

Liedtke, W. Experiences with blocks in kindergarten. *Arithmetic Teacher*, 1975, 22, 406–412.

Lilley, I., *Friedrich Froebel: A selection from his writings*. Cambridge, MA: Cambridge University Press, 1967.

National Institute of Education (DHEW). *The national conference on achievement testing and basic skills. March 1–3, 1978. Conference proceedings*, 1978. (ED 171 784, 38 pp.)

Placek, C. Kindergarten cooks. *Day Care and Early Education*. 1976, 4, 23–25.

Pratt, C., & Stanton, J. *Before books*. New York: Adelphi Co., 1926.

Ross, E. D. *The kindergarten crusade: The establishment of preschool education in the United States*. Athens, OH: Ohio University Press, 1976.

Synder, A. *Dauntless women in childhood education*. Washington, DC: Association for Childhood Education International, 1972.

Spodek, B. Needed: A new view of kindergarten education. *Childhood Education*, 1973, 49, 191–197.

Spodek, B. Early childhood education: A synoptic view. In N. Nir-Janiv, B. Spodek, & D. Steg (Eds.), *Early child education: International perspectives*. New York: Plenum, 1982.

Spodek, B. Early childhood education: A synoptic view. In N. Nir-Janiv, B. Spodek, & D. Steg (Eds.), *Early child education: International perspectives.* New York: Plenum, 1982.

Spodek, B., & Davis, M. C. The changing nature of early childhood teacher education programs. Paper presented at annual conference of the National Association for the Education of Young Children, Detroit, MI, November 1981.

Spodek, B., & Saracho. O. N. The preparation and certification of early childhood personnel. In B. Spodek (Ed.), *Handbook of research in early childhood education.* New York: Free Press, 1982.

Tanner, L. N. Unanticipated effects of federal policy: The kindergarten. *Educational Leadership,* 1973, *31,* 49–52.

Vanderwalker, N. C. History of kindergarten influences in elementary education. In M. J. Holmes (Ed.), *The kindergarten and its relation to elementary education.* 6th Yearbook of the National Society for the Study of Education, Pt. 2. Bloomington, IL: Public School Publishing Co., 1907.

Vanderwalker, N. C., *The kindergarten in American education.* New York: Macmillan, 1908.

Wagner, B. J. Alice Beck of Hubbard Woods: Portrait of a kindergarten teacher. *Elementary School Journal,* 1977, *77,* 343–349.

Warfield, J. A. A visit to the world of the four-year-old: Implications for the kindergarten art program. *Art Teacher,* 1973, *3,* 3–5.

Weber, E. *The kindergarten: Its encounter with educational thought in America.* New York: Teachers College Press, 1969.

Whipple, G. M. (Ed.), *preschool and parental education.* 28th Yearbook of the National Society for the Study of Education. Bloomington, IL: Public School Publishing Co., 1929.

PART THREE

Practice With Young Children

Chapter 5 Play   107

Chapter 6 Learning Environments   130

Chapter 7 Sound Practice   150

CHAPTER 5 Play

5.1 FRIEDRICH FROEBEL

The School and the Family

Friedrich Froebel's writings on how young children should be educated were based on his observations as a teacher in Germany. Born in 1782, Froebel spent years studying with Swiss educator Johann Pestalozzi and others, and he then established several innovative schools that allowed him to refine his concept of a free environment where young children could explore and manipulate simple playthings. His philosophy was a departure from the rigid schools of the time, which emphasized a great deal of memory work and recitation, with minimal child activity.

Froebel envisioned learning taking place much like the growth of a plant under the watchful eye of a gardener who provides the necessary elements for growth and only intervenes when something may impede growth. Froebel's gardener analogy led him to coin the term *kindergarten,* literally translated, "children's garden." He used the word *kindergartner* for the teacher, who he envisioned as a nurturer of the children. The teacher's responsibilities were not to bend, shape, and mold the child but to guide and excite a child to grow through play. Froebel stated that he did not want his new setting called a school, because he did not want children to be schooled but to explore and develop freely under gentle guidance. The materials Froebel developed for the children became known as eleven "gifts," which were objects for discovery, and eight "occupations," which were activities for creativity. Froebel's philosophy and his gifts and occupations are elaborated on in the following selection from his book *The Education of Man* (D. Appleton, 1897). Today, Froebel's perception of play seems overly symbolic and inflexible; however, it stood in sharp contrast to the prevailing rote-learning practices of his day.

The political climate of the time led the leaders of a divided Prussia to become concerned about Froebel's deviation from strict control over young children. They accused Froebel of atheism and prohibited kindergartens just before his death in 1852.

Man is developed and cultured toward the fulfillment of his destiny and mission, and is to be valued, even in boyhood, not only by what he receives and absorbs from without, but much more by what he puts out and unfolds from himself.

Experience and history, too, teach that men truly and effectively promote human welfare much more by what they put forth from themselves than by what they may have acquired. Every one knows that those who truly teach, gain steadily in knowledge and insight; similarly, every one knows, for nature herself teaches this, that the use of a force enhances and intensifies the force. Again, to learn a thing in life and through doing is much more developing, cultivating, and strengthening, than to learn it merely through the verbal communication of ideas. Similarly, plastic material representation in life and through doing, united with thought and speech, is by far more developing and cultivating than the merely verbal representation of ideas. Therefore, this subject of instruction necessarily follows the subjects just considered.

The life of the boy has, indeed, no purpose but that of the outer representation of his self; his life is, in truth, but an external representation of his inner being, of his power, particularly in and through (plastic) material.

In the forms he fashions he does not see outer forms which he is to take in and understand; but he sees in them the expression of his spirit, of the laws and activities of his own mind. For the purpose of teaching and instruction is

> to bring ever more *out* of man rather than to put more and more *into* him; for that which can get *into* man we already know and possess as the property of mankind, and every one, simply because he is a human being, will unfold and develop it out of himself in accordance with the laws of mankind. On the other hand, what yet is to come *out* of mankind, what human nature is yet to develop, that we do not yet know, that is not yet the property of mankind; and, still, human nature, like the spirit of God, is ever unfolding its inner essence.

However clearly this might and should appear from the observation of our own and all other life, even the best among us, like plants near a calcareous spring, are so encrusted with extraneous prejudices and opinions, that only with greatest effort and self-constraint we give even limited heed to the better view. Let us confess at least that, when, with the best intentions toward our children, we speak of their development and education, we should rather say *en*velopment and *in*duction; that we should not even speak of culture which implies the development of the mind, of the will of man, but rather of stamping and molding, however proudly we may claim to have passed beyond these mind-killing practices.

Those to whom we intrust our children for education may, therefore, well be full of anxiety. . . .

The outer material representation of the spiritual in man must begin with efforts on his part to spiritualize the corporeal about him by giving it life and a spiritual relation and significance.

This is indicated in the course of development of mankind itself: the corporeal material with which the representation of the spiritual is to begin must present and distinctly declare even in its external form the laws and conditions of inner development—it must be rectangular, cubical, beam-shaped, and brick-shaped.

The formations made with this material are either external aggregations—*constructive*—or developments from within—*formative.*

Building, aggregation, is first with the child, as it is first in the development of mankind, and in crystallization.

The importance of the vertical, the horizontal, and the rectangular is the first experience which the boy gathers from his building; then follow equilibrium and symmetry. Thus he ascends from the construction of the simplest wall with or without cement to the more complex and even to the invention of every architectural structure lying within the possibilities of the given material.

Laying or arranging tablets beside one another on a plane has much less charm for the boy than placing or piling them on one another—a clear proof of the tendency of the mind for all-sided development, manifested in all his activities.

The joining of lines seems to come still later. Thus, the course of human development and culture seems to free itself more and more from corporeality, to become more and more spiritualized; drawing takes the place of the joining of concrete lines or splints; painting, the place of tablet-work; true modeling, the corporeal development from cubical forms, the place of corporeal building.

In spite of this obvious, living, progressive development from the external and corporeal to the inner and spiritual, in spite of this continuous progression in the growth of human culture, some nevertheless are inclined to doubt the utility of these exercises for children.

And yet even these could not have reached the degree of general culture they enjoy, if Providence—ruling in secret—had not led them on this very way, either without their knowledge or through their own perseverance against the opposition of their surroundings.

Man should, at least mentally, repeat the achievements of mankind, that they may not be to him empty, dead masses, that his judgment of them may not be external and spiritless; he should mentally go over the ways of mankind, that he may learn to understand them. Nevertheless some are inclined to consider these things useless in the boyhood of their children.

Perhaps, however, it is not necessary to go so far; but you do know that your sons need energy, judgment, perseverance, prudence, etc., and that these things are indispensable to them; and all these things they are sure to get (in the course indicated), and by far more, for idleness, ennui, ignorance, brooding, are the most terrible of poisons to growing childhood and boyhood, and their opposites a panacea of mental and physical health, of domestic and civil welfare.

The course of instruction here, too, determines itself, as it does, indeed, in all cases when we have found the true starting-point, when we have apprehended the subject of instruction and grasped its purpose.

The material for building in the beginning should consist of a number of wooden blocks, whose base is always one square inch and whose length varies from one to twelve inches. If, then, we take twelve pieces of each length, two sets—e.g., the pieces one and eleven, the pieces two and ten inches long, etc.—will always make up a layer an inch thick and covering one square foot of surface; so that all the pieces, together with a few larger pieces, occupy a space of somewhat more than half a cubic foot. It is best to keep these in a box that has exactly these dimensions; such a box may be used in many other ways in instruction, as will appear in the progress of the boy's development.

The material next to this will consist of building-bricks of such dimensions that eight of them will form a cube of two inches to the side. In the former set of blocks there was the same number of each kind and length. In this set, the greatest number of blocks—at least five hundred—are of the described brick-shape and size; in addition there are successively smaller numbers of twice, thrice, to six times the length indicated, as well as some of half the length.

The first thing the boy should learn is to distinguish, name, and classify the material according to size. During the progress of building, too, it should always be carefully arranged according to size. In the next place, all that has been produced should be carefully and accurately described by the boy—e.g., I have built a vertical wall with vertical ends, a door, and two windows at equal distances; the bricks are placed alternately, or so that in each upper row each brick rests on and covers the ends of two bricks below.

Subsequently, a simple building with only one door may be put up; then, the number of doors and windows is increased; at last, partitions, another story, etc., are added.

Similar considerations control the work with tablets, although the forms are more complicated. Still greater diversity is attainable with linear splints one half to five inches long, with special reference to writing, drawing, and building.

Modeling with paper and paste-board has its peculiar progressive course.

Still more profitable, but only for those who have attained a certain degree of mental power, is the modeling of plastic soft material in accordance with the laws indicated by the cubical form. However, this, as well as the free modeling of the same material, belongs to a later part of the period of boyhood.

[In this and the succeeding paragraphs we have the first indications of the system of *gifts and occupations* subsequently developed in Froebel's kindergarten. Even at the date of the publication of "Education of Man," Froebel appreciated the value of simple playthings, but, as the paragraphs here translated show, his ideas on the subject were still crude. Not before 1835, he gained from some children playing ball in a meadow near Burgdorf the inspiration that *the ball* is the simplest and as such should be made the first plaything of the little child. In 1836 he had reached the first five gifts, and even among these the second gift lacked the cylinder, and the *fifth gift* consisted of twenty-seven entire cubes. The cylinder was added to the *second gift,* probably not before 1844, when the idea of the *external mediation of contrasts* in educational work was first clearly seen and formulated by him. In a weekly journal which Froebel began to publish in 1850, a *System of Gifts and Occupations,* similar to the one now used in kindergartens, is described. These are arranged by Hanschmann in thirty-six gifts, by Marenholtz-Bülow in eleven gifts and eight occupations, with the promise of more for advanced work. A few modifications and additions have been made since Froebel's death. So far as they seem to be in accordance with Froebel's thought, they have been embodied with the *Synoptical Table* given below. This table gives a concise description of each gift where this appeared desirable; and, in the first six gifts, a few words are added in brackets,[], designating in order the chief external (1) and internal (2) characteristic of the gift, and the essential lesson (3) which the gift, could it speak, is meant to teach the child.

SYNOPTICAL TABLE OF GIFTS AND OCCUPATIONS.

Gifts.

A. BODIES (Solids).

   I. [Color (1);—Individuality (2);—"We are here!" (3).] Six colored worsted balls, about an inch and a half in diameter.—*First Gift.*
   II. [Shape (1);—Personality (2);—"We Live!" (3).] Wooden ball, cylinder, and cube, one inch and a half in diameter.—*Second Gift*
   III. [Number (divisibility) (1);—Self-activity (2);—"Come, play with us (3)."] Eight one-inch cubes, forming a two-inch cube ($2 \times 2 \times 2$). —*Third Gift.*
   IV. [Extent (1);—Obedience (2);—"Study us!" (3).] Eight brick-shaped blocks ($2 \times 1 \times \frac{1}{2}$), forming a two-inch cube.—*Fourth Gift.*
   V. [Symmetry (1);—Unity (2);—"How beautiful!" (3).] Twenty-seven one-inch cubes, three bisected and three quadrisected diagonally, forming a three-inch cube ($3 \times 3 \times 3$).—*Fifth Gift.*
   VI. [Proportion (1);—Free obedience (2);—"Be our master!" (3).] Twenty-seven brick-shaped blocks, three bisected longitudinally and six bisected transversely, forming a three-inch cube.—*Sixth Gift.*

B. SURFACES.—Wooden tablets.—*Seventh Gift.*

   I. *Squares* (derived from the faces of the second or third gift cubes).
      1. *Entire* squares (one-and-a-half in. square or one-inch square).
      2. *Half* squares (squares cut diagonally).
   II. *Equilateral triangles* (length of side, one inch, or one inch and a half).
      1. *Entire* triangles.

2. *Half* triangles (the equilateral triangle is cut in the direction of the altitude, yielding right scalene triangles, acute angles of 60° and 30°).
3. *Thirds* of triangles (the equilateral triangle is cut from the center to the vertices, yielding obtuse isosceles triangles, angles 30° and 120°).

C. LINES.—*Eighth Gift.*

    I. Straight. (Splints of various lengths.)
    II. Circular. (Metal or paper rings of various sizes; whole circles, half circles, and quadrants are used.)

D. POINTS.—Beans, lentils, or other seeds, leaves, pebbles, pieces of card-board or paper, etc.—*Ninth Gift.*

E. RECONSTRUCTION.—(By analysis the "system" has descended from the solid to the point. This last gift enables the child to *reconstruct* the surface and solid synthetically from the point. It consists of softened pease or wax pellets and sharpened sticks or straws.)—*Tenth Gift.*

Occupations.

A. SOLIDS. (Plastic clay, card-board work, wood-carving, etc.)
B. SURFACES. (Paper-folding, paper-cutting, parquetry, painting, etc.)
C. LINES. (Interlacing, intertwining, weaving, thread games, embroidery, drawing, etc.)
D. POINTS. (Stringing beads, buttons, etc.; perforating, etc.)

The distinction between the *gifts* and *occupations,* though never clearly formulated by Froebel, is very important. The *gifts* are intended to give the child from time to time new universal aspects of the external world, suited to a child's development. The *occupations,* on the other hand, furnish material for practice in certain phases of skill. Anything will do for an occupation, provided it is sufficiently plastic and within the child's powers of control; but the gift in form and material is determined by the cosmic phase to be brought to the child's apprehension, and by the condition of the child's development at the period for which the gift is intended. Thus, nothing but the *First Gift* can so effectively arouse in the child's mind the feeling and consciousness of a world of individual things; but there are numberless occupations that will enable the child to become skillful in the manipulation of surfaces.

The gift gives the child a new cosmos, the occupation fixes the impressions made by the gift. The gift invites only arranging activities; the occupation invites also controlling, modifying, transforming, creating activities. The gift leads to discovery; the occupation, to invention. The gift gives insight; the occupation, power.

The occupations are one-sided: the gifts, many-sided, universal. The occupations touch only certain phases of being; the gifts enlist the whole being of the child.

Froebel has formulated four conditions which true *gifts* should satisfy:

1. They should, each in its time, fully represent the child's outer world, his macrocosm.
2. They should, each in its time, enable the child to give satisfactory expression in play to his inner world, his microcosm.
3. Each gift should, therefore, in itself represent a complete, orderly whole or unit.
4. Each gift should contain all the preceding, and foreshadow all the succeeding gifts.

In short, each gift should, in due time and in the widest sense, aid the child "to make the external internal, the internal external, and to find the unity between the two."—*Tr.*]

Social Participation Among Pre-School Children

The early nursery schools that were developed during the 1920s and 1930s afforded researchers the opportunity to observe groups of children. Until that time, children had been studied informally and often individually or in very small groups. The nurseries allowed teachers and researchers to observe for specific behaviors or interactions and to focus on group/peer interaction. Throughout the first part of the twentieth century, various studies were carried out on groups of children around the United States.

When Mildred B. Parten became interested in the field of social development, she chose the nursery school as the setting for her study, which is described in the following selection from "Social Participation Among Pre-School Children," *The Journal of Abnormal and Social Psychology* (vol. 27, 1932–1933). While at the Institute of Child Welfare at the University of Minnesota, Parten observed 42 children in the nursery school. From October 1926 to June 1927, she observed the children during the free choice time for an hour every day. Children were allowed to play with any materials and with any other children in the group. Her study examined the interactions of children and led her to conclude that social play increases with a child's age.

Parten classified play in the following categories: solitary play; parallel group activity; associative group play; and organized, cooperative group play. Her work allows us to view isolated and parallel play in developmental terms, not just as an indication of children's temperament. In more recent studies, solitary play has been redefined as independent, goal-oriented activity, rather than a sign of immaturity. Although it has been modified and challenged, Parten's typology continues to be used to study the links between play and social development.

DESCRIPTION OF SUBJECTS AND OF METHOD OF OBSERVATION

This investigation was carried on in the Nursery School of the Institute of Child Welfare at the University of Minnesota. The applicability of the findings of this study to children as a whole is a function of the similarity of the subjects studied to children in general. In so far as these individuals are representative children, and if the sample is sufficient, the generalizations should hold true. The 42 children observed are summarized as to intelligence, sex, occupational category of the father, age and size of family in Table 1.

The intelligence tests which have been given to the children seem to indicate that their average mental ability is above normal, although the I.Q.'s range from 81 to 145. The occupations of the fathers were grouped into categories based upon the Barr Scale for Occupational Intelligence and the Taussig Industrial Classification.[1] Group I is composed of the highest or professional class while the semi-skilled laborers constitute Group V. The occupations are representative of the economic groups of the city of Minneapolis, except for the fact that there is an over-weighting with children from the professional classes. The children were from mixed national stock and came from families where the number of children ranged from one to five.

Period of Observation

The observations extended from October 26, 1926, to June 10, 1927, with the majority of the observations during the months from January to April. The records from October to January were made when the technique of observing was being developed. During May and June the records were not kept daily because weather conditions permitted the children to play outside and it was thought that elements might enter into outside play which did not exist in indoor play. To complete records, however, some observations on outdoor play were made for subjects who entered the nursery school late in the year.

In order to provide a minimum of variation in the conditions of observation, the investigation was carried on at the same hour every day that the children were in the nursery school. The hour selected for observation was a morning period from 9:30 to 10:30 during the free-play period. At this hour every child is permitted to play with any toys he wishes and with any children, or with none at all, as he desires. The teachers make relatively few suggestions to the children, but are in sight of the children in order to help settle any problems that may arise. The sandboxes are opened at the beginning of the hour, the kiddie-kars are placed in the gymnasium upstairs, and practically all toys are accessible to the children without assistance from adults in the room. Since there are not enough toys of every type to supply each child, there is a ruling that the child who gets a toy first, may play with it until he leaves it, or in the case of the swings and large apparatus, the children must take turns. A few activities are directed by adults during this hour, such as painting water-color pictures, washing dolls' clothes, or making valentines; but in no case are the children solicited to join in these activities. If they do join, it is of their own volition.

There are about two assistants or teachers to every room. Occasionally there are four or five observers who sit quietly near the door, and who do not speak to anyone except to nod a reply to the questions from the children. As a

TABLE 1

Distribution of the Children of This Study in Age, Sex, I.Q., Paternal Occupation and Family Size

Age at October, 1926	No. Cases Boys	Girls	I.Q.	Cases	Occupational Class	Cases	Family Size	Cases
Under 2	2	2	80–89	2	Group I	13	1 child	5
2–2, 11	9	5	90–99	3	Group II	6	2 children	15
3–3, 11	8	6	100–109	8	Group III	11	3 children	11
4–4, 11	3	7	110–119	11	Group IV	6	4 children	5
			120–129	11	Group V	6	5 children	6
			130–139	3				
			140–149	4				
Total	22	20		42		42		42

rule, the players are quite oblivious to the presence of adults and pursue their activities as if no grown-ups were around.

Categories of Social Participation

Two aspects of social participation may be considered, *extensity,* or the number of social contacts made by an individual, and *intensity,* or the kind of groups participated in and the rôle of the individual in those groups. The number of social contacts may be measured by recording the number of different groups in which a child played. Such a record, however, fails to bring out the differences in social participation between the child who is actively playing in a group and one who is merely an accidental member. Intensity of participation may be determined in two ways: first, by the extent of group integration, i.e., whether the group is organized in such a way that certain duties and responsibilities are demanded of its members, or whether it is only a congregation of independent individuals; and second, by the status of the individual in the group, i.e., whether or not he is helping to shape the plans and activities of the group, i.e., that is to say, his leadership.

After several weeks of preliminary observation of the children at play the extensity and group integration were combined in such a way that a scale of social participation with rigidly defined categories was worked out. One child, for example, did not seem to be playing at all. He usually stood in the middle of the room, pulling at a handkerchief which was tied to his blouse. His head dropped from one shoulder to the other. If asked what he wanted to do, he would merely shake his head; if a toy were placed in front of him, he would not look at it. This type of behavior was called *unoccupied,* although the child was really playing in the manner designated by Stern as the play limited to the child's own body. In order not to confuse this type of play with solitary play, unoccupied behavior was defined as follows:

> *Unoccupied behavior*—The child apparently is not playing, but occupies himself with watching anything that happens to be of momentary interest. When there is nothing exciting taking place, he plays with his own body, gets on and off chairs, just stands around, follows the teacher, or sits in one spot glancing around the room.

Closely related to the unoccupied behavior is the play in which the child observes a group of children playing, but he himself does not overtly enter into the play activity. He is an *onlooker*. Such behavior was described as follows:

> *Onlooker*—The child spends most of his time watching the other children play. He often talks to the children whom he is observing, asks questions, or gives suggestions, but does not overtly enter into the play himself. This type differs from the unoccupied in that the onlooker is definitely observing particular groups of children rather than anything that happens to be exciting. The child stands or sits within speaking distance of the group so that he can see and hear everything that takes place.

A third type of play behavior is that which is usually called playing alone or *solitary play*. Contrary to general opinion there is no clear-cut distinction between group and solitary play. This is particularly true when the play space available for thirty-six children is too meager to permit them to get out of speaking or hearing distance of one another. For this reason, in borderline cases, a purely arbitrary distinction was used to discriminate between group and non-group play. It was decided that a child who played with toys different from those of the children within speaking distance of himself, and one who centered his interest upon his own play, making no effort to get close to and speak to other children, was playing alone. This play was defined thus:

> *Solitary independent play*—The child plays alone and independently with toys that are different from those used by the children within speaking distance and makes no effort to get close to other children. He pursues his own activity without reference to what others are doing.

Closely related to such individual play is a type of group play which was called:

> *Parallel activity*—The child plays independently, but the activity he chooses naturally brings him among other children. He plays with toys that are like those which the children around him are using, but he plays with the toy as he sees fit, and does not try to influence or modify the activity of the children near him. He plays *beside* rather than *with* the other children. There is no attempt to control the coming or going of children in the group.

A common example of this type of play may be observed in the group who congregate around the sandbox. Several children stand close to one another around the sandbox, each child going after and using the toys with which he wishes to play in the sand (usually cups). Children come and go all the time, but those remaining at the sandbox pay no attention to the movements of others; they are absorbed in their own activities. This type of play is not solitary play, yet it is independent play in a group. To what extent children choose to play with toys because they bring them into physical proximity to other children one can not observe; only the overt facts, not the motives, are observable. Suffice it to say that parallel play better resembles group play, and is a more socialized form of play than solitary independent play.

Two other types of group play were *associative* play and *coöperative* or *organized supplementary play*. Associative play is group play in which there is an overt recognition by the group members of their common activity, interests, and personal associations. Organized supplementary play is the most highly organized group activity in which appears the elements of division of labor, group censorship, centralization of control in the hands of one or two members, and the subordination of individual desire to that of the group. Associative play is a less well organized form of the group activity in which the children play with one another, while organized supplementary play is the type in which the efforts of one child are supplemented by those of another for the attainment of a final goal. They were characterized as follows:

> *Associative play*—The child plays with other children. The conversation concerns the common activity; there is a borrowing and loaning of play material; following one another with trains or wagons; mild attempts to control which children may or may not play in the group. All the members engage in similar if not identical activity; there is no division of labor, and no organization of the activity of several individuals around any material goal or product. The children do not subordinate their individual interests to that of the group; instead each child acts as he wishes. By his conversation with the other children one can tell that his interest is primarily in his associations, not in his activity. Occasionally, two or three children are engaged in no activity of any duration, but are merely doing whatever happens to draw the attention of any of them.
>
> *Coöperative or organized supplementary play*—The child plays in a group that is organized for the purpose of making some material product, or of striving to attain some competitive goal, or of dramatizing situations of adult and group life, or of playing formal games. There is a marked sense of belonging or of not belonging to the group. The control of the group situation is in the hands of one or two of the members who direct the activity of the others. The goal as well as the method of attaining it necessitates a division of labor, taking of different rôles by the various group members and the organization of activity so that the efforts of one child are supplemented by those of another.

To illustrate the difference between parallel, associative and organized supplementary play, the sandbox situation may be cited.

Mildred B.
Parten

Parallel activity—Several children are engaged in filling cups in the sandbox. Each child has his own cup and fills it without reference to what the other children are doing with their cups. There is very little conversation about what they are making. No one attempts to tell who may or may not come to the sandbox, so children are coming and going all the time. Occasionally one finds a child who remains at the sandbox during the entire period. The children play *beside* rather than *with* one another.

Associative play—The children begin to borrow one another's cups, they explain why they need two cups; they advise and offer sand to one another. They call a child to the sandbox, and ask those present to make room for him. The others may or may not move over, depending upon their own wishes. No child or children dictate what the various children shall make, but each makes whatever he pleases. Someone may suggest that they all make a road but in that case each child makes his own road, or none at all, as he chooses, and the other children do not censor him. There is much conversation about their common activity.

Organized supplementary play—One child suggests that they are all making supper. Soon the various family rôles are assigned or adopted and the children speak about their shares in preparing the meal. Domination by one or more of the children occurs, one child being informed that he can't cook because he's the baby. The group becomes closed to some children and open to others, depending upon the wishes of the leaders. The children are criticized by one another when they do not play their rôles correctly. They are not permitted to leave the sandbox unless it is known what they are going to do next.

NOTE

1. Descriptions of both of these scales may be found in Terman *et al.*, "Genetic Studies of Genius", Stanford University Press, 1925, pp. 66–72.

Learning Through Play and Experience in the Here-and-Now World

In 1916 Harriet Johnson, Caroline Pratt, Emily Dewey, Lucy Sprague Mitchell, and eight others established the Bureau of Educational Experiments, a private educational corporation in New York City. Their mission was to collect information on children, support innovative "free education" experiments, and publish resource materials.

They used Pratt's City and Country School with the addition of a new nursery as the first setting for their experiments. Regular field trips throughout the city provided firsthand content for the curriculum, and Mitchell's unique approach to literature provided reinforcement. By 1930 the researchers realized that they needed to train teachers to match the goals of their expanding programs, so they moved to new quarters at 69 Bank Street and entered into teacher education. Mitchell's discussion in the following selection, which is from her book *Our Children and Our Schools: A Picture and Analysis of How Today's Public School Teachers Are Meeting the Challenge of New Knowledge and New Cultural Needs* (Simon & Schuster, 1951), is based on experiences at this school, known as the Bank Street School. In the selection, Mitchell writes about play experiences for kindergarten, first-, and second-grade children, focusing on the development of creativity in its many forms.

Mitchell (1878–1967) was strongly influenced by the work of John Dewey, whose experimental Laboratory School of the University of Chicago was based on a philosophy of active learning through direct experience. After graduating from Radcliffe College, Mitchell took a succession of positions leading to an appointment as one of the first women faculty members at the University of California. Following her marriage to a colleague at the university, the couple moved to New York City, where Mitchell took courses under John Dewey in Teachers College at Columbia University. She quickly became an integral player in "educational experiments" that were performed in the city. Mitchell continued as the head of the Bank Street School's governing board as well as a teacher, and she authored over 20 children's books.

121

Lucy Sprague
Mitchell

CURRICULUM EXPERIENCES FOR KINDERGARTEN, FIRST- AND SECOND-GRADE CHILDREN

We [the staff at the Bank Street School] . . . have basic convictions about how young children learn which, from previous experimental work, we had long since come through to. Our immediate job with the teachers of kindergarten, first- and second-grade children was not to state these convictions. Rather, it was to plan with the teachers and help them carry out curriculum experiences for their young children and through follow-up discussions with these teachers bring out what the children learned through these experiences. When we began, most of the kindergarten and first-grade teachers, and, to a lesser extent, the second-grade teachers, welcomed a here-and-now approach for their young children. Yet some, perhaps most of them, regarded trips as impossible for large groups or just fun for the children; and play in the classroom as interludes for relaxation, a necessary concession to children's immaturity but not as a genuine learning situation. The techniques which they wished us to show them they regarded as "extras" tacked on to their real work in teaching academic tool subjects and "good" behavior. As already said, we had faith that if these teachers once became convinced that their children were learning and growing through firsthand experiences—gathering information themselves on neighborhood trips, playing back and discussing their trips and other experiences in the classroom—they would enter into these experiences, sharing them with the children actively and with relish.

With adults as well as with children, interests and attitudes are not built up through words but through direct experiences—in this case experiences of watching and analyzing their children's reactions to the various learning situations which the new teaching techniques afforded. So we philosophized little in the beginning but began to work actively with individual teachers in what they called "demonstration teaching" in one technique after another.

THE THEME: LIVING IN THE HOME, SCHOOL AND NEIGHBORHOOD

We knew from our contacts with the Board of Education committee working on curriculum revision that the theme in social studies for kindergarten, first and second grades was to be *Living in the Home, School, and Neighborhood.* This theme placed the curriculum experiences and activities squarely in the here-

and-now world in which these young children so largely live. It afforded a perfect approach to learning through firsthand experiences. It gave full opportunity to have the children follow their interest drives—to find out about things and people that interested them in the world around them, and to organize and express their thinking and feelings about what they had found out. In educational jargon, this theme could well be interpreted through interrelated "intake" and "outgo" experiences by which we believe children really learn.

We began by watching the children in their classrooms to find out what they were doing there and what leads to direct experiences this gave us. Very soon, we began going on trips with teachers and their children in these three younger classes to see work and workers in the school and neighborhood, with follow-up discussions and dramatic play in the classrooms. In the kindergarten, where the children were emotionally centered around their homes and their information was largely about things and people in their homes, we began with dramatic domestic play.

Why did we emphasize work and workers? Because work and workers are a significant part of the world in which children early show great interest. Kindergarten children come to school with this interest in how thing and people work already well developed. *Their homes are children's first laboratory.* There they learn about the work processes going on around them which are closely tied up with their personal lives: going to bed and getting up, getting dressed and undressed, taking baths, watching their food being cooked, perhaps seeing it delivered at the door, perhaps buying it at the store along with mother. And this work in their homes is done by the people who are intimately tied up with their emotional lives, with the people who take care of them, above all with their mothers or often with mother substitutes. In their homes, too, these children have already been living over their own experiences in dramatic play. In their play they are "identifying" with people they have known at first hand— their mothers and fathers, or the milkman bringing the milk to them, or the groceryman selling food to their mothers.

DRAMATIC PLAY BEGINNING WITH HOME EXPERIENCES

When these young children come to school, the situation changes. Home and mother are gone. They are lost in a world of strange things and people. But does it have to change completely? How can a teacher use these deep home experiences which kindergarten children bring to school with them? By giving them a chance to play out all their home, their personal, experiences in school. That is what is meant by "dramatic domestic play." Such play is greatly furthered by equipment through which children can play back these precious memories—dolls, which to the child can be symbols of himself or symbols of these vanished grownups whom he knows personally; doll beds and covers; small washtubs with real water to wash dolls' clothes in; small-sized irons to play ironing clothes; blocks with which he can build almost anything—a house, a bed, a stove, a store for the use of his doll people. This dramatic play needs floor space—chairs and tables should be movable, not screwed down. The kindergarten child, though he is in school, is still oriented in his home. He still needs a chance to express his own home experiences in his own way, to express his close identification with the people who make up his world at home.

All this, most of the kindergarten teachers sympathized with. They had some dolls and toys in their rooms but little that suggested *related group* play. Nor did they have the technique of guiding the play into constructive channels. So this is where the Bank Street member started. She worked directly in their rooms with individual teachers on equipment and techniques of getting dramatic play started.

THE NEIGHBORHOOD AS A LABORATORY

But even kindergarten children's world has not been limited entirely to the home. They have been on neighborhood streets. The neighborhood is already a laboratory for them. And what has interested them in this neighborhood laboratory? Objects that move such as autos, trains, boats, and airplanes and how these objects work. With whom have they identified in this neighborhood laboratory? With workers who are doing something, making some of these objects move, building a house, selling at a store.

Again, we know that these are the interests of five-year-old children because of their spontaneous dramatic play. In their play they *become* the train, the airplane, the auto, the boat. Or they become the worker who is controlling these moving things, the worker building a house, the groceryman, the milkman. At first, they regard these workers who do something as almost a part of the work process. For instance, the milkman is someone who delivers milk—not a man with a home and a family, who earns money through his work, and needs good working conditions. All that kind of interest in workers comes much later. The younger the child, the more his interest is centered on *how* the work is done, and the worker is a part of this *how.*

So our trips with kindergarteners were to see how work was done—work that was closely tied up with their personal lives. The trips had to be near by, for these children had not been on group trips and had no idea of the kind of behavior which is necessary in a group for safety. The first trips were within the school—to talk with the school nurse; to talk with the principal; to see the food being cooked for the lunchroom; to see the older children getting ready the little milk bottles they were later to bring to these kindergarten children; to see the pile of coal in the cellar and the custodian's helper shovel the coal into the furnace; to see the pipes that went from the furnace and along the ceiling and finally appeared connected with the radiators in their own room. Perhaps to see the coal truck and watch the driver grind up the truck, put up the chute, take the cover off the hole in the sidewalk, and let the coal rattle down to the school cellar. Perhaps a walk around the block (with no street crossing) to see what they could see. Perhaps a pause to watch the shoemaker putting new soles on shoes, or the laundryman ironing clothes, or the man with the grindstone sharpening scissors and knives, or the grocer selling vegetables, fruit, and other groceries. After each trip, the Bank Street member discussed with an individual teacher or the teachers of the three younger groups at after-school meetings what the children could do in the classrooms to express and organize the information and feelings they had experienced on the trips. Again, most of the teachers wanted to be shown *how* to follow up a trip. So a Bank Street member, after a day or two had passed, led short simple talks with the children in which, as much by gestures as by words, they told what they had seen or heard or felt. In these discussions the Bank Street member acted as a guide, sometimes asking questions, sometimes contributing memories of her own. She did not try for any very logical or articulate expression from these young children. Then the children were turned loose to put their images and their thinking into action in dramatic play. Again, this play needed suggestive equipment. Small dolls, made of wood or pipe cleaners—the children called them "little people"; small autos, boats, trains—anything important that the children had noticed on the street—and plenty of blocks for building. Now the play expanded to "city play," not merely domestic play, though always many children built houses and carried on domestic family play there. Autos chugged down the street to stores; coal trucks delivered coal at the school; there were grocery stores, sometimes a movie house, sometimes boats moving on the Hudson River. Through teacher guidance, this play became more related, more group play. The housewives with their children went from their homes to buy food at the store; sometimes they ordered coal to be delivered; trucks delivered vegetables, fruit, and milk to the grocery store. The neighborhood work and workers, as the little children knew them, appeared in action on the kindergarten floor. All this did not happen suddenly. But it did happen.

At the same time the Bank Street member was working with teachers of the first and the second grade. The trips with first-graders, particularly if they had had trips and related play in the kindergarten, could take them farther afield in their neighborhood experiences. The Hudson was familiar—only two blocks from the school. Now these children crossed Manhattan Island to see what was happening on another river, the East River. Now, too, the children took in more complicated work processes. At the request of the teachers, the Bank Street member drew up a way for first-grade children to study the neighborhood. She also explored the neighborhood to find situations where the children could see various steps in a work process more fully—such, for instance, as a trip to Harlem River, to see coal barges and the workers unloading the coal with great derricks and other workers filling their trucks with coal and driving off; or trips to different kinds of bakeries.

The teachers of the second grade organized their work more definitely into units. They were more ambitious to have their children learn "subject matter" and were more concerned to have this subject matter in books in order to help the children learn to read. Whatever the unit the teacher had chosen, we found related work and workers for them to explore. These second-grade children are interested in still more elaborate work processes and in those less immediately related to their personal lives—post office work and postmen; keeping the streets clean, and street cleaners; city markets and food coming into the city by trains, trucks, and boats; traffic and policemen; pipes under the street that carry water, electric wires, and gas to their homes and stores and school, and the various workers they can see working with these pipes when the street is torn up or the cover of a manhole is removed. The play that followed such trips was more organized than that in the younger groups. It was more mature dramatic play.

YOUNG CHILDREN'S ART EXPRESSIONS

We have talked only about dramatic play as a way in which young children express and organize their thinking and feelings. But, given a chance, young children will use all the art media for expression of themselves. The teachers recognized the art element in their children's dramatic play—the way the children transformed an actual experience through their imagination. They did not so readily recognize the play element in art expressions. The teachers of these younger groups in our school wanted their children, however, to have art work. Among the courses of study in the old curriculum were drawing, music, dancing (largely games), and the language arts (which, however, did not include language as an art). In drawing and painting, some of them set models of adult pictures for the children to trace or copy and judged the children's products by the faithfulness of their imitation of adult products. More of them encouraged "free" painting—that is, they let the children experiment with the media, paint or draw what they wanted to, and were satisfied with the product if the child was satisfied. Most of the teachers recognized that a child's crude painting was art on a young level. We recall the picture of a boat painted by one of our second-grade children after a trip to see boats on the Hudson. It is a gay red boat with tipsy smokestacks such as never sailed on any sea. The teachers, most of them, recognized that such a painting sprang from a deep experience of color, shapes, sounds, movements, and that these images were translated by the child's imagination into his own expression. The teachers recognized that this boat meant more to the child than the pictures made by adults which were hung in many of the classrooms.

In music and dancing, the teachers had much more the attitude of teaching the children techniques. They did not commonly try to have children express their own experiences. For instance, kindergarten children were taught steps to imitate Indians; first-grade children learned traditional singing games like Looby Loo. And language was seldom treated as an art medium for children to use themselves. Art experience in language was primarily exposing children to "literature"—episodes of reading them verse. To "cultivate children's imagination" they read them fairy tales. The teachers were far more concerned with correcting the children's incorrect use of adult forms of speech than with preserving their children's spontaneous use of rhythm, sound quality, and patterning of words—all elements in adult literature.

Here as elsewhere, the Bank Street worker kept notes of what children did and said. She also began "demonstration teaching" in all the arts. She happened to be a musician, a dancer, a writer, as well as a teacher of young children. She assembled songs about things in the world around them in which the children had shown interest. She arranged the songs in ingenious books with the subjects on tabs so that a teacher could quickly find and use a song related to some play or remarks of the children. Often the children's gestures suggested a dance. On the piano, she played appropriate music and suggested that the children dance they were trains or boats or airplanes; that they were shoveling coal into the furnace (if they had had a trip to the school cellar) or were steam shovels (if they had been to Harlem River). The children under encouragement began to created their own simple songs and their own dances.

GETTING CREATIVE LANGUAGE STARTED

On trips and in classroom play the Bank Street worker asked the teachers to notice the *way* children said things—not merely *what* they said. Some of them began to jot down rhythmic expressions that they heard from the children or anything that showed how the children were taking in the world through their senses—eyes, ears, noses, and muscles—and giving back these sense and muscle images in their own child language. In a discussion with one first-grade class, the Bank Street worker asked the children what they thought was "the quietest thing in the world." Here is a list of the things the children named:

horse (when asleep)	sheets on a bed
sleep	covers on a bed
snow	alligators
rain	reindeers are quiet when they come on
sun	Christmas
house	fish,
clouds	seeds
bulbs	orange seeds
moon	

This list she left with the teacher. Here is some of the verse that the children later composed with this teacher.

Cold cold cold
Steam steam steam
Hats sweaters ear muffs
   mittens coats and
     mackinaws
Cold cold cold

See the man on the street
He has a wagon full of concrete
Tall houses
Middle-sized houses
Little houses

Ten floors high
Four floors high
Houses on the Drive, streets and avenues
Houses all around us

I like to see the coal truck
  when it backs up
I like to see the coal slide
  down the slide
It makes such a clatter
  Bump, bump bump
  Br—br-br-br-br
  S S S S S

Pull the coal barges
Pull the train barges
Puff, puff, puff
I am a little tug.

    The teacher used such creative language of her children as early reading charts.

    All these art expressions, in painting, modeling, music, dance, language, sprang from the children's experiences but none of them were limited to a mere rehearsal of experiences. These children were genuine artists, though young ones. Like all artists the children selected from their experiences what had meaning to them; they transformed or heightened their reality by their imagination, through a creative use of the media.

    The question of creative language came up in all the groups from kindergarten through sixth grade. It led to several talks at our meetings by a Bank Street worker on children's language and how to preserve and develop children's pleasure in the "play of language"—the use of the art elements in language—which they lose if language is treated only as a utilitarian method of communication in which correct adult forms are the goal. These talks also led to an additional supplemental "Writers' Workshop" held after school, where some teachers wrote stories for their children.

    These young children were also given an opportunity to find out how things in the natural world behave. This is the beginning of science. However, we shall postpone a fuller discussion of science, since science experiences concerned all the teachers and were discussed in grade levels with all in our after-school meetings.

    As these children became spatially oriented in the neighborhood their floor play began to reflect the beginnings of map thinking and human geography—the relation of work to earth situations. Here again we refer forward to the Workshop discussions on map thinking and human geography with all the teachers.

THE TEACHERS' THINKING AT THE END OF
A YEAR AND A HALF OF WORK

In our small weekly meetings with the kindergarten, first- and second-grade teachers, we discussed what the children were getting out of these experiences—trips, related dramatic play, free painting, music, dance, creative language. From the beginning, they thought their children were enjoying their school life. Later they felt, or most of them did, that their children were not merely having a good time, nor were they merely gathering factual information: they were *learning how to think*. They were beginning to see the relationships, and, as we have said, seeing relationships is thinking. Kindergarten and first-grade children began to see the relationship of the work around them to their own lives; of one step of a work process to another step. The five-year-old kindergarten children thought primarily in details of *how* things and people work—such as trains and engineers. By six, the children began to think of the *function* of the train—to carry people, food, and other things. And *they played out related work* in dramatic group play. The second-grade children were beginning to grasp new relationships which built on the relationships they had played out in first grade, such as: the city does work so that the city people can have water, light, telephone, gas in their houses—all the things we call "city housekeeping"; a sense that there are faraway workers whose work makes it possible for city people to have all these things and also to have food.

The teachers felt that this thinking, even on a young level, was satisfying to the children and that it laid a foundation for more mature thinking up through the grades and up to adulthood about work and workers that they could not experience directly. They felt that their children were identifying with an ever-broadening group of people and that this laid the foundation for identifying later with people they could not know personally.

All this thinking on the part of the teachers was reflected in the way they thought of their job. They began to think not in separate units or curriculum experiences, not in techniques but in related programs of experience in which children found out about things and people and expressed what they had found out in their own creative ways. They began to watch their children's play and to realize that whatever a child spontaneously plays has deep significance to him; and to listen to how their children used language as an art, not merely as communication. They began to think of these techniques of trips, related play, discussion, art expressions not as ends in themselves but as means through which they could give their children learning experiences. Some of them began exploring the neighborhood for situations that would clarify for the children some relationship their children were beginning to grasp. This, in turn, aroused their adult interest in the work pattern of New York. They began to ask to have Workshop talks on background content for themselves. They were taking on their "new" job. They found it hard work but it gave deep satisfaction.

This growth in thinking and attitudes of the teachers did not happen suddenly nor to all the teachers at the same time. But by the end of a year and a half of our Workshop, these teachers had moved far toward the conception of curriculum building as differentiated from separate curriculum experiences, and far toward the conception of their role as a guide as differentiated from a dispenser of information.

CHAPTER 6 Learning Environments

6.1 MARIA MONTESSORI

How the Lessons Should Be Given

Maria Montessori (1850–1972) has left an indelible mark on our educational system. She was born in Italy and became the first woman to earn an M.D. in that country. She became interested in the education of mentally impaired children, so she developed an educational program and materials for them. The successes of these children, who had less than average mental abilities, brought her much recognition. In 1906 she started her first school in Rome, the Casa dei Bambini, or "Children's House." It was here that she developed her ideas on how children learn through a prescribed set of materials in a properly prepared environment. Less than 10 years later, the first Montessori nursery school opened in New York City. After World War I the British Montessori Society was founded, and schools for teachers opened in Rome and London.

Montessori wrote and lectured on educational practices throughout her career. She travelled around the world to speak at annual congresses on her methods. Her philosophy is still in practice worldwide. The Montessori method provides an opportunity for children to explore the materials at their own pace, although the materials were originally intended to be used didactically. The materials found in a Montessori classroom are high-quality, wooden, monochromatic items. Some call her method "autoeducation" because of its reliance on self-teaching, self-discipline, and self-expression. In this setting, teaching is significantly different from teaching in other programs. Montessori describes the role of the teacher in the following selection from *The Montessori Method: Scientific Pedagogy as Applied to Child Education in "The Children's Houses"* (Robert Bentley, 1965). She believes that the adult's role is to guide, rather than teach, the child.

Given the fact that, through the régime of liberty the pupils can manifest their natural tendencies in the school, and that with this in view we have prepared the environment and the materials (the objects with which the child is to work), the teacher must not limit her action to *observation*, but must proceed to *experiment*.

In this method the lesson corresponds to an *experiment*. The more fully the teacher is acquainted with the methods of experimental psychology, the better will she understand how to give the lesson. Indeed, a special technique is necessary if the method is to be properly applied. The teacher must at least have attended the training classes in the "Children's Houses," in order to acquire a knowledge of the fundamental principles of the method and to understand their application. The most difficult portion of this training is that which refers to the method for discipline.

In the first days of the school the children do not learn the idea of collective order; this idea follows and comes as a result of those disciplinary exercises through which the child learns to discern between good and evil. This being the case, it is evident that, at the outset the teacher *cannot give* collective lessons. Such lessons, indeed, will always be *very rare,* since the children being free are not obliged to remain in their places quiet and ready to listen to the teacher, or to watch what she is doing. The collective lessons, in fact, are of very secondary importance, and have been almost abolished by us.

CHARACTERISTICS OF THE INDIVIDUAL LESSONS:— CONCISENESS, SIMPLICITY, OBJECTIVITY

The lessons, then, are individual, and *brevity* must be one of their chief characteristics. Dante gives excellent advice to teachers when he says, "Let thy words be counted." The more carefully we cut away useless words, the more perfect will become the lesson. And in preparing the lessons which she is to give, the teacher must pay special attention to this point, counting and weighing the value of the words which she is to speak.

Another characteristic quality of the lesson in the "Children's Houses" is its *simplicity*. It must be stripped of all that is not absolute truth. That the teacher must not lose herself in vain words, is included in the first quality of conciseness; this second, then, is closely related to the first: that is, the carefully chosen words must be the most simple it is possible to find, and must refer to the truth.

The third quality of the lesson is its *objectivity*. The lesson must be presented in such a way that the personality of the teacher shall disappear. There shall remain in evidence only the *object* to which she wishes to call the attention of the child. This brief and simple lesson must be considered by the teacher as an explanation of the object and of the use which the child can make of it.

In the giving of such lessons the fundamental guide must be the *method of observation*, in which is included and understood the liberty of the child. So the teacher shall *observe* whether the child interests himself in the object, how he is interested in it, for how long, etc., even noticing the expression of his face. And she must take great care not to offend the principles of liberty. For, if she provokes the child to make an unnatural effort, she will no longer know what is the *spontaneous* activity of the child. If, therefore, the lesson rigorously prepared in this brevity, simplicity and truth is not understood by the child, is not accepted by him as an explanation of the object,—the teacher must be warned of two things:—first, not to *insist* by repeating the lesson; and second, *not to make the child feel that he has made a mistake*, or that he is not understood, because in doing so she will cause him to make an effort to understand, and will thus alter the natural state which must be used by her in making her psychological observation. A few examples may serve to illustrate this point.

Let us suppose, for example, that the teacher wishes to teach to a child the two colours, red and blue. She desires to attract the attention of the child to the object. She says, therefore, "Look at this." Then, in order to teach the colours, she says, showing him the red, "This is *red*," raising her voice a little and pronouncing the word "red" slowly and clearly; then showing him the other colour, "This is *blue*." In order to make sure that the child has understood, she says to him, "Give me the red,"—"Give me the blue." Let us suppose that the child in following this last direction makes a mistake. The teacher does not repeat and does not insist; she smiles, gives the child a friendly caress and takes away the colours.

Teachers ordinarily are greatly surprised at such simplicity. They often say, "But everybody knows how to do that!" Indeed, this again is a little like the egg of Christopher Columbus, but the truth is that not everyone knows how to do this simple thing (to give a lesson with such simplicity). To *measure* one's own activity, to make it conform to these standards of clearness, brevity and truth, is practically a very difficult matter. Especially is this true of teachers prepared by the old-time methods, who have learned to labour to deluge the child with useless, and often, false words. For example, a teacher who had taught in the public schools often reverted to collectivity. Now in giving a collective lesson much importance is necessarily given to the simple thing which is to be taught, and it is necessary to oblige all the children to follow the teacher's explanation, when perhaps not all of them are disposed to give their attention to the particular lesson in hand. The teacher has perhaps commenced her lesson in this way:—"Children, see if you can guess what I have in my hand!" She knows that the children cannot guess, and she therefore attracts their attention by means of a falsehood. Then she probably says,—"Children, look out at the sky. Have you ever looked at it before? Have you never noticed it at night when it is all shining with stars? No! Look at my apron. Do you know what colour it is? Doesn't it seem to you the same colour as the sky? Very well then, look at this colour I have in my hand. It is the same colour as the sky and my apron. It is *blue*. Now look around you a little and see if you can find something in the room which is blue. And do you know what colour cherries are, and the colour of the burning coals in the fireplace, etc., etc."

Now in the mind of the child after he has made the useless effort of trying to guess there revolves a confused mass of ideas,—the sky, the apron, the cherries, etc. It will be difficult for him to extract from all this confusion the idea which it was the scope of the lesson to make clear to him; namely, the recognition of the two colours, blue and red. Such a work of selection is almost impossible for the mind of a child who is not yet able to follow a long discourse.

I remember being present at an arithmetic lesson where the children were being taught that two and three make five. To this end, the teacher made use of a counting board having coloured beads strung on its thin wires. She arranged, for example, two beads on the top line, then on a lower line three, and at the bottom five beads. I do not remember very clearly the development of this lesson, but I do know that the teacher found it necessary to place beside the two beads on the upper wire a little cardboard dancer with a blue skirt, which she christened on the spot the name of one of the children in the class, saying, "This is Mariettina." And then beside the other three beads she placed a little dancer dressed in a different colour, which she called "Gigina." I do not know exactly how the teacher arrived at the demonstration of the same, but certainly she talked for a long time with these little dancers, moving them about, etc. If *I* remember the dancers more clearly than I do the arithmetic process, how must it have been with the children? If by such a method they were able to learn that two and three make five, they must have made a tremendous mental effort, and the teacher must have found it necessary to talk with the little dancers for a long time.

In another lesson a teacher wished to demonstrate to the children the difference between noise and sound. She began by telling a long story to the children. Then suddenly someone in league with her knocked noisily at the door. The teacher stopped and cried out—"What is it! What's happened! What is the matter! Children, do you know what this person at the door has done? I can no longer go on with my story, I cannot remember it any more. I will have to leave it unfinished. Do you know what has happened? Did you hear? Have you understood? That was a noise, that is a noise. Oh! I would much rather play with this little baby (taking up a mandolin which she had dressed up in a table cover). Yes, dear baby, I had rather play with you. Do you see this baby that I am holding in my arms?" Several children replied, "It isn't a baby." Others said, "It's a mandolin." The teacher went on—"No, no, it is a baby, really a baby. I love this little baby. Do you want me to show you that it is a baby? Keep very, very quiet then. It seems to me that the baby is crying. Or, perhaps it is talking, or perhaps it is going to say papa or mamma." Putting her hand under the cover, she touched the strings of the mandolin. "There! did you hear the baby cry? Did you hear it call out?" The children cried out—"It's a mandolin, you touched the strings, you made it play." The teacher then replied, "Be quiet, be quiet, children. Listen to what I am going to do." Then she uncovered the mandolin and began to play on it, saying, "This is sound."

To suppose that the child from such a lesson as this shall come to understand the difference between noise and sound is ridiculous. The child will probably get the impression that the teacher wished to play a joke, and that she is rather foolish, because she lost the thread of her discourse when she was interrupted by noise, and because she mistook a mandolin for a baby. Most certainly, it is the figure of the teacher herself that is impressed upon the child's mind through such a lesson, and not the object for which the lesson was given.

6.2 HARRIET M. JOHNSON

The Physical Environment —Activities and Materials

Harriet M. Johnson (1867–1934) was a nurse and a teacher who, together with Lucy Sprague Mitchell and other educators, established a nursery school in New York City in 1919 under the auspices of the Bureau of Educational Experiments (later called Bank Street). Johnson, the school's first director, worked with teachers to develop behavior records for the two- to five-year-olds. The records were used in combination with family histories and physicians' files to establish maturity levels of the children. Using comprehensive data in a new way, the records created by Johnson were quite detailed and are just one example of the many ways Bank Street demonstrated "applied science" in the programs.

The curriculum of the nursery school was experimental, modern, and urban. The curriculum content was the city, and the children's outdoor playground was the roof. Roof play is no longer allowed by most licensing agencies, but in the 1920s, the roof served as the only play area for many children in New York City. In the following selection, from *Children in the Nursery School* (John Day, 1928), Johnson discusses materials for roof play and inside play. She believed that the same materials should be available in all schools.

The list of materials is significant for a number of reasons. First, almost 100 percent of the materials on the list form the foundation of materials available in quality preschool programs today. Second, the list includes materials that foster the different areas of development, including physical, social, creative, emotional, and cognitive. There are programs operating today that are still using materials purchased in the 1920s. Quality sets of unit blocks, cylinders, and chairs can withstand generations of use if cared for properly.

I shall try to define what I mean by [a "suitable" environment for nursery school children] and how we have tried to meet its requirements.

In the terms of our experiment suitable must mean favorable for growth. An environment might be planned with specific phases of growth in mind. It would then vary as the aims of the group responsible for it varied. It might, of course, mean favorable for training in certain special abilities, favorable for gaining facility in language, favorable for developing readiness in rhythmic response, favorable for overcoming malnutrition or untoward tendencies which might lead to serious disfunctioning. We are however quite specifically not establishing a system of training, though studies in the acquisition of different abilities and in the development of individual differences might well result from our researches. Our environment must be one in which the processes of growth go on fully and at an adequate rate. By growth I do not mean increase in bulk alone but increase in power and control and in maturation. Development means to us all the progress toward maturity. The moment we begin to look at it from this point of view, we see the importance of giving each phase of development an opportunity to mature. We can trace in many adults immaturities in gait, in attitude toward this or that situation, in taste or what not. The infantile crops up in even the normal adult sometimes and he shows that some experience or lack of it has interfered with the growth process.

Our environment then, as far as concerns the material equipment and the physical arrangements, is based upon what we know of growing children. Practically we make our decisions regarding equipment upon the observation of the behavior of small children. We see them putting forth all the energy they can summon. We observe them pushing, rolling, hauling, pulling; we watch them running, climbing, balancing and, given unimpeded space and suitable accessory material, we see them gaining balance and control of their bodies through the exercise of the big muscles of trunk and chest and of the arm-shoulder and the leg-pelvis girdles. We see them touching, handling, manipulating, looking, listening, feeling, tasting or feeling with the mouth. We see them applying this method not only to their external environment but also to their own bodies, in the process of which they learn to use their hands and fingers with nicety. They include in their investigations the bodies and possessions of their associates, at first in a purely objective fashion but from a very early age with interest and, given opportunity, we can see their progress from their first assaults to a realization of a sort of social relationship with other children. . . .

Concluding certain physiological needs from the observation of behavior, nursery schools have tried to meet these needs in their equipment. This does not mean that we can find identical apparatus and play material wherever we find nursery school children. The adults responsible for the set-up interpret children's needs in varying fashion. The more literal minded may provide materials that reproduce literally types of activity sought by the children,— boards on rockers because they roll, beads and pegboards because they investigate small objects. The academically inclined may attempt to seize the experimenting impulse as a training opportunity and, looking forward to a future when certain performances will be demanded, seek to prepare in advance and specifically for it. This group will probably stress self-help and manners, correct technique at table, counting and the use of numbers, and a prereading program.

Out of doors and in, we have in the first place, space. We believe that it is more necessary for the runabout baby than for the older child who is absorbed in more concentrated play with materials. Have you thought what it would be like suddenly to acquire levitation: to find that you could propel yourself through space, not soaring perhaps but just freely floating without the contact of feet against pavements and without the slow pace consequent upon the method? You might find that at first you would not be able to gauge the distance above an obstacle that you must allow for—or that you could manage your corners and street crossings well if you were alone but that you needed to acquire more skill when you had companions or were meeting vehicles. Would you not wake eager to make sure that your new-found power was with you? Would you not try all sorts of tricks to increase speed and accuracy, and would you not be so filled with the joy and interest in your skill and the power it made possible to you that the day would hardly be long enough for you to practice it? Reading, study, the movies and social events would lose their charm till your body was sure of this facility. I believe the acquisition of loco-motion brings a comparable experience into the life of a child. He has not of course a background which enables him to analyze either his process in acquir-ing the art of locomotion or the possibilities which the new power has opened up to him. However, everyone who has watched babies from fourteen to eight-een or twenty months, has noted their absorbed and incessant practice of the new accomplishment. They have a wide stance and their balance of control is poorly developed, so space is a prime requisite—indoors and out.

To us the play activity of children is a dynamic process, stimulating growth and the integration of the entire organism as no system of training however skillfully devised could to. Therefore in our choice of equipment we have tried to provide materials which would not only develop the bodies of children, but which would also have genuine play content and would follow the lines of genuine play interests. That is, in providing wagons and kiddy kars, pails and shovels, springboards, seesaws and swings, slides, steps and packing boxes, blocks, dolls, crayons and clay, we are thinking of their play use as well as of the effect of exercise with them upon muscular development. We mean for the most part to avoid what might be called static material. By static material I mean things that have a simple and limited use. An example would be a set of blocks cut so they could make only one sort of construction. We try on the contrary to choose things that have a variety of uses or the possibility of progressive use. The blocks are the most striking illustrations. The smallest nursery children who play with them at all carry them about,—handling, ma-nipulating, then shifting from one place to another,—stacking them in a mass without form or design or apparent purpose other than that of putting out energy. From this use to the construction of an elaborate design or a building which is named and with which the children play, stretches a period of months at least, during which various action patterns are maturing. Much of the mate-rial is actually novel to the children. Its form, or structure, and its other proper-ties are unknown and must be made a part of their experience. At first it means nothing in terms of the dynamic relationship between "that" and "me." They see things and persons as undifferentiated wholes and use them in an objective fashion which takes little account of cause and effect. They push the swing and are unprepared for the resulting blow; they do not place their blocks evenly and are unaware that they cannot stand securely on the tottering pile; they stride the kiddy kars but are very likely to walk, carrying them between their legs instead of sitting upon them. A block conveys one impression when it is a block-on-the-floor and quite another when it is a block-in-a-pile which is the construction of another child. Awareness of differences, discrimination, interest and initiative in choosing and using the material, the feel of the pattern possibilities, whether as design or construction, are stages through which we believe a child passes at his own individual rate. The stage of the true construction—a building designed to serve an end and used after it is completed—comes later, often after he has left our group.

Blocks are, as has been said, unusually simple and clear examples of educational material, but in all the types of playthings and apparatus mentioned there can be traced the growth processes involved in their use. The use of the swing seems more limited. If, however, the growth and development of the pattern is followed it is found that a great elaboration of the first simple method takes place. The completed pattern shows the ability to use the apparatus and to control the body in a variety of ways, to sit and propel oneself, to stand and pump alone or with another child, to twist and spin and to approach near enough to push a child in the swing without allowing it to hit one on the rebound. When the finished product is compared with the performance of a small child to whom none of the qualities is known and who has continually to be protected from disaster, it can be seen that here again is material which can be used more or less efficiently and elaborately as the child is more or less matured in physical control, and more or less captured by the rhythmic and balancing possibilities of the apparatus. Like most dynamic material there can be traced through an analytic study of its use marked individual differences.

In choosing materials we avoid those that prove to require in their use adult supervision beyond what is needed to safeguard a child's initiation to them. Materials which are too heavy or cumbersome for the children to manage or which must be used with a degree of caution beyond their powers, we discard. An example of such toys is a large box which the children wished to load upon one of their express wagons. It was too bulky and heavy for them to lift or to mount safely. Another example of unsuitable material was a small shovel which was hinged and equipped with a sharp prong so that it could be tipped and become a hoe and pick. The adjustment, with a ring which slipped down over the pick when the shovel was in use, was too difficult for most of our children, the sharp instrument served as a dangerous weapon and we found no especially suitable and legitimate use for it in our environment. Hammers might fall into the same category except that driving nails and crushing small pebbles are profitable occupations and therefore we undertake to carry on a period of supervision till a child can be trusted with the tool.

Besides the importance of gaining an integrated use of the muscular equipment a return to our study of children's behavior shows us that they need opportunity for sense experiences. We might devise a graded series of weights, of color cards and of other selected training material which could be presented at intervals to the children, and in that way trace the process of learning under controlled conditions. We use, however, the same criterion here that we did in the choice of the other equipment. We present the children with a situation that holds in it inherent play possibilities and we encourage them to deal with it in their own way. It is our belief that this method leads to the development of a ready initiative and an inquiring experimental attitude toward the environment which are more fruitful than the degree of skill which might be attained by deliberate training. We do not believe that sense experiences should be given by training, but by providing materials the use of which leads to sense discrimination because again we are convinced that with self-initiated use comes power. Our children play with things of different weights and sizes: boxes, blocks, pails empty and pails filled with sand; with things of different colors: crayons, clothing, dolls, covers, blocks; with things of different textures and consistencies, and as they use these materials they are becoming aware of differences and likenesses, of qualities and relationships which will lead to sensory acuity. They then perceive the qualities in their relation to the phenomena in which they are seen, not as isolated sensations.

Language discrimination may not go along at an equal rate. A child will often choose the superior kiddy kar long before he can tell his reasons. Our records show that a child can often match colors before he can name them correctly. Color as an affect is more important in growth than color as a name, and it may be that the insistence upon naming qualities delays rather than hastens on the process of discrimination. In an atmosphere where children are encouraged to experiment with language as well as with other materials, the interest in naming seems to appear spontaneously however, and most nursery children name accurately and with interest the colors they are using before they leave us.

Another consideration governing our choice of equipment is that of permanent or progressive use. Our age range is wide, though less so than in many nursery groups. Our equipment is unsatisfactory if it fails to meet the needs of our children as they progress in age. Little children come to us with a very limited experience. When the dramatic element enters into their play it represents an attempt at reproducing details of their experience. The block pushed over the floor may be a boat or train. The play is brief and undertaken largely for the motor and sensory enjoyment of the push across the floor, generally to a vocal accompaniment. There is at first no attempt at even an approach to representative form in the construction. A single block will serve the purpose and the "choo choo" sound may be the only train noise that is given. Gradually more qualities emerge and this mass which is a train shows further details which are reproduced. The bell and whistle sounds, the noise of escaping steam, smoke stacks, sand domes and then wheels are added, and after a time—though usually not before five years—a railway system with tracks, station, turn table and signals develops. The same is true of the domestic play that so absorbs little children. Dolls are used, at first usually to put to bed but gradually the entire cycle of personal care which the baby has experienced so intimately and for so many months is reproduced in play. Maternal solicitude and discipline are represented with real histrionic skill and all the domestic processes from laundry to dressmaking are carried on.

The child sees additional possibilities in an environment of materials which he can adapt to his purposes, but his constructive attack upon it depends first upon the sort of growth patterns that are developing and second upon whether life is bringing him experiences which stimulate his play purposes. The baby will play out all that he has of content and will elaborate his play as his content becomes organized. The importance of educational principles such as these must be recognized in planning a nursery school environment.

In presenting a list of the play materials used in our school it must not be understood that it is done with the recommendation that identical equipment should be used in all schools. The school in the large city has to invent opportunities which the country or small town school can find present in its environment. Experience with turf and growing things brings something to a child that can not be imitated in a brick and mortar environment. An urban situation must be faced as an urban situation and attacked and developed for what it is worth, not as a poor substitute for the country. The country environment must be treated in the same way. City life offers vital experiences to a child which he cannot get in the country, and our task is to provide an environment in which the child's developing needs are met, whether it be under green trees or in a city back yard.

We have come to believe that the city roof playground is preferable to the park or yard. It can usually be placed so that it receives sun for most of the day and consequently the snow and wet clear from it rapidly. The expanse of sky, the clouds, the smoke, the occasional sparrows and the building and repair operations carried on nearby are of vital interest to the children. The noise and confusion that continually assault us may well dull city-bred ears to fine auditory discrimination and especially to the enjoyment of listening and identifying what we hear. The sounds that come from the streets and in some neighborhoods from the river or harbor are clearer and more easily recognizable from the roof than they are from a lower level, and bring to children the opportunity for auditory experience. . . .

PLAY EQUIPMENT

Roof

Slide, 5 feet high, chute 10 feet long—set in pebble pit.

Four low swings, all four corners of seats pierced for ropes which are bound together about two feet above seats. This is more secure than the ordinary single rope swing with a narrow seat.

Two double planks, about 12 feet long, 17 inches wide, of fitted tongue and groove boards. These are set up as inclines of varying steepness, up and down which the children may walk, ride kiddy kars, haul wagons or leap as on a springboard. Bridging two packing cases, they afford opportunity for developing confidence and balance on heights.

Seesaw planks, 12 feet long, 1 foot wide, which can be set at different heights according to the age and skill of the children.

Two sawhorses, 20 inches high, used as supports for planks or seesaw or to raise the end of slide chute or occasionally in construction and dramatic play.

Two large packing cases, 23½″ × 42½″ × 29½″, and 48″ × 38″ × 30″, the latter being slatted at each end which facilitates climbing and converts the box into a "cage" when turned upside down.

Set of three steps, 18 inches high, top step 9 inches wide, others 7 inches wide, which are moved about to facilitate climbing on packing cases, walls, etc.

Two sandboxes—one of cement, 5¾′ × 4′, with sloping wooden top, waterproof canvassed, which hooks back against a wall; one of wood, also with canvas covered Top, 7⅔′ × 3⅔′ × 9½″, cover fitted with castors and with three sides only, so that it may be rolled off forming in this position a convenient surface for sand play.

Skylight peak, 27 inches high, enclosed by a seat 15 inches high which can be lifted off skylight and used by itself when desired.

Work bench—for adult use.

Four dozen hollow yard blocks (closed boxes) 4″ × 10″ × 10″, weight three pounds. These blocks were devised by Caroline Pratt and in larger sizes are used in the City and Country School. They are described in the *Catalogue of Play Equipment*, Bulletin VIII, published by the Bureau of Educational Experiments. We have them in only one size, scaled down for the nursery children. They can usually be obtained from a packing box factory, which will furnish boxes of any size desired.

Four dozen spruce blocks, 8½″ × 5¼″ × 3⅜″ (exact size depending on obtainable ready-cut lumber) called "paving blocks" because of their resemblance to those used in street paving—weight about 2½ pounds each.

Boards, 4′ × 7½″ × ¾″, light enough for the children to load into wagons and to use for construction purposes.

Pails with bails, made of heavy tin.

Perforated sink shovels, used in the sand chiefly; small shovels; wooden spoons.

Small tin pans for sand play.

Kiddy kars of two sizes, largest 10 inches high, lowest 9 inches.

Large and small express wagons, one rubber tired, the others with metal-rimmed wheels.

Two "trailer" carts with hooks on the handle so they may be easily attached to kiddy kars or other wagons.

Toy wheelbarrows.

Brooms.

Coal shovels and snow shovels, both used in the snow.

Rubber balls, various sizes.

Basketball.

Hammers, full size, light weight.

Nails—one-inch wire with large head. When the children begin to use hammers and nails, we set the nails for them with points just piercing the top of our yard blocks which are closed boxes, thus making it possible for even the younger children really to drive them in. Later we set the points just into the wood. Still later the children learn to set their own nails.

Indoor slide, reached by a flight of eight rather steep open steps with handrails, a balcony of two levels providing extra room and height at top, and chute 12 feet long, end resting on a gym mat. The lower balcony is roughly square, 6½' × 6½', and is 5 feet 5 inches from the floor. The upper is about 6' 3" × 2' 3", and is raised about 11 inches above the other, making a high step to climb from one to the other. The stairway measures 6 feet 7 inches, and has a light pipe railing which goes through wooden slots at the top so that the steps can be hooked up out of the way when supervision is impossible. The treads are 9½ inches apart.

Small folding tables with linoleum covered tops to provide a durable and easily cleaned surface. These tables are particularly durable and stable.

Small chairs. We have not considered it necessary to be especially exact in fitting our tables and chairs to the height of our children, which sounds like rank heresy and neglect. When we equipped the nursery for our first group we did so, giving each child a chair in which he could sit with his feet flat upon the floor, with his buttocks well back. His table was just high enough so that as he sat in this position his forearm with elbow flexed rested easily upon it. As the groups have varied since then we have tried to give the appropriate chair and table to each child but we have not followed our early standards. Our children spend a minimum of time at their tables—only while they are eating and the short periods when they are using crayons and paper. The group varies from year to year so much that if we fitted chairs and tables to the fourteen months old children they might the next year be quite unsuitable for any child in the group since we keep the children till they are three years old.

Kegs—painted nail kegs, 14½ inches high, heads 1 foot in diameter, both heads set in; used to roll about on floor, or to roll on and over, astride or head first, and to stand, climb and walk upon.

Rubber balls, various sizes.

Three two-wheeled carts, 15" × 8", converted from gayly painted boxes of which there are eight, used for bedding dolls, to hold cubes or to drag about.

Painted wooden covers for boxes and carts.

Blocks—City and Country school unpainted wooden bricks, half bricks and multiples of that size up to three feet in length, triangles of two sizes and turned pillars.

Nine dozen paving blocks, described above.

Montessori Pink Tower and Brown Stair Blocks.

Milton Bradley 1-inch cubes in primary colors, pierced for stringing.

Interlocking blocks, 5" × 2" × 1½", head at one end, notch at the other so that they may be linked together into "trains" and pushed or pulled about.

Nested boxes, largest about 11½" × 9½" × 6½".

Montessori Cylinders—two sets, No. 1 and No. 2.

Wooden jointed dolls, 11½ inches, Schoenhut.

Covers about 16" × 14" of various colors and textiles, used with dolls or flatirons—more easily manipulated by small children than dolls' clothes. There have been many attempts to devise dolls' clothing which could be used by very young children. An admirable garment is made kimono style with a wide neck into which an elastic is fastened. This can be stretched over the doll's head and is so simple that the arms can easily be thrust into the wide sleeves. Children below three seem to be more satisfied with such covers as we provide and get such a variety of uses from them that we no longer offer clothing. A favorite play is spreading the covers out on the floor and putting the dolls into them. The technique of holding a cover by the corners and flipping it out so that it will lie smoothly on the floor is acquired only after quite a practice period. Children keep at it till they have acquired proficiency in it—and longer because that particular arrangement is used in their play with dolls and with irons. The older children ask for safety pins and make "suits" or sleeping bags for the dolls.

Doll's bedstead with mattress and pillows.

Flatirons—sad iron variety.

Plastilene.

Manila drawing paper and large size octagonal crayons—Milton Bradley.

Four Swiss tuned bells, key of E flat. These can be ordered from R. H. Mayland, 54 Willoughby Avenue, Brooklyn. The price is five dollars for each bell.

Musical bells, set at either end of a handle, dumb-bell fashion.

Scuffers—unit blocks with handles, covered with sandpaper.

Bags 10" × 14", made of stout cloth, filled with paper. These may be thrown about or at one another by the children without fear of injury, and are used as a substitute for the block-throwing impulse which breaks out from time to time.

There are also in the play room a piano and a table and chairs for adult use.

6.3 SYBIL KRITCHEVSKY, ELIZABETH PRESCOTT, AND LEE WALLING

How to Analyze Play Space

Sybil Kritchevsky, Elizabeth Prescott, and Lee Walling of Pacific Oaks College in California have developed a method for calculating the necessary amount of materials for play. Their method is based on a three-year study of how children behave in play spaces. They found that children will vary their behavior according to their perceptions of spatial contents and arrangement. They found that the play environment, more than all other factors, seems to be the predictor of program quality. For this reason they advocate that teachers pay careful attention to play materials and their arrangement. Kritchevsky, Prescott, and Walling expand on their ideas about utilizing play space in the following selection from *Planning Environments for Young Children: Physical Space* (National Association for the Education of Young Children, 1969).

What the three colleagues learned about physical space is helpful for teachers who are often left without any guidelines as to whether or not there are appropriate types or amounts of play materials in a classroom. The formula for calculating play spaces and play units can be applied by any teacher to any classroom.

Play units are classified by the authors as simple, complex, or super, based on the number of children that can be involved and the amount of creativity and interaction involved in the activity. Play units can be created in the classroom or the outside play area. The play environment can be enhanced by including materials that are complex or super and that require time and imagination for the play to develop.

Space communicates with people—in a very real sense it tells us how to act and how not to act. What it tells us to do is related to what is in the space and how these things are arranged or organized. Just as adults behave in one way at a table set for a formal dinner, and in a very different way at the same table set for a poker game, children tend to behave in ways suggested by spatial contents and arrangement. If play space is interesting to children, they are likely to play in an interested way, provided the rest of the setting is not excessively distracting. Even the talented story teller presenting a favorite tale is likely to find the activity disrupted by the unexpected presence of a lively and friendly dog; and children in a play room well equipped with interesting material are likely to shift their attention frequently if the area is congested.

In other words, it is necessary to understand both the parts of a play space (the contents and the empty space around the contents) and how these parts function as a whole, since it is apparently the total setting which children perceive and to which they respond.[1]

THE CONTENTS OF PLAY SPACE

The contents of play space which appear to matter most to children are **play units** and **potential units.**

Potential Units

A potential unit is simply some empty space which is surrounded in large part by visible and/or tangible boundaries. For instance, an empty table, the empty corner of a room or yard, a shady area under a tree or umbrella, are all potential units to which it is easy to add play material of one kind or another. Potential units can be used for greater spatial variety from day to day and thus provide flexibility for the staff. However, a staff-unrecognized potential unit can be a source of trouble. Access to space under stairs, if off limits, may need to be boarded up. If children are attracted to cozy play in an off-limits closet, a high hook may need to be placed on the door.

Play Units

Play units, in contrast to potential units, contain something to play with, and may or may not have visible and/or tangible boundaries. The sides of a play house or shelves surrounding a block play area do provide tangible boundaries, but much equipment needs some surrounding empty space to function effectively. For example, the jump-off-walk-around space surrounding the slide, the space outside a jungle gym where children swing their legs and stretch their arms, the space surrounding a table where children shift their chairs or stand just watching, all belong to the respective play units. This surrounding empty space is not really free for other uses. If other children need to use this play unit space to move through a room or yard, there will quite naturally be conflicts and interruptions of play.

Types of Play Units: Complexity   Play units can be classified in two major ways. In the first place, they can be classified according to differences in the kind of activity in which they invite children to participate: climbing, digging, building, etc. These differences are discussed below under the heading of **variety.** In the second place, they can be classified according to differences in what we have called relative **complexity:** the extent to which they contain potential for active manipulation and alteration by children. Elaborating on this distinction, it is possible to discern three types of play units—simple, complex and super, which vary both in their relative capacity to keep children interested, and in the relative number of children they can accommodate at one time. Our basis for classifying play equipment considers its possible use based on its internal complexity.

> **Simple:** A play unit that has one obvious use and does not have sub-parts or a juxtaposition of materials which enable a child to manipulate or improvise. (Examples: swings, jungle gym, rocking horse, tricycle.)

> **Complex:** A play unit with sub-parts or juxtaposition of two essentially different play materials which enable the child to manipulate or improvise. (Examples: sand table with digging equipment; play house with supplies.) Also included in this category are single play materials and objects which encourage substantial improvisation and/or have a considerable element of unpredictability. (Examples: all art activities such as dough or paints; a table with books to look at; an area with animals such as a dog, guinea pigs or ducks.)

> **Super:** A complex unit which has one or more additional play materials, i.e., three or more play materials juxtaposed. (Examples: sand box with play materials and water; dough table with tools; tunnel, movable climbing boards and boxes, and large crates.)

A super unit can be likened to a large sponge which soaks up a lot of water; it accommodates the most children at one time and holds their interest longest. A complex unit is like a smaller sponge and ranks second in degree of interest and number of children it is likely to accommodate at one time. A simple unit is like a paper towel, indispensable but short-lived, and ranks third.

The relative complexity of a space or setting (the number of complex and super units) is a measure of the capacity of the space to keep children continuously interested. Except for an occasional spring-horse, tumbling mat or pull toy, simple equipment is not often found indoors in California. Outdoors, however, many play units tend to be simple. If children are expected to play in an area for any length of time, high complexity seems virtually essential.

Complex and super units can be formed most easily by rearranging simple units and/or adding props of some kind. A crawl barrel, a large crate, and a couple of old benches might be used to surround a dirt area and create a complex unit. Children could climb up, over, through, around and in—and maybe do some rearranging of their own. If shovels or trucks or dramatic play props such as parasols or costumes were added, a super unit would be formed. Boxes and boards added to the jungle gym make a complex unit. A box with a steering wheel becomes complex if engineer hats are added. To be complex trikes need some place to go, or an interesting way of going. If crates and boxes can be arranged so riders can thread their way through, or stop and go signs added, trikes become complex.

Children often create their own complex or super units. A table with kitchen equipment placed a foot or two from a sand box is a super unit to a child, and if sand must stay in the box it is wise to move the table, either away from or into the sand box. Some conflict in preschool settings is related to the presence of complex and super units unrecognized by staff.

It is probably obvious that if children are expected to stay in any play area for only a short time, high complexity may well lead to unhappy children unwilling to leave their play. But if children are expected to stay in a play area for a long time without complexity, teachers probably will need to compensate, through their own active participation, for the failure of the setting to provide enough play ideas.

Types of Play Units: Variety   The other important way in which play units can be classified is according to the particular activity they invite from children. The number of different kinds of units (only in terms of differences in activity, and regardless of whether they are simple, complex or super) can be called the degree of variety and is a measure of the relative capacity of the space to elicit immediate interest from children. Some of the categories we have used are rockers, digging areas, vehicles, climbing units and house play units. For example, a play yard with 12 vehicles, a rocking boat, a tumble tub (all single); a jungle gym with boxes and boards and a dirt area with scooper trucks (both complex); and a well-equipped sand table with water (a super unit), has only four different kinds of things to do. Even though there are 17 separate play units, and two complex and one super unit, the space offers choice only of riding, rocking, digging or climbing.

Occasionally, though a space does contain a healthy variety of things to do, a disproportionately large amount of one kind of thing overwhelms the eye, so that the choice may seem to be between climbing and digging, and climbing and riding, and climbing and swinging, and so on. Or, for example, so much shelf space may contain blocks, that other things to do may fade into the invisible category of "toys."

Possibilities for increasing variety often exist within the framework provided by what is already present. For instance, some play units have potential for more than one kind of activity. If there are two units which invite children to crawl inside and be cozy, such as a crate and a crawl barrel, it might be expedient to exploit the climbing potential of one and the containing potential of the other; or routinely, to introduce different kinds of play ideas by adding props like trucks, hats, etc. If there is an excessive number of certain toys such as trikes or blocks, some might be stored away, or traded for other needed equipment, or dismantled and their parts used in novel ways. Like complexity, variety appears of greatest importance when children are expected to play freely for some length of time and to make their own choices about what to play with.

Complexity and variety then, are measures of interest. Complex and super units invite children to make an ongoing series of meaningful choices in altering the contents of a particular play unit, and thus tend to keep them continuously involved. Wide variety invites children to make choices among many different kinds of activities, and thus tends to elicit immediate interest from children who are ready to find something to do.

Amount to Do per Child

A particular space may contain a wide variety of units including many complex and super units, and thus appear to provide a good deal of choice to children. Still the question remains: Given the number of children expected to use the space, what is the likelihood that these play units will actually be available for children's choices? Based on the relative value of simple, complex and super units, we devised a method for approximating what might be called the number of play places that a room or yard actually has. To do this we assign a value of **four** to complex units, on the basis that complex units will generally accommodate about four children at once. Considering the unique potential of super units, we felt they were worth two complex units and so we valued them at **eight**. Though many simple units can be used by more than one child at a time, the fact that they are less continuously interesting than complex units led us to assign a value of **one** to simple units. When the total number of play places of a yard or room is determined, this sum can be divided by the number of children expected to use the space. This ratio gives the approximate number of play places available to each child at any given time. For instance, in the example given under Variety, the yard would have a total of 30 play places.

Number of Play Units	Type of Unit	Number of Play Places
12 vehicles	simple	12
1 rocking boat	simple	1
1 tumble tub	simple	1
1 jungle gym with boxes and boards	complex	4
1 dirt area plus scoop trucks	complex	4
1 equipped sand table with water	super unit	8
	Total play places	30

If the yard had 15 children, there would be 2.0 play places per child; if the yard had 25 children, there would be 1.2 play places per child.

The implications of this dimension are most easily expressed through an analogy in which play is likened to a game of musical chairs. However, for the purposes of the analogy we shall assume that the objective of the game is not to eliminate participants, but to provide each child with a chair each time the music stops. In a game with 20 chairs and 10 children (2.0 chairs per child), when the music stops children can easily find an empty chair without help. If there are 10 children and 15 chairs (1.5 chairs per child), some children probably will have difficulty finding an empty chair. The closer the number of chairs is to the number of children, the more likely it will be that a teacher will need to help children find the empty chairs. If there are fewer chairs than children, either some one (or more) must stand every time the music stops, or children must double up on chairs. If the teacher is in charge of the music, shifting from chair to chair will take place for all children at once and be much as described above. However, if the teacher wants the children to listen to their own "inner music," further difficulties are introduced. When the number of chairs is close to one per child, and a child wants to change chairs, choice will be severely limited, and the teacher probably will need to help. If several children want to change chairs in close succession, the demands on the teacher and the limitations on the children will be extreme. Through this analogy, the importance of having enough to do per child can perhaps be felt.

The amount to do per child in a space can be increased most readily either by scheduling smaller groups of children in the space, or by adding complex and super units.

The Importance of Contents

Complexity, Variety and Amount to do per child as aspects of play ideas available to children, have been discussed. Unless staff have a clear conception of the relationship between goals and the play environment which they have created by their choice of contents, they may force behavior which acts against the achievement of desired goals. For instance, teachers may want to support the development of autonomy by giving children many opportunities to make their own choices, and yet the amount to do per child may be so low that choice is constantly thwarted. Or teachers may want to support the lengthening of attention span by actively helping children remain interested in their self-chosen activity, and yet the complex or super type of play unit which invites doing lots of different things within one play unit (i.e., invites children to stay with an activity for a long time) may be virtually absent. It becomes important then, in examining space, to be sure the content necessary to support the goals is present.

NOTE

1. There is another side to a child's response to particular space which relates to the child's background. For instance, what is spacious and roomy and provides ease of movement in a familiar way to one child, may be apprehended as cold and distant and even unpleasantly threatening to another.

CHAPTER 7 Sound Practice

7.1 JOHN DEWEY

Three Years of the University Elementary School

John Dewey's life (1859–1952) spanned nearly a century of major advances in industry and science. His progressive philosophy, rooted deeply in democratic principles and the scientific method, encouraged teachers to develop curricula based on what was happening in the lives of children, not totally on academic disciplines. His influence on the American educational system is clearly visible in schools today. Teachers who use a localized curriculum, integrate subjects, involve the children in extended projects, utilize curriculum webbing, or encourage critical thinking are employing techniques that have evolved from Dewey's educational philosophy.

In the following selection, Dewey asks, "How can teachers bring the school into closer relationship with the home and neighborhood life—instead of the school being a place where the child comes solely to learn certain lessons?" This has become a critical question in the 1990s. "Three Years of the University Elementary School" (February 1899), a stenographic report of a speech given by Dewey at a meeting of the Parents' Association of the University Elementary School, is an account of Dewey's experimental school at the University of Chicago. His "learning by doing" program required new curricula, new methods, and new furniture. A kindergarten was later added, prompted by the mid-1890s wave of child study in America.

Dewey's pragmatic philosophy and his interest in kindergarten made him a leader of the Progressives, who were advocating for changes in educational practices. He wrote widely on subjects such as imagination, education in a democracy, pedagogy, experimentalism, ethics, and evolution. Dewey's *Democracy and Education* (1916) is considered by many to be his masterpiece.

*T*he school was started the first week in January, three years ago. I shall try this afternoon to give a brief statement of the ideas and problems that were in mind when the experiment was started, and a sketch of the development of the work since that time. We began in a small house in Fifty-seventh street, with fifteen children. We found ourselves the next year with twenty-five children in Kimbark avenue, and then moved in January to Rosalie court, the larger quarters enabling us to take forty children. The next year the numbers increased to sixty, the school remaining at Rosalie court. This year we have had ninety-five on the roll at one time, and are located at 5412 Ellis avenue, where we hope to stay till we have a building and grounds of our own.

The children during the first year of the school were between the ages of six and nine. Now their ages range between four and thirteen—the members of the oldest group being in their thirteenth year. This is the first year that we have children under six, and this has been made possible through the liberality of friends in Honolulu, H.I., who are building up there a memorial kindergarten along the same lines.

The expenses of the school during the first year, of two terms only, were between $1,300 and $1,400. The expenses this year will be about $12,000. Of this amount $5,500 will come from tuitions; $5,000 has been given by friends interested in the school, and there remains about $1,500 yet to be raised for the conduct of the school. This is an indication of the increase of expenses. The average expense per pupil is about the same since the start, *i.e.*, $120 per child per school year. Relatively speaking, this year the expenses of the school took something of a jump, through the expense of moving to a new building, and the repairs and changes there necessary. An increase in the staff of teachers has also enlarged the work as well as the debits of the school. Next year (1899–1900) we hope to have about 120 children, and apparently the expenses will be about $2,500 more than this. Of this amount $2,000 will be met by the increase in tuition from the pupils. The cost of a child to the school, $120 a year, is precisely the tuition charged by the University for students and is double the average tuition charged by the school. But it is not expected that the University tuition will come anywhere near meeting the expense involved there. One reason for not increasing the tuition here, even if it were advisable for other reasons, is that it is well to emphasize, from an educational point of view, that elementary as well as advanced education requires endowment. There is every reason why money should be spent freely for the organization and maintenance of foundation work in education as well as for the later stages.

The elementary school has had from the outset two sides: one, the obvious one of instruction of the children who have been intrusted to it; the other, relationship to the University, since the school is under the charge, and forms a part of the pedagogical work of the University.

When the school was started, there were certain ideas in mind—perhaps it would be better to say questions and problems; certain points which it seemed worth while to test. If you will permit one personal word, I should like to say that it is sometimes thought that the school started out with a number of ready-made principles and ideas which were to be put into practice at once. It has been popularly assumed that I am the author of these ready-made ideas and principles which were to go into execution. I take this opportunity to say that the educational conduct of the school, as well as its administration, the selection of subject-matter, and the working out of the course of study, as well as actual instruction of children, have been almost entirely in the hands of the teachers of the school; and that there has been gradual development of the educational principles and methods involved, not a fixed equipment. The teachers started with question marks, rather than with fixed rules, and if any answers have been reached, it is the teachers in the school who have supplied them. We started upon the whole with four such questions, or problems:

1. What can be done, and how can it be done, to bring the school into closer relation with the home and neighborhood life—instead of having the school a place where the child comes solely to learn certain lessons? What can be done to break down the barriers which have unfortunately come to separate the school life from the rest of the everyday life of the child? This does not mean, as it is sometimes, perhaps, interpreted to mean, that the child should simply take up in the school things already experienced at home and study them, but that, so far as possible, the child shall have the same attitude and point of view in the school as in the home; that he shall find the same interest in going to school, and in there doing things worth doing for their own sake, that he finds in the plays and occupations which busy him in his home and neighborhood life. It means, again, that the motives which keep the child at work and growing at home shall be used in the school, so that he shall not have to acquire another set of principles of actions belonging only to the school—separate from those of the home. It is a question of the unity of the child's experience, of its actuating motives and aims, not of amusing or even interesting the child.

2. What can be done in the way of introducing subject-matter in history and science and art, that shall have a positive value and real significance in the child's own life; that shall represent, even to the youngest children, something worthy of attainment in skill or knowledge; as much so to the little pupil as are the studies of the high-school or college student to him? You know what the traditional curriculum of the first few years is, even though many modifications have been made. Some statistics have been collected showing that 75 or 80 per cent. of the first three years of a child in school are spent upon the form—not the substance—of learning, the mastering of the symbols of reading, writing, and arithmetic. There is not much positive nutriment in this. Its purpose is important—is necessary—but it does not represent the same kind of increase in a child's intellectual and moral experience that is represented by positive truth of history and nature, or by added insight into reality and beauty. One thing, then, we wanted to find out is how much can be given a child that

is really worth his while to get, in knowledge of the world about him, of the forces in the world, of historical and social growth, and in capacity to express himself in a variety of artistic forms. From the strictly educational side this has been the chief problem of the school. It is along this line that we hope to make our chief contribution to education in general; we hope, that is, to work out and publish a positive body of subject-matter which may be generally available.

3. How can instruction in these formal, symbolic branches—the mastering of the ability to read, write, and use figures intelligently—be carried on with everyday experience and occupation as their background and in definite relations to other studies of more inherent content, and be carried on in such a way that the child shall feel their necessity through their connection with subjects which appeal to him on their own account? If this can be accomplished, he will have a vital motive for getting the technical capacity. It is not meant, as has been sometimes jocosely stated, that the child learn to bake and sew at school, and to read, write, and figure at home. It is intended that these formal subjects shall not be presented in such large doses at first as to be the exclusive objects of attention, and that the child shall be led by that which he is doing to feel the need for acquiring skill in the use of symbols and the immediate power they give. In any school, if the child realizes the motive for the use and application of number and language he has taken the longest step toward securing the power; and he can realize the motive only as he has some particular—not some general and remote—use for the symbols.

4. Individual attention. This is secured by small groupings—eight or ten in a class—and a large number of teachers supervising systematically the intellectual needs and attainments and physical well-being and growth of the child. To secure this we have now 135 hours of instructors' time per week, that is, the time of nine teachers for three hours per day, or one teacher per group. It requires but a few words to make this statement about attention to individual powers and needs, and yet the whole of the school's aims and methods, moral, physical, intellectual, are bound up in it.

I think these four points present a fair statement of what we have set out to discover. The school is often called an experimental school, and in one sense that is the proper name. I do not like to use it too much, for fear parents will think we are experimenting upon the children, and that they naturally object to. But it is an experimental school—at least I hope so—with reference to education and educational problems. We have attempted to find out by trying, by doing—not alone by discussion and theorizing—*whether* these problems may be worked out, and *how* they may be worked out.

Next a few words about the means that have been used in the school in order to test these four questions, and to supply their answers, and first as to the place given to hand-work of different kinds in the school. There are three main lines regularly pursued: (*a*) the shop-work with woods and tools, (*b*) cooking work, and (*c*) work with textiles—sewing and weaving. Of course, there is other hand-work in connection with science, as science is largely of an experimental nature. It is a fact that may not have come to your attention that a large part of the best and most advanced scientific work involves a great deal of manual skill, the training of the hand and eye. It is impossible for one to be a first-class worker in science without this training in manipulation, and in handling apparatus and materials. In connection with the history work, especially with the younger children, hand-work is brought in in the way of making implements, weapons, tools, etc. Of course, the art work is another side—drawing, painting, and modeling. Logically, perhaps, the gymnasium work does not come in here, but as a means of developing moral and intellectual control through the medium of the body it certainly does. The children have one-half hour per day of this form of physical exercise. Along this line we have found that hand-work, in large variety and amount, is the most easy and natural method of keeping up the same attitude of the child in and out of the school. The child gets the largest part of his acquisitions through his bodily activities, until he learns to work systematically with the intellect. That is the purpose of this work in the school, to direct these activities, to systematize and organize them, so that they shall not be as haphazard and as wandering as they are outside of school. The problem of making these forms of practical activity work continuously and definitely together, leading from one factor of skill to another, from one intellectual difficulty to another, has been one of the most difficult, and at the same time one in which we have been most successful. The various kinds of work, carpentry, cooking, sewing, and weaving, are selected as involving different kinds of skill, and demanding different types of intellectual attitude on the part of the child, and because they represent some of the most important activities of the everyday outside world: the question of living under shelter, of daily food and clothing, of the home, of personal movement and exchange of goods. He gets also the training of sense organs, of touch, of sight, and the ability to coördinate eye and hand. He gets healthy exercise; for the child demands a much larger amount of physical activity than the formal program of the ordinary school permits. There is also a continual appeal to memory, to judgment, in adapting ends to means, a training in habits of order, industry, and neatness in the care of the tools and utensils, and in doing things in a systematic, instead of a haphazard, way. Then, again, these practical occupations make a background, especially in the earlier groups, for the later studies. The children get a good deal of chemistry in connection with cooking, of number work and geometrical principles of carpentry, and a good deal of geography in connection with their theoretical work in weaving and sewing. History also comes in with the origin and growth of various inventions, and their effects upon social life and political organization.

Perhaps more attention, upon the whole, has been given to our second point, that of positive subject-matter, than to any one other thing. On the history side the curriculum is now fairly well worked out. The younger children begin with the home and occupations of the home. In the sixth year the intention is that the children should study occupations outside the home, the larger social industries—farming, mining, lumber, etc.—that they may see the complex and various social industries on which life depends, while incidentally they investigate the use of the various materials—woods, metals, and the processes applied—thus getting a beginning of scientific study. The next year is given to the historical development of industry and invention—starting with man as a savage and carrying him through the typical phases of his progress upward, until the iron age is reached and man begins to enter upon a civilized career. The object of the study of primitive life is not to keep the child interested in lower and relatively savage stages, but to show him the steps of progress and development, especially along the line of invention, by which man was led into civilization. There is a certain nearness, after all, in the child to primitive forms of life. They are much more simple than existing institutions. By throwing the emphasis upon the progress of man, and upon the way advance has been made, we hope to avoid the objections that hold against paying too much attention to the crudities and distracting excitements of savage life.

History of the Unifying of Kindergarten and First-Grade Education

Samuel Chester Parker and Alice Temple were professors at the University of Chicago. They coauthored the book *Unified Kindergarten and First-Grade Teaching* (Ginn & Company, 1925), from which the following selection has been excerpted, just prior to Parker's death. The book represents one of the earliest attempts to assist teachers in plotting a course for kindergarten in the public school system and to adjust the first-grade curriculum to accommodate children who had had a kindergarten experience.

Temple (1871–1946) studied under Anna E. Bryan at the Chicago Free Kindergarten Association and John Dewey at the University of Chicago. In 1913, after four years of work at the University of Chicago, Temple succeeded in forming a new department called Kindergarten and Primary Education. In this program, a student was able to attain the Kindergarten-Primary Certificate in two years. Temple based her work on the belief that kindergarten teachers should have some preparation in primary education and that primary teachers should be exposed to kindergarten methods and materials. During that time kindergartens served children ages four through six.

Temple served as president of the International Kindergarten Union from 1925 to 1927. This association merged with the National Council of Primary Education in 1931 to become the Association for Childhood Education (which added the word *International* to its name in 1946).

In examining the incorporation of kindergartens into the public schools and tracking their acceptance, one can see evidence of resistance to change. First-grade teachers were perplexed by the role the new kindergartens had taken as the child's first school experience. In response, Parker and Temple examined the overlap of curriculum, the mental ages of children, and unified teacher training, areas that are still considered critical today.

THE UNIFIED KINDERGARTEN AND FIRST GRADE . . .

Extension of Kindergarten Activities into the First Grade

THREE INFLUENCES OF KINDERGARTEN ON FIRST GRADE   The influence of the kindergarten movement in modifying the old-fashioned American first grade worked along three lines: namely, (1) a change in the general spirit of the work so as to make it more active and playful; (2) modification in the teaching of some of the standard first-grade subjects, such as music, which had been added to some of the old-fashioned American first grades during the nineteenth century, (3) the introduction of new subjects, such as handwork and games.

METHOD OF INFLUENCE   *Teachers visited kindergartens.*—A pleasing suggestion of how these first-grade changes were stimulated through visits of first-grade teachers to kindergartens is contained in the following paragraph by Miss Vandewalker:

The primary teacher who visited a kindergarten could not fail to be impressed by the kindergartner's attitude toward her children—by her coöperation with them in the spirit of comradeship, and by her sympathetic insight into their interests and needs. She was impressed no less by the children's attitude toward their work, by the spontaneity of their interest, and by their delight in the use of the bright-colored material. The games were a revelation to her, since they showed that there could be freedom without disorder; the interest which the children took in the kindergarten songs made her own drill on scales and intervals seem little better than drudgery; and the attractiveness of the kindergarten room gave her helpful suggestions concerning the value of beauty as a factor in education. In short, recognizing that there was possible an order of things very different from that to which she was accustomed, she determined to profit by the lesson. If kindergarten procedure could be made so interesting, why not school procedure as well? Why, she asked, should there not be pictures upon the walls and plants in the windows in the primary room as well as in the kindergarten? Why should the kindergarten children have bright-colored material and the primary children none? Why could not the songs and many of the games used in the kindergarten be used also in the primary department? The educational leaders were beginning to ask the same questions, and to urge the utilization of childish activity in the primary grades, but no arguments were half so convincing as the example of the kindergarten itself. As a result, the characteristic features of the kindergarten were to a greater or less degree adopted by the school. Exercises with kindergarten material became common, and kindergarten songs and games were incorporated into the procedure of the primary school.

Dewey's laboratory school adopted kindergarten principles.—Among the schools in which this transformation of the primary work was greatly influenced by kindergarten principles and practices was the famous laboratory or experimental school conducted at The University of Chicago by Professor John Dewey from 1896 to 1901. In speaking of this influence Dewey said:

> One of the traditions of the school is of a visitor who, in its early days, called to see the kindergarten. On being told that the school had not as yet established one, she asked if there were not singing, drawing, manual training, plays and dramatizations, and attention to the children's social relations. When her questions were answered in the affirmative, she remarked, both triumphantly and indignantly, that that was what she understood by a kindergarten, and she did not know what was meant by saying that the school had no kindergarten. The remark was perhaps justified in spirit if not in letter. At all events, it suggests that in a certain sense the school endeavors throughout its whole course—now including children between four and thirteen—to carry into effect certain principles which Froebel was perhaps the first consciously to set forth.[1]

EXTENSION WELL UNDER WAY BY 1910   Through such influences as these, the first grades in many schools became permeated with the kindergarten spirit and kindergarten activities by 1910. We shall now consider the extension of certain first-grade activities into the kindergarten.

Extension of First-Grade Activities into the Kindergarten

THE PROBLEM   Our problem here is to determine the place that arithmetic, writing, and reading have had and may properly have in the kindergarten.

ARITHMETIC   *Some kindergartens doing more than some first grades.*— Strange to say, arithmetic, in the form of counting and measuring, has been more highly developed in some kindergartens than in many first grades. This is due to the fact that the games and the handwork of the kindergarten offer many natural opportunities for using counting and measuring; hence the pupils gain considerable facility in the practical use of simple numbers, including even easy fractions such as one half. On the other hand, in those first grades where games and handwork are lacking, these natural opportunities for practice with numbers are lost. Since the original Froebelian kindergarten contained such number work, while the old-fashioned first grade frequently lacked it, we are here confronted not so much with the extension of a first-grade activity into the kindergarten as with the problem of fully utilizing in both grades the natural possibilities for arithmetical thinking that the activities of the children offer.

HANDWRITING   *Delayed by immature motor development.*—When we turn to handwriting, however, the opposite situation exists. The difficulty that even first-grade children have in making small movements has resulted in the minimizing of handwriting even in that grade. Hence psychologically organized first grades call for only a small amount of handwriting, and this consists of large letters made either on the blackboard or with soft pencils on paper. The same fact concerning the psychological strain from small movements led progressive kindergartens to abandon such activities as weaving and interlacing with small materials, which were carried on in the earlier kindergartens. Consequently we see that handwriting can have little place in the kindergarten.

READING   *Complex problem resulting from variation in mental ages.*—The subject of reading offers a different case from either arithmetic or handwriting, because, although the teaching of reading was seldom found in the isolated kindergarten, it is quite appropriate and valuable for certain kindergarten children who are mentally capable of making easy progress with it. On the other hand, it is clearly not adapted to other kindergarten children of lower grades of mental ability, just as it is not adapted to some first-grade children of low intellectual ability. Thus the introduction of reading into the kindergarten offers a much more complex problem than we encountered in considering arithmetic and handwriting. We may approach this problem in a reasonable manner by reviewing and applying the two sets of facts brought out in our history of the old-fashioned first grade and the isolated kindergarten. The first of these will show the social value of reading; and the second, its psychological adaptation to many kindergarten children of high mental ability.

Social value. Reading is the great tool of civilization.—From our study of the old-fashioned first grade we learned that when society in the past organized a primary school to meet a definite social need, the one essential social skill that it emphasized first was skill in reading. We found this true not only in the case of commercial needs but also in the case of the most idealistic religious and civic needs. If space had permitted, we could have shown that while handwriting was frequently omitted from important primary schools (as in Boston), and while arithmetic was frequently omitted except in the large commercial cities (as in New Netherland), reading was always present. Thus society regarded reading as of primary value in meeting its well-defined social needs; reading was the primary social tool, the primary subject in the primary school. Moreover, it takes little insight into the essentials of civilization as contrasted with barbarism to see that society has always been right in placing this high social value on skill in the art of reading.

NOTE

1. *Elementary School Record*, Vol. I (June, 1900), p. 142. Republished in the revised edition of Dewey's *The School and Society* (The University of Chicago Press, 1915), p. 111.

Meeting the Challenge of Diversity

In "Meeting the Challenge of Diversity," *Young Children* (January 1992), from which the following selection is taken, Elizabeth Jones and Louise Derman-Sparks address common inappropriate approaches that can occur intentionally or unintentionally in programs. Then they define obstacles teachers face when attempting to implement an antibias curriculum. They also offer ways to gather support for making changes in programs serving young children.

Jones and Derman-Sparks teach at Pacific Oaks College in Pasadena, California. Both have a long history in early childhood education. Derman-Sparks taught at the original Perry Preschool, a high-quality educational program for disadvantaged four- and five-year-olds, in Ypsilanti, Michigan, in the 1960s. She was one of the first educators to address the need for teachers to become familiar with the various lifestyles and cultural influences that are a major part of a young child's life with her book *Anti-Bias Curriculum: Tools for Empowering Young Children* (National Association for the Education of Young Children, 1989). Derman-Sparks is also the director of the Anti-Bias Leadership Project at Pacific Oaks.

Jones holds a Ph.D. in sociology from the University of Southern California. She has been a resource support team leader for the Partnership Project between Pacific Oaks College and the Pasadena Unified School District. Her publications reveal her extensive experiences teaching preschool, primary grades, and college. Jones tells of the personal journeys of others in *The Play's the Thing: The Teachers' Roles in Children's Plays* (Teachers College Press, 1992), coauthored with Gretchen Reynolds, and *Growing Teachers' Partnerships in Staff Development*. She describes her own personal journey in *Teaching Adults: An Active Learning Approach* (National Association for the Education of Young Children, 1986).

As the NAEYC accreditation criteria (National Academy of Early Childhood Programs, 1984) make clear, meeting the challenge of diversity is an essential component of quality early childhood programs. We live in a diverse society in a multicultural world; not to understand and value diversity is to shortchange oneself and others. Experience with the accreditation process has thus far shown that this criterion is among those least likely to be fully satisfied by programs applying for accreditation (Bredekamp & Apple, 1986).

What do the accreditation criteria ask for? Under "Interactions among Staff and Children" . . .

> Staff equally treat children of all races, religions, and cultures with respect and consideration. Staff provide children of both sexes with equal opportunities to take part in all activities. (1984, p. 9)

. . . and under "Curriculum" . . .

> Developmentally appropriate materials and equipment which project heterogeneous racial, sexual, and age attributes are selected and used. (p. 12)

"Of course," you may say. "That's what we believe and that's what we do." It sounds easy, but it isn't. In teaching young children and teachers and observing a wide variety of programs, we have seen several types of inappropriate approaches to diversity provided intentionally or unintentionally in early childhood programs.

CAN ANY OF THESE INAPPROPRIATE APPROACHES BE FOUND IN YOUR CENTER?

Teachers Believe They're Not Prejudiced.

At the personal level it may well be true that an individual does not hold bigoted beliefs; however, we all learn prejudices beginning in our childhood (Derman-Sparks & the A.B.C. Task Force, 1989). The practices and sterotypes that support institutional racism are all around us, even in curriculum materials in early childhood education. As one example, inaccurate, hurtful images of "Indians" abound in alphabet books, cartoons, and Western movies. They permeate our daily language.

> At an AEYC conference, a workshop presenter said, "But what can you do when the children are running around like wild Indians . . . ?"
> A Native American woman in the audience stood up. "What you've just said is offensive to me," she said.
> "And did any of the White women present say anything?" asked the educator to whom this story was told by a White member of the audience.
> "No, none of us did," was the reply. "I hadn't really noticed the words when the speaker said them. . . ."

We don't notice. Our unawareness and the lack of actions that challenge bias help to perpetuate oppressive beliefs and behaviors. Prejudice is real for its recipients, regardless of whether is was intentional.

Teachers Are Proud of Being "Colorblind."

Asked about the racial/ethnic composition of her class, the teacher proudly declared, "I don't know what color my children are. I never notice. They are all just children to me. I treat them all alike."

The children in her class are predominantly African Americans. The pictures of nursery rhyme characters on the walls, the dolls, and the books are nearly all white and reflect only the dominant Euro-American culture. The teacher is sure, however, that she is teaching all the children equally.

This teacher reflects a color-denial philosophy of education. Originally a progressive argument against racial bigotry, it implicitly establishes the dominant (Euro-American) culture experience as the norm and ends up equating "we are all the same" with "we are all White." Moreover, "colorblindness" ignores what we know about children's development of identity and attitudes as well as the realities of racism in the daily lives of people of color.

Teachers Believe That White Children Are Unaffected by Diversity Issues.

I don't see why I have to do multicultural curriculum. My class is all White. We don't have any problems with prejudice like teachers do in classrooms that are mixed.

All children are living in a society in which diversity is an ever-increasing reality. And all children are exposed to the biases still pervasive in our country—biases based on gender, age, and disability as well as race, language, and culture. Curriculum that does nothing to counter the biases that dominant-culture children absorb as they go about their daily lives ill-equips them to live effectively and fairly with diversity.

Teachers Assume That the Children They Teach Are "Culturally Deprived."

"My children come from deprived homes. Their parents don't even teach them good English before they come to school. They don't know how to be an American. My job is to teach them how to fit in," said one teacher to another.

Her colleague agreed. "You should *see* the homes they come from," she said. "They're so much better off here at the center. I don't think these parents really care about their children."

These teachers believe that "these children" need experiences that fill the void left by inadequate or inferior parenting; therefore, sharing different families' lifestyles, language, and values is not part of the curriculum. Children's behaviors, including language, that reflect their home culture are stopped and corrected.

Where children are defined as culturally deprived, curriculum is often developmentally inappropriate. Learning through play and spontaneous language is seen as an unaffordable luxury for children who must work hard to "catch up." Working with parents, these teachers give advice on childrearing, leaving no room for questions about the desirability of some of the dominant culture's values or for examining the value of other cultures' childrearing practices.

Teachers Seek Out Resources to Develop Multicultural Curriculum.

Many teachers are making conscientious efforts to introduce multicultural activities into their classrooms. Their intent is positive: Let's teach children about each other's cultures so they will learn to respect each other and not develop prejudice. In practice, however, activities frequently deteriorate into a tourist approach to diversity: "visiting other cultures" from time to time by way of a special bulletin board, a "multicultural" center, an occasional parent visit or holiday celebration, or even a week's unit—and then a return to "regular" daily activities that reflect only the dominant culture. Paradoxically, these curricula usually do not study the Euro-American culture because that is what happens in the regular curriculum.

Tourist curriculum emphasizes the "exotic" differences between cultures by focusing on holidays and ignoring the real-life daily problems and experiences of different peoples. When activities about diversity are only occasionally added to the curriculum, rather than integrated on a daily basis, such limited exposure misrepresents cultural realities and perpetuates stereotyping.

HOW CAN YOU MAKE CHANGES?

Antibias Curriculum: Tools for Empowering Young Children (by Louise Derman-Sparks and the A.B.C. Task Force, 1989) addresses both the daily-life realities of diversity and the biased attitudes and unfair behavior that are part of this reality. It recognizes that children begin to develop awareness both of differences and of socially prevailing biases by the time they're two or three. It asks adults to challenge children to practice critical thinking and activism, while integrating diversity into the daily program.

Teachers who begin to question their previous perceptions and behaviors face several potential obstacles when they consider implementing an antibias approach. Issues of bias stir up painful feelings, threatening both self-esteem and existing relationship patterns. Teachers may have feelings such as these:

164 "It Sounds Like Everything I've Been Doing is Wrong."

Chapter 7
Sound Practice

This is an awful feeling. It's faced by everyone who comes up against a new set of assumptions governing behavior. In many public schools these days, it's being faced by traditional kindergarten and primary teachers who are being encouraged to adopt developmentally appropriate practice.

Challenged to examine our biases, many of us become defensive, especially if we have always seen ourselves as unbiased and fair to everyone. Disequilibrium is never comfortable, but as Piaget has made clear, it's a necessary condition for constructing new ways of thinking and doing. Colleagues need to nurture each other through this process, just as they do children. It's OK to not be perfect, to be a learner.

"But What If I Say the Wrong Thing?"

A public school teacher challenged to move beyond her annual classroom Christmas celebration protested, "I don't really teach about Hannukah because I just don't know how to pronounce all those words." A teacher who habitually diverted rather than confronted racial name-calling explained, "I'm embarrassed and I don't know what to say." It's important to teachers to be knowledgeable, to feel competent. Practicing new behaviors, we may indeed say the "wrong thing." It is hard to know what to say in the face of bias; we don't have many models. It is hard to broaden the cultural base of our curriculum when what we know and love best are the stories and songs and customs of our own culture. If we try introducing new ideas, we'll be learning with the children instead of teaching them.

"I Want My Classroom to Be a Happy Place."

Many women have been socialized to be nice, to be nurturing, and to keep relationships running smoothly. We are very comfortable reminding children that we're all friends here and helping them solve problems peacefully. We are comfortable with a multicultural curriculum that emphasizes the attractive differences among celebrations, food, and music. We are not at all comfortable with an antibias curriculum that asks us to examine negative attitudes toward differences, including our own. We have no wish to make waves or take risks. If confronted by colleagues or supervisors, we are likely to feel both pain and anger at the threat this poses to pleasant, cooperative relationships among staff and with parents.

"I'm Ready to Address Antibias Issues With Children, but I Worry About My Relationships With Other Staff, Parents, and Administration If I Do. What Will They Say About Me?"

A teacher who is the only adult in a classroom may have some privacy to try new curriculum and new dialogues. If she is a member of a team, negotiation becomes necessary. And what about parents? How will they react if familiar holidays aren't observed, if race and disability are talked about openly, if boys are encouraged to play with "girls' things"? Unlike young children, who are willing to explore differences and to think critically about bias, many adults have learned that these are things we don't talk about. In *The Emperor's New Clothes*, no adult had the courage to mention the emperor's nakedness; it was up to a child to make the observation.

Implementation of antibias curriculum sometimes produces conflict situations. Teachers skilled in conflict resolution are aware of the ingredients necessary to make it work: (a) a caring relationship with the children; (b) practice in using problem-solving strategies that empower all the parties to the conflict and enable them to generate creative solutions; and (c) the ability to accept strong feelings, appropriately expressed. Working in this way with young children provides an excellent base for undertaking encounters with other adults around issues likely to generate conflict. It is important that adults have established caring relationships with each other that provide the base of safety from which it is possible to challenge each other.

"I'd Like to Develop Antibias Curriculum, but I Just Don't Have the Materials I'd Need."

It's true that there are large gaps in the range of appropriate materials available; but there are more than you might think, especially from the smaller suppliers (see Derman-Sparks & the A.B.C. Task Force, 1989, for resource lists). Some materials can be improvised; families can be invited to share others. Stories can be collected from parents, children, colleagues, and your own imagination.

HOW DO YOU FIND SUPPORT FOR MAKING CHANGES?

If you have faced up to these potential obstacles and still fear that the consequences of *not* broadening your curriculum—thus leaving children ill-equipped to "play fair" with others in a diverse world—will be worse than the consequences of taking action, what could you do next?

Buddy Up With a Sympathetic Colleague or Two in Your School or Community.

Talk about changes you'd like to create in your classroom. Share your fears of potential obstacles. Commit to working together and help each other get started. Arrange to observe in each other's classrooms (it's amazing how rarely teachers do this) and then raise questions and make suggestions to each other. You might agree to focus your first observation on the room environment or how children are using different materials. Make a commitment to be both caring and direct. Tell each other about new things you try and what happens.

Begin Step-By-Step in Your Own Classroom.

Get ideas from reading and from workshops. Identify one thing you want to change—in the environment, in children's behavior, or in your behavior. Decide whether you want to address all the areas of bias or just one, and whether you want to begin with the one easiest for you (for some people that's gender equity) and then go on to a harder one, or start out by tackling the one that is your biggest challenge. Be alert to opportunities offered by things that children say and do. Remember that children are forgiving. If something feels wrong one day, bring it up again the next day: "You know, yesterday I said something that I've been thinking about some more. I'm not sure that was a good idea. What do you think?" As Vivian Paley (1986) has pointed out, children are eager to discuss issues of feelings and fairness; those are their preoccupations, too. They'll help you if you ask them.

Develop Strategies for Sharing Your Learning With Other Teachers, Parents, Administrators, and the Professional Community.

- Before approaching other staff, consider the following: Is there a climate of trust and caring in your program, among peers and with administrators? If not, that's your first priority to work on, through resolving other issues or just through getting to know each other better. One relevant approach is to schedule time at meetings for personal sharing of "family albums": Where do you come from? Tell us about your family and culture and neighborhood, your experiences with differences. Anti-bias issues should not be tackled with coworkers unless the existing relationships are emotionally safe and caring.
- If trust exists, bring up the issue with your school staff as a concern you'd like to share. Are others interested? Identify your allies: Who else shares your concern? Is there enough interest for an in-service, or do you need a voluntary study/task group? Consider whether to identify interested parents and invite them to participate with staff in such a group.
- Agree on a clear structure for study/task group meetings, with rules of order and a designated facilitator for each session. There will be issues of territory and mistrust; you will encounter both personal and institutional obstacles to change.
- Give it time; expect to continue meeting for a year or more. Plan to go back and forth between discussion and action, making a commitment to both learning and change-making. Apply the same rules of acceptance of each person that govern your work with children.

*Elizabeth Jones
and Louise
Derman-Sparks*

Am I Creating An Antibias Environment?

To gain a sense of whether you're creating an antibias environment in your program, score yourself on this checklist. Rather than relying on memory, have this checklist with you in the classroom. If your answer to an item is "a lot," give yourself 2 points; if your answer is "a little," give yourself 1 point; and if your answer is "no," give yourself 0.

Do I use materials/do activities that teach about . . .

* all the children, families, and staff in my program?
* contemporary children and adults from the major racial/ethnic groups in my community, my state, and American society in their families, at work, and at play?
* diversity within each racial/ethnic group?
* women and men of various ethnic backgrounds doing "jobs in the home"?
* women and men of various ethnic backgrounds doing "jobs outside the home" including blue collar work, pink collar work, white collar work, and artistic work?
* elderly people of various backgrounds doing a variety of activities?
* differently abled people of various backgrounds working, being with their families, and playing?
* diversity in family lifestyles, including single mom or dad; mom works, dad's at home; dad works, mom's at home; mom and dad work; two moms and two dads; extended families; interracial and multiethnic families; foster families; families by adoption; families with differently abled members; low-income families, middle-class families?
* individuals of many different backgrounds who contribute to our lives, including participants in movements for justice?

Now Total Your Points and Examine the Results

If your score is between *16* and *18*, you are using an antibias approach.

If your score is between *11* and *15*, you are moving away from a tourist approach is some areas.

If your score is between *5* and *10*, you are using a tourist approach.

If your score is *4* or below, you are using a dominant (Euro-American) culture-centered approach.

Antibias work begins with the assumption that, like yourself, other early childhood educators want to grow and improve. Most adults working with young children value fairness, self-esteem, and respect for individual differences. This shared value base is a starting point for questioning each other: "I've been wondering about . . . (the pictures on our walls, the holidays we celebrate, the dramatic play props we provide, some of our books)." Are they fair? What messages do they give children about themselves and about other people?

The other important assumption is that growth takes time. Other adults' priorities may be different from yours. Respect and learn from their priorities while advocating your own. Recognize the slowness of the process and people's right not to change even though you think they should. Remember that you are creating disequilibrium when others may be seeking equilibrium in their lives and in their work.

Early childhood educators committed to developmentally appropriate practice—in which children's competence and motivation to grow and learn are trusted, developmental and individual differences are respected, and adult-child relationships are more egalitarian than authoritarian—have a solid foundation for meeting the challenges of diversity. Integrating an antibias approach into developmentally appropriate practice takes time, persistence, courage, and the conviction that children are worth the struggle.

REFERENCES

Bredekamp, S., & Apple, P. L. (1986). How early childhood programs get accredited. An analysis of accreditation decisions. *Young Children, 42*(1), 34–37.

Derman-Sparks, L., & the A.B.C. Task Force (1989). *Anti-bias curriculum: Tools for empowering young children.* Washington, DC:NAEYC.

National Academy of Early Childhood Programs. (1984). *Accreditation criteria and procedures.* Washington, DC:NAEYC.

Paley, V. (1986). On listening to what the children say. *Harvard Educational Review, 56*(2), 122–131.

7.4 NATIONAL ASSOCIATION FOR THE EDUCATION OF YOUNG CHILDREN

NAEYC Position Statement on Developmentally Appropriate Practice in the Primary Grades Serving 5- Through 8-Year-Olds

The National Association for the Education of Young Children (NAEYC), established in 1925 as the National Association for Nursery Education, is the largest early childhood professional organization in the country. It serves over 96,000 professionals dedicated to the care and education of young children from birth through age eight.

During the 1980s educational practices for young children followed no consistent order and varied tremendously, from rigid academic programs in which young babies were taught how to read to totally open, free settings where minimal structure and guidance were provided. Both extremes were viewed by the NAEYC as inappropriate educational experiences. The association therefore published a small volume entitled *Developmentally Appropriate Practice in Early Childhood Programs Serving Children from Birth Through Age 8* (1987). This book has encouraged much thought and discussion on the best educational practices for young children. The book, with its simple format, has been read by teachers, administrators, and parents. Available at a reasonable cost, it quickly became required reading for early childhood professionals. The guidelines include appropriate practices for infants through the primary grades. The following selection is an excerpt from the section of the book on primary grades (kindergarten through third grade).

*T*he current trend toward critical examination of our nation's educational system has recently included concerns about the quality of education provided in elementary schools (Bennett, 1986; Office of Educational Research and Improvement, 1986). Concerns have been raised because, in response to calls for "back to basics" and improved standardized test scores, many elementary schools have narrowed the curriculum and adopted instructional approaches that are incompatible with current knowledge about how young children learn and develop. Specifically, rote learning of academic skills is often emphasized rather than active, experiential learning in a meaningful context. As a result, many children are being taught academic skills but are not learning to apply those skills in context and are not developing more complex thinking skills like conceptualizing and problem solving (Bennett, 1986).

The National Association for the Education of Young Children (NAEYC), the nation's largest organization of early childhood educators, defines early childhood as the years from birth through age 8. NAEYC believes that on index of the quality of primary education is the extent to which the curriculum and instructional methods are developmentally appropriate for children 5 through 8 years of age. The purpose of this position statement is to describe both developmentally appropriate and inappropriate practices in the primary grades. This position statement reflects the most current knowledge of teaching and learning as derived from theory, research, and practice. This statement is intended for use by teachers, parents, school administrators, policymakers, and others who make decisions about primary grade educational programs. . . .

BACKGROUND INFORMATION

Classrooms serving primary-age children are typically part of larger institutions and complex educational systems with many levels of administration and supervision. Classroom teachers may have little control over the curriculum or policies they implement. However, ensuring developmentally appropriate practice in primary education requires the efforts of the entire group of educators who are responsible for planning and implementing curriculum—teachers, curriculum supervisors, principals, and superintendents. At the same time, ensuring developmentally appropriate practice is the professional obligation of each individual educator. No professional should abdicate this responsibility in the absence of mutual understanding and support of colleagues or supervisors. This position statement is intended to support the current appropriate practices of many primary-grade programs and to help guide the decisions of administrators so that developmentally appropriate practices for primary-age children become more widely accepted, supported, and followed.

Curriculum derives from several sources: the child, the content, and the society. The curriculum in early childhood programs is typically a balance of child-centered and content-centered curriculum. For example, good preschools present rich content in a curriculum that is almost entirely child-centered. As children progress into the primary grades, the emphasis on content gradually expands as determined by the school, the local community, and the society. The challenge for curriculum planners and teachers is to ensure that the content of the curriculum is taught so as to take optimum advantage of the child's natural abilities, interests, and enthusiasm for learning. . . .

INTEGRATED COMPONENTS OF APPROPRIATE AND INAPPROPRIATE PRACTICE IN THE PRIMARY GRADES

Curriculum Goals

Appropriate Practice: Curriculum is designed to develop children's knowledge and skills in all developmental areas—physical, social, emotional, and intellectual—and to help children learn how to learn—to establish a foundation for lifelong learning.

Inappropriate Practice: Curriculum is narrowly focused on the intellectual domain with intellectual development narrowly defined as acquisition of discrete, technical academic skills, without recognition that all areas of children's development are interrelated.

Appropriate Practice: Curriculum and instruction are designed to develop children's self-esteem, sense of competence, and positive feelings toward learning.

Inappropriate Practice: Children's worth is measured by how well they conform to group expectations, such as their ability to read at grade level and their performance on standardized tests.

Appropriate Practice: Each child is viewed as a unique person with an individual pattern and timing of growth. Curriculum and instruction are responsive to individual differences in ability and interests. Different levels of ability, development, and learning styles are expected, accepted, and used to design curriculum. Children are allowed to move at their own pace in acquiring important skills including those of writing, reading, spelling, math, social studies, science, art, music, health, and physical activity. For example, it is accepted that not every child will learn how to read at 6; most will learn to read by 7; and some will need intensive exposure to appropriate literacy experiences to learn to read by age 8 or 9.

Inappropriate Practice: Children are evaluated against a standardized group norm. All are expected to achieve the same narrowly defined, easily measured academic skills by the same predetermined time schedule typically determined by chronological age and grade level expectations.

Teaching Strategies

Appropriate Practice: The curriculum is integrated so that children's learning in all traditional subject areas occurs primarily through projects and learning centers that teachers plan and that reflect children's interests and suggestions. Teachers guide children's involvement in projects and enrich the learning experience by extending children's ideas, responding to their questions, engaging them in conversation, and challenging their thinking.

Inappropriate Practice: Curriculum is divided into separate subjects and time is carefully allotted for each with primary emphasis given each day to reading and secondary emphasis to math. Other subjects such as social studies, science, and health are covered if time permits. Art, music, and physical education are taught only once a week and only by teachers who are specialists in those areas.

Appropriate Practice: The curriculum is integrated so that learning occurs primarily through projects, learning centers, and playful activities that reflect current interests of children. For example, a social studies project such as building and operating a store or a science project such as furnishing and caring for an aquarium provide focused opportunities for children to plan, dictate, and/or write their plans (using invented and teacher-taught spelling), to draw and write about their activity, to discuss what they are doing, to read nonfiction books for needed information, to work cooperatively with other children, to learn facts in a meaningful context, and to enjoy learning. Skills are taught as needed to accomplish projects.

Inappropriate Practice: Instructional strategies revolve around teacher-directed reading groups that take up most of every morning, lecturing to the whole group, total class discussion, and paper-and-pencil practice exercises or worksheets to be completed silently by children working individually at desks. Projects, learning centers, play, and outdoor time are seen as embellishments and are only offered if time permits or as reward for good behavior.

Appropriate Practice: Teachers use much of their planning time to prepare the environment so children can learn through active involvement with each other, with adults and older children serving as informal tutors, and with materials. Many learning centers are available for children to choose from. Many centers include opportunities for writing and reading, for example a tempting library area for browsing through books, reading silently, or sharing a book with a friend; a listening station; and places to practice writing stories and to play math or language games. Teachers encourage children to evaluate their own work and to determine where improvement is needed and assist children in figuring out for themselves how to improve their work. Some work is corrected in small groups where children take turns giving feedback to one another and correcting their own papers. Errors are viewed as a natural and necessary part of learning. Teachers analyze children's errors and use the information obtained to plan curriculum and instruction.

Inappropriate Practice: Teachers use most of their planning time to prepare and correct worksheets and other seatwork. Little time is available to prepare enriching activities, such as those recommended in the teacher's edition of each textbook series. A few interest areas are available for children who finish their seatwork early or children are assigned to a learning center to complete a prescribed sequence of teacher-directed activities within a controlled time period.

Appropriate Practice: Individual children or small groups are expected to work and play cooperatively or alone in learning centers and on projects that they usually select themselves or are guided to by the teacher. Activity centers are changed frequently so children have new things to do. Teachers and children together select and develop projects. Frequent outings and visits from resource people are planned. Peer tutoring as well as learning from others through conversation while at work or play occurs daily.

Inappropriate Practice: During most work times, children are expected to work silently and alone on worksheets or other seatwork. Children rarely are permitted to help each other at work time. Penalties for talking are imposed.

Appropriate Practice: Learning materials and activities are concrete, real, and relevant to children's lives. Objects children can manipulate and experiment with such as blocks, cards, games, woodworking tools, arts and crafts materials including paint and clay, and scientific equipment are readily accessible. Tables are used for children to work alone or in small groups. A variety of work places and spaces is provided and flexibly used.

Inappropriate Practice: Available materials are limited primarily to books, workbooks, and pencils. Children are assigned permanent desks and desks are rarely moved. Children work in a large group most of the time and no one can participate in a playful activity until all work is finished.

Integrated Curriculum

Appropriate Practice: The goals of the language and literacy program are for children to expand their ability to communicate orally and through reading and writing, and to enjoy these activities. Technical skills or subskills are taught as needed to accomplish the larger goals, not as the goal itself. Teachers provide generous amounts of time and a variety of interesting activities for children to develop language, writing, spelling, and reading ability, such as: looking through, reading, or being read high quality children's literature and nonfiction for pleasure and information; drawing, dictating, and writing about their activities or fantasies; planning and implementing projects that involve research at suitable levels of difficulty; creating teacher-made or child-written lists of steps to follow to accomplish a project; discussing what was read; preparing weekly class newspaper; interviewing various people to obtain information for projects; making books of various kinds (riddle books, *what if* books, books about pets); listening to recordings or viewing high quality films of children's books; being read at least one high quality book or part of a book each day by adults or older children; using the school library and the library area of the classroom regularly. Some children read aloud daily to the teacher, another child, or a small group of children, while others do so weekly. Subskills such as learning letters, phonics, and word recognition are taught as needed to individual children and small groups through enjoyable games and activities. Teachers use the teacher's edition of the basal reader series as a guide to plan projects and hands-on activities relevant to what is read and to structure learning situations. Teachers accept children's invented spelling with minimal reliance on teacher-prescribed spelling lists. Teachers also teach literacy as the need arises when working on science, social studies, and other content areas.

Inappropriate Practice: The goal of the reading program is for each child to pass the standardized tests given throughout the year at or near grade level. Reading is taught as the acquisition of skills and subskills. Teachers teach reading only as a discrete subject. When teaching other subjects, they do not feel they are teaching reading. A sign of excellent teaching is considered to be silence in the classroom and so conversation is allowed infrequently during select times. Language, writing, and spelling instruction are focused on workbooks. Writing is taught as grammar and penmanship. The focus of the reading program is the basal reader, used only in reading groups, and accompanying workbooks and worksheets. The teacher's role is to prepare and implement the reading lesson in the teacher's guidebook for each group each day and to see that other children have enough seatwork to keep them busy throughout the reading group time. Phonics instruction stresses learning rules rather than developing understanding of systematic relationships between letters and sounds. Children are required to complete worksheets or to complete the basal reader although they are capable of reading at a higher level. Everyone knows which children are in the slowest reading group. Children's writing efforts are rejected if correct spelling and standard English are not used.

Appropriate Practice: The goal of the math program is to enable children to use math through exploration, discovery, and solving meaningful problems. Math activities are integrated with other relevant projects, such as science and social studies. Math skills are acquired through spontaneous play, projects, and situations of daily living. Teachers use the teacher's edition of the math textbook as a guide to structure learning situations and to stimulate ideas about interesting math projects. Many math manipulatives are provided and used. Interesting board and card, paper-and-pencil, and other kinds of games are used daily. Noncompetitive, impromptu oral "math stumper" and number games are played for practice.

Inappropriate Practice: Math is taught as a separate subject at a scheduled time each day. A math textbook with accompanying workbooks, practice sheets, and board work is the focus of the math program. Teachers move sequentially through the lessons as outlined in the teacher's edition of the text. Seldom is time available for recommended "hands-on" activities. Only children who finish their math seatwork are permitted to use the few math manipulatives and games in the classroom. Timed tests on number facts are given and graded daily. Competition between children or groups of children (boys vs. girls, Row 1 vs. Row 2) is used to motivate children to learn math facts.

Appropriate Practice: Social studies themes are identified as the focus or work for extended periods of time. Social studies concepts are learned through a variety of projects and playful activities involving independent research in library books; excursions and interviewing visitors; discussions; the relevant use of language, writing, spelling (invented and teacher-taught), and reading skills; and opportunities to develop social skills such a planning, sharing, taking turns, and working in committees. The classroom is treated as a laboratory of social relations where children explore values and learn rules of social living and respect for individual differences through experience. Relevant art, music, dance, drama, woodworking, and games are incorporated in social studies.

Inappropriate Practice: Social studies instruction is included occasionally after the reading and math programs are completed. Social studies projects, usually related to holidays, consist of completing brief activities from the social studies textbook or reading a commercially developed weekly newspaper and doing the accompanying seatwork.

Appropriate Practice: Discovery science is a major part of the curriculum, building on children's natural interest in the world. Science projects are experimental and exploratory and encourage active involvement of every child. The science program takes advantage of natural phenomena such as the outdoors, and the classroom includes many plants and pets for which children provide care daily. Through science projects and field trips, children learn to plan; to dictate and/or write their plans; to apply thinking skills such as hypothesizing, observing, experimenting, and verifying; and many science facts related to their own experience.

Inappropriate Practice: Science is taught mainly from a single textbook or not at all. Children complete related worksheets on science topics. Science consists of memorizing facts or watching teacher-demonstrated experiments. Field trips occur rarely or not at all. A science area may have a few plants, seashells, or pine cones that have been there many months and are essentially ignored by the children.

Appropriate Practice: A variety of health and safety projects (such as nutrition, dental health, handwashing) are designed to help children learn many personalized facts about health and safety; to integrate their learning into their daily habits; to plan and to dictate and/or write their plans; to draw and write about these activities; to read silently and aloud; and to enjoy learning because it is related to their lives.

Inappropriate Practice: Health is taught with the aid of posters and a textbook. A health lesson is scheduled once a week or a unit on health is completed once a year.

Appropriate Practice: Art, music, movement, woodworking, drama, and dance (and opportunities for other physical activity) are integrated throughout each day as relevant to the curriculum and as needed for children to express themselves aesthetically and physically and to express ideas and feelings. Specialists work with classroom teachers and children. Children explore and experiment with various art media and forms of music.

Inappropriate Practice: Art, music, and physical education are taught as separate subjects only once a week. Specialists do not coordinate closely with classroom teachers. Representational art, evaluated for approximations to reality, is emphasized. Children are expected to follow specific directions resulting in identical projects. Crafts substitute for artistic expression.

Appropriate Practice: Multicultural and nonsexist activities and materials are provided to enhance individual children's self-esteem and to enrich the lives of all children with respectful acceptance and appreciation of differences and similarities.

Inappropriate Practice: Cultural and other individual differences are ignored. Children are expected to adapt to the dominant culture. The lack of a multicultural component in the curriculum is justified by the homogeneity of the group, ignoring the fact that we live in a diverse society.

Appropriate Practice: Outdoor activity is planned daily so children can develop large muscle skills, learn about outdoor environments, and express themselves freely.

Inappropriate Practice: Outdoor time is limited because it is viewed as interfering with instructional time or, if provided, is viewed as recess (a way for children to use up excess energy).

Guidance of Social-Emotional Development

Appropriate Practice: Teachers promote prosocial behavior, perseverence, industry, and independence by providing many stimulating, motivating activities; encouraging individual choices; allowing as much time as needed for children to complete work; and ensuring moments of private time alone with the teacher or with a close friend.

Inappropriate Practice: Teachers lecture about the importance of appropriate social behavior and use punishment or deprivations (such as no recess) when children who become restless and bored with seatwork whisper, talk, or wander around or when children dawdle and do not finish their work in the allotted time. Teachers do not have time for private conversations with children and only the most able students finish their work in time for special interests or interaction with other children.

Appropriate Practice: Children have many opportunities daily to develop social skills such as helping, cooperating, negotiating, and talking with the person involved to solve interpersonal problems. Teachers facilitate the development of social skills at all times, as part of the curriculum.

Inappropriate Practice: Little time is available for children to practice social skills in the classroom because they are seated and doing silent, individual work or are involved in teacher-directed groups. The only opportunities for social interaction occur on the playground, but the teacher is not present unless it is her playground duty day; therefore, children don't have a consistent, familiar adult to help them with problems.

Appropriate Practice: Teachers promote the development of children's consciences and self-control through positive guidance techniques including: setting clear limits in a positive manner; involving children in establishing rules for social living and in problem solving of misbehavior; redirecting children to an acceptable activity; and meeting with an individual child who is having problems or with children and their parents. Teachers maintain their perspective about misbehavior, recognizing that every infraction does not warrant attention and identifying those that can be used as learning opportunities.

177

*National
Association for
the Education
of Young
Children*

Inappropriate Practice: Teachers place themselves in an adversarial role with children, emphasizing their power to reward acceptable behavior and punish unacceptable behavior. Their primary goal is maintaining control of the classroom. Teachers spend considerable time enforcing rules, giving external rewards for good behavior, and punishing infractions. When social conflicts arise, the teacher intervenes, separating and quieting participants, avoiding the social issue. Whether or not the teacher intends, her attitude often feels demeaning to the child.

Appropriate Practice: Teachers limit or contain overexposure to stimulation such as exciting, frightening, or disturbing real or fantasy events (including holidays, television programs or films, overwhelming museum exhibits, and depictions of disasters). When such events occur, teachers help children deal with excitement or fear and express feelings. Teachers know that although schoolchildren can discriminate between fantasy and reality, their capacity for absorbing stimulation is limited. Teachers recognize signs of overstimulation such as when children become silly, overly excited, and carried away in chasing or wrestling; when children try to unduly scare others by relating dramatic accounts of events or experiences; when children are unable to calm down and focus on the activity at hand; or when they become preoccupied with a frightening event. Teachers' strategy is to prevent these behaviors rather than punishing them and to provide an alternative calming activity.

Inappropriate Practice: Teachers are not sensitive to signs of overstimulation in children and treat such demonstrations as misbehavior that must be punished or teachers escalate the situation by encouraging children to release pent-up energy in uncontrolled activity.

Motivation

Appropriate Practice: Teachers build on children's internal motivation to make sense of the world and acquire competence. The teacher's role is to work with the child in a supportive way toward shared goals, such as reading, writing, learning about the world, exploring science and math, and mastering the rules and skills of sports. Teachers guide individual children to see alternatives, improvements, and solutions.

Inappropriate Practice: Teachers attempt to motivate children through the use of external rewards and punishments. The teacher's role is to correct errors and make sure the child knows the right answer in all subject areas. Teachers reward children for correct answers with stickers or privileges, praise them in front of the group, and hold them up as examples.

Appropriate Practice: Through the relationship with the teacher, the child models her or his enthusiasm for learning, identifies with the teacher's attitudes toward conscientious work, and gains in self-motivation.

Inappropriate Practice: The child, sensing that the teacher is struggling to keep her composure and get through the day, identifies with this attitude and emulates it.

Appropriate Practice: Teachers point out how good it feels to overcome a hurdle, to try hard to achieve success, and to live up to one's own standards of achievement. The reward for completing a task is an opportunity to try something even more self-challenging, for example "Now that you've finished this book, you can choose another book you want to read."

Inappropriate Practice: Teachers try to motivate children by giving numerical (85%) or letter grades, stickers, gold stars on charts, candy, or privileges such as extra minutes of recess.

Parent-Teacher Relations

Appropriate Practice: Teachers view parents as partners in the educational process. Teachers have time for periodic conferences with each child's parents. Parents' visits to school are welcomed at all times and home visits by teachers are encouraged. Teachers listen to parents, seek to understand their goals for their children, and are respectful of cultural and family differences.

Inappropriate Practice: Teachers are not given time for work with parents although many exceptional teachers do it on their own time. Subtle messages convey that schools are for teachers and children, not parents. Teachers view parents' role as carrying out the school's agenda.

Appropriate Practice: Members of each child's family are encouraged to help in the classroom (sharing a cultural event or language, telling or reading a story, tutoring, making learning materials or playing games); to help with tasks related to but not occurring within the classroom (sewing costumes, working in the school library); and to assist with decision-making where appropriate.

Inappropriate Practice: Schedules are so tight that parents are seen as one more frustration to teachers who need to cover the curriculum. A policy exists for parent participation, but it receives little time or effort. Teachers go to occasional PTA/PTO meetings and sit quietly in the audience. Teachers make formal contacts with parents through report cards and one yearly conference.

Evaluation

Appropriate Practice: No letter or numerical grades are given during the primary years. Grades are considered inadequate reflections of children's ongoing learning.

Inappropriate Practice: Grades are seen as important in motivating children to do their work.

Appropriate Practice: Each child's progress is assessed primarily through observation and recording at regular intervals. Results are used to improve and individualize instruction. No letter or number grades are given. Children are helped to understand and correct their errors.

Inappropriate Practice: Children are tested regularly on each subject. Graded tests are sent home or are filed after children see their grades. To ease children's stress caused by the emphasis placed on test scores, teachers "teach to the test."

Appropriate Practice: Children's progress is reported to parents in the form of narrative comments following an outline of topics. A child's progress is reported in comparison to his or her own previous performance and parents are given general information about how the child compares to standardized national averages.

Inappropriate Practice: Children's progress is reported to parents in letter or numerical grades. Emphasis is on how well the child compares to others in the same grade and to standardized national averages.

Appropriate Practice: Children are not "promoted" nor do they "fail." Because children progress through sequential curriculum at different paces, they are allowed to progress in all areas as they acquire competence. Retention is avoided because of its serious impact on children's self-esteem and the fact that the practice of retaining children in a grade for another year disproportionately affects male, minority, very young, and low-income children. The program is designed to serve the needs of the children; the children are not expected to change to fit the program.

Inappropriate Practice: Children repeat a grade or are placed in a special "transition" grade if they have not mastered the expected reading and math skills. It is assumed that their performance will improve with repetition or as they mature. Placement decisions are based on children's ability to sit still and complete paperwork, follow directions, and read at or near grade level.

Grouping and Staffing

Appropriate Practice: Size of classroom groups and ratio of adults to children is carefully regulated to allow active involvement of children and time for teachers to plan and prepare group projects that integrate learning and skills in many subject areas and relate to children's interests; to plan for and work with individual children having special needs or interests; to plan and work with parents; and to coordinate with other teachers, teams of specialists, and administrators involved in each child's school experience. Groups of 5-, 6-, 7-, and 8-year-olds are no larger than 25 with 2 adults, one of whom may be a paraprofessional, or no larger than 15 to 18 with one teacher.

Inappropriate Practice: Groups of 25 to 35 children with one teacher are considered acceptable because they are economical and possible with strict scheduling and discipline, use of prepaced textbooks and workbooks, and devoting little attention to individual needs or interests, allowing minimal parent involvement, and allowing no time for coordination among teachers and specialists. Kindergarten teachers must teach a total of 50 or more children in separate morning and afternoon sessions without the assistance of a paraprofessional.

Appropriate Practice: Classroom groups vary in size and composition depending on children's needs. Some groups consist mostly of 5- and 6-year-olds or 6- and 7-year-olds, while others span 3 chronological years (5-, 6-, and 7-year-olds or 6-, 7-, and 8-year-olds) or are composed mainly of same-age children. Children are placed where it is expected that they will do their best, which may be in a family grouping and which is more likely to be determined by developmental than by chronological age. Persistent difficulties of individual children are handled in small groups with more intensive help and the composition of these groups is flexible and temporary.

Inappropriate Practice: Classrooms consist of 25 to 35 children without opportunity for teachers to place children in smaller classes when needed (except children diagnosed as eligible for special or remedial education). Children are grouped by chronological age whenever possible, although inconsistencies arise due to dates of birth and the retention of some children. Children are tracked into homogeneous groups according to ability level.

Appropriate Practice: Five- through 8-year-old children are assigned a primary teacher and remain in relatively small groups of 15 to 25 because so much of their learning and development is integrated and cannot be divided into specialized subjects to be taught by special teachers. Specialists assist the primary adult with special projects, questions, and materials.

Inappropriate Practice: Departmentalized settings and groups of 80 or more children with a team of teachers are common. Teachers teach their special areas of interest and what they know best in isolation from one another and children rotate among different teachers.

Appropriate Practice: Care is taken to integrate special needs children into the mainstream classroom socially as well as physically. Care is taken to avoid isolating special needs children in a segregated classroom or pulling them out of a regular classroom so often as to disrupt continuity and undermine their feeling of belonging to the group.

Inappropriate Practice: Special needs children are nominally assigned to a regular class, but almost all their instruction occurs with special teachers elsewhere in the building. These children have only a vague sense of what is happening in their regular classroom and the classroom teacher spends little time with them because she assumes they are getting intensive treatment from the special education teacher. Special needs children may be seated together in a designated area of their regular classroom.

Teacher Qualifications

Appropriate Practice: Teachers are qualified to work with 5- through 8-year-olds through Early Childhood Education degree programs or Elementary Education degree programs with a specialty in Early Childhood Education that includes supervised field experience with this age group and required coursework in child development and how children learn, in integrated curriculum and instructional strategies, and in communication with families.

Inappropriate Practice: Elementary or secondary teachers with no specialized training or field experience working with 5- through 8-year-olds are considered qualified because they are state certified regardless of the grade level for which their coursework prepared them.

Appropriate Practice: Ongoing professional development opportunities are provided for primary grade teachers to ensure developmentally appropriate curriculum and instruction and to help teachers become more competent, confident, and creative.

Inappropriate Practice: Teachers participate in continuing professional development to maintain certification although development opportunities are not necessarily related to the primary age group.

Before- and After-School Care

Appropriate Practice: The before- or after-school program is staffed by people trained in early childhood education, child development, and/or recreation. The program offers a wide variety of choices for children (including nutritious snacks) and features private areas, good books, sports, expeditions, clubs, and many home activities like cooking and woodworking. Children may do homework for a short period of time if they choose.

Inappropriate Practice: The before- and after-school program is staffed by unqualified persons with little or no training in child development or recreation. The before- or after-school program is operated as an extension of the structured school day with children expected to do homework or occupy themselves with paper-and-pencil activities OR the program is considered babysitting and children are warehoused in large groups with few available materials.

Transitions

Appropriate Practice: Children are assisted in making smooth transitions between groups or programs throughout the day by teachers who provide program continuity, maintain ongoing communication, prepare children for the transition, involve parents, and minimize the number of transitions necessary.

Inappropriate Practice: A child's day is fragmented among many different groups and programs with little attempt by adults to communicate or coordinate successful transitions.

PART FOUR

Teaching Young Children

Chapter 8 Teacher Preparation and Development 185

Chapter 9 Observation and Assessment 211

Chapter 10 Parenting 246

CHAPTER 8 Teacher Preparation and Development

8.1 SUSAN E. BLOW

Kindergarten Education

Susan E. Blow (1843–1916) was the director of the first public school kindergarten, established in 1873 in St. Louis, Missouri. Her work and writing were greatly influenced by German educator Friedrich Froebel's methods of involving children with materials that appeal to their nature and lead to self-activity. From her study with Froebel in Germany, Blow came to believe that just as knowledge is presented, moving the child from perception to intelligence, so is moral truth, moving the child from intuition to comprehension. Froebel and Blow placed emphasis on a deeper, more spiritual side of the development of the child. Blow called it "double development."

Under Blow's kindergarten program, activities were to be both reflective and productive, demanding that teachers pay close attention to ways children use materials to transform and create. To prepare for Froebel's methods, teachers would study the child, and the kindergarten would be the university. This was a radical change from traditional teacher training of the time. Shortly after establishing the kindergarten, Blow opened the first training school for teachers.

Blow wrote a monograph entitled "Kindergarten Education" for the U.S. exhibit at the Paris Exposition of 1900 to inform people of the changes taking place in kindergarten and teacher preparation across America. She

186

*Chapter 8
Teacher
Preparation
and
Development*

wrote of her frustration that kindergarten was either regressing into a "mere" play school or moving dangerously close to the primary school, and that teacher education was eroding. She seemed to disregard the flood of new scientific data from the child study movement that was changing kindergarten philosophy from pedagogical mysticism to pragmatism.

As you read the following selection from "Kindergarten Education," which was published in Nicholas Murray Butler, ed., *Education in the United States* (J. B. Lyon, 1900), keep in mind that Blow refers to teachers (not students) as "kindergarteners."

*I*t is greatly to be desired that all cities establishing kindergartens in connection with their public schools, should insist upon having a specially qualified supervisor. Without watchful and intelligent guidance the kindergarten tends either to relapse into a mere play school or to become too closely conformed to the primary school. The ideal supervisor stands to the individual kindergartener in a relation similar to that which the latter occupies toward her children. She quickens their intellectual and moral aspiration, deepens in them the complementary impulses of self-culture and child-nurture, points out practical errors and suggests the ways and means of overcoming them. She must thoroughly understand the method of the kindergarten, its psychologic implications and its relationship to education as a whole. She must unite intellectual insight with moral earnestness and practical sagacity. Hence only the most gifted and illuminated kindergartners are adequate to the work of supervision.

Two great dangers assail the kindergarten and threaten to impede its progress towards the realization of Froebel's ideal. The first of these dangers is reversion to instinctive games and traditional toys. In some kindergartens, children are taught to play street games, while it has recently been urged that "peg boards, tops, bean bags, kites, dolls, jackstraws, hoops, spool, chalk and wire games and the whole toy world" should be added to the Froebelian instrumentalities. Tendencies such as these indicate a complete failure to comprehend what Froebel has done. He recognized in traditional games the deposit of unconscious reason; preserved what was good and omitted what was crude and coarse in these products of instinct; supplied missing links and presented a series of games wherein each is related to all the others and which, by means of dramatic and graphic representation, poetry and music, win for the ideals they embody a controlling power over the imagination. In like manner, from among traditional toys he selected those which possessed most educative value, ordered them into a related series and suggested a method by which they might be consciously used to interpret the child's experiences and develop his creative power. If this transfiguration of traditional games and toys is valueless, then the kindergarten has no *raison d'etre*. But if Froebel has translated the hieroglyphic of instinctive play and found means which, without detriment to the child's spontaneity, influence the growth of character and the trend of thought, then the clamor for street games and promiscuous toys is educational atavism.

The second danger which threatens the integrity of the kindergarten is the substitution of exercises which attempt to wind thought around some arbitrarily chosen center for those Froebelian exercises whose confessed aim is to assist thought to unwind itself. Too many kindergartners have allowed themselves to be betrayed into selecting some object such as a pine tree or a potato, and making all songs, games, stories and gift exercises revolve around it. Between these so-called cores of interest and the exercises clustered around them there is no valid connection. The clustering like the subject depends wholly upon the caprice of the teacher. Could such exercises succeed in their object, the pupils of different teachers would have their thoughts set to revolving around different centers and more than this around arbitrary and contingent centers. That such a procedure directly contradicts Froebel's ideal will be apparent to all who have understood his writings. That it likewise contradicts every true ideal of education will be evident to all who understand that the function of education is to substitute objective and universal for subjective and contingent associations. The discovery of related qualities in nature, the disclosure of their causes and the reduction of these causes to a system is the great work of science. The discovery of the related activities of mind and their genetic evolution is the work of psychology. The portrayal of the universal and divine man latent in each individual is the supreme achievement of literature and art. To lead pupils away from what is capricious, arbitrary and accidental, and thus capacitate them to receive and augment their scientific, aesthetic, literary and psychologic inheritance is the great duty of education. The substitution of arbitrary for necessary cores of thought wherever attempted is, therefore, the parody of education.

The future of the kindergarten in the United States is largely dependent upon the work of the normal schools for kindergarteners. The friends of the system must, therefore, view with disapprobation and even with dismay the rapid multiplication of schools with low standards of admission and a low conception of the training they should give. Inexperienced students are attracted to such schools, and the result is that the whole country is flooded with so-called kindergartners who are ignorant of the first principles of all true education.

In the early days of the Froebelian movement it was believed that in a single year young girls could be prepared to conduct a kindergarten. In most reputable training schools the course has now been extended to cover two years. The requirements for admission into these schools are, generally, graduation from a high school, or an education equivalent thereto. The courses of study include theory of the kindergarten gifts and occupations, study of the Mother Play, practice in songs and games, physical culture, lessons in singing, drawing, modeling and color, lectures on the art of story telling, and more or less observation of the practical work of the kindergarten. Finally, some trainers insist that their normal pupils shall not only observe but assist in actual work with the children.

In addition to this specific training, the best normal schools offer courses in science, literature, psychology, and the history of education.

188

*Chapter 8
Teacher
Preparation
and
Development*

Prominent among private training schools are those of Miss Garland, Miss Symonds, Miss Wheelock and Miss Page in Boston; that of Mme. Kraus-Boelte in New York; that conducted by Miss H. A. Niel in Washington, in connection with the work, established and sustained by Mrs. Phoebe A. Hearst, and that of the Kindergarten institute of Chicago, which is co-operative with the social settlement work in that city. Conspicuous among normal departments conducted under the auspices of kindergarten associations, is the training school of Miss C. M. C. Hart in Baltimore, which, in addition to a two years' course for kindergartners, offers a fine post-graduate course, and a course preparatory for normal work. Other training schools connected with kindergarten associations are the normal departments of the Froebel association, and the Free kindergarten association of Chicago, and the training schools conducted under the auspices of the Louisville and Golden Gate associations.

Kindergarten departments have been established in several great *quasi*-public institutions. Among the most notable of these are the kindergarten department of Pratt institute, Brooklyn, and of Teachers college, Columbia university, and of Workingman's institute, New York.

Of the 164 public normal schools in the United States 36 provide some kind of kindergarten training, the courses varying in length from about two years to six months. . . .

The public normal schools whose kindergartens are most worthy of mention are those of Boston and Philadelphia. In general, however, the kindergarten work in public normal schools is inferior to that of private training schools, kindergarten associations and the great institutions to which reference has been made above.

Kindergartners are admitted to surpass all other teachers as students of educational literature. They are also distinguishing themselves by zealous and persistent attendance upon post-graduate courses in pedagogics, science, literature, history and psychology. Between the years 1880 and 1888 large numbers of St. Louis kindergartners participated in classes organized during successive winters for the study of Herodotus, Thucydides, Sophocles, Homer, Dante and Goethe. They also followed lecture courses in psychology and philosophy, and constantly attended classes devoted to the deeper study of Froebel's educational principles and the illustration of his method. Through the efforts of the Chicago kindergarten college post-graduate work of a high order has become a feature of Froebelian activity in that city, and for many years there has been conducted each winter a literary school whose lecturers are recognized as the greatest interpreters in America of the supreme works of literature. During successive winters Miss Laura Fisher, director of the public school kindergartens of Boston, has organized post-graduate classes in the study of the Mother Play and the Pedagogics for the Kindergarten and has also conducted valuable courses in literature and psychology. Through the efforts of Miss C. P. Dozier, supervisor of the New York kindergarten association, and Miss Mary D. Runyan, head of the kindergarten department of Teachers college, Columbia university, post-graduate work has been organized in New York city. Classes in psychology, literature and the philosophy of history are conducted by Miss Hart in Baltimore, and courses in literature and psychology are already given in connection with the young but flourishing work of Miss Niel in Washington. In Philadelphia, Pittsburgh, Buffalo and other cities post-graduate work is less developed, but good beginnings have been made.

The power of the kindergarten over the minds of its students arises from the fact that it connects the ideal of self-culture with the ideal of child-nurture. The true woman does not wish to "deck herself with knowledge as with a garment, or to wear it loose from the nerves and blood that feed her action." Therefore, she responds with whole heart to the appeal to learn all she can, be all she can, and devote all she is and all she knows to the service of childhood.

Rooted in maternal impulses it would be strange indeed if the kindergarten did not appeal to mothers. That classes for mothers should come into existence was a predestined phase of the Froebelian movement. Whoever has studied the writings of Froebel knows that the education of mothers was one of the most important features of his endeavor. Practically, however, the work in this direction amounted to very little until a mothers' department was established in that unique institution, the Chicago kindergarten college. I call this institution unique because it has consciously attempted the transformation of the girls' college into a school for motherhood. The colleges for men offer many different courses. Why should not the colleges for women offer at least elective courses in subjects fitting their students for the vocation of mother and home maker? Why should not the study of Froebel's Mother Play, the use of kindergarten gifts and the practice of kindergarten games be made one of these elective courses? Why should not all institutions which ignore the mission of woman as nurturer be supplanted by institutions like the Chicago kindergarten college, which, while giving general culture, make it their supreme aim to fit women for the work, which, if there be any meaning in the process of natural evolution, is theirs by divine appointment? And, finally, why should not such institutions give instruction not only to young girls but to mothers themselves? During the single year 1891–92 the mothers' department of the Chicago college gave instruction to 725 mothers. In the eight years since its foundation it has given whole or partial courses to nearly five thousand mothers. The effects of such instruction in enhancing the sanctity and uplifting the ideals of family life can hardly be exaggerated. Recently the work of this department has been extended by holding convocations for the discussion of all phases of child-nurture. Four of such convocations have already been held, each of which had nine sessions of from two to two and one-half hours in length. The attendance was from three to five thousand persons.

While the maternal ideal is dominant in the Chicago college it is not exclusive. This organization supports a number of kindergartens wherein students learn to apply Froebelian principles. It has departments for kindergarteners, kindergarten trainers and primary teachers. It has also departments of literature and publication and a philanthropic department, these several departments being all in the hands of competent specialists. Finally, it has developed and extended the literary and historic courses begun in St. Louis and by adding courses in science and art has connected the kindergarten with the total round of man's spiritual activity.

Radiating from the kindergarten college as its center the maternal movement is spreading throughout the United States. It is the highest reach of the

190

*Chapter 8
Teacher
Preparation
and
Development*

Froebelian ideal and means nothing more nor less than the attempted regeneration of all human life through the regeneration of the family.

Froebel's supreme claim to our grateful remembrance rests upon the fact that consciously repeating the unconscious process of social evolution he set the little child in front of the great army of advancing humanity. Science affirms that the feebleness of infancy created the family and that from the family have been evolved the higher institutions. "Without the circumstances of infancy," writes one of our leading scientists, "we might have become formidable through sheer force of sharpwittedness. But except for these circumstances we should never have comprehended the meaning of such phrases as self-sacrifice or devotion. The phenomena of social life would have been omitted from the history of the world and with them the phenomena of ethics and religion." In his cry, "Come, let us live for the children," Froebel utters in articulate speech the ideal whose unconscious impulsion set in motion the drama of human history. The little child was pioneer of the process which created human institutions. We must make him the pioneer of their perfection.

8.2 MARGARET McMILLAN

The Training of the Teachers

"Others are going to teach a big girl history or a big boy Latin. [The nursery school teacher] is going to modify or determine the structure of brain centres." In light of the most recent science of the brain, which is capable of catching the mind in the very act of thinking, Margaret McMillan's statement in 1919 was prophetic.

McMillan (1860–1931) began her London nursery school in 1914, a time when psychoanalysis, mental hygiene, and child psychology were newly developing fields. The speech center of the brain had recently been identified, making intensive investigation of the way children learn possible. Economic conditions in London were abysmal for poor people, and many young children were living in the streets, orphaned or abandoned. Medical care for newborns and infants was just coming into existence. Teaching was rapidly evolving in conjunction with these societal changes.

The following selection is from *The Nursery School* (E. P. Dutton, 1919), McMillan's account of the open-air school and training center she established with her sister Rachel. Their method of teacher preparation began with student-teachers working in every section of the nursery so that everything learned would be "big with meaning." Although *The Nursery School* is written in a stream-of-consciousness style, it conveys the significance of this urban nursery experiment. McMillan believes that new societal circumstances require new environments for the youngest children and new ways of teaching.

Not long ago it was held by most people that any nice motherly girl would do as a nurse for little children. The well-to-do classes believed this, so they engaged a good motherly woman, who in some cases turned out very well, because she had some natural gifts. Often a young woman of humble education was taken on as a nurse, and a great deal of mischief was done in a quiet way, mischief that no future education would ever really undo. As for the working-class mothers and fathers, their children were left to them altogether, and without help or hindrance they did what they could. Parental love was believed by even great thinkers like Herbert Spencer to be a tremendous safe-

192

*Chapter 8
Teacher
Preparation
and
Development*

guard. Without discussing the rightness or wrongness of these views, we can now open the records or reports of the Chief Medical Officer of the Board of Education and others. It is sad to learn that in some districts a fifth or more of all the children born, die in early childhood. Many of the survivors are to be seen in our new school clinics, and the records of the doctors and nurses all tell one tale. The *causes* that killed so many do not spare the children who appear to escape. They are maimed and weakened. Above all, the work of the Open Air Nursery-School has flung over the evil results of bad environment a pitilessly searching light.

We compare our regular attendants of years standing in the Nursery with the newcomers, and with the average child of the district. Then the truth cannot be gainsaid. The Nursery child has a fairly good physique. Not only do his neighbours in the slum fall far short of him: his "betters" in good districts, the middle-class children, of a very good type, fall short of him. It is clear that something more than parental love and "parental responsibility" are wanted. Rules of thumb have all broken down. "Parental love" without knowledge has broken down. Child nurture has not broken down. It is very highly skilled work. Here and there on the world's surface comparatively good results may be had indeed, even in poor districts. Connemara mothers may do more to keep down infant mortality than a finely-equipped clinic and a brace of medical officers of health in Bradford. These good results are due to natural feeding to start with, and life in the open with simple diet to go on with. These things depend not on choice, but on accident. They prove that in some places it is difficult to go very far and very fatally wrong! In most places it is only too easy to go fatally wrong, and that is why our children's death-rate is still so high.

If "Parental responsibility" is limited by the degree of intelligence a parent has or has not, the responsibility of a "nice motherly girl" is limited in the same way. Certainly we did not at first realise how large and varied should be the equipment of people who aspire to give real nurture to children under seven. That had to be learned gradually, now we know that the help, not of one, but of various specialists is needed. Also that in no other trade or profession is every kind of *real* skill and vision so useful as in this work. Our results in this camp are said to be wonderful. They do not come without any kind of effort. There is nothing occult about them, but they mean labour of every kind. They can be won for the millions of young children in every land and district. Many workers will have to co-operate. Dentists and (at first) doctors, specialists, trained teachers, and mothers will have to co-operate. At last out of all their help and striving will come the new and beautiful thing that is going to change the face of the world.

So there is need, first of all, of training. What kind of training? Are we to turn to Spencer or Herbart, Froebel or Séguin? Who is to be the supreme guide and teacher? We answer, "All of these," in the sense that we may learn something from each. None of these in the sense we should follow any of them blindly. Our task is new. It has never before been attempted. The arts our new teachers have to learn are not so much as named in any scheme or almost in any syllabus of to-day.

All the examinations of our leading societies, their diplomas and certificates and distinctions, steer clear of problems we have to face. All the teachings of the greatest men and women halt long before they come abreast of our needs. Therefore we have to do our own research work.

Sensing the trouble all round them, vaguely conscious of new demands made on them, teachers stand to-day in a kind of dream. Many fall back on old cries. "We are not going to be nurses," say many voices. "Why should we go far in any subject but child care, if we are only going into nursery-schools?" ask others. Before each we stand to-day with a new gospel. These cries as of wanderers emerging suddenly in a cloudy place call for guidance. We must not be afraid of seeking, or of telling what we know.

Most of our children are ill. Many are half-alive. That did not matter yesterday. There was no Nursery-School legislation, and no new desire to give nurture. Mr. Forster's Bill of 1871 set out to give us a people who can read. This was done. Most people can read nowadays. The new Bill goes farther. The new Bill in effect says, "Most people, all people at least must have nurture," which is the beginning of culture. The teachers stand a little aghast. This nurture is very well, but it is not their business. Not their business! Then nothing of the greatest things, the removal of disease and vice and dullness, is their business! They are not going on then to lead us, but only to find a simplified way of spelling? And we have just discovered that it is not only their business, but that all they have learned and done has prepared them to give nurture. The teacher of little children is not merely giving lessons. She is helping to make a brain and nervous system, and this work which is going to determine all that comes after, requires a finer perception and a wider training and outlook than is needed by any other kind of teacher.

Others are going to teach a big girl history or a big boy Latin. *She* is going to modify or determine the structure of brain centres.

So we had first of all to work out a new art in the only way possible, that is by taking on new tasks and doing them with a new motive. We took young girls and some older girls also who were already certificated teachers, and said to them. "Forget that you were teachers, forget even that you are students, and try to help these children." The little ones were delicate. Many were dirty. All had more or less bad habits in diet and behaviour, and everyone went home at night to its parents. These teachers who were now nurses had many things to learn that are not taught in training colleges. They had to bathe and dress, to feed and take care of the children. They did all this as the nurses had never done it. Their work was, as we say, "blessed." They began to teach, not writing, but washing, not art, but how to use one's hand, and lo! this was true education. This was not merely service, but the means for research.

Perhaps it would be well to dwell on this success a little. We were reminded of it at once when, after a year's work, our students went back to books and paint-boxes, and the usual work of students. Teachers better trained and better educated in many ways took their places. The school fell off at once. The nose-drills ceased, and the hair was not so pretty. The school became a poor school. Again the children were poor children, they matched the poor walls instead of glowing like flowers in a cottage garden. On the other hand, the teachers who had served, began to teach the three R's with great success. One of these, not very well qualified, excelled all the others in her results. Why? We do not know. But should we now go back to the old order. Oh no! We

194

*Chapter 8
Teacher
Preparation
and
Development*

had found a better one! There was something lacking in the training of yesterday and having caught a glimpse of better things one could not go back. We must take the culture-work of yesterday and give it a new foundation.

Séguin, our greatest modern teacher, learned by teaching defective children. They opened to him the doors of new truth. Our teachers go back to the poorest class of child and serve him. Into dark homes they go doing work that is new to them, and lo! this work opens new doors to them, and they see what was hid from them in former days and in more "cultured" places.

There is no risk in these visits, for the whole adult population is friendly, and the nursery holds them by strong ties through the love both places have in common for their children. Yet the first wave of new experience is new and startling. There are mothers who drink and fight and stay out late, so that the little ones are locked out.

Teddy's mother was one of these. She lives in a cellar, and neglects him for long spells, when she is out "enjoying" herself. Yet she is suggestible, and our Miss S. has got a hold of her somehow, through her goodness to Teddy. Miss S. dives into the cellar and makes a glow there with her soft fresh face and bright uniform. "You do look a posy coming in," says the heavy-eyed woman in the gloom. "You make me think of the country." And after a few weeks Teddy makes her think of the country every evening, when he comes back all fresh and rosy from the nursery. Our Miss S. has rigged up a cheap apparatus for heating water in the cellar and she has got Teddy's mother to give him his bath at the week-end, and to wash his home-clothes, and send him in bright and sweet on a Monday morning. She has done this for other children, and she has done it by getting friendly with mothers.

Full of resource is this "lass from Lancashire." She encourages a kind of rivalry in the matter of clothes and hair-dressing. "Patience was so spotless to-day that she did not have a bath!" "Rosy was a picture this morning when she came in at the gate!" And she describes Rosy. Perhaps it would be trivial to write down all that she says and does, but the result of it all is not trivial. It is to be found in a troop of little children who lighten up the streets like a posy, and who make the idle men standing at the corner gaze at them with a wistful, half-stupefied air, as if a waft of something new and long forgotten had come down the air. It is Miss S.'s glory to see them turn in at the gate looking as fair and fit as any children of the best suburbs. To send them out looking so fair is a triumph. To see them come in so fair and so sweet, is a greater triumph.

The week-end falling away has to be tackled in nearly every case. At first nearly all the children used to come in on Monday morning with the digestive system all upset. Teddy's mother did not relate all this to anything she had given him to eat on Sunday. In a friendly visit one can tackle this question and settle it, if only the friendship is real and strong enough. Teddy's mother will do almost anything for our Miss S.

Some of the children of our school were nearly always heavy-eyed and weary. They had short and troubled nights in crowded and foetid rooms. Adored and lovely toddlers were cherished all day! How did they fare at night?

"I heard Tommy crying last night in the street. It was eleven o'clock, dark and cold, and I heard his voice in the street," said Tommy's nurse.

In this case also nothing is much use except the magic touch of a new friendship. Under it miracles can be wrought; the dirty staircase and poor rooms can be cleaned up, and a corner found for a little bed. Even if there is noise all round his bed it may be screened from glaring light, and Tommy may be placed in it at eight o'clock. Some children began to come in bright-eyed of a morning and without any gross signs of wrong feeding.

Our students have to know their new neighbours. They have to get some idea of housing, of the cost of food, and the needs of a family who live always on the brink of a financial precipice! They must not turn their eyes away from the horrors of a bad neighbourhood, just as a nurse may not flinch near the battle-front or in the hospital. They are quite safe in a slum as they would be in Belgravia—in fact, a great deal safer. This we have proved by experience, and by the fact that we have slept and still sleep with open doors in the heart of a so-called "bad" neighbourhood. But the grim street, the public-house, and pawnshop area, the drunkenness, the cruel rack-renting, the epidemics and high death-rate concern the teachers just as bombs and gangrene and broken limbs concern the nurse in a war hospital.

The Disadvantaged Child

Behind the phrase "self-fulfilling prophecy" is the idea that one person's expectations can affect another's behavior. Self-fulfilling prophecy is not limited to teaching, for it takes place in everyday life. For example, work quotas established on the job can make employees tense and less likely to reach them. Or when hospital staff are led to believe a new drug has been introduced in patient treatment, they may assess it as very effective, even though it is actually a placebo (an inactive substance).

When self-fulfilling prophecy refers to education, it often involves a teacher's expectation of students' intellectual abilities. The students who are expected to perform competently do so, while those who are expected to perform incompetently tend to do poor work.

Robert Rosenthal and Lenore Jacobson studied the results of teacher expectations on "educationally disadvantaged" children and concluded that the sources of disadvantages are not all economic, social, cultural, or linguistic. Teacher attitudes and reactions can also contribute to children's lack of success. How children are treated, based on their appearance, their family origin, or their behavior, translates into their performance. Rosenthal and Jacobson discuss their findings in the following selection from *Pygmalion in the Classroom: Teacher Expectation and Pupils' Intellectual Development* (Holt, Rinehart & Winston, 1968).

How teachers interact with children to cause some to bloom and some to wither is subtle and complex. Results of experimental studies conducted since self-fulfilling prophecy was first applied to teaching in the 1960s have been mixed. Newer research, which focuses on brain chemistry, multiple intelligences, and inclusion strategies, attends to the learner almost exclusively. The teacher is not viewed as a potent variable in the teaching-learning setting.

*I*t is usually in September that school opens, and thousands of near-six-year-olds from every conceivable kind of home start first grade. It is an anxious

time for them, a mixture of uncertainty and excitement, confused with antici-
patory feelings. "Will the teacher like me? When will I learn to read? Will she
like *me?*"

Entering the first-grade classroom is a big step for a child. It can be a
glowing or a devastating experience. The teacher smiles at the children, looking at them to see what the year will bring. The well-groomed white boys and
girls will probably do well. The black- and brown-skinned ones are lower-class
and will have learning problems unless they look exceptionally clean. All the
whites who do not look tidy and need handkerchiefs will have trouble. If the
teacher sees a preponderance of lower-class children, regardless of color, she
knows her work will be difficult and unsatisfying. The teacher wants her children to learn, all of them, but she knows that lower-class children do not do
well in school, just as she knows that middle-class children do do well. All this
she knows as she smiles at her class for the first time, welcoming them to the
adventure of first grade, measuring them for success or failure against the
yardstick of middle-classness. The children smile back at her, unaware as yet
that the first measurements have been taken. The yardstick will be used again
when they speak to her, as she hears words spoken clearly or snuffled or
stammered or spoken with an accent. And later they will be measured for
readiness for reading or intelligence. Many times that first year the children
will be examined for what they are, for what they bring with them when they
come to school.

Down the hall, the second-grade teacher knows that most of *her* lower-
class students are behind those of the middle class. All through the schools that
first day in September the teachers look at their classes and know which children will and will not do well during the year. Sometimes the results of formal
and informal measurement modify that first day's perception; a dirty child
may be very bright, a brown child may learn rapidly, a black child may read
like an angel, a tidy middle-class child may be hopelessly dull. Sometimes.
Usually, the teacher is right when she predicts that middle-class children generally succeed in school and lower-class children generally lag behind and eventually fail.

THE DISADVANTAGE OF POVERTY

Currently attention has focused glaringly upon the educationally disadvantaged children in our schools, spotlighting their scanty experience with formal
language, ignorance of school culture and concomitant poor school achievement. Numerous reports indicate that the IQ scores of disadvantaged children
are lower than those of middle-class children, their reading is substandard,
their attitudes are negative, and their behavior is annoying to teachers (Becker,
1952; B. Clark, 1962; David and Dollard, 1940; Sexton, 1961). Disadvantaged
children by definition come from lower socioeconomic groups where low income is married to values alien to the school culture. A larger proportion of
disadvantaged children than middle-class children are failing in school.

Havighurst, who refers to the children as socially disadvantaged, predicts
that American schools will spend the next ten years in a "prodigious attempt to

198

*Chapter 8
Teacher
Preparation
and
Development*

wipe out the social disadvantage that has prevented some fifteen percent of our children from learning anything useful in school . . . and this means some thirty percent of children in the low-income sections of our big cities" (Havighurst, 1965, p. 31). The U. S. Department of Health, Education, and Welfare is encouraging this effort through making available vast sums of money for schools in low-income attendance areas. This resulted from the Elementary and Secondary Education Act of 1965, Title I, which "places the major emphasis of this new law on meeting the special needs of educationally deprived children through the largest federal grant program ever authorized for such a task" (U.S. Office of Education, 1965).

The generally low educational achievement of lower-class children has caused consternation on the federal level because of the close tie between education and the development of talent, and talent gets top place in the marketplace today. Technological innovations and international political crises demand educated manpower, which means that those disadvantaged children who have not benefited from schooling represent a waste of future national skilled manpower.

There has been in the past few years an almost overwhelming amount of literature describing the educationally disadvantaged learner, his home, family, neighborhood, and teachers, as well as the frustrations he encounters in the process of learning in the climate of a middle-class school. The sources of the disadvantages variously have been laid to economic, social, cultural, and/or linguistic factors, depending upon the orientation of the writer. Here we can only touch on some of the factors implicated.

Income and School Success

Sexton's (1961) study on the relation between income and educational opportunity revealed that where the average family income exceeded $7000, achievement was above grade level; and where the income was below $7000, achievement was below grade level. Apparently, poor achievement is cumulative; that is, by grade eight, the lowest-income students were at least two years behind the highest-income students, a fact that confirmed Becker's (1952) widening gap, as well as being in accord with Kahl's (1961) findings that "common man" boys performed at much lower levels than high-status boys of equal intelligence by the time they were ready for grade nine, even though the boys had achieved similarly in their early school years.

Sexton found further differentiation between income groups in "Big City's" gifted-child program: out of 436 students selected for the program, not one came from an income group below $5000, whereas 148 were selected from the above $9000 group.

Achievement Training

Research in the area of achievement motivation points out that there are class and cultural differences in family training for achievement (McClelland,

1961), differences that may cause conflict when the child attends school where middle-class values are emphasized. It is known that middle-class children, notorious for their competitiveness, have been encouraged to achieve since diaper days because the child-rearing practices of American middle-class families radiate about the concept of achievement. Children from subcultures that have a similar achievement orientation also find the school culture familiar and nurturing (Rosen, 1959; Strodtbeck, 1961). Florence Kluckhohn's (1953) value orientations show a modal profile of the dominant American who is trained at home for an activity culture with emphasis on values that lead to an achieving personality. "A child who has not acquired these particular value orientations in his home and community is not so likely to compete successfully with youngsters among whom these values are implicitly taken for granted" (Cloward and Jones, 1963, pp. 193–194).

Impoverished Training

Another theoretical explanation for the failure of the disadvantaged child is also based on family training, or, rather, the lack of it. Some writers postulate that the type of language spoken in lower-class families causes difficulty in children's learning at school. Working-class families use a restricted form of language whereas middle-class families use a more elaborate form. Bernstein (1960) believes that this difficulty is likely to increase as the child goes through school unless he learns the middle-class language used in the school. Loban (1964), in identifying deviations from standard English among children, found a consistent relationship between social class and communication facility.

Social-class elements other than language also appear to affect learning. Deutsch (1963) states that lower-class children have not learned to "pay attention." Their habits of seeing, hearing, and listening have not been trained in the family situation. The middle-class child, conversely, is encouraged from babyhood in discrimination of sound, sight, and judgment, all of which constitute reading readiness.

POVERTY PROGRAMS

The findings are extensive on the disparity between middle-class and lower-class children in school performance and tested ability. In fact, the relationship of school success to social-class status has been confirmed to the extent that it may be regarded as "empirical law" (Charters, 1963, pp. 739–740). Educators, in current attempts to make this relationship historical, are establishing experimental programs to increase the educational opportunity for lower-class children—with pressure for action being levered by federal agencies. The United States Office of Education has sponsored programs for the educationally disadvantaged over the past few years. And the Elementary and Secondary Education Act signed by President [Lyndon B.] Johnson in April 1965 focused an even

200

*Chapter 8
Teacher
Preparation
and
Development*

larger spotlight on the disadvantaged children in the United States when it authorized, under Title I, over one billion dollars for them for 1966.

Faced with the chance to upgrade achievement for poverty-pocket children at federal expense, schools have been formulating programs subject to agency approval. Many of the programs are longitudinal in structure so that findings will not be conclusive for a while. Ultimate goals appear to be in accord: increase of educational opportunity through improved self-image, potential, and aspiration. The programs seem most fundamentally to be attempts to overcome learning handicaps by means of acting on the child—remedial reading, counseling and guidance, cultural experiences, parental involvement, and health and welfare services. These programs are constructed to emphasize deficiencies within the child and the home, and they are all compensatory approaches (see Wrightstone, McClelland, Krugman, Hoffman, Tieman, and Young, undated). Apparently, the varied research findings have been interpreted to mean that the disadvantaged child is somehow deficient, and that educators should be concerned about his impoverished early training and his subculturally determined differences in achievement orientation.

The premises for these expensive, special programs contain only some suggestion that the school itself may be harboring deficiencies. The premises too rarely suggest that teacher attitudes and behavior might be contributing factors to pupil failure. And yet, teacher reaction to lower-class children may well be intertwined inextricably in their lack of success.

TEACHER VARIABLES

To say that the role of the teacher has been neglected in programs for the disadvantaged child is not to say that the teacher has been neglected by either theory or research. As will be seen from the dates of their publications, good theory was written and good research conducted even long before it was fashionable and advantageous to be concerned with the disadvantaged. Becker (1952) for example, found in his Chicago studies that teachers in slum schools use different techniques that do teachers in middle-class schools, teachers and administrators expect less from lower-class children, the gap in learning widens through the grades, teachers are offended by the attitudes and hygiene of the children, and teachers transfer to "better" schools as soon as they can. Similar findings were presented even earlier by Davis and Dollard (1940) who analyzed the operation of social-class standards in the classroom and found that the lower-class child is punished for what he is; and they found that "he is stigmatized by teachers and their favored students on grounds of the 'ignorance' of his parents, the dialect which he speaks, the appearance of his clothes, and, very likely, the darkness of his skin" (Davis and Dollard, 1940, pp. 284–285). Warner, Havighurst, and Loeb (1944) presented findings of differential attitudes in the school toward persons in different positions in the social structure.

The important work of Deutsch (1963) and Wilson (1963) lent further support to the position taken by the earlier workers. Deutsch (1963) suggested that "It is in the school situation that the highly charged negative attitudes toward learning evolve" (p. 178), that the responsibility for disadvantagedness is the school's because the lower-class child learns his negative attitudes there. Wilson (1963) suggested after studying three socially stratified schools that the normalization of diverging standards by teachers is responsible to some degree for the divergence between aspirations and achievement among underprivileged youth; that is, that "variations in teachers' expectations and standards contribute to differences in pupil attainment and aspirations" (Passow, 1963, p. 183). Teachers in lower-class schools did not set standards as high as those in middle-class schools, nor were they as concerned with bringing their children up to grade level. Lower-strata children were overevaluated on the basis of tested performance, and high-strata children were underevaluated.

Burton Clark's (1962) reaction to Becker's findings also holds implications for the premises upon which poverty programs are built:

> The large and continuing growth of Negro and other dark-skin minority populations in northern cities makes teacher reaction a critical aspect of the education of minorities. The northern urban situation is one in which prejudice alone is not the major factor. It is a matter of the way in which the characteristics (other than skin color and race) of the minority child affect teachers and the operation of the schools. In an important sense, doing away with prejudice would not do away with the minority problem; for as long a sizable share of the children from culturally deprived and lower-class backgrounds are dirty, violent, and unmotivated—or appear so in the eyes of their teachers—the teachers are likely to handle them differently, teach them less, and want to escape. (p. 99)

Riessman (1965) expresses his concern through his teacher-training program "whose objective is the development of interest in and respect for low-income *culture*, as distinct from appreciating the difficulties of low income *environment*. The theory is that this will lead to an honest 'expect more and get more' from the children and their parents" (p. 16).

Riessman's primary argument appears to be that the disadvantaged child has been underestimated and that there are positive characteristics of lower socioeconomic groups, a stand that should be adopted as a "working hypothesis, a positive myth, because by so doing we can work *with* the underprivileged rather than *upon* them" (1962, p. 106).

These writers are in agreement about at least one formulation: children defined as disadvantaged are expected by their teachers to be unable to learn. Other writers and observers agree. In his paper entitled "Not Like Other Children," Bernard Asbell (1963) reports on his visits to schools and with teachers. *"Teachers everywhere I went seemed preoccupied with the idea of 'what to expect,' so seldom with what they might effect"* (p. 116).

Kvaraceus (1965) who discusses the programs for the disadvantaged as "programs of promise or pretense" maintains, "We must stop projecting failure for the disadvantaged. The HARYOU studies indicate a low performance expectancy on the part of teachers which acts as a self-fulfilling prophecy. Frequently teachers use psychological tools and tests to reinforce and justify their low predictions" (p. 30).

202

*Chapter 8
Teacher
Preparation
and
Development*

MacKinnon (1962) observed: "If our expectation is that a child of a given intelligence will not respond creatively to a task which confronts him, and especially if we make this expectation known to the child, the probability that he will respond creatively is very much reduced" (p. 493). The same position has been stated by Kenneth Clark (1963), Hillson and Myers (1963), Katz (1964), Rivlin (undated), and Rose (1956). Kenneth Clark speaks of the deprived child becoming "the victim of an educational self-fulfilling prophecy" (1963, p. 150). Perhaps the most detailed statement of this position is that made by the authors of *Youth in the Ghetto* [Harlem Youth Opportunities Unlimited, Inc., (HARYOU), 1964]: "When teachers and principals have a low opinion of the children's learning ability, the children seldom exceed those expectations" (p. 203). Effective poverty programs, the authors continue, "will come only from a firm belief and insistence that pupils *can* perform" (p. 244). Of their judgment of the central importance of teacher expectancy they say: "The whole weight of modern social science confirms this judgment" (p. 244). This statement means that modern social theorists often feel expectation variables to be important, but there is something more to social science than social theory, and this something more is evidence.

The evidence presented for the importance of the educational self-fulfilling prophecy was in the form of data to show that disadvantaged children fall further and further behind as they go from third to sixth grade. Data of that kind, although important to some purposes, are not enough to demonstrate the effects of teachers' expectancies. To be sure, teachers' self-fulfilling prophecies might have been responsible but so might a host of other factors.

From the theory and evidence presented so far, the most we can reasonably conclude is that disadvantaged children are not expected to do well in school. Now we need ask whether there is any good evidence that a teacher's expectations or prophecies made any difference in either her evaluation of her pupils or in their actual performance.

PUPIL EVALUATION

When certain things are known or believed about a pupil, other things about him, true things or not, are implied. That is nothing more than the so-called halo effect, and it is well illustrated by a recent experiment by Leonard Cahen (1966), who was interested in determining whether false information about pupils' aptitudes would influence teachers' scoring of pupils' tests. Each of 256 teachers-in-training was asked to score a new test of "learning readiness." Each was told that children who scored higher on reading tests and on IQ tests also scored higher on this new test. On the front of each of the test booklets the pupil's IQ and reading level were indicated. Sometimes these fictitious scores were high, sometimes low, Cahen's results showed clearly that when the teachers-in-training scored the tests of allegedly brighter children, they gave them much greater benefit of the doubt than when they scored the tests of allegedly duller children. When one "knows" a child is bright, his behavior is evaluated as of a higher intellectual quality than is the very same behavior shown by a child "known" to be dull. Such halo effects have also been shown to occur in the scoring of responses to individually administered standardized tests of intelligence for children (Sattler, Hillix, and Neher, 1967).

It has often been suggested that children from minority ethnic groups, particularly dark-skinned groups, are especially likely to suffer the disadvantages of unfavorable halo effects (HARYOU, 1964). A recent study by Jacobson (1966) serves as illustration.

Two groups of teachers were asked to rank a set of unknown children's photographs on their American or Mexican appearance. ("American" was not defined.) The teachers agreed highly on their rankings. Then these same groups of teachers were asked to rank in the same manner photographs of Mexican children who were unknown to one group but were students in the school of the other group of teachers. Here there was little agreement. The teachers at the school attended by the Mexican children saw those with higher IQs as looking more American. The significant correlation of IQ and appearance was present only where the IQ scores were available. Apparently, teachers agree in their perception of "Mexican-looking" until they know how a child tests, and then perception is changed.

This study provided further information related to disadvantaged children in the classroom. The highest achieving (in reading) Mexican children in grades one and two were seen by both teacher groups as looking significantly more Mexican. This correlation reversed itself in grades three and four, and still more so in grades five and six; that is, the highest achievers in the upper grades looked more American to both groups of teachers. The study presented the possibility that if a Mexican child looked more American (that is, Anglo-Saxon) to a teacher, academic expectations for him might be like expectations for middle-class children as compared to those for the Mexican child who looked more Mexican, or lower-class, with resultant differences in performance.

Teachers' evaluations of pupils are determined by many variables. Sometimes the teacher recognizes disadvantages and perhaps, sometimes, she creates them. An evaluation of a child, lowered or raised by halo effects, may lead to a specific expectation of performance which is communicated to the child who then may go on to fulfill the teacher's prophecy.

PUPIL PERFORMANCE

Teacher expectations of pupil performance can derive from more than the pupil's skin color, apparent affluence, or background information. One of the most important sources of teachers' expectations about their pupils' intellectual competence comes from standardized tests of intelligence and achievement (Deutsch, Fishman, Kogan, North, and Whiteman, 1964; Gibson, 1965; Goslin, 1966; Péquignot, 1966). Even when the administration of one of these tests is more or less appropriate and valid, the results may influence the teacher's prophecy about the child's subsequent intellectual performance. In a sense, that is the purpose of aptitude and ability testing, and the advantages and disadvantages of this purpose have been as much discussed in the popular

204

*Chapter 8
Teacher
Preparation
and
Development*

press as in the technical literature. Sometimes, however, there are special circumstances surrounding the administration of standardized tests of intelligence that throw into bolder relief the effects of test results on teachers' expectations. In such situations it may be suspected that the test results are not valid. Some examples of this type follow.

Tina was a small, mentally retarded child who spent two years in kindergarten and three in the first grade. She was tested annually because she was part of the class. Her last two scores from first grade gave her an IQ of over 140. She had memorized the preprimer and "read" it faultlessly. Her last first-grade teacher, college-fresh, until she learned of this, believed Tina to be her star pupil.

Billie, an average sixth-grade girl, in taking an achievement test for junior high school placement, used the wrong section on her IBM card and came out with a second-percentile score. The year before she had been absent for the achievement test. She was scheduled for classes for nonlearners in the new school and could not be changed until testing time at the end of the year. She spent the year, stone-faced, in her classes, and has since become a nonproductive truant.

Generally, one test will be considered along with others when children are to be placed in learning tracks or ability groups. Exceptions primarily arise during the first grade or when children transfer to a new school without former records. In kindergarten where children are first tested for IQ and first-grade placement, the cycle of expectancy may begin. High-spirited children often distract the teacher, causing a disturbance and their subsequent removal from class; frequently, the background required for taking placement tests (practicing making marks with a crayon, listening to directions, learning to turn the page, and so on) is not received. One such young man was Pedro—aggressive, bossy, boisterous, and unpredictable. Experimentally, the principal confided to his kindergarten teacher that Pedro showed all indications of being a leader. "Wasn't it marvelous to see a child today so unrestricted, a free spirit, uninhibited by middle-class artificialities?" "What would happen to this boy when he was assigned to a teacher who would seek to drain the joyousness away?" The teacher began to see Pedro in a new light, and Pedro, recognizing her approval, turned to her and became her best pupil that year. His self-pride was evident. Further, his test scores and her recommendations placed him in a top-level first grade where he continued enthusiastically through school, charming all of his teachers, the first in his large family to be an academic success.

One family came to an American school from Mexico, and the administrator, on a hunch, placed all four of the children in top-level, fast-moving classes, telling each teacher that each youngster was bright, and she need not worry that year about anything excepting encouragement in learning English. At the end of the year, the teachers asked the administrator to excuse the children from testing because their English, although fast-developing, was not sufficient for fair testing. All four children were recommended for continuance in top groups. At the end of the second year, the children scored in both intelligence and achievement where their classmates did, above average.

8.4 LILIAN G. KATZ

Developmental Stages of Preschool Teachers

Although early childhood teachers are familiar with developmental stages of young children, they have not always applied the theory to themselves. Professional development may be a high priority for early childhood educators, but, in the past, it has not been well defined. The following selection from "Developmental Stages of Preschool Teachers," *The Elementary School Journal* (vol. 23, no. 1, 1972) marks the introduction of a pattern to teachers' professional growth. In it, Lilian G. Katz defines four stages—survival, consolidation, renewal, and maturity—marking the career span from the first year of teaching to longevity. She believes that at each stage teachers are able to fulfill certain developmental tasks. To ensure successful transition from stage to stage, Katz recommends specific training activities for teachers.

Katz (b. 1932) has been a professor of education at the University of Illinois since 1968. As director of the ERIC Clearinghouse on Elementary and Early Childhood Education, editor of the *Current Topics in Early Childhood Education* series, and president of the National Association for the Education of Young Children, she has influenced the shape of early childhood education. Her philosophical perspective is evident in such areas of the field as the functions and dispositions of teachers, parents as partners in education, and in-depth learning through the project approach.

*T*eachers can generally be counted on to talk about developmental needs and stages when they discuss children. It may be equally meaningful to think of teachers themselves as having developmental sequences in their professional growth patterns (Katz and Weir 1969). The purpose of the present discussion is to outline the tasks and associated training needs of each suggested developmental stage, and to consider the implications for the timing and location of training efforts.

206

*Chapter 8
Teacher
Preparation
and
Development*

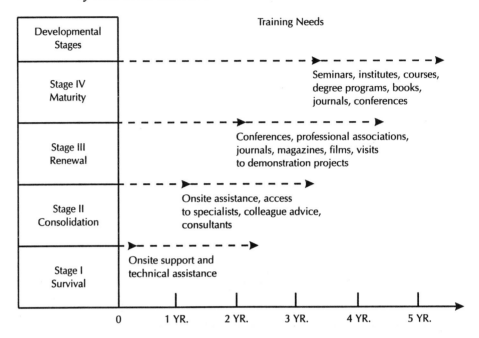

It seems reasonable to suggest that there may be at least four develop-mental stages for teachers. Individual teachers may vary greatly in the length of time spent in each of the four stages outlined below and schematized in Figure 1.

STAGE I—SURVIVAL

Developmental Tasks

During this stage, which may last throughout the first full year of teach-ing, the teacher's main concern is whether or not she can *survive*. This preoccu-pation with survival may be expressed in terms like these: "Can I get through the day in one piece? Without losing a child? Can I make it until the end of the week—the next vacation? Can I really do this kind of work day after day? Will I be accepted by my colleagues?" Such questions are well expressed in Ryan's (1970) enlightening collection of accounts of first year teaching experiences.

The first full impact of responsibility for a group of immature but vigor-ous young children (to say nothing of encounters with their parents) inevitably provokes teacher anxieties. The discrepancy between anticipated successes and classroom realities intensifies feelings of inadequacy and unpreparedness.

During this period the teacher needs support, understanding, encouragement, reassurance, comfort, and guidance. She needs instruction in specific skills and insight into the complex causes of behavior—all of which must be provided on the classroom site. Onsite trainers may be senior staff members, advisers, consultants, or program assistants. Training must be constantly and readily available from someone who knows both the trainee and her teaching situation well. The trainer should have enough time and flexibility to be on call as needed by the trainee. Schedules of periodic visits which have been arranged in advance cannot be counted on to coincide with trainees' crises. Cook and Mack (1971) describe the British pattern of onsite training given to teachers by their headmasters (principals). Armington (1969) also describes the way advisers can meet these teacher needs.

STAGE II—CONSOLIDATION

Developmental Tasks

By the end of the first year the teacher has usually decided that she is capable of surviving. She is now ready to consolidate the overall gains made during the first stage and to differentiate specific tasks and skills to be mastered next. During Stage II, teachers usually begin to focus on individual problem children and problem situations. This focus may take the form of looking for answers to such questions as: "How can I help a clinging child? How can I help a particular child who does not seem to be learning?"

During Stage I, the neophyte acquires a baseline of information about what young children are like and what to expect of them. By Stage II the teacher is beginning to identify individual children whose behavior departs from the pattern of most of the children she knows.

Training Needs

During this stage, onsite training continues to be valuable. A trainer can help the teacher through mutual exploration of a problem. Take, for example, the case of a young teacher from a day care center who was eager to get help and expressed her problem in the question, "How should I deal with a clinging child?" An onsite trainer can, of course, observe the teacher and child *in situ* and arrive at suggestions and tentative solution strategies fairly quickly. However, without firsthand knowledge of the child and context, an extended give-and-take conversation between teacher and trainer may be the best way for the trainer to help the teacher to interpret her experience and move toward a solution of the problem. The trainer might ask the teacher such questions as, "What have you done so far? Give an example of some experiences with this

208

*Chapter 8
Teacher
Preparation
and
Development*

particular child during this week. When you did such and such, how did the child respond?" . . .

Also, in this stage the need for information about specific children or problem children suggests that learning to use a wider range of resources is needed. Psychologists, social and health workers, and other specialists can strengthen the teacher's skills and knowledge at this time. Exchanges of information and ideas with more experienced colleagues may help teachers master the developmental tasks of this period. Opportunities to share feelings with other teachers in the same stage of development may help to reduce some of the teacher's sense of personal inadequacy and frustration.

STAGE III—RENEWAL

Developmental Tasks

Often, during the third or fourth year of teaching, the teacher begins to tire of doing the same old things. She starts to ask more questions about new developments in the field: "Who is doing what? Where? What are some of the new materials, techniques, approaches, and ideas?" It may be that what the teacher has been doing for each annual crop of children has been quite adequate for them, but that she herself finds the recurrent Valentine cards, Easter bunnies, and pumpkin cutouts insufficiently interesting! If it is true that a teacher's own interest or commitment to the projects and activities she provides for children contributes to their educational value, then her need for renewal and refreshment should be taken seriously.

Training Needs

During this stage, teachers find it especially rewarding to meet colleagues from different programs on both formal and informal occasions. Teachers in this developmental stage are particularly receptive to experiences in regional and national conferences and workshops and profit from membership in professional associations and participation in their meetings. Teachers are now widening the scope of their reading, scanning numerous magazines and journals, and viewing films. Perhaps during this period they may be ready to take a close look at their own classroom teaching through videotaping. This is also a time when teachers welcome opportunities to visit other classes, programs, and demonstration projects.

Perhaps it is at this stage that the teacher center has the greatest potential value (Silberman 1971; Bailey 1971). Teacher centers are places where teachers can gather together to help each other learn or relearn skills, techniques and methods, to exchange ideas, and to organize special workshops. From time to time specialists in curriculum, child growth, or any other area of concern which teachers identify are invited to the center to meet with teachers.

Developmental Tasks

Maturity may be reached by some teachers within three years, by others in five or more. The teacher at this stage has come to terms with herself as a teacher. She now has enough perspective to begin to ask deeper and more abstract questions, such as: "What are my historical and philosophical roots? What is the nature of growth and learning? How are educational decisions made? Can schools change societies? Is teaching a profession?" perhaps she has asked these questions before. But with the experience she has now gained, the questions represent a more meaningful search for insight, perspective, and realism.

Training Needs

Throughout maturity, teachers need an opportunity to participate in conferences and seminars and perhaps to work toward a degree. Mature teachers welcome the chance to read widely and to interact with educators working on many problem areas on many different levels. Training sessions and conference events which Stage II teachers enjoy may be very tiresome to the Stage IV teacher. (Similarly, introspective and searching discussion seminars enjoyed by Stage IV teachers may lead to restlessness and irritability among the beginners of Stage I.)

SUMMARY

In the above outline, four dimensions of training for teaching have been suggested: (1) developmental stages of the teacher; (2) training needs of each stage; (3) location of the training; and (4) timing of training.

Developmental Stage of the Teacher. It is useful to think of the growth of teachers as occurring in stages, linked very generally to experience gained over time.

Training Needs of Each Stage. The training needs of teachers change as experience occurs. For example, the issues dealt with in the traditional social foundations courses do not seem to address themselves to the early survival problems which are critical to the inexperienced. However, for the maturing teacher, those same issues may help to deepen her understanding of the total complex context in which she is trying to be effective.

Location of Training. The location of training should be moved as the teacher develops. At the beginning of the new teacher's career, training resources must be taken *to* her so that training can be responsive to the particular (and possibly unique) developmental tasks and working situation the trainee

210

*Chapter 8
Teacher
Preparation
and
Development*

faces in her classroom. Later on as the teacher moves on past the survival stage, training can move toward the college campus.

Timing of Training. The timing of training should be shifted so that more training is available to the teacher *on* the job than *before* it. Many teachers say that their preservice education has had only a minor influence on what they do day-to-day in their classrooms, which suggests that strategies acquired before employment will often not be retrieved under pressure of concurrent forces and factors in the actual job situation.

However, even though it is often said that experience is the best teacher, we cannot assume that experience teaches what the new trainee should learn. To direct this learning, to try to make sure that the beginning teacher has *informed* and *interpreted* experience, should be one of the major roles of the teacher trainer.

REFERENCES

Armington, D. "A Plan for Continuing Growth." Mimeographed. Newton, Mass.: Educational Development Center, 1969. ED 046 493.

Bailey, S. K. "Teachers' Centers: A British First." *Phi Delta Kappan* 53, no. 3 (November 1971): 146–149.

Cook, A., and Mack, M. *The Headteacher's Role.* New York: Citation Press, 1971.

Katz, L. G., and Weir, M. K. "Help for Preschool Teachers: A Proposal." Mimeographed. Urbana, Ill.: ERIC Clearinghouse on Early Childhood Education, 1969. ED 031 308.

Ryan, K., ed. *Don't Smile Until Christmas: Accounts of the First Year of Teaching.* Chicago: University of Chicago Press, 1970.

Silberman, A. "A Santa's Workshop for Teachers." *American Education* 7, no. 10 (December 1971): 3–8.

CHAPTER 9

Observation and Assessment

9.1 DOROTHY H. COHEN AND VIRGINIA STERN

Recording a Child's Use of Materials

Why and how should teachers record what young children do? In the following selection, Dorothy H. Cohen and Virginia Stern explore this question by showing how children are thinking and growing through the use of materials. Their work provides clear instruction on observing the details of children's behavior. Cohen and Stern believe that when teachers pay attention not only to what children do but also to how they feel, they are responding to the whole, integrated behavior of children. This comes from looking at children and writing about them in terms of the quality of their interrelatedness with people and materials. The authors teach the skill of observation and recording by example, guiding teachers to compose records that take the form of stories.

When Cohen and Stern discuss interpreting a child's behavior, they advise teachers to rely on their own personal experience and knowledge. They regard the combination of objective data and subjective interpretation as the complete professional skill of observation. They believe that one without the other makes the recording less effective.

The following selection is from Cohen and Stern's *Observing and Recording the Behavior of Young Children* (Teachers College Press, 1958). Since its publication, the book has been reprinted numerous times and used extensively in teacher preparation and inservice professional development programs. Cohen was the director of Graduate Programs and Stern was a research associate at the Bank Street College of Education when they coauthored this classic reference work.

THE MEANING OF MATERIALS TO CHILDREN

Play materials are as integral a part of school life as routines, but their function in the development of personality is somewhat different. If we tend to see play materials as a means of keeping idle hands busy, or if we evaluate their use in terms of work, we are likely to miss the special role they do play.

Materials, ordinary play materials, are a bridge between the child's inner self and the outside world. They are the means by which a child captures impressions of the world outside himself and translates them into forms he can understand; they are the means of pulling out of himself what he feels and giving it concrete expression. His inexperience limits his grasp of the world he lives in, and his speech is not yet the most efficient tool for the expression of ideas and feelings about this world. Materials (toys, blocks, sand, paint, clay, wood, paper, crayons, pencils, etc.) help him to . . .

. . . transform feelings into action.
> Anger or high spirits get pounded into clay.
> The desire to be big and strong goes into building "the tallest building in the world."
> The mood of spring sunshine is gently painted in pinks, yellows, and pale greens.

. . . translate ideas into forms, concepts into shapes.
> A house of blocks, like a real house, has to be closed in and around; a road of blocks rambles on and on; a bridge is high up and across.

. . . turn impressions into products.
> A cookie of clay must be round and flat; a crayoned grown-up has long legs and a big smile.

Even if his impressions of a tree, a cow, and his daddy all come out looking like a blob of red paint, a child feels he has made a good try! Through his use of materials, a child externalizes impressions and feelings, develops muscles and skills, grows in his powers of reasoning and logic. He gains in inner strength as he clarifies his hazy, incomplete understanding of the real world of objects, phenomena, and people.

A child approaches materials as he approaches life itself, with directness or shyness, with attack or withdrawal, with fear and hesitancy or with courage and self-confidence. Do all children plunge into soapsuds with the same zest? Do all children build daring block towers? Do all children sprawl paints across every inch of paper? Don't we all know the tidy child who handles clay and paint almost daintily? Or the cheerful little fellow who is never willing to stop playing and put toys away, makes the most mess at the clay table, carries the mess over into an orgy of soap and water in the bathroom, and disappears just when he's needed to clean up! And what of the many others who confine themselves to a limited few of the materials we offer them, as though starving themselves in the midst of plenty? Or the sad child who does not play with anything? There is a consistency of style and approach to materials that reveals much about children's responses.

Children will take any material, shape, or form and breathe a bit of themselves into it. The more shapable, or "unstructured," the material is, the better it serves for them to project feelings and ideas. At first contact, a material is something outside oneself, and a curiosity for that reason. It has to be explored as an item of the world outside of self. Then there is experimentation with it for its own sake: What are its properties and possibilities? Does it stick, stretch, break, fall, crush, smear? Eventually the material becomes a medium for expression and projection, and it is *used* for the child's own purposes. When a child is fairly well able to break down the details that pertain to objects and people, and he has the physical coordination for detailed work, he may use materials representationally to crystallize that clarity. If he is confused about some details, the confusion is set down too. Interestingly enough, if his feelings are stronger than his intellectual curiosity or creativity, he may seem to misuse the material, as when he makes mud out of clay or uses a doll for poking and throwing, or deliberately breaks block buildings. At such a point, he may need materials that are especially suited to his needs.

Materials that have a specific use and function, like dolls and bikes, are "structured" materials. Children use these for the implied purpose, but they will also project feelings onto them. (The doll is naughty and rebellious or is crying and upset.) Or children use them as a means for carrying out ideas, desires, or fantasies. (The bike is a plane, the doll is a big girl, the lotto cards are tickets, etc.)

Semi-structured materials, like blocks (not as fluid as paint or clay, nor as finally formed as a toy car), give the satisfaction of construction and three-dimensional solidity.

But beyond this analysis, there remains the wonder of children's imagination: If they need a plane, a car or a stick can become one, and if they want to make a person, they will struggle with the material until the essence of *person* is there.

In short, materials are used by children in the way children themselves need and want to use them. The manner and style, however, is unique to each child.

DETAILS TO OBSERVE IN RECORDING
A CHILD'S USE OF MATERIALS

THE SETTING

Include the nearby significant people and activities, as in routines, and also such things as the abundance or scarcity of materials, availability of supplies, amount and kind of adult supervision, etc.

THE STIMULUS

How does the child come to use the material? (teacher-suggested; group procedure; imitation of another child; self-initiated; suggested by another child, etc.)

RESPONSE TO *Paint*

What colors does the child use? Does he mix colors (in jars or on the paper)? Are the colors separated on paper?

Does he paint one color over another?

Is he able to control the drips?

Does he try to control the drips? Does he deliberately drip?

Does he confine himself to one small spot or bit of space, or does he spread out? Does he paint off the paper?

What forms, if any? (vertical lines, curves, circles, fill-ins, letters, dots, numbers, blotches of color, representation, etc.)

Does he paint over the forms?

What kind of brush strokes? (scrubbing, dotting, gliding, etc.)

How many paintings? Does he paint quickly? Does he work for a long time on one?

Does he name the painting? In detail? In general?

RESPONSE TO *Clay*

How does he handle the clay physically? (pounding, rolling, pulling apart; squeezing, poking, making mush, making balls, snakes; slapping it, stamping on it; patting, stroking, scraping, etc.)

Does he use supplementary tools, such as tongue depressors? (sticks, toothpicks, scissors, beads, etc.)

Is there representation? (naming; size of products; accuracy of detail)

How does he use material in the space available? Does he work in his own area or does he spread out? (off the board, over the table, etc.)

RESPONSE TO *Blocks*

What blocks does the child select? (size and type of blocks; supplementary materials—dolls, small blocks, cars, wedgies, etc.)

What forms does he construct? (up in the air, crisscross, along the floor, piling, enclosures, recognizable structures, etc.)

How does he use space? (confined, spread out; close to shelves; aware of obstacles; etc.)

Is the structure named? Is it used in dramatic play? Is the child interested primarily in the process of building?

Two-year-old Penny at the sandbox:

Penny runs to sandbox carrying tablespoon, empty orange juice can, and toy plastic teacup. She climbs down into sandbox, sits down in corner, and silently and intently begins to fill can with sand, using spoon. She is oblivious to several other children around her. She stands up, dumps sand from can onto asphalt outside sandbox. She bangs can down on sand several times, then gently pats sand with open palm, saying "Cake." Rene, aged four, comes up. She starts to take can from Penny, saying, "Can I have that?" Penny pulls the can away and stands still, staring at Rene. Teacher gives Rene a small spoon and plastic cup. She stands beside Penny and they both begin to spoon sand, occasionally smiling at each other. Penny climbs out of the sand to bench where teacher is sitting. She dumps the sand onto the bench and then spoons it back into can. She dumps it onto the bench again, and pats it gently. "I'm making cake." She takes a spoonful of sand and puts it on teacher's hand. She looks up and sees Patty on the swing. She runs over to her, carrying spoon with her . . .

Four-year-old Leo at the paints:

Leo wanders into the art room, pausing at the door to watch Polly, who is painting at the easel, and Mary and Ellen who are drawing with chalk.

"Guess I'll paint, O. K.?"

Without awaiting an answer, Leo carefully lifts smock from hook, carries it, bundled in his arms, to teacher. "Mrs. S., put this on for me?" Teacher helps him into smock and he bounces over to easel next to Polly. Looks into jars on her easel, looks at colors in his own jars.

"I have red. And yellow too."

Picks up a brush in each hand, hands rotate in opposite directions. Stops, still holding brushes aloft. Looks at paper and smiles. "That's the way spiders are made. Spiders are nice. When I was a snake I was friendly with them and I liked it."

Dips brushes into paint and resumes swirling motions, dripping paint with gay abandon.

"I don't like to wipe on the edge of jars. I just do it this way. Don't you think I'm covering this whole paper up? I am."

Dips brushes again. "There's hard painting at the bottom, Teacher." (sediment) Inspects tips of brushes and paints drip off onto floor. Looks at teacher, frowning and worried-looking. "It's all right if paint gets on the paper, isn't it?" Waits, brushes held over tray, for reply. When reassured, he makes a few tentative jabs at the paper with the brushes.

"That's all for me." Replaces brushes carefully in correct colors, unbuttons smock slowly, and strips it off, dropping it to floor.

"I'll save my brushes till tomorrow, right?" Strolls out to sink, rolling up sleeves as he goes.

THE UNIQUE QUALITY OF THE CHILD, OR *HOW* HE DOES *WHAT*

Thus far we have recorded a child's use of materials in such a way as to get a fairly inclusive picture of *what* he is doing. But we do not see from this picture what the special meaning of the experience is to him. We are not getting down *how* he does the thing he is doing.

To show a child's feelings as he uses materials, we must consciously and deliberately include, along with the actual action itself, the signs that show feeling. When we record *gross* movement, such as "he reached for a block," "he lifts the brush," "he grabbed the sponge," we are recording actions completely objectively, but without their life-pulse, or even our own response to their meaning. A child might be reaching for that block stealthily, hesitantly, or victoriously; perhaps he grabbed the sponge angrily, defiantly, efficiently, or just quickly; and he could lift the brush suspiciously, hastily, or absentmindedly. It is not enough to record what he does (i.e., he reached for a block); we must tell HOW he does WHAT. In the above descriptions, the meaning of each activity is different with each qualifying word. The descriptive adjective or adverb sums up the details we have been recording, and indicates the unique character of the gross action.

As we live and work with people, we react spontaneously to their range of feelings without ever thinking about how we know they feel as they do. We just sense it. With children, we certainly sense when they are delighted with themselves, when they are unhappy, when they are tense, when they are completely at ease. Actually, we take into our mind's eye a wide variety of cues that the other person sends out and get a composite picture which we then interpret according to our own experience and associations. Often we jump to conclusions before we get all the clues. It helps, therefore, to break down the nuances of behavior so that we are able to include them in the record. Even though something of our own interpretation will be there, the evidence to support us will be there too.

These clues to feeling that we must record are the involuntary, non-controlled, non-directed movements and gestures that accompany any gross action and give it its character. They are unique for every child and every action, for no child works at materials, or any form of play, without a variety of accompanying behavior. Thus, as we pick up his motions . . .

. . . we include the sounds that he makes and the language he speaks.
    If he is using his voice, what is it like? (jubilant, wavering, ringing, well-modulated, whining, etc.)
    To whom is it directed? (himself, other children, teacher, no one in particular, etc.)
    What does he say? (direct quote) (chants, sings; nonsense syllables, phrases, stories, etc.)
. . . we note the movements of his body as he uses materials.
    What is his posture like? (erect, rigid, hunched, floppy, straight, curled, squat, etc.)

What is the rhythm of his body movement? (jerky, smooth, easy, jumpy, staccato-like, flowing, etc.)

What is the tempo of his body movement? (rapid, sluggish, measured, slow, swift, leisurely, deliberate, speedy, hasty, moderate, unhurried, etc.)

How much and what kind of effort does he expend? (a great deal, excessive, very little, moderate; strained, laborious, easy, vigorous, forceful, feeble, etc.)

What kind of freedom does he show in his body movement? (sweeping movements; cramped, tiny movements; free-flowing; restrained, tight, restricted, etc.)

. . . we identify the details of facial expression.

Eyes—(glint, dullness, brightness, shine, teariness, blinking, etc.)

Mouth—(grin, quiver, pucker, tongue between lips, biting lips, smiling, wide open, drawn tight, etc.)

From these details we can surmise the child's emotional response to the materials, e.g., excitement, contentment, frustration, self-criticalness, confidence, squeamishness, stimulation, overstimulation, taking in stride, intense interest, preoccupation, etc.

REACTIONS TO PEOPLE AROUND HIM

The feelings which the child reveals may be reactions to things other than the materials he is using. We include in the record, therefore, what we see of his reactions to the people around him:

Is there any socializing with children as the child uses materials?

How does the child show awareness of children about him? (talking, showing materials and products, touching others, etc.; using products in dramatic play; helping others, criticizing; calling for attention to what he is doing, etc.)

Does he work alone or with others?

What are his relations to adults while using materials?

(calls for help, approval, supplies, etc.)

(is suggestible, defiant, indifferent, heedless, mindful, etc., regarding adult offers of help, adult participation, reminders of rules and limitations, offers of suggestions, etc.)

How does the experience end?

What events and feelings follow immediately after? (puts things away, puts his work on the storage shelf, destroys his work, shows things to the children or teachers, leaves everything and goes to another activity, dances around the room, etc.)

RECORDS ILLUSTRATING DETAIL

The following records show increasing attention to detail. The first is primarily a recording of gross movements and sequence of events.

Marsha, age 5:

Marsha came directly to the outdoor table on which teachers had prepared a basket of scissors, crayons, paste in a six-ounce jar with a spoon in it, and small 1½-inch cups. The children were encouraged to help themselves to the paste and to put it in a cup. There was also a stack of paper and two aluminum plates filled with paper collage, string and wool, and cloth collage in various shapes.

"I wanna paste, I wanna paste, I wanna paste."

Teacher, busy with another child, "Yes, Marsha. It's Debby's turn now. . . . It will be yours next. Help yourself, Marsha."

(Marsha can be very self-sufficient, but now and again becomes completely helpless, usually with a smile on her face as though she knows she is acting.)

Standing in the same place, and not looking at teacher, Marsha says, in a babyish, whiny tone, "I wanna paste, I wanna paste." She looks along the table at the others who are cutting, crayoning, pasting. She moves around a child, and helps herself to the entire basket of crayons, placing it in front of her seat. She helps herself to paper, sits down, and makes a few crayon marks. As though realizing that this was not what she had planned to do, she calls, "Mrs. M.?"

"Yes?"

"I wanna paste."

"The jar is down at the end of the table, Marsha."

Marsha goes for the paste and gives herself some. Back at her seat she pastes a piece of collage on her paper, helps herself to another piece, and pastes that. She works intently, lips parted. Spends more time than needed pushing her finger around and around in the paste on the paper, as though enjoying the feel of it. She pastes wool, lace, paper and cloth. A piece of string frustrates her. T. approaches.

"May I help you?"

"Yes," whiny and a little pouty. T. puts a short line of paste on the paper and lays the string on it.

"Now you show me how you want your string to go and we will put some paste there," Marsha accepts this idea.

"Now you put the paste where you want the string to be." She does.

"I'm finished!"

"O.K."

She smears, smears the paste around on her hands.

"I wanna wash."

"There's water and towels on the tree stump," says the teacher.

Marsha washes and runs off to the trikes. She had not spoken to any child while she worked.

This record gives us some of the teacher's assessment of the child she is observing.

Freddy, age 5, at clay:

After hanging up his snowsuit Freddy entered the playroom in a manner which for him was thoughtful and quiet, a great contrast to his voluble propulsion, as if shot out of a cannon. He edged into a chair at the end of a table where no one else sat, his eyes dreamily watching in an unfocused manner the actions of others at two other tables as they rolled, punched, and pounded the clay they were using. Like a sleepwalker he accepted a hunk of clay and in an absent manner rolled it under the palm of his right hand, his head turned to the side, eyes directed toward the ten or twelve in the room.

A few minutes passed thus. Then he picked up the hunk of clay and let it fall "kerplunk" on the table. Instantly his mood changed, like pressing a button and changing a still picture into an animated one. "Boom!" he shouted, "I got a ball! Look at my ball, teacher! Bounce! Bounce!" He banged it down a few times. Then he started rolling it into a long thin piece. "Here's a snake. I'm making a rattlesnake. Are you making a rattlesnake, Donna?" he asked the child nearest him at the other table.

To David, who had a moment before entered the room and started to work at Freddy's table, "That's a snowman, David. Now I'm making a snowman. . . . Now I'm making a snake big as Edward's." Freddy held it up and chortled with glee. "Hee-hee-hee. . . ."

"Look what I made. I twist it here." He dropped it on the table and began pounding it.

"Now I'm making a pancake. Look at my pancake. Taste my pancake, teacher."

Flop! he dropped it on the table again, rolling it over and over, faster-faster, his motions in keeping with his words. Head and shoulders were hunched over the table, his lips and tongue stumbled over each other in an effort to increase the speed of his words. "Chee-ee-ee-eeeeeeeee. . . ."

Everything slowed down. He was quiet, absorbedly working for a moment. Then in sharp staccato and prideful tone: "Look what I made, teacher."

"Look what I made, Donna."

"Look at my wrist watch."

At this point it was necessary for the teacher to help another child, and she was in a stooping position, with her back to Freddy. He poked her insistently in the back to add emphasis to his exhortation.

"Look at me, teacher!"

She turned to find the clay covering Freddy's upper lip. His head was tilted back to prevent its slipping off. "It's a mustache. Ha-ha-ha (he laughed uproariously). Now it's a hat." He quickly transferred the clay to his head.

"Teacher, look at my hat."

It seems that Freddy's satisfaction in all he does comes not only from his creative use of materials but from the response of individuals, especially adults, present.

INTERPRETATION—THE LAST DIMENSION

Even though we spot the separate, small parts of an action, we actually respond to the whole, integrated behavior of a child, such as his anger, joy, surprise. Our response follows a spontaneous, unspoken assessment of the child's feeling which is drawn from our personal experience and understanding. To some extent we must rely on this subjectivity to define or interpret a child's behavior. We are dependent, however, on correct descriptive words about significant details to place that feeling on record. The value of a record that includes details such as those suggested in the preceding sections is that our interpretation (he is happy, he is sad) is rather better bolstered by objective evidence. We are therefore less likely to be assuming that a feeling is present in a child because we happen to be identifying with him as the underdog or victim, or because we are reacting with subjective antagonism to an aggressor or uncouth person, or because for any other reason we are putting ourselves into the situation irrationally. Interpretation represents the sum total of our background of understanding. Professionally valuable interpretation relies heavily on objective data.

A NOTE OF CAUTION

It is impossible to get everything into every record. No child ever does everything possible in human behavior, nor could a teacher get it all down if he did. Don't try to use these suggestions as a checklist! While busily checking off what seems important to look for, the child may be doing something we never thought of at all, and you would miss it. Keep your eyes on the youngster not on the printed page! It is not *how much* you record, but *what* and *how*, that makes a record valuable.

ON-THE-SPOT RECORDS LEAD TO SUPPORTED GENERALIZATIONS

The review of a child's use of materials over a period of time will be a mirror of his growth in this area. We will get to know many things about him that we might have missed without these concentrated observations of his activity. We will see a profile of his tastes and his ideas and learn how much confidence he has in his own imagination and capacity. We will note his dependency on adults and children for standards and security, his concern with standards or his indifference to them, his pleasure in doing or his anxiety about doing things

wrong. These responses are evaluated best when seen against the backdrop of
a child's general coordination, maturity, experience, and age, as well as against
the usual behavior of children in his age group.

*Dorothy H.
Cohen and
Virginia Stern*

PERSISTENT OR CHANGING PATTERNS OF BEHAVIOR IN RELATION TO MATERIALS: A SUMMARY

As with the summary on routines, we look for patterns of behavior—over-all
patterns that indicate a general approach to materials and specific patterns
relating to different materials. Here are suggestions for what to include in such
a summary:

1. How the child uses the various materials—paint, clay, blocks, etc.—
   over a period of time, in persistent or changing ways
   • How he comes to use the material generally (on his own initiative,
   on the suggestion of the teacher or another child, through imitation of
   other children)
   • Coordination (his physical ability to carry out techniques)
   • Techniques (include the state of development—manipulative, exploratory, representational—in relation to child's age and background
   of experience. For example, painting dots, rolling clay or piling cubes
   are techniques which can be early steps in the use of new materials,
   typical techniques of an age group, or excessively simple usage of
   material by a child who has the age and background for more complex
   approaches)
   • How he works (concentration and care used; exploratory; competently, skillfully, intensively, carelessly, tentatively, distractible, in different ways)
   • Language or sound accompaniments
   • Mannerisms
   • Products (creativity, imagination, originality shown)
   • Attention span (in general, and in relation to specific material and
   activities)
   • Use of materials in dramatic play—which materials are so used?
   • Does he complete what he starts?
   • Adult role and child's response (Indicate rules, limitations, participa-
   tion, what is permitted, and how child accepts all these.)
2. How the child seems to feel about the materials
   • Number, variety, frequency of materials and activities enjoyed, used,
   avoided. (Including changing and static interest.)
   • General attitudes—enthusiastic, eager, confident, matter-of-fact, cau-
   tious, etc. (Include attitude toward new as well as familiar materials.)
   • Importance of given areas to the child—interest, intensity of pleas-

ure, preoccupation, fears, avoidance, resistance.
• In relation to which materials the child apparently feels satisfaction, frustration, self-confidence, inadequacy, etc.
• How he reacts to failure, to success (What constitutes failure or success? What is the level of aspiration?)
3. How the child's use of color and form compares with what most children in the group seem to be doing
4. Child-adult relationship revealed via materials
   Independence—dependence
5. Special problems
   Distress over breakage, avoidance of messiness, concentration on only one material or idea, inability to concentrate and enjoy

Following are examples of two children's over-all use of materials. The various items from the records, when brought together in a summary of persistent or changing patterns, are easily written up as a sketch of a youngster's use of materials. In time this sketch becomes part of the end-of-the-year record of the child.

Records of Over-all Response to Materials

Lee, age 4 yrs. 5 mos.:
Lee's work with creative materials has been largely teacher-initiated. Before he begins any activity he usually spends more time watching the other children. Then, when he apparently feels sure of himself, he begins. His attention span is adequate to complete the activity. He works deliberately and quietly, absorbed and interested in the task at hand. It is quite evident that this is real work. His work is neat and carefully done. When he abandons this approach to materials he seems worried, seeks reassurance from the teacher that this untidiness is accepted comfortably by her. He verbalizes as he works, a running commentary to teacher, children, or no one. He shows pride in accomplishment and again often seeks approval from the teacher. His work with clay is delightful and imaginative and he seems to feel more freedom here than in the use of other media.

Iris, age 3:
Materials most used by Iris are sand, mud, crayons, easel paints, finger paints, and water. Just recently she has begun to use the clay to make cakes with cooky cutters or make imprints with any article handy. At first her attitude toward materials was one of indifference, but now she is interested in what she is making and comes to show it to the teachers or children. Paste on her hands at first annoyed her so that she did not want to use it. Today she was pasting and I was delighted to see a paste smear in her hair, and Iris concentrating intently on her creation.
When a new material was introduced she looked at it but did not attempt to play with it. Recently we received train and track, musical bells, new dishes

Dorothy H. Cohen and Virginia Stern

and started a new project of covering our rug chest. She wanted to be part of each group, except dishes, and went from one thing to another as fast as she could. This was so unusual that we almost gasped in surprise. The part that gave us the biggest thrill was this morning when two children were taken upstairs to cover the chest. Iris went to the toilet and on the way back noticed what was going on. Going up to a big five-year-old she said, "Give me hammer" in a demanding voice. Teacher said she could have a turn next. Stamping foot, trying to pull hammer from Lucy's hand, she replied, "Now, I want it right now." Not receiving it instantly, she came down to tell the other teacher her trouble. She did get a turn and then went to the musical bells. While there are still materials she has not touched, such as blocks, setting table with dishes, cars, she is adding to her play more materials each day. Outside equipment is now, and has been from the beginning, used without fear of falling. Every piece of equipment has been used by her, and with good control of muscles, expression and movement of body indicating extreme satisfaction. The swing is the one place where she always hums and sings.

Early Mental Growth

Arnold Gesell (1880–1961) began his pioneer work in the mental growth of babies in 1911, a time when very little attention was paid to the educational development of children under age six. With the rise in popularity of educational nurseries and developmental centers, babies and toddlers became subject to study. New standards were needed, and Gesell, as director of the Yale Psycho-Clinic, undertook a program of research into the norms of infant mental and behavioral development. The norms were based on comprehensive data, including photographs, of a large number of "unselected" preschool children to age five. Gesell was the first to use the motion picture camera as a scientific instrument for recording children's everyday activity.

Because Gesell considered mental and physical development to be maturational processes, governed by laws common to both, norms were a well-received standard. Gesell et al.'s *The First Five Years of Life: A Guide to the Study of the Preschool Child* (Harper & Row, 1940), from which the following selection has been taken, has been the child development sourcebook for generations of parents, pediatricians, and teachers. The selection, "Early Mental Growth," defines the theory behind Gesell's norms for children's growth.

Gesell was a tireless advocate for public school kindergarten, believing that it should not be separate from schools, welfare programs, and public health organizations. He discusses the need for kindergarten to be an organic part of a unified system of public health and education in *The Preschool Child*, written in 1923. His views were influenced by G. Stanley Hall, his former professor and one of the founders of modern American child psychology, and by the distressing economic and medical conditions of the early 1900s that led to high levels of childhood mortality and morbidity. Gesell believed that kindergarten children had a fundamental right to physical health. He deplored the rise of infectious diseases that came as the result of kindergarten indoor life, a lack of muscle work, and large classes.

In a biological sense the span of human infancy extends from the zero hour of birth to the middle twenties. It takes time to grow. It takes about twenty-four years for an American youth to reach the stature of maturity. For convenience one may think of this cycle of growth as a succession of four stages of six years each: (1) the preschool years, (2) the elementary years, (3) the secondary school years, (4) the preadult years.

We are now beginning to see this cycle of growth in its true perspective. Thus far, for sound social reasons, the middle twelve years have received most of the attention of the public school system. These are indeed important years for the transmission of cultural inheritance, but the demands of society and the findings of science are compelling us to see a new significance in the preschool years—the fundamental years which come first in the cycle of life and which therefore claim a certain priority in all social planning.

Social Significance of the Preschool Years

Every eighth person in the population is a preschool child. There are in the United States sixteen million children under the age of 6 years, a total of about thirteen per cent of the population. In recent decades the proportion of preschool children has been diminishing; the proportion of aging and elderly adults is increasing. Families with no child or with an only child are more frequent. These populational trends are augmenting the importance of the preschool child.

The environmental conditions which surround the preschool children of the nation vary enormously. Man of these children are ushered into the world without the protection of medical service; many grow up without medical supervision, reared by parents who have received no guidance from the community in the most elementary principles of child care.

At the other extreme is the infant who is born in a hospital, safe-guarded by medical supervision even prior to birth. This privileged infant is fed, weighed, bathed, sunned, aired, inoculated, examined, and re-examined at intervals, prescribed or periodic. When he is 2 years old an automobile transports him daily to a nursery school. At 5 he graduates into a progressive kindergarten. His mother has been trained to pay attention to his psychological as well as to his physical welfare.

Over 5,000,000 preschool children in rural, village, and tenement areas are underfed, underclothed, underhoused, and undereducated. About 75,000 children are enrolled in approximately 2,000 emergency nursery schools established through federal grants in aid. A similar number of children attend various forms of day nurseries, relief nurseries, and nursery-kindergartens. A few thousand attend laboratory nursery schools and tuition preschools. Only about one child out of four of eligible age attends a tax-supported kindergarten.

Some 1,500 institutions and 350 child placing agencies in a given year care for approximately 250,000 neglected and dependent children. Fully one-fourth of these are of preschool age. At conservative estimate, 65,000 infants each year are born out of wedlock. (One illegitimate birth for every thirty-five of the total population; one such birth in every sixty-one of the white population.) The death rate of these children is approximately three times that of other children; but those who survive create peculiarly intricate and exacting problems of social control. They make the most searching of all challenges to psychological understanding and diagnosis.

A Committee of the White House Conference on Child Health and Protection estimated the total number of handicapped children of all ages in the United States to be more than 10,000,000. Ten major types of handicap occur. They are listed below in an ascending order of frequency: (1) visual handicap, (2) epilepsy, (3) motor disability, (4) cardiac defect, (5) tuberculosis and pre-tuberculosis, (6) speech defect, (7) deafness and impaired hearing, (8) nervous and behavior disorders, (9) mental deficiency and subnormality, (10) malnutrition.

In the vast majority of cases the foregoing handicaps are either present at birth or arise during the first five years of life. To some extent the defects can be prevented; to a large extent they can be ameliorated during infancy and early childhood. Whether a handicap is classified as physical or mental, it inevitably involves problems of psychological understanding and of psychological guidance.

The great problem of physical accidents also proves to have a psychological aspect. Street and highway accidents, but more especially household accidents—burning, scalding, falls, poisoning, smothering, and play injuries—take a disproportionately heavy toll in the preschool years. Many of these accidents have their origin in controllable psychological factors in parent and child; many of them arise out of the limitations of the child's immaturity. Another reason, both social and personal, for attaining a better understanding of the preschool child.

The present volume is chiefly concerned with the normal aspects of mental growth. It makes no attempt to consider systematically the specialized clinical procedures necessary for the early diagnosis of the graver handicaps of child development. In the period of infancy and young childhood, however, it is not always possible to draw a significant line between normal and abnormal symptoms. Moreover, in early life defects are often veiled beneath a plausible exterior of "mere immaturity." Incompleteness, weakness, and inadequacy are overlooked; or they are too readily excused on the blind faith that the infant will "outgrow" his difficulties. Wishful thinking becomes easy when a defect is suspected. To reduce such errors of interpretation we need critical norms of development cautiously applied.

It happens also that errors are often made in the reverse direction. The normal is misinterpreted as abnormal. Under the spell of anxiety or of oversophistication, parents impute dire meaning to symptoms of development which are really benign. They misjudge the child because they do not perceive his imcompleteness, weakness, and inadequacy in terms of immaturity. This kind of misinterpretation is the most common of all. It can be overcome only by a more intelligent appreciation of the *process* of mental growth.

Then there are the uncounted everyday misinterpretations which all of us are bound to make because of sheer ignorance of the nature and needs of the child's psychology. We lack knowledge of the ways in which he grows and learns. We accept the fact that he is not a miniature adult, but we do not know enough about the traits which make him different from the adult.

A rational approach to the problems of child psychology can remove many misconceptions but it is not infallible. There is always a temptation to over-use new-found scientific data. For example, an excessive emphasis on the measurement of intelligence has tended to blind us to other very important factors in the child's economy. Individual differences in personality make-up, in emotional predispositions, and in innate growth characteristics demand more consideration particularly in children of preschool age. A superficial adoption of the doctrines of the conditioned reflex and of habit training likewise has led to faulty aims and methods of child care. Even the modern nursery school is too much influenced by a conventional psychology of learning and by the traditional patterns of public school organization. The preschool child is in danger of being regarded as a miniature school child.

The only corrective for this danger is an increased insight into the distinctive developmental needs and hygiene of the early years. There are profound social reasons why our understanding of preschool children should be deepened and humanized. The age period between one year and three years is peculiarly liable to misunderstanding and mismanagement. And between the ages of three and six there is the prospect that we shall once more use mental ages, intelligence quotients, and achievement tests in a pseudo-technical manner, prejudicial to the developmental welfare of the children concerned.

The nursery school movement as an educational and social experiment has yielded invaluable data relating to the preschool child. It would, however, be a mistake to propagate the nursery school as a subprimary addition to our present graded school system—as virtually another stratification to be administered like a schoolroom. Our public school system is already over-stratified. We must organize our social provisions for the preschool years in new patterns which will preserve the constructive forces of home life and vitalize parental responsibility.

This means that the problems of school entrance, of kindergarten and prekindergarten, and of the nursery school cannot be successfully divorced from the problems of infant welfare. Adequate protection of the preschool child demands continuous safeguards, beginning with birth and the prenatal period. From the standpoint of social control such protection can be achieved only through a coordination of medical supervision, parental guidance, preparental education, and special educational provisions in health and guidance centers. Social planning has already recognized the importance of housing, and the influence of favorable domestic surroundings on child life. Progressive housing programs may in the end prove a wholesome counterbalance to excessive physical expansion of the public school system.

These considerations all bear upon the subject of our chapter: Understanding the Preschool Child. It is difficult to separate cause and effect. However blind and impersonal social forces seem to be, it is certain that our understanding and evaluation of the preschool child will have a determining effect upon the form of the environment which is ultimately created for him. Psychology as a science makes a social contribution when it helps to specify the optimal environmental needs of the preschool child. Not even the architecture of a nursery school or of a child health center can be truly functional until we define the behavior characteristics and the developmental requirements of children of varying ages. An adequate understanding of the preschool child will promote favorable social provisions for him. A narrow application of psychological techniques will have an opposite effect. . . .

THE NATURE OF MENTAL GROWTH

Mental growth is a rather elusive reality. Growth is a process so subtle that it cannot be perceived. And for ordinary vision the mind is utterly insubstantial. Yet the growth of the mind in its first years constitutes the subject matter of the present volume. How can we make this elusive reality less elusive?

First of all we must agree to think of growth not as an empty abstraction but as a living process, just as genuine and as lawful as digestion, metabolism, or any physiological process. We must also think of "the mind" as being part and parcel of a living organism. As such the mind has form, contour, tendency, and direction. It has "architecture." It is as configured as the body with which it is identified. It reveals this configuration in modes of reaction, in patterns of behavior. Mental growth is a process of behavior patterning which organizes the individual and brings him toward a stage of psychological maturity.

The metaphysics of the relationship between body and mind need not concern or confuse us here. We simply suggest that there are laws of growth and mechanisms of development which apply alike to body and mind. Growth is a patterning process whether we think of its physical or its mental manifestations. The embryologist is particularly interested in the transformations of bodily structure; the genetic psychologist, in transformations of behaviors. Both embryologist and psychologist investigate the shape of things to come and the shape of things becoming.

For example: The embryologist finds in the tiny human embryo at the fourth week of intra-uterine life, a pair of "buds" just behind the gill arches or neck region of the trunk. They are limb buds. They grow. Note the remarkable transformations of this pair of diminutive stumps. (1) Cells penetrate into the stumps causing them to elongate. (2) Some of these cells change into a skeleton or framework of three segments (future arm, forearm, and hand). (3) The outer segment (future hand) assumes the shape of a paddle. (4) Five lobes appear on the edge of the paddle. (5) A skeleton penetrates into each lobe and provides it with three or four bony segments.

Thus the paddle transforms into a five-fingered hand. Muscles and tendons attach themselves to the skeleton of arm and hand. Nerve fibers penetrate the muscular tissue; nerve endings ramify into the joints; end organs by the thousands, like so many sentinels, establish themselves in the sensitive skin which envelops the growing hand and arm.

Soon, very soon, this arm and even the fingers will make characteristic movements, spontaneous, reflex, and induced. The mind has begun to grow!

For what are characteristic movements but patterns of behavior? And mental growth is a process of behavior patterning.

Even in the limb bud stage, when the embryo is only 4 weeks old, there is evidence of behavior patterning: the heart beats. In two more weeks slow back and forth movements of arms and legs appear. Before the twelfth week of uterine life the fingers flex in reflex grasp. Increasingly complicated postural movements take form: the trunk curves and straightens; legs and arms flex, extend, rotate; the head moves from side to side and up and down. By the time the embryo, now properly called a fetus, is 5 lunar months old, it has an astonishing repertoire of behavior patterns.

At this age the future infant is a foot in length and a pound in weight, but he is already far advanced in his bodily and behavioral organization. He is distinctly human in his lineaments. He is not unduly compressed by the confines of the uterus, but maintains a partially free existence in its fluid medium. His postural attitudes somewhat resemble those which he will assume in his bassinet. He makes lashing movements of arms and legs (quickening). His skin is sensitive and responds to stimuli. He even makes rhythmic movements of the chest—pre-respiratory movements in preparation for the event of birth, another five months hence, when the breath of postnatal life will rush into his lungs.

It is well to realize that even at this early age the fetus has attained such a high degree of behavior organization. It seems as if Nature hastens the growth of the organism as a safeguard against the contingency of premature birth. Fortunately, if the attendant complications are not too severe, an infant born eight weeks before normal term may survive and undergo a relatively normal behavior development.

The fetus at the age of 5 months is already in possession of twelve billion (or more) nerve cells which make up the human nervous system. This is the full quota, all that the individual will ever have. Many of these cells have already established functional connections among each other and with muscle fibers; many more cells, particularly those of the brain cortex, are still fallow. As the fetus grows, as the infant grows, and as the child grows, these nerve cells become organized into patterns of responsiveness, or into reaction systems. These neuron patterns determine behavior. They are influenced by the constitution of the blood, by endocrine hormones, and by electro-chemical regulators; but in a fundamental sense, the patterning of the mind is inseparably identified with the microscopic and ultramicroscopic patterning of nerve cells.

This neuron patterning pervades the entire organism. The fibers and fibrils of neurons proliferate within the extensive gastro-intestinal tract, the walls of blood vessels, the respiratory apparatus, the genito-urinary system, the sphincters of rectum and bladder, the mucous, sweat, salivary and tear glands, and the ductless glands of internal secretion. A vast network of autonomic and sympathetic neurons thus organizes the vegetative and visceral functions.

Another vast network of sensory neurons supplies numberless sensitive areas in the skin and the mucous membranes, in the joint surfaces and tendons, and in a dozen special organs of sense. Motor neurons with innumerable collaterals ramify within the musculature of head, neck, trunk, and extremities. This network constitutes the sensory-motor system.

A third network of neurons concerned with memory, language, ideation, and with adaptations to past and impending experience, mediates the voluntary, symbolic, and imaginal forms of behavior.

These three neuron nets are in reality a single fabric, because the organism is an integrated whole and grows as a unit rather than by discrete installments. This single fabric preserves the unity of the organism; it embodies and implements the psychological individuality of fetus, infant, and child.

It is permissible to speak of the individuality of the fetus, for even newborn infants display significant individual differences in their physiological processes, in their reactions to internal and extrinsic stimuli, in their patterns of feeding, sleeping, and waking activity, and in perceptivity. These neonatal expressions of individuality are largely the end products of the primary mental growth which was accomplished in the long period of gestation.

The neonatal period lasts about four weeks. By that time the stump of the umbilical cord has separated and the infant is well advanced in his physiological adjustment to a postnatal environment. The period of infancy may be regarded as extending to the second year. Conventionally the years between two and six are known as the preschool years. They terminate with the eruption of the sixth year molar. With second dentition the child is usually ready for the elementary grades.

These conventional age periods are in a measure justified by distinguishable differences in mental maturity. But from a biological standpoint, there are no sharp transitions in the continuum of mental growth. Even birth does not bring about a unique and abrupt transition, because *in utero* the fetus has already anticipated to a great degree the reactions of early neonatal life. He has been prepared; the very arrangement and relationships of his neurons have pointed to the future. In preliminary and provisional form these relationships were laid down by intrinsic patterning prior to and independent of actual experience. This preliminary prospective kind of patterning is mental maturation. It operates not only *in utero* but throughout the whole cycle of mental growth.

Environment inflects preliminary patterns; it determines the occasion, the intensity, and the correlation of many aspects of behavior; but it does not engender the basic progressions of behavior development. These are determined by inherent, maturational mechanisms.

Such mechanisms account for those characteristics of behavior growth which are universal in the species, and they also account for resemblances between human and infra-human growth. In all vertebrate creatures the general direction of behavior organization is from head to foot. The sequence of motor patterning in the human infant clearly reflects this law of developmental direction. The lips lead, eye muscles follow, then neck, shoulders, arms, trunk, legs, and lastly feet.

The tide and trend of preschool development may be outlined, tersely, as follows:

In the *first quarter* of the first year the infant gains control of twelve tiny muscles which move his eyes.

In the *second quarter* (16–28 weeks) he comes into command of the muscles which support his head and move his arms. He reaches out for things.

In the *third quarter* (28–40 weeks) he gains command of his trunk and hands. He sits. He grasps, transfers and manipulates objects.

In the *fourth quarter* (40–52 weeks) he extends command to his legs and feet; to his forefinger and thumb. He pokes and plucks. He stands upright.

In the *second year* he walks and runs; articulates words and phrases; acquires bowel and bladder control; attains a rudimentary sense of personal identity and of personal possession.

In the *third year* he speaks in sentences, using words as tools of thought; he shows a positive propensity to understand his environment and to comply with cultural demands. He is no longer a "mere" infant.

In the *fourth year* he asks innumerable questions, perceives analogies, displays an active tendency to conceptualize and generalize. He is nearly self-dependent in routines of home life.

At *five* he is well matured in motor control. He hops and skips. He talks without infantile articulation. He can narrate a long tale. He prefers associative play; he feels socialized pride in clothes and accomplishment. He is a self-assured, conforming citizen in his small world.

The psychological growth which is achieved in the first five years of life is prodigious. Both in scope and speed, the transformations of the preschool years exceed those of any other half decade.

The purpose of the succeeding chapters is to define the steps and stages by which the child accomplishes these developmental transformations. Our first task will be to characterize ascending levels of maturity in terms of typical behavior patterns. Such characterizations will provide a series of normative portraits outlining the directions and trends of psychological growth. In order that the lines of growth may be more apparent, each portrait will consider in turn four major fields of behavior, namely (1) Motor Characteristics, (2) Adaptive Behavior, (3) Language Behavior, (4) Personal-Social Behavior.

1. *Motor characteristics* include postural reactions, prehension, locomotion, general bodily coordination and specific motor skills.
2. *Adaptive behavior* is a convenient category for those varied adjustments, perceptual, orientational, manual, and verbal, which reflect the child's capacity to initiate new experience and to profit by past experience. This adaptivity includes alertness, intelligence, and various forms of constructiveness and exploitation.
3. *Language* embraces all behavior which has to do with soliloquy, dramatic expression, communication, and comprehension.
4. *Personal-Social behavior* embraces the child's personal reactions to other persons and to the impacts of culture; his adjustments to domestic life, to property, to social groups, and community conventions.

These four major fields of behavior comprise most of the visible patterns of child behavior. They do not, of course, fall neatly into separate compartments. The child always reacts as an interger. The underlying organ and instrument of his behavior it will be recalled is a single fabric. Our categorical classification, therefore, is simply for convenience, to facilitate observation and diagnostic analysis. Judgment is necessary to evaluate the psychological import of any given behavior. Behavior values overlap and they change with age. A behavior pattern may be regarded as "adaptive" at one age, and as "motor" at another age. The reactions to a behavior test may be observed and interpreted from two or more aspects at any given age. Take for example the test, *Draws a horizontal stroke responsively to demonstration.* First of all we may be interested to observe whether the child persists in making a vertical stroke or whether he has the motor maturity required for a lateral movement. This is a *motor* value. We may also note how intently he looks at the demonstration and how discriminatingly he begins and ends his stroke. This is an *adaptive* behavior value. There may even be accompanying verbal or emotional expressions which also have symptomatic value. It is evident that many behavior tests might be assigned to two or more categories. The classifications adopted in the present volume are for clinical convenience; but are not intended to obscure the fact that mental life normally is integrated.

Mental growth is a process of organization. It is synthetic and manifests itself in patterned wholes. All behavior items need interpretation because of the ever-present factor of developmental relativity. Unqualified psychometric ratings of behaviors as absolute abilities will prevent a sympathetic understanding of the young child's psychology.

The normative portrait sketches which follow attempt to call attention to the developmental contexts which color behavior at different age levels. The child's mind does not grow by simple linear extension. He has a persisting individuality, but his outlook on life and on himself transforms as he matures. He is not simply becoming more "intelligent" in a narrow sense of this much misused term. He alters as he grows. His personality sense, his appreciation of his own personal status, his assertiveness of this status, undergo profound developmental changes evidenced particularly in his personal-social behavior, but also in language and in "adaptive" behavior. The whole task of understanding the preschool child becomes more interesting and rewarding if we focus attention, not on his abilities, but upon the organizing processes of growth.

9.3 SAMUEL J. MEISELS

Uses and Abuses of Developmental Screening and School Readiness Testing

For many years, the Gesell School Readiness Screening Test and similar tests have been used to label young children's developmental stages. Developmental screening and readiness tests are considered objective measures for determining which children will be assigned to particular school programs. Schools regard them as reliable measures for making decisions about young children. Thus, when Samuel J. Meisels confronted professionals for misusing such tests, he triggered great debate.

Meisels, a research scientist at the University of Michigan, is convinced that developmental screening and readiness tests are commonly used for exclusionary reasons, to keep children from the services and programming they need. He criticizes the Gesell tests in particular for delaying school entrance for children who are found to be "not ready." Whenever and wherever this occurs, according to Meisels, it indicates that children must "conform to school programs, rather than schools adjusting to the needs of children." His arguments led to a debate with the Gesell Institute. The following selection from "Uses and Abuses of Developmental Screening and School Readiness Testing," *Young Children* (January 1987) presents both sides of the issue of whether or not readiness screening tests are an effective means to enhance developmentally appropriate education.

Public school involvement in early childhood education is growing rapidly, bringing with it new responsibilities for schools to identify children who may be at risk for learning problems and to place these children in appropriate educational environments. This process of identification and placement has been complicated by several basic confusions about screening and readiness

233

tests that have resulted in young children being denied a free and appropriate public education. This exclusion is based not, as in the past, on being handicapped, coming from impoverished backgrounds, or being members of minority groups, but as a result of such labels as *young, developmentally immature,* or *not ready.* Moreover, these labels have been assigned on the basis of tests with unknown validity by testers who have had little training and usually no supervision.

One test that has been in widespread use nationally for identification and placement is the Gesell School Readiness Screening Test (Ilg & Ames, 1972). The purpose of this article is to analyze the uses and abuses that can be traced to the Gesell and other similar tests. I will first discuss developmental screening tests and readiness tests in general. Then I will focus on the Gesell tests, specifically addressing their validity, and questioning their current use, given the type of information the tests were designed to produce. This article will conclude with a discussion of the implications of using readiness tests for assigning children to particular school programs.

Uses and Abuses of Screening and Readiness Tests

Elsewhere I have defined and analyzed the differences between developmental screening tests and readiness tests and have listed examples of each (Meisels, 1984, 1985). The two types of tests are different and were designed to accomplish different objectives. Developmental screening tests provide a brief assessment of a child's developmental abilities—abilities that are highly associated with future school success. Readiness tests are concerned with those curriculum-related skills a child has already acquired—skills that are typically prerequisite for specific instructional programs. Table 1 compares the differences between the two types of tests in terms of purpose, content, type of test, and psychometric properties.

Screening Tests During the years, professionals have misused and abused both screening and readiness tests. The most frequent abuse of developmental screening results from using tests that have no established reliability and validity. Reliability is an indicator of a test's consistency. It measures how often identical results can be obtained with the same test. Validity is a measure of a test's accuracy. Technically, validity concerns the overall degree of justification for test interpretation and use. It tells us whether a test does what it claims to do. Because young children grow and change so rapidly from day to day and week to week, it is critical that tests used to assess these children be stable and accurate.

Tests without reliability and validity are inherently untrustworthy and should not be used to identify and place children. We do not know if such tests provide different results when administered by different testers, whether children from certain socioeconomic or ethnic backgrounds are disadvantaged by them, or whether they are strongly related to some stable, external criterion or outcome measure—such as the results of a diagnostic assessment, a systematic

TABLE 1

Contrasts Between Developmental Screening Tests and Readiness Tests

Samuel J. Meisels

	Developmental Screening Tests	Readiness Tests
Purpose	to identify children who may need early intervention or special education services	to facilitate curriculum planning
	to identify children who might profit from a modified or individualized classroom program	to identify a child's relative preparedness to benefit from a specific academic program
Content	items that display a child's ability or potential to acquire skills	items that focus on current skill achievement, performance, and general knowledge
Type of test	norm-referenced	most are criterion-referenced; some are norm-referenced
Psychometric properties	reliability predictive validity	reliability construct validity

teacher report form, or report card grades—that permits the test results to be interpreted and the findings to be generalized.

Yet, professionals persist in using invalid and unreliable tests. In a survey of 177 school districts in New York State, Joiner (1977) found that 151 different tests or procedures were used for screening. At best, only 16 of these tests could be considered even marginally appropriate. In a recent survey in Michigan, 111 tests were being used for preschool, kindergarten, and pre-first grade programs (Michigan Department of Education, 1984). Fewer than 10 of these tests were appropriate in terms of the age group and purpose to which they were being put. What is taking place in these two states, as well as elsewhere nationwide, is a proliferation of screening tests, many developed locally, that have never been assessed in terms of reliability, validity, or other general criteria that have been established for developmental screening tests (see Meisels, 1985). In the absence of satisfying these criteria—particularly the criterion of validity—children who need special services are being overlooked; some children who are not at risk are being identified as being at risk; parents are becoming alarmed, teachers and administrators upset, and resources squandered. More than 25 states currently mandate developmental screening for 3- to 6-year-olds (Meisels, 1986). A test with known, high-level validity and reliability should always be used when this type of testing is performed. Nothing less than strict psychometric standards are acceptable for other kinds of tests, such as diagnostic assessments or school achievement tests. Using screening tests that lack validity data is an abuse of testing procedures and of the trust the community

FIGURE 1 *Relationship of Screening and Readiness Tests to Assessment and School Performance*

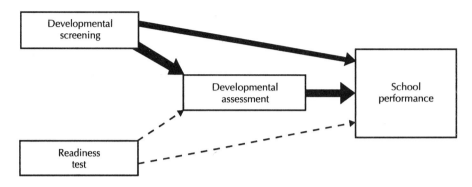

places in professional educators (see American Educational Research Association, American Psychological Association, & National Council on Measurement in Education, 1985).

Readiness Tests   Another major abuse is the substitution of readiness tests for screening tests. This substitution frequently occurs inadvertently, through confusion about the difference between screening and readiness testing. As a brief sorting device, readiness tests can be loosely considered screening tests. But, because of the type of information they yield and their lack of predictive validity, they cannot correctly be considered developmental screening tests. Readiness tests should be used to facilitate curriculum planning, not to identify children who may need special services or intervention.

One of the differences between developmental screening and readiness tests lies in the predictive relationships of these tests to such outcome measures as comprehensive developmental assessments and school performance. In general, individual readiness tests, as contrasted to multivariate reading readiness batteries that incorporate several different kinds of assessments (see Barnes, 1982; Satz & Friel, 1978), do not have a strong predictive relationship to outcome measures. Most correlations between reading success and reading readiness tests are moderate at best (Knight, 1979). Figure 1 portrays the general relationship between developmental screening, individual readiness tests, developmental assessments, and school performance. The figure portrays the conclusions from several different studies, rather than a strict quantitative representation of specific empirical findings (see Lichtenstein, 1981; Rubin, Balow, Dorle, & Rosen, 1978; Wiske, Meisels, & Tivnan, 1982). The wide, dark lines represent strong relationships, the narrower dark lines suggest moderate relations and the broken lines indicate weak relationships.

Figure 1 suggests that readiness tests have a much weaker relationship to developmental assessments and school performance than developmental screening tests. At first glance, such a statement may seem counterintuitive because readiness tests are intended to assess readiness for a specific school program. Nonetheless, readiness tests best describe *child entry characteristics;* they are not intended to *predict child outcomes.* Thus, children who perform poorly on readiness tests may profit proportionately more from school programs than children with higher initial skills because they have more to gain. Conversely, those with well-developed entry level skills may profit less from kindergarten than children who do poorly on readiness tests. Hence, neither the potential of those who score well nor the potential of those who score poorly is accurately assessed by single-measure readiness tests. These tests are best used by teachers for making *initial curriculum decisions about individual children*. While this function is critically important, the data from readiness tests should not be used to attempt to identify developmental problems that may affect a child's chances for school success. Mistaking readiness tests for predictive developmental screening instruments misrepresents the purpose and scope of both tests.

Uses and Abuses of Gesell Testing

One of the most widely adopted tests used for both readiness and developmental screening is the Gesell School Readiness Screening Test (Ilg & Ames, 1972). Also known as the Gesell Preschool Test (Haines, Ames, & Gillespie, 1980), this test, or set of tests, is a shortened version of the Gesell Developmental Schedules—full-scale evaluations used to assess personal-social, fine motor/adaptive behavior; language and reasoning; and gross motor development of children younger than age 6. This article will focus on the Preschool Readiness Tests, not the Developmental Schedules.

In recent years the Preschool Tests have become increasingly popular. According to the Gesell Institute, thousands of public, private, and parochial schools nationwide have adopted them. In addition to the tests, the Gesell Institute conducts week-long workshops on developmental placement. These workshops prepare kindergarten teachers and other professionals to use the Gesell test results to place children in readiness or developmental kindergartens, to recommend that the child delay entering kindergarten for a year, or to suggest conventional kindergarten placement. In other words, the Gesell *readiness* tests are explicitly presented as performing the functions of *developmental screening tests*. According to Ames, Gillespie, Haines, and Ilg (1979), "perhaps 50% of school failures could be prevented or cured by proper placement based on a child's behavior age" (p. 182). Claims like these are responsible for the tremendous interest that educators have shown in Gesell testing in recent years.

Nevertheless, despite their widespread popularity and the amount of time and energy expended on them, the Gesell Preschool Tests are based on an outmoded theory of child development, lack reliability and validity, and use a concept of developmental age that has never been empirically verified. The remainder of this article will be devoted to substantiating these assertions and drawing conclusions from them.

Gesell's Theory The Gesell tests reflect a maturationist theory of development. They view behavior as a function of structure, changing in a patterned, predictable way. The stages through which most behaviors develop are considered to be highly similar from child to child.

According to this theory, behavior is almost entirely the result of maturation, and neither chronological age nor environmental intervention is considered to be highly correlated with so-called developmental age (Gesell, 1954). In other words, maturational theory links behavior with pre-formed, genetically determined biological structures. In the absence of unusual environmental conditions, this theory focuses on *time* as the crucial variable in behavior change, not environmental stimulation or intervention, but time to grow, mature, and endogenously develop. According to Gesell, developmental diagnosis implies prognosis (Shonkoff, 1983).

Although the importance of maturational change in development cannot be ignored, this strict Gesellian approach is at odds with research ranging from Piaget to the Perry Preschool Project. Numerous researchers have identified the ameliorative effects of environmental intervention on childhood development (see, for example, Berrueta-Clement, Schweinhart, Barnett, Epstein, & Weikart, 1984; Clarke & Clarke, 1976; Clarke-Stewart & Fein, 1983; Lazar & Darlington, 1982; Meisels & Anastasiow, 1982; and Zigler & Valentine, 1982). Modern-day researchers view maturation as only one aspect of development. Other factors include socioeconomic variables, familial factors, encounters with the physical and social environment, sex differences, and the internal regulations of new information with preexisting schemes of action. To assume, as do the Gesell theorists, that behavior is equivalent to age-related maturational growth is to confuse a description of experience with its cause. In other words, although it may be possible to describe development in terms of patterned, sequential behaviors, doing so does not imply that development occurs *because* of these behaviors. Nor does it imply that teachers and other professionals are powerless to work with children until children spontaneously achieve these behaviors (i.e., school readiness). Few teachers today would willingly accept such a passive approach to education as that which is implied by a maturationist theory. Yet, unknowingly, that is what they are doing when they subscribe to the Gesellian approach to developmental placement and readiness.

Certainly, all children are not equally ready for school when they become 4 or 5 years of age. However, identifying these differences in readiness only suggests the need for differences in curriculum planning. Other information is required before a valid judgment can be made about whether a child should attend a particular program, or should be labeled *at risk.* This is particularly true for children from linguistic or cultural groups who may be at a disadvantage because of the limitations of the tests being used.

Validity of the Gesell Tests   Although the Gesell schedules were first published in 1940 (Gesell et al.) and have been used in numerous research studies and clinical investigations, no systematic study of the validity of these tests has ever been conducted. In 1966 a subset of items covering the first 2 years of life were selected as a developmental screening test for infants—the Developmental Screening Inventory (DSI) (Knobloch, Pasamanick, & Sherard, 1966). The data that accompanied this test were insufficient to support its validity as a screening test (see McCall, 1982, for a discussion of the DSI). No other validation studies have been published. Jacqueline Haines, director of training at the Gesell Institute, confirms that the Gesell tests have not been validated. In 1984 she noted that the Gesell "documents normative responses by age. The validity of the work has been through years of experience in application. A validity study has not been completed at the present time" (personal communication, March 28, 1984).

This situation raises several problems for users of the Gesell tests. In the absence of predictive validity data, it is impossible to evaluate the claims set forth by Gesell theorists. For example, Ames and her colleagues state that "behavior develops in a patterned and highly predictable way and can be evaluated by means of simple, basic test situations" (Ames et al., 1979, p. ix). This may be true, but there is no evidence to support the position that the behavior evaluated by the Gesell Preschool Tests accurately predicts subsequent development.

A test that only "documents normative responses by age" cannot be used appropriately for prediction unless the predictive relationship has been tested and demonstrated. That is, children whose behavior is non-normative—either delayed or advanced—could, theoretically, be identified by means of the Gesell, but claims about their future performance would be purely speculative in the absence of studies that demonstrate the predictive accuracy of these normative assessments.

Another issue concerns the norms used by the Gesell tests. The original norms were developed by Gesell in 1928 and published in 1940. These norms were based on data obtained from a small, uncontrolled sample of primarily upper middle-class children and were rated by observers who were neither independent of each other nor free from potential bias. New norms have now been established for the Preschool Tests (Ames et al., 1979), but they still leave many questions unanswered. The norms are based on 640 children stratified by sex, age (eight 6-month intervals, from 2½ to 6 years), and parental occupational level. Unfortunately, nearly all of the children were Caucasian, and all lived in Connecticut. Further, no effort was made to test for the effects of differences in birth order, parental education, number of parents in the home, or prior preschool or child care experience. Also, no data are provided concerning the reliability of the standardization procedure: We do not know how many examiners participated, what the level of interobserver agreement was, whether there was intertester stability, or what the standard error of measurement was. Thus, inadequate sampling procedures, absence of validity data, inattention to issues of reliability, and sources of variance in recording performances render the entire normative foundation of the Gesell tests questionable.

Developmental Age and School Placement One of the foremost uses of the Gesell tests is developmental placement. Ames et al. (1979) note that "of all the possible uses of the Gesell Behavior battery, its use in relation to determining the most favorable time for starting school or for subsequent promotion of students may turn out to be one of its most substantial contributions" (p. 184). According to Gesell theorists, the purpose of Gesell testing is to make examiners aware of age-related behaviors. Children's responses then show the level, or developmental age, at which they are functioning. "Regardless of either birthday age or Intelligence Quotient, in most instances a child does best in school if started and subsequently promoted on the basis of developmental age" (Ames et al., 1979, p. 6).

Clearly, the validity of the concept of developmental age hinges on the mechanism for establishing this age. Because that mechanism is the Gesell Preschool Tests—nonstandardized tests excerpted from the full-scale Gesell Developmental Schedules—the notion of developmental age is highly suspect.

Only one published study examines the predictive validity of developmental age by comparing results of kindergarten-age children on the Gesell School Readiness Screening Test with school success (Wood, Powell, & Knight, 1984). The study claims that developmental age provides a useful predictive measure of later school performance. Unfortunately, the study had major problems; the study population was small and not highly generalizable (N = 84, all Caucasian and middle class); the outcome measure of school success (special needs status versus nonspecial needs) was undefined and unvalidated; and the study was not predictive as claimed, but at best postdictive or possibly concurrent. That is, the children were first referred for special services, then 3 months later the Gesell was administered. Because the Gesell test was given *after* the special needs designation was assigned, the study authors linearly adjusted scores back by 3 months. This circular procedure assumes the validity of the developmental age concept, which is precisely what the study was intended to prove.

In short, the use of the Gesell School Readiness Screening Test—based as it is on a set of tests with unknown validity and reliability, a theory that is outmoded and unsubstantiated, an unverified notion of developmental age, and a racially and ethnically narrow normative base—for developmental screening and class placement is empirically unjustified and professionally suspect. The Gesell tests can be used effectively as school readiness tests for initial curriculum planning for individual children, but there currently is no evidence to support more extensive application.

Implications for Early Childhood and Kindergarten Educators

Testing in early childhood and kindergarten should only be used to make better and more appropriate services available to the largest number of children. There are several kinds of tests that, if used as designed and intended, can assist professionals in making appropriate decisions for young children. Children who need special services can be identified by developmental screening and assessment. Children in need of modified classroom programming or individualized attention in preschool or kindergarten can be identified by readiness tests and, to a certain extent, by developmental screening inventories. Tests that exclude children from public education services or that delay their access to the educational mainstream, however, are antithetical to legal and constitutional rights to free education and equal protection. In addition, such tests and practices are incompatible with the belief systems, theoretical perspectives, and best practices of most early childhood educators.

The use of exclusionary tests suggests that children should conform to school programs, rather than schools adjusting to the needs of children. Nowhere is this reversal of the child-centered tradition more evident than in the Gesellian practice that recommends a year's delayed school entrance for children who are not ready for kindergarten. Ames and her colleagues claim that "if a 5-year-old child is still behaving like a 4- or 4½-year-old, he will in all likelihood not be ready for the work of kindergarten, regardless of what the law allows" (Ames et al., 1979, p. 6). This approach is unjustified because it is based on the assumption that the Gesell tests are valid predictors of school performance—an assumption that has not been proven. Also unproven is the assumption that all not ready or developmentally immature children develop similarly and cannot benefit from kindergarten, even if their peers who are ready can. The reality of individual differences is that even in classrooms where all the children have been certified as ready, some will be more ready than others.

Proponents of the developmental readiness concept frequently recommend that children who are immature or not ready be enrolled in *developmental* kindergartens instead of having to enter school late. These programs, also known as readiness kindergartens, usually precede a regular year of kindergarten.

Readiness kindergartens are a fast-growing phenomenon. In Michigan alone 161 school districts offered such programs during the 1983–84 school year, with 67 more districts slated to add them in the 1984–85 school year. These programs—most of which (65%) have existed for less than 5 years—served 5,700 students from 1983 to 1984 at a cost of $3,430,000 (Michigan Department of Education, 1984).

All developmental kindergartens do not subscribe to a Gesellian philosophy. Indeed, most of them are highly eclectic in approach, but they nevertheless share the same kinds of problems as Gesell-oriented programs. Specifically, these types of programs have not been systematically studied or evaluated. Among the questions that need further exploration are the following: On what basis are children placed in these programs? Are minority or poor children overrepresented in them? Are parents accorded due process in placement? What impact do these programs have on children's long-term development?

In practice, many developmental kindergartens contain a disproportionate number of younger children—those with birth dates late in the year. But the research evidence does not support this type of age grouping. Other factors in addition to simple immaturity play important roles in the explanation of school failure and learning problems (Diamond, 1983; Gredler, 1978; Maddux, Stacy, & Scott, 1981). Changing the standard of school readiness or the entry age cutoff only changes the composition of the group that is youngest or least ready—it does not eliminate it.

Many of these practices seem to result from pressures placed on kindergarten teachers to implement academically oriented programs in order to prepare children for the heavy academic emphasis seen in most first through third grades. The developmental readiness movement, as well as the widespread popularity of the Gesell tests, can be seen, in part, as well-meaning responses to these pressures, in which some children are excluded from kindergarten or enrolled in kindergarten for 2 years in order to reduce the likelihood of subsequent failure.

But this situation should cause grave professional concern. It signifies that schools are placing such institutional needs as obtaining higher achievement test scores and adopting more academically oriented early elementary curricula ahead of children's needs. To the extent that these priorities deny slowly developing or at-risk children access to public school programs, they are incompatible with child development research, contemporary social policy, and exemplary early childhood practice. Rather than label children, schools should devote their resources to helping teachers fashion individually responsive curricula that embrace a wide range of childhood abilities and readiness levels.

The National Association for the Education of Young Children's *Position Statement on Developmentally Appropriate Practice in Early Childhood Programs Serving Children Birth Through Age 8* (NAEYC, 1986) notes that high quality, developmentally appropriate programs typically include children with a range of developmental levels in a single classroom. The statement further notes that "It is the responsibility of the educational system to adjust to the developmental needs and levels of the children it serves; children should not be expected to adapt to an inappropriate system" (p. 16). Nor, it might be added, should children or their parents expect not to be served at all because children's skill levels do not conform to some external, preestablished norm or because they are being tested with an inappropriate instrument. In such situations, the schools and professionals who advocate these positions are demonstrating a failure of readiness, not the children.

Editor's Note: When Dr. Meisels's article was accepted for publication by *Young Children*, the Gesell Institute was invited to respond. These are the Institute's remarks:

THE GESELL INSTITUTE RESPONDS

As a pioneer in the field of child development and a leading architect in applying developmental understanding to the classroom, the Gesell Institute accepts its responsibilities as a leader in today's movement toward a developmentally sound, theoretically consistent use of knowledge concerning children's growth applied to school readiness.

Through extensive clinical observation, Arnold Gesell and his colleagues developed innovative observational techniques and established norms that remain the reference point for pediatric milestones, child development stages, and school readiness screening tests today (1925, 1940). When the original norms were compared to current samples in the 1970s controlled for age, sex, and socioeconomic background, the stability of the norms over time were reconfirmed (Ames, Gillespie, Haines, & Ilg, 1979; Knobloch, 1980).

Dr. Gesell was not merely a student of human behavior, but was interested in applying scientific knowledge to the creation of social environments conducive to maximizing the mental health and education of children (1930). Through their work with children in the public schools, Drs. Ilg and Ames helped to accomplish this. Drs. Ilg and Ames recognized that many children were not succeeding in school because they did not have the maturity to effectively undertake the tasks presented. They refined the clinical procedures used in their clinic so that the child's maturity level could be determined by trained educational professionals in schools. This resulted in the development of the Gesell School Readiness Screening, the Gesell School Readiness, and the Gesell Preschool Assessments.

These assessments are designed to assess a child's developmental functioning, using tasks most closely associated with maturationally related aspects of school readiness. *School readiness,* as defined by the Gesell Institute, is the capacity to simultaneously learn and cope with the school environment. *School success* is defined as the ability to learn and have enough energy left over to be a competent, growing human being in all areas of living. The Gesell approach takes into account a child's emotional, social, physical, and adaptive capacities as being of equal concern to human development as intelligence. To define school readiness as having only to do with intelligence, or as having only to do with achievement, or as having only to do with being given previous learning experiences, contradicts longstanding research and experience.

The Gesell assessments are used by schools to gain fuller developmental understanding of the child. If an assessment reveals that a child is developmentally young for kindergarten placement, for example, educational settings more consistent with that child's development can be considered. Rather than excluding a child from kindergarten, the information provided by the assessment assures that responsible recommendations for placement can be made so that the child can be included in an appropriate kind of kindergarten program at an appropriate time and pace. The Gesell assessments do not label children as at risk, handicapped, or remedial. Rather, they tell how the child is functioning on the developmental path of normalcy. Children whose developmental rate is far from that path on the Gesell assessment can be further evaluated.

Gesell readiness assessments have been predictive of school success. A longitudinal study by Ames and Ilg (1964) established a positive relationship between predictions for kindergarten readiness and school performance in the 6th grade. That the assessments measure primarily maturity and not intelligence or experience (Kaufman, 1971), is evidence of the impact maturity has on school readiness. Kaufman also reported that although test interpretation was qualitative in nature, examiners interpreted the records similarly (interrater reliability was .87),. Most recently Wood (Wood, Powell, & Knight, 1984) found that developmental age was a more effective predictor of success or failure in kindergarten than chronological age. Gesell Institute is aware that many researchers want further statistical information to judge the usefulness of the assessments. This is presently one of our major thrusts. Additional statistical data pertaining to the Gesell assessment will soon be available.

A growing body of convincing evidence about the effective use of the Gesell instruments comes from schools. In diverse communities throughout the country, schools are pursuing their own studies of the assessments and the concept of developmental placement. These studies are confirming the predictive ability of the assessments. Such variables as achievement, school adjustment, discipline patterns, parental and teacher satisfaction, child self-concept, retention rates, and the need for special services have all shown positive changes with use of the Gesell Screening Test and developmental placement. Schools as diverse as Broward County Schools in Florida, St. Charles Parish Schools in Louisiana, Avondale Schools in Michigan, and Oxford Central Schools in New York have all reported positive results.

Respecting the process of maturity, the process of development as it unfolds, and the individual pace of each child is what the Gesell philosophy entails. The Gesell School Readiness Screening Test, as a reflection of this philosophy, is a valuable tool for recognizing the forces of maturity in our individual students and thus is an effective means to enhance developmentally appropriate education.

Editor's Note: The following are Dr. Meisels's comments on the Gesell Institute's response.

BUT DR. MEISELS IS NOT CONVINCED

Knowing of my concerns about the Gesell School Readiness Test, a colleague recently asked me whether my doubts would be relieved by a systematic validity study that supported the Gesell Institute's claims. I replied that a carefully designed research study would eliminate many of my concerns. However, past experience casts doubt on the likelihood that such validity data can or will ever appear.

The Gesell Institute has promised statistical data for generations, as they do yet again. But all they provide are difficult-to-prove assertions about "the forces of maturity"—assertions based on faith in Dr. Gesell's admittedly pioneering efforts. It is time to move beyond the faith of the 1930s to the reason of the 1980s.

In their published response, the Institute restates its central claim that "Gesell readiness assessments have been predictive of school success" (Gesell Institute, 1987, p. 00). The burden of proof is on the Institute to support this key assertion, but the burden proves too heavy and the evidence too weak.

First, they cite Ames and Ilg (1964) as establishing a positive relationship between predictions of kindergarten readiness and school performance in the 6th grade. Yet this relationship is reported only in terms of correlations, thereby making impossible an analysis of the proportions of accurate and inaccurate predictions. Furthermore, because the highest level of agreement between predictors and outcomes was for children at the extremes of ability, the correlation reflects these extremes rather than the performance of the majority of children tested.

Second, they suggest that Kaufman (1971) confirmed that the tests measure maturity—not intelligence or experience. However, Kaufman reports that the factor structure of the Readiness Tests suggests that the tests measure intelligence and experience as well as maturity. Moreover, Shepard and Smith

(1985) have shown that the Gesell tests lack discriminate validity from IQ tests. Naglieri (1985) also notes that the test items on the Preschool Test "are very similar and in some cases identical to those found in current IQ tests. . . . The major difference between the Gesell and current intelligence tests appears to be the lack of emphasis on the psychometric properties of the scale" (p. 608).

Third, the Institute cites the study by Wood, Powell, and Knight (1984) as evidence of predictive validity. Already criticized in my original article, the results presented in their study have been further analyzed by Shepard and Smith (1986). They note that only one half of the children identified as potential school failures by the School Readiness Test were accurately identified. Shepard and Smith note that for every potential failure accurately identified by the test, a successful child was falsely identified. In other words, the study by Wood, Powell, and Knight documents the predictive *inaccuracy* of the Gesell.

As the use of the Gesell tests proliferate, the problems associated with false predictions and false identifications continue to grow. Children are said to be *overplaced, developmentally young,* or simply *not ready,* when in fact the tests used to make these judgments are invalid, their norms unrepresentative, and their claims unsubstantiated. Reviews of the Gesell Preschool and School Readiness Tests have repeatedly demonstrated the limitations of the tests, concluding that the authors "ignore their responsibilities as testmakers and do not report the type of information that is mandated as essential by American Psychological Association guidelines" (Kaufman, 1985, p. 607). "The lack of emphasis on psychometric attributes of the scale leads to a potential for misuse or misinterpretation" (Naglieri, 1985, p. 608). "The test developers offer no set of cutoff scores that might be useful in making decisions about the placements, nor do they provide evidence that students who are placed according to scores on the test really benefit over the long term from such placement" (Bradley, 1985, p. 609).

The time has come for faith to give way to reason. The claims made for the Gesell should be modified, and its use as a placement and screening instrument correspondingly curtailed.

CHAPTER 10 Parenting

10.1 BETTYE M. CALDWELL

What Is the Optimal Learning Environment for the Young Child?

Every day across America, many infants and toddlers are cared for in a wide variety of child centers and family care homes. These environments are intended to nurture and to provide opportunities for developing children's full potential.

Prominent educator Bettye M. Caldwell (b. 1924) has held university positions in Missouri, Illinois, and New York, and most recently at the University of Arkansas. She received a Ph.D. from Washington University in St. Louis, Missouri. When Caldwell was the president of the National Association for the Education of Young Children (1982–1984), she led the organization to adopt several position papers on child-care licensing, family day-care regulation, nomenclature, benefits, and wages. Caldwell, who has studied and defined infant and toddler programming, promotes the term *educare* for the care and education of very young children. Her theoretical model for the systematic educare of children as young as six months involves arranging the environment in such a way that growth-inducing events can occur.

Caldwell considers the implications of this model in "What is the Optimal Learning Environment for the Young Child?" *American Journal of Orthopsychiatry* (January, 1967), from which the following selection is taken. After stating the operating principle guiding optimal environments, that the child is cared for at home by the mother, Caldwell poses a series of questions that challenge hidden assumptions. Using studies to bolster her discussion, Caldwell concludes that letting nature take its course is not the best position to take in early learning. In spite of what is known today about the personal-social and cognitive development of infants and toddlers, her basic premise and assumptions still raise some questions about the education of the very young.

A truism in the field of child development is that the milieu in which development occurs influences that development. As a means of validating the principle, considerable scientific effort has gone into the Linnaean task of describing and classifying milieus and examining developmental consequences associated with different types. Thus we know something about what it is like to come of age in New Guinea (Mead, 1953) in a small Midwestern town (Barker and Wright, 1955), in villages and cities in Mexico (Lewis, 1959), in families of different social-class level in Chicago (Davis and Havighurst, 1946) or Boston (Maccoby and Gibbs, 1954; Pavenstedt, 1965), in a New York slum (Wortis *et al.*, 1963), in Russian collectives (Bronfenbrenner, 1962), in Israeli Kibbutzim (Irvine, 1952; Rabin, 1957; Spiro, 1958), in the eastern part of the United States (Provence and Lipton, 1962), and in a Republican community in Central New York (Caldwell *et al.*, 1963). Most of these milieu descriptions have placed great stress on the fact that they were just that and nothing more, i.e., they have expressed the customary scientific viewpoint that to describe is not to judge or criticize. However, in some of the more recent milieu descriptions which have contrasted middle- and lower-class family environments or highlighted conditions in extreme lower-class settings (Pavenstedt, 1965; Wortis *et al.*, 1963), often more than a slight suggestion has crept in that things could be better for the young child from the deprived segment of the culture. Even so, there remains a justifiable wariness about recommending or arranging any environment for the very young child other than the type regarded as its natural habitat, viz., within its own family.

Of course, optimizing environments are arranged all the time under one guise or another. For example, for disturbed children whose family environments seem effectively to reinforce rather than extinguish psychopathology, drastic alterations of milieu often are attempted. This may take the form of psychotherapy for one or both parents as well as the disturbed child, or it may involve total removal of the child from the offending environment with temporary or prolonged placement of the child in a milieu presumably more conducive to normal development. Then there is the massive milieu arrangement formalized and legalized as "education" which profoundly affects the lives of all children once they reach the age of five or six. This type of arrangement is not only tolerated but fervently endorsed by our culture as a whole. In fact, any subculture (such as the Amish) which resists the universalization of this pattern of milieu arrangement is regarded as unacceptably deviant and as justifying legal action to enforce conformity.

For very young children, however, there has been a great deal of timidity about conscious and planned arrangement of the developmental milieu, as though the implicit assumption has been made that any environment which sustains life is adequate during this period. This is analogous to suggesting that the intrauterine environment during the period of maximal cellular proliferation is less important than it is later, a suggestion that patently disregards evidence from epidemiology and experimental embryology. The rate of proliferation of new behavioral skills during the fist three years of life and the increasing accumulation of data pointing to the relative permanence of deficit acquired when the environment is inadequate during this period make it mandatory that careful attention be given to the preparation of the developmental environment during the first three years of life.

CONCLUSIONS FROM INADEQUATE ENVIRONMENTS

It is, of course, an exaggeration to imply that no one has given attention to the type of environment which can nourish early and sustained growth and development. For a good three decades now infants who are developing in different milieus have been observed and examined, and data relating to their development have made it possible to identify certain strengths and deficiencies of the different types of environments. Of all types described, the one most consistently indicated by the data is the institution. A number of years ago Goldfarb (1949) published an excellent series of studies contrasting patterns of intellectual functioning shown by a group of adopted adolescents who had been reared in institutions up to age three and then transferred to foster homes or else placed shortly after birth in foster homes. The development of the group that had spent time in the institution was deficient in many ways compared to the group that had gone directly into foster homes. Provence and Lipton (1962) recently published a revealing description of the early social and intellectual development of infants in institutions, contrasting their development with that of home-reared children. On almost every measured variable the institutional infants were found wanting—less socially alert and outgoing, less curious, less responsive, less interested in objects, and generally less advanced. The findings of this study are almost prototypic of the literature in the field, as pointed out in excellent reviews by Yarrow (1961) and Ainsworth (1962).

Although there are many attributes in combination that comprise the institutional environment, the two most obvious elements are (1) absence of a mother and (2) the presence of a group. These basic characteristics have thus been identified as the major carriers of the institutional influence and have been generalized into an explicit principle guiding our recommendations for optimal environments—learning or otherwise—for young children whenever any type of milieu arrangement is necessary. This principle may be stated simply as: the optimal environment for the young child is one in which the child is cared for in his own home in the context of a warm, continuous emotional relationship with his own mother under conditions of varied sensory input. Implicit in this principle is the conviction that the child's mother is the person best qualified to provide a stable and warm interpersonal relationship as well as the necessary pattern of sensory stimulation. Implicit also is the assumption that socio-emotional development has priority during the first three years and that if this occurs normally, cognitive development, which is of minor importance during this period anyway, will take care of itself. At a still deeper level lurks the assumption that attempts to foster cognitive development will interfere with socio-emotional development. Advocacy of the principle also implies endorsement of the idea that most homes are adequate during this early period and that no formal training (other than possibly some occasional supervisory support) for mothering is necessary. Such an operating principle places quite an onus on mothers and assumes that they will possess or quickly acquire all the talents necessary to create an optimal learning environment. And this author, at least, is convinced that a majority of mothers have such talents or proclivities and that they are willing to try to do all they can to create for their children the proper developmental milieu.

But there are always large numbers of children for whom family resources are not available and for whom some type of substitute milieu arrangement must be made. On the whole, such attempts have followed the entirely logical and perhaps evolutionary approach to milieu development—they have sought to create substitute families. The same is usually true when parents themselves seek to work out an alternate child-care arrangement because of less drastic conditions, such as maternal employment. The most typical maneuver is to try to obtain a motherly person who will "substitute" for her (not supplement her) during her hours away from her young child.

Our nation has become self-consciously concerned with social evolution, and in the past decade a serious attempt has been made to assimilate valid data from the behavioral and social sciences into planning for social action. In this context it would be meaningful to examine and question some of the hidden assumptions upon which our operating principle about the optimal environment for the young child rests.

EXAMINING THE HIDDEN ASSUMPTIONS

1. Do intermittent, short-term separations of the child from the mother impair the mother-child relationship or the development of the child?

Once having become sensitized to the consequences of institutionalization, and suspicious that the chief missing ingredient was the continued presence of the mother, the scientific and professional community went on the *qui vive* [alert] to the possibly deleterious consequences of any type of separation of an infant from its mother. Accordingly, a number of studies (Caldwell *et al.*, 1963; Gardner *et al.*, 1961; Hoffman, 1961; Radke, 1961; Siegel and Hass, 1963) investigated the consequences of short-term intermittent separation and were unable to demonstrate in the children the classical syndrome of the "institutional child." In reviewing the literature, Yarrow (1961) stressed the point that available data do not support the tendency to assume that maternal deprivation, such as exists in the institutional environment, and maternal separation are the same thing. Apparently short cyclic interruptions culminated by reunions do not have the same effect as prolonged interruptions, even though quantitatively at the end of a designated period the amount of time spent in a mother-absent situation might be equal for the two experiences. Also in this context it is well to be reminded that in the institutional situation there is likely to be no stable mother-child relationship to interrupt. These are often never-mothered rather than ever-mothered children, a fact which must be kept in mind in generalizing from data on institutional groups. Thus until we have data to indicate that such intermittent separation-reunion cycles have similar effects on young children as prolonged separations, we are probably unjustified in assuming that an "uninterrupted" relationship is an essential ingredient of the optimal environment.

2. Is group upbringing invariably damaging?

In studies done in West European and American settings, social and cognitive deficits associated with continuous group care during infancy have been frequently demonstrated. Enough exceptions have been reported, however, to warrant an intensification of the search for the "true" ingredient in the group situation associated with the observed deficits. For example, Freud and Dann (1951) described the adjustment of a group of six children reared in a concentration camp orphanage for approximately three years, where they were cared for by overworked and impersonal inmates of the camp, and then transported to a residence for children in England. The children, who had never known their own mothers but who had been together as a·group for approximately three years, were intensely attached to one another. Although their adjustment to their new environment was slow and differed from the pattern one would expect from home-reared children, it was significant that they eventually did make a reasonably good adjustment. That the children were able to learn a new language while making this emotional transition was offered as evidence that many of the basic cognitive and personality attributes remained unimpaired in spite of the pattern of group upbringing. The accumulation of data showing that Kibbutz-reared children (Rabin, 1957) do not have cognitive deficits also reinforces the premise that it is not necessarily group care *per se* that produces the frequently reported deficit and that it is possible to retain the advantages of group care while systematically eliminating its negative features. Grounds for reasonable optimism also have been found in retrospective studies by Maas (1963) and Beres and Obers (1960) although in both cases the authors found evidence of pathology in some members of the follow-up sample. Similarly Dennis and Najarian (1957) concluded from their data that the magnitude of the deficit varied as a function of the type of instrument used to measure deficit, and Dennis (1960) showed that in institutions featuring better adult-child ratios and a conscious effort to meet the psychological needs of the infants the development of the children was much less retarded than was the case in a group of children residing in institutions with limited and unsophisticated staff. It is not appropriate to go into details of limitations of methodology in any of these studies; however, from the standpoint of an examination of the validity of a principle, it is important to take note of any exceptions to the generality of that principle.

In this context it is worth considering a point made by Gula (1965). He recently has suggested that some of the apparent consistency in studies comparing institutionalized infants with those cared for in their own homes and in foster homes might disappear if it were possible to equate the comparison groups on the variable of environmental adequacy. That is, one could classify all three types of environments as good, marginal, or inadequate on a number of dimensions. Most of the studies have compared children from palpably "inadequate" institutions with children from "good" foster and own homes. He suggests that, merely because most institutions studied have been inadequate in terms of such variables as adult-child ratio, staff turnover, and personal characteristics of some of the caretakers, etc., one is not justified in concluding *ipso facto* that group care is invariably inferior or damaging.

3. Is healthy socio-emotional development the most important task of the first three years? Do attempts to foster cognitive growth interfere with social and emotional development?

These paired assumptions, which one finds stated in one variety or another in many pamphlets and books dealing with early child development, represent acceptance of a closed system model of human development. They seem to conceptualize development as compartmentalized and with a finite limit. If the child progresses too much in one area he automatically restricts the amount of development that can occur in another area. Thus one often encounters such expressions as "cognitive development at the *expense* of socio-emotional development." It is perhaps of interest to reflect that, until our children reach somewhere around high school age, we seldom seem to worry that the reverse might occur. But, of course, life is an open system, and on the whole it is accurate to suggest that development feeds upon development. Cognitive and socio-emotional advances tend on the whole to be positively, not negatively correlated.

The definition of intelligence as *adaptivity* has not been adequately stressed by modern authors. It is, of course, the essence of Piaget's definition (1952) as it was earlier of Binet (Binet and Simon, 1916). Unfortunately, however, for the last generation or so in America we have been more concerned with how to measure intelligent behavior than how to interpret and understand it. Acceptance of the premise that intelligent behavior is adaptive behavior should help to break the set of many persons in the field of early child development that to encourage cognitive advance is to discourage healthy socio-emotional development. Ample data are available to suggest that quite the reverse is true either for intellectually advanced persons (Terman *et al.*, 1925; Terman and Oden, 1947) or an unselected sample. In a large sample of young adults from an urban area in Minnesota, Anderson and associates (1959) found that the best single predictor of post-high school adjustment contained in a large assessment battery was a humble little group intelligence test. Prediction based on intelligence plus teacher's ratings did somewhat better, but nothing exceeded the intelligence test for single measure efficiency.

It is relevant here to mention White's (1959) concept of competence or effectance as a major stabilizing force in personality development. The emotional reinforcement accompanying the old "I can do it myself" declaration should not be undervalued. In Murphy's report (1962) of the coping behavior of preschool children one sees evidence of the adjustive supports gained through cognitive advances. In his excellent review of cognitive stimulation in infancy and early childhood, Fowler (1962) raises the question of whether there is any justification for the modern anxiety (and, to be sure, it is a modern phenomenon) over whether cognitive stimulation may damage personality development. He suggests that in the past severe and harmful methods may have been the culprits whenever there was damage and that the generalizations have confused methods of stimulation with the process of stimulation *per se*.

4. Do cognitive experiences of the first few months and years leave no significant residual?

Any assumption that the learnings of infancy are evanescent appears to be a fairly modern idea. In his *Emile*, first published in 1762, Rousseau (1950) stressed the point that education should begin while the child is still in the cradle. Perhaps any generalization to the contrary received its major modern impetus from a rather unlikely place—from longitudinal studies of development covering the span from infancy to adulthood. From findings of poor prediction of subsequent intellectual status (Bayley, 1949) one can legitimately infer that the infant tests measure behavior that is somewhat irrelevant to later intellectual performance. Even though these behaviors predictive of later cognitive behavior elude most investigators, one cannot infer that the early months and years are unimportant for cognitive development.

Some support for this assumption has come from experimental studies in which an attempt has been made to produce a durable effect in human subjects by one or another type of intervention offered during infancy. One cogent example is the work of Rheingold (1956), in which she provided additional social and personal stimulation to a small group of approximately six-month-old, institutionalized infants for a total of eight weeks. At the end of the experimental period, differences in social responsiveness between her stimulated group and a control group composed of other babies in the institution could be observed. There were also slight but nonsignificant advances in postural and motor behavior on a test of infant development. However, when the babies were followed up approximately a year later, by which time all but one were in either adoptive or boarding homes or in their own natural homes, the increased social responsiveness formerly shown by the stimulated babies was no longer observed. Nor were there differences in level of intellectual functioning. Rheingold and Bayley (1959) concluded that the extra mothering provided during the experimental period was enough to produce an effect at the time but not enough to sustain this effect after such a time as the two groups were no longer differentially stimulated. However, in spite of their conservative conclusion, it is worth nothing that the experimentally stimulated babies were found to vocalize more during the follow-up assessments than the control babies. Thus there may have been enough of an effect to sustain a developmental advance in at least this one extremely important area.

Some very impressive recent unpublished data obtained by Skeels, offer a profound challenge to the assumption of the unimportance of the first three years for cognitive growth. This investigator has followed up after approximately 25 years most of the subjects described in a paper by Skeels and Dye (1939). Thirteen infants had been transferred from an orphanage because of evidence of mental retardation and placed in an institution for the retarded under the care of adolescent retardates who gave them a great deal of loving care and as much cognitive stimulation as they could. The 13 subjects showed a marked acceleration in development after this transfer. In contrast a group of reasonably well matched infants left on the wards of the orphanage continued to develop poorly. In a recent follow-up of these cases, Skeels discovered that the gains made by the transferred infants were sustained into their adult years, whereas all but one of the control subjects developed the classic syndrome of mental retardation.

The fact that development and experience are cumulative makes it difficult ever to isolate any one antecedent period and assert that its influence was or was not influential in a subsequent developmental period. Thus even though it might be difficult to demonstrate an effect of some experience in an adjacent time period, delayed effects may well be of even greater developmental consequence. In a recent review of data from a number of longitudinal studies, Bloom (1964) has concluded that during the first three to four years (the noncognitive years, if you will) approximately 50 per cent of the development of intelligence that is ever to occur in the life cycle takes place. During this period a particular environment may be either abundant or deprived in terms of the ingredients essential for providing opportunities for the development of intelligence and problem solving. Bloom states:

> The effects of the environments, especially of the extreme environments, appear to be greatest in the early (and more rapid) periods of intelligence development and least in the later (and less rapid) periods of development. Although there is relatively little evidence of the effects of changing the environment on the changes in intelligence, the evidence so far available suggests that marked changes in the environment in the early years can produce greater changes in intelligence than will equally marked changes in the environment at later periods of development. (pp. 88–89)

5. Can one expect that, without formal planning, all the necessary learning experiences will occur?

There is an old legend that if you put six chimpanzees in front of six typewriters and leave them there long enough they eventually will produce all the works in the British Museum. One could paraphrase this for early childhood by suggesting that six children with good eyes and ears and hands and brains would, if left alone in nature, arrive at a number system, discover the laws of conservation of matter and energy, comprehend gravity and the motions of the planets, and perhaps arrive at the theory of relativity. All the "facts" necessary to discern these relationships are readily available. Perhaps a more realistic example would be to suggest that, if we surround a group of young children with a carefully selected set of play materials, they would eventually discover for themselves the laws of color mixture, of form and contour, of perspective, of formal rhythm and tonal relationships, and biological growth. And, to be sure, all this *could* occur. But whether this will necessarily occur with any frequency is quite another matter. We also assume that at a still earlier period a child will learn body control, eye-hand coordination, the rudiments of language, and styles of problem solving in an entirely incidental and unplanned way. In an article in a recent issue of a popular woman's magazine, an author (Holt, 1965) fervently urges parents to stop trying to teach their young children in order that the children may learn. And, to be sure, there is always something to be said for this caution; it is all too easy to have planned learning experiences become didactic and regimented rather than subtle and opportunistic.

As more people gain experience in operating nursery school programs for children with an early history deficient in many categories of experience, the conviction appears to be gaining momentum that such children often are not able to avail themselves of the educational opportunities and must be guided into meaningful learning encounters. In a recent paper dealing with the preschool behavior of a group of 21 children from multiproblem families, Malone (1966) describes the inability of the children to carry out self-directed exploratory maneuvers with the toys and equipment as follows:

> When the children first came to nursery school they lacked interest in learning the names and properties of objects. Colors, numbers, sizes, shapes, locations, all seemed interchangeable. Nothing in the room seemed to have meaning for a child apart from the fact that another child had approached or handled it or that the teacher's attention was turned toward it. Even brief play depended on the teacher's involvement and support. (p. 5)

When one reflects on the number of carefully arranged reinforcement contingencies necessary to help a young child learn to decode the simple message, "No," it is difficult to support the position that in early learning, as in anything else, nature should just take its course.

6. Is formal training for child-care during the first three years unnecessary?

This assumption is obviously quite ridiculous, and yet it is one logical derivative of the hypothesis that the only adequate place for a young child is with his mother or a permanent mother substitute. There is, perhaps unfortunately, no literacy test for motherhood. This again is one of our interesting scientific paradoxes. That is, proclaiming in one breath that mothering is essential for the healthy development of a child, we have in the very next breath implied that just any mothering will do. It is interesting in this connection that from the elementary school level forward we have rigid certification statutes in most states that regulate the training requirements for persons who would qualify as teachers of our children. (The same degree of control over the qualifications and training of a nursery school teacher has not prevailed in the past, but we are moving into an era when it will.) So again, our pattern of social action appears to support the emplicit belief in the lack of importance of the first three years of life.

In 1928, John B. Watson wrote a controversial little trade book called *The Psychological Care of Infant and Child.* He included one chapter heretically entitled, "The Dangers of Too Much Mother Love." In this chapter he suggested that child training was too important to be left in the hands of mothers, apparently not because he felt them intellectually inadequate but because of their sentimentality. In his typical "nondirective" style Watson wrote:

> Six months' training in the actual handling of children from two to six under the eye of competent instructors should make a fairly satisfactory child's nurse. To keep them we should let the position of nurse or governess in the home be a respected one. Where the mother herself must be the nurse—which is the case in the vast majority of American homes—she must look upon herself while performing the functions of a nurse as a professional woman and not as a sentimentalist masquerading under the name of "Mother." (p. 149)

At present in this country a number of training programs are currently being formulated which would attempt to give this kind of professional training called for by Watson and many others. It is perhaps not possible to advance on all fronts at the same time, an the pressing health needs of the young child demanded and received top priority in earlier decades. Perhaps it will now be possible to extend our efforts at social intervention to encompass a broader range of health, education, and welfare activities.

7. Are most homes and most parents adequate for at least the first three years?

Enough has been presented in discussing other implicit assumptions to make it unnecessary to amplify this point at length. The clinical literature, and much of the research literature of the last decade dealing with social-class differences, has made abundantly clear that all parents are not qualified to provide even the basic essentials of physical and psychological care to their children. Such reports as those describing the incidence of battered children (Elmer, 1963; Kempe *et al.*, 1962) capture our attention, but reports concerned with subtler and yet perhaps more long-standing patterns of parental deficit also fill the literature. In her description of the child-rearing environments provided by low lower-class families, Pavenstedt (1965) has described them as impulse determined with very little evidence of clear planfulness for activities that would benefit either parent or child. Similarly, Wortis and associates (1963) have described the extent to which the problems of the low-income mother so overwhelm her with reactions of depression and inadequacy that behavior toward the child is largely determined by the needs of the moment rather than by any clear plan about how to bring up children and how to train them to engage in the kind of behavior that the parents regard as acceptable or desirable. No social class and no cultural or ethnic group has exclusive rights to the domain of inadequate parentage; all conscientious parents must strive constantly for improvement on this score. However, relatively little attention has been paid to the possibly deleterious consequences of inadequacies during the first three years of life. Parents have been blamed for so many problems of their children in later age periods that a moderate reaction formation appears to have set in. But again, judging by the type of social action taken by the responsible professional community, parental inadequacy during the first three years is seldom considered as a major menace. Perhaps, when the various alternatives are weighed, it appears by comparison to be the least of multiple evils; but parental behavior of the first three years should not be regarded as any more sacrosanct or beyond the domain of social concern than that of the later years. . . .

SUMMARY

Interpretations of research data and accumulated clinical experience have led over the years to a consensual approximation of an answer to the question: what is the optimal learning environment for the young child? As judged from our scientific and lay literature and from practices in health and welfare agencies, one might infer that the optimal learning environment for the young child is that which exists when (a) a young child is cared for in his own home (b) in the context of a warm and nurturant emotional relationship (c) with his mother (or a reasonable facsimile thereof) under conditions of (d) varied sensory and cognitive input. Undoubtedly until a better hypothesis comes along, this is the best one available. This paper has attempted to generate constructive thinking about whether we are justified in overly vigorous support of (a) when (b), (c) or (d), or any combination thereof, might not obtain. Support for the main hypothesis comes primarily from other hypotheses (implicit assumptions) rather than from research or experimental data. When these assumptions are carefully examined they are found to be difficult if not impossible to verify with existing data.

The conservatism inherent in our present avoidance of carefully designed social action programs for the very young child needs to be re-examined. Such a re-examination conducted in the light of research evidence available about the effects of different patterns of care forces consideration of whether formalized intervention programs should not receive more attention than they have in the past and whether attention should be given to a professional training sequence for child-care workers. The careful preparation of the learning environment calls for a degree of training and commitment and personal control not always to be found in natural caretakers and a degree of richness of experience by no means always available in natural environments.

REFERENCES

Ainsworth, Mary. 1962. Reversible and irreversible effects of maternal deprivation on intellectual development. *Child Welfare League of America*, pp. 42–62.

American Women. 1963. A report of the President's Commission on the Status of Women (Washington, D.C.: Superintendent of Documents).

Anderson, J. E., *et al.* 1959. *A survey of children's adjustment over time* (Minneapolis, Minn.: University of Minnesota).

Barker, R. G., and H. F. Wright. 1955. *Midwest and its children: the psychological ecology of an American town* (New York: Harper & Row).

Bayley, Nancy. 1949. Consistency and variability in the growth of intelligence from birth to eighteen years. *J. genet. Psychol.*, 75, pp. 165–196.

Beres, D., and S. Obers. 1950. The effects of extreme deprivation in infancy on psychic structure in adolescence. *Psychoanal. Stud. of the Child*, 5, pp. 121–140.

Binet, A., and T. Simon. 1916. *The development of intelligence in children.* Translated by Elizabeth S. Kite (Baltimore, Md.: The Williams & Wilkins Company).

Bloom, B. S. 1964. *Stability and change in human characteristics* (New York: John Wiley & Sons, Inc.).

Bronfenbrenner, Urie. 1962. Soviet studies of personality development and socialization. In American Psychological Association, Inc., *Some views on Soviet psychology*, pp. 63–85.

Caldwell, Bettye M., *et al.* 1963. Mother-infant interaction in monomatric and polymatric families. *Amer. J. Orthopsychiat.*, 33, pp. 653–664.

___, and J. B. Richmond. 1964. Programmed day care for the very young child—a preliminary report. *J. Marriage and the Family*, 26, pp. 481–488.

Davis, A., and R. J. Havighurst. 1946. Social class and color differences in child-rearing. *Amer. Sociol. Rev.*, 11, pp. 698–710.

Dennis, W. 1960. Causes of retardation among institutional children. *J. genet. Psychol.*, 96, pp. 47–59.

___, and P. Najarian. 1957. Infant development under environmental handicap. *Psychol. Monogr.*, 71, 7, Whole No. 536.

Elmer, Elizabeth. 1963. Identification of abused children. *Children*, 10, pp. 180–184.

Fowler, W. 1962. Cognitive learning in infancy and early childhood. *Psychol. Bull.*, 59, pp. 116–152.

Freud, Anna, and Sophie Dann. 1951. An experiment in group upbringing. *Psychoanal. Stud. of the Child*, 6, pp. 127–168.

Gardner, D. B., G. R. Hawkes, and L. G. Burchinal, 1961. Noncontinuous mothering in infancy and development in later childhood. *Child Develpm.*, 32, pp. 225–234.

Goldfarb, W. 1949. Rorschach test differences between family-reared, institution-reared and schizophrenic children. *Amer. J. Orthopsychiat.*, 19, pp. 624–633.

Gula, M. January 1965. *New concepts for group care.* A paper given at the conference on Group Care for Infants and Young Children (Washington, D.C.: Children's Bureau, Department of Health, Education, and Welfare).

Hoffman, Lois Wladis. 1961. Effects of maternal employment on the child. *Child Develpm.*, 32, pp. 187–197.

Holt, J. 1965. How to help babies learn—without teaching them. *Redbook*, 126(1), pp. 54–55; 134–137.

Irvine, Elizabeth E. 1952. Observations on the aims and methods of child-rearing in communal settlements in Israel. *Human Relat.*, 5, pp. 247–275.

Kempe, C. H., *et al.* 1962. The battered-child syndrome. *J. Amer. Med. Assn.*, 181, pp. 17–24.

Lewis, O. 1959. *Five families* (New York: Basic Books, Inc.).

Maas, H. 1963. Long-term effects of early childhood separation and group care. *Vita Humana*, 6, pp. 34–56.

Maccoby, Eleanor, and Patricia K. Gibbs. 1954. Methods of child-rearing in two social classes. In W. E. Martin and Celia B. Stendler (eds.), *Readings in child development* (New York: Harcourt, Brace & World, Inc.), pp. 380–396.

Malone, C. A. 1966. Safety first: comments on the influence of external danger in the lives of children of disorganized families. *Amer. J. Orthopsychiat.* **36**, pp. 3–12.

Mead, Margaret. 1953. *Growing up in New Guinea* (New York: New American Library of World Literature, Inc.).

Murphy, Lois B., *et al.* 1962. *The widening world of childhood* (New York: Basic Books, Inc.).

Pavenstedt, E. 1965. A comparison of the child-rearing environment of upper-lower and very low-lower class families. *Amer. J. Orthopsychiat.*, **35**, pp. 89–98.

Piaget, J. 1952. *The origins of intelligence in children.* Translated by Margaret Cook (New York: International Universities Press, Inc.).

Provence, Sally, and Rose C. Lipton. 1962. *Infants in institutions* (New York: International Universities Press, Inc.).

Rabin, A. I. 1957. Personality maturity of Kibbutz and non-Kibbutz children as reflected in Rorschach findings. *J. proj. Tech.*, pp. 148–153.

Rheingold, Harriet. 1956. The modification of social responsiveness in institutional babies. *Monogr. Soc. Res. Child Develpm.*, **21**, p. 63.

___, and Nancy Bayley. 1959. The later effects of an experimental modification of mothering. *Child Develpm.*, **30**, pp. 363–372.

Rousseau, J. J. 1950. *Emile (1762)* (Woodbury, N.Y.: Barron's Educational Series, Inc.).

Siegel, Alberta E., and Miriam B. Hass. 1963. The working mother: a review of research. *Child Develpm.*, **34**, pp. 513–542.

Skeels, H., and H. Dye. 1939. A study of the effects of differential stimulation on mentally retarded children. *Proc. Amer. Assn. on ment. Defic.*, **44**, pp. 114–136.

Spiro, M. 1958. *Children of the Kibbutz* (Cambridge, Mass.: Harvard University Press).

Terman, L. M., *et al.* 1925. Genetic studies or genius: Vol. 1. *Mental and physical traits of a thousand gifted children* (Stanford, Calif.: Stanford University Press).

___, and Melita H. Oden. 1947. *The gifted child grows up: twenty-five years' follow-up of a superior group* (Stanford, Calif.: Stanford University Press).

Watson, J. B. 1928. *Psychological care of infant and child* (London: George Allen & Unwin Ltd.).

White, R. W. 1959. Motivation reconsidered: the concept of competence. *Psychol. Rev.*, **66**, pp. 297–333.

Wortis, H., *et al.* 1963. Child-rearing practice in a low socio-economic group. *Pediatrics*, **32**, pp. 298–307.

Yarrow, L. J. 1961. Maternal deprivation: toward an empirical and conceptual re-evaluation. *Psychol. Bull.*, **58**, pp. 459–490.

Yarrow, Marian Radke. 1961. Maternal employment and child rearing. *Children*, **8**, pp. 223–228.

10.2 MARGARET O'BRIEN STEINFELS

Larger Questions: Day Care, the Family, and Society

Why do some people fear that child care can weaken the family? Why is it that child care is sometimes viewed as a way to limit and control the family?

Historian Margaret O'Brien Steinfels (b. 1941) first raised these questions in *Who's Minding the Children? The History and Politics of Day Care in America* (Simon & Schuster, 1973), a discussion of the historical and political issues surrounding child care in America. In the following selection from the book, she tackles the issue of family values and children living in an individualistic society. Since the 1970s the particulars may have changed, yet the broad questions of childrearing and the family's role in it largely remain unanswered today.

One of the major difficulties is that through the years society's laws and policies have extended further and further into childrearing. Steinfels notes, for example, that compulsory schooling laws created a new expectation for how children's time was to be spent outside the family. One result of more schooling was greater dependency on parental support, which impacted family economics. Regulations on child labor, health, television, and discipline represent society's efforts to improve the lives of children. According to Steinfels, such regulations and policies, benevolent though they may be, have stressed families' child-rearing capabilities. She argues that society's values have actually weakened families rather than strengthened them. From a historian's perspective, Steinfels claims that society demands much of families yet does little to assist them in meeting those demands, particularly in the task of childrearing.

Steinfels holds degrees from Loyola University and New York University. Her writings focus on topics related to families and work.

Day care will not destroy the family. Day care will not replace the family. Day care will not become the arbiter of child-rearing in America. Depending on the degree of its future development, or lack of it, day care will have a substantial impact on the family. The extent and nature of that impact hinges on many decisions yet to be made about the control, financing, administration, and programming of day care services—decisions which President Nixon's 1971 veto of the Comprehensive Child Development Act postponed but did not resolve. The possibility that these questions may never be resolved, that the present, small, piecemeal and inadequate system will continue, is in itself, a decision too, one that will have consequences for family life as powerful as those that could flow from a decision to expand day care services. The rigid limitation of government-subsidized day care, for example, could encourage the growth of custodially oriented for-profit centers where the child care is often poor and where the only parental control is through the cashbox.

The questions one ought to pose about day care's effects upon the family are not those most frequently asked nor those coming from our most illustrious public figures.

The question is not: Shall America have day care? We already have day care. The question is: What kind of day care shall we have? Excellent, good, or bad?

The question is not: Will day care destroy the family? In their one hundred years of limited but effective existence, day care services have never attempted or unwittingly managed to do that. The question is: Will day care support family and community or will it continue to be an instrument of government social policy offered and withdrawn solely in response to Washington's attitude on welfare and regulation of the poor? . . .

The new ingredient in the debate is the influence of early childhood education and development. As day care has more and more come under its influence, shedding, to a considerable extent, the image of a custodial institution, it has become highly attractive to a broad range of families—far more than would ever have been attracted by the turn-of-the-century day nursery or the child welfare establishment of three, four, and five decades ago. This normalization of day care has presented, largely to lower-middle and middle-income families, a new option in child-rearing along with an enlarged potential for increasing family income by allowing more women to work. How well this new usage can fit old welfare-oriented definitions is a matter of speculation. Can a service granted begrudgingly to the poor and desperate meet the needs and expectations of the not-so-poor and hopeful?

. . . There is, in a real sense, no such thing as "the American Family"; nor is there, the accusations against Dr. Spock notwithstanding, an American system of child-rearing; nor, in fact, is there common agreement about the kind of child the American child should be. One has only to observe child-rearing in France or Germany or Russia or China to appreciate American diversity and heterogeneity in family styles, in child-rearing practices, and in the range of relationships allowed between American parents and their children. Whether this variety is based on personal choice, class, race, ethnic group, religion, or region, differences do exist, and they ought to be acknowledged in any discussion of day care and the family.

And even beyond these child-rearing differences there is a broad range of family size, behavior, and organization. After all, not every American Family is made up of Mama, Papa, and 2.7 children, although our art, literature, and television situation comedies usually bring the patriarchal nuclear family most readily to mind as the archetypical form. Many nuclear families are not patriarchal at all. The mother may work, the father sharing in more than a minimum of child care and domestic tasks. Other differences also exist. Many nuclear families have only one parent, and unless the family is on welfare or rich, this parent must meet not only the nurturance needs of his or her children but also be the sole breadwinner. Many cooperative efforts among families, be they something so simple as a babysitting exchange or something more complicated, like a cooperative nursery school or cooperative meal-planning and cooking, have moved many families out of the nuclear, isolation trap. The incidence of communal living remains very small, but it, too, serves as an important alternative model, suggesting to many people that the nuclear household need not be the only way to organize family life. Acknowledging this considerable variety of structures and styles brings us along the first steps toward demythologizing the American family and understanding why day care, or almost any form of cooperative, community-shared child care, has great appeal to so many families.

The relationship between day care and the family is not then a one-to-one matching of two givens, like one molecule of sodium and one molecule of chloride that put together produce common table salt. It is a rather more complicated chemical reaction. A variety of day care services that are, after all, totally voluntary, combined with a variety of family styles and child care needs, need not result in the demise of the family but in greater flexibility, choice, and opportunity for a greater number of families. Furthermore, day care could represent for many families participation in a child-centered community that removes the parents from the isolation, frustration, and sheer difficulty of going it alone in their child-rearing tasks. Good day care, in a center or in a family day care home, from a certain point of view and a certain level of commitment, could be considered a reconstitution of the extended family—the larger Family to which so many nuclearized, mobile, and isolated little families need to belong.

From this point of view, day care is not the unknown future but a return to common sense, a recognition that, just as individuals do not exist alone, neither do families; that children do not belong just to their parents but to other adults and a community larger than the nuclear family. . . .

Does the economy weaken or strengthen the family? In money terms it supports some families very well; it supports other families decently if there are two wage earners; other families it supports very poorly, or not at all. In terms of life quality, wages, job assignments, transfers, work hours, and working conditions, employers are not particularly concerned with families, with children's needs, or with their schooling. Admittedly this is how it has always been, and more humane personnel policies and employment practices probably make the present working situation of many people better than it was fifty years ago. But, except as ornamentation, a man or woman's family needs and responsibilities are given little consideration in the job market. But the struggle to survive, or the need to make a living, has always been a prime determinant of family behavior and a powerful shaper of family adaptations.

Most families' lives are organized around the job situation of the bread-winner or breadwinners. The amount of money there is to spend, the hours at which meals are eaten (if they are eaten in common), the time people rise and go to bed, the amount of time a father or employed mother can spend with their children, the kinds of goods and services, housing, and schools are tied to their employment (or unemployment) situation. Quite clearly an agricultural economy allowed a considerable amount of family cohesiveness; in contrast, our technological and "almost post-industrial" society is notable for fracturing and alienating family members. The absence of the father from the home and his considerably diminished influence is a by-product of industrialization. The effect of jobs and employment on families passes largely unnoticed by most employers and economic planners. Salaries are pegged not to the number of people who must live on them, but on the skills and job classification of the breadwinner. The United States stands practically alone among Western nations in its failure to pay a family allowance to compensate for the inequities of its economic system. Most families meet this situation by tailoring expenditures and their living conditions to their income. But certain inequities built into the economic system mean that some families can never have sufficient income to attain a decent standard of living and a decent standard of child-rearing. The female-headed family is one example. Still considered secondary workers, most women, those whose husbands work, as well as those who are the sole support of their families, are systematically paid less than men doing the same job. The chronically under-employed are another example of men and women who though willing to work can never find steady employment through which to support their families. Coal miners in depressed areas of Appalachia and unskilled or semi-skilled blacks in the city are both groups that get the short end of the economic stick. That regularly employed people cannot make a family wage, that some men must work at two or three jobs to support their families, is a powerful, telling indictment against our present system of income distribution and an indicator of how little concern there actually is for the family in areas where it really matters. And one does not have to concentrate at the lower end of the income scale to support this point. Even at higher income levels, men and women may not have any more time to raise their children than the man who works two or three jobs. Frequently enough higher pay and more satisfying work requires longer hours and greater job responsibilities. And at every income level the supposed merit of the nuclear family in an industrial society—its mobility and adaptability—takes its toll. Our high level of geographic and social mobility has its effect on families, removing them from a larger community of support whether that be defined in terms of parents, neighborhoods, baseball teams, or old friends. The frequency with which so many families move, while making them free-floating and efficient units in the economy, serves to weaken the bonds which make communities possible and family life tolerable.

John Demos describes the situation in which so many families find themselves:

> The family is important not so much as the foundation for an ideal social order, but as the foil to an actual state of social disorder. It forms a bulwark against the

outside world—destroy it, and anarchy reigns everywhere. It forms, too, a bulwark against anxieties of the deepest and most personal kind. For we find in the family, as nowhere else in our "open society," an indispensable type of protection against the sense of utter isolation and helplessness.

What kind of retreat can the family really provide from outer social chaos? Relatively little. For families isolated from supportive communities, whether that community be geographically, psychologically, or religiously defined, have little feeling of being able to cope either with the outer or inner world. Indeed, in Demos' description one can find little purpose for the family except as a pressure vent for the individual's anxieties and struggles with the larger society. The family becomes an arena for taking things out, for relieving individual members from their sense of frustration with the economic, social, and psychological happenings outside the family.

The fact that the family continues to exist despite such pressures may be a tribute to its marvelous flexibility but it could not long survive if it did not allow people a way out when and if the pressures become intolerable. And divorce is, for most people, the way out, with desertion for those who cannot observe legal niceties. Divorce is not only a concomitant necessity to our highly romantic notions of love, unrealistic expectations about marriage and life in a nuclear family, but it serves as well to relieve individuals from the intolerable situations created in families by their economic and social situations. Like economic circumstances, divorce is both result and cause of changes in family life and has particularly affected the families' child-rearing capabilities. We have considerably revised and upgraded our standards of personal happiness; the idea that an unhappy couple should remain together for the sake of raising their children has come to seem as masochistic a notion as it once was considered selfish and irresponsible for an unhappy couple not to remain together, at least until after their children were grown. While marital fidelity and family stability may be an ideal in our society it is now legally permissible and socially acceptable for husband and wife to separate, divorce and remarry without particular reference to the effect on their children, except, of course, for what the parents are capable of observing and remedying themselves. Part of the trade-off then for our notions of marriage, family life, and economic organization is a high divorce rate, a loosening of family ties and rearing children in one-parent families.

Finally there are attitudes and values which penetrate the family and affect children quite without reference to parental desires. Television is paramount among these influences; whatever the merits or demerits of the "global village," television perhaps more than any other medium, like comic books, or other institutions, like the schools, has influenced and intruded upon the child-rearing task of parents. The exact nature and effect of this intrusion has not yet been clearly analyzed but a number of facts are commonly agreed upon. The first and most striking is the number of hours that the average child watches television. It is calculated that by the age of 18 an American child will have spent twenty thousand hours in front of the tube, according to Ben Bagdikian "more time than he has spent in classrooms, churches, and all other educational and cultural activities." Not only then does television consume a great amount of time, it does so at the expense of parents and children doing other things together. In fact, watching television may be the only thing many parents and children do do together. The second fact is that the social, moral, and economic values underlying most of television have at best a dubious effect on children; at worst, they are positively detrimental to the proper socialization of children.

In this area there remains a great amount of conjecture, but violence on television has been shown to encourage violent behavior in a significant minority of children. Worse than the violent behavior itself is the systematic desensitization to violence, pain, and suffering that characterizes the attitude of so many children *and adults.* Furthermore, the bumbling father, the dreary housewife, the foolish older people that are the stock-in-trade of so many situation comedies and commercials help form attitudes that do a disservice to a child's understanding of other people's roles and ages. Even so simple a matter as what families eat is settled by which cereal company sponsors the children's favorite programs. A somewhat frivolous example perhaps but indicative that something so simple as a family's eating habits are formed outside of parental control by cereal manufacturers whose chief interest is not, after all, proper nutrition but making money. Television has radically intruded upon family-centered child-rearing, becoming, in Bagdikian's phrase, the "electronic teacher-playmate-babysitter-parent."

The fear that day care has family-weakening implications must be seen in this context which suggests that a large measure of our social and economic life, too, has its family-weakening, or, at least, family-changing implications. A high level of personal and geographic mobility, the pursuit of personal happiness, the pressures of a consumer society, a continually rising standard of living, the influence of television, among many facets of American society, create almost insurmountable pressures against the requisites we claim to have established for sound child-rearing: family cohesion and stability, intensive and exclusive care of children by mothers.

In an attempt to preserve the family most Americans are certainly not willing to return to the constraints that eighteenth- and nineteenth-century families lived with. We are not willing to return to a situation in which the family defined society as it did in seventeenth-century New England; to return to a time when people lived miserably in unhappy marriages; when the confines of a child's view were limited to what his parents knew, or what they were willing to have the child know; when our economy was inefficient and there were many more poor people than there are now. But we cannot have changed our economic and social lives without expecting that the family too would change. Having created a flexible, mobile, sometimes overheated family, we must recognize that its needs will be different from the family life that characterized our past.

The present situation of the family might be characterized as one in which parents have total responsibility for children while having almost no control over the larger social forces which impinge on the lives of their children; parents have a rather extensive set of duties toward their children but they receive little moral or psychological support from the larger society in carrying out those duties. While as a society we expect a good deal from those who are parents, we do not create an ambience in which parental responsibilities are easy to meet or in which children's needs are taken into consideration. As compensation for this lack in our society we console ourselves with the thought that with child-dominated homes and permissiveness, at least we are kind to children. But rather than a thought-out system of child-rearing, aren't these signs of parental withdrawal? Or, as Urie Bronfrenbrenner has written, of psychological abandonment, before a nearly hopeless and unrewarding task which results in parents and children resenting rather than respecting one another? We have collectively forgotten how to make "human beings human."

> We are experiencing a breakdown in the process of making human beings human. By isolating our children from the rest of society, we abandon them to a world devoid of adults and ruled by the destructive impulses and compelling pressures both of the age-segregated peer group and the aggressive and exploitive television screen. By setting our priorities elsewhere and putting children and families last, by claiming one set of values while pursuing another, we leave our children bereft of standards and support and our own lives impoverished and corrupt.

These sentences from the 1970 White House Conference on Children suggest how far we really are from family-centered child-rearing. We cling to that catchword—family-centered—because it permits us to ignore the responsibilities and reordering of priorities that would go along with a social and economic system that would make the raising of children, the "making of human beings human" an important task. We are well into community-centered child-rearing without, unfortunately, having devised many successful means to accomplish it. We are horrified by the unruly young and call for greater family supervision when on every front we have diluted parental authority and capabilities.

In a time when the family is being so radically transformed by policies, both purposeful and intended, and unconscious and uncontrolled, the question is not whether day care will destroy the family but how to construct and foster a system of day care that will support, encourage, and strengthen the family in its child-rearing task. The chief danger of day care to the family is not that day care exists but that it will be organized in such a way as to foster the kind of division, intrusion, and separation that have already attenuated the ties between parents and children. A day care system, neighborhood-based, community-oriented, and parent-controlled, could go a long way toward giving families the Family they need to belong to. As an autonomous unit the family cannot long survive the pressures it now experiences; as one of many units in which there is a shared concern for children the family could meet its own need and enlarge our capacities for raising children and making human beings human.

Parent Education and Parent Involvement: Retrospect and Prospect

In the 1960s Ira J. Gordon was a professor of education at the University of Florida and the director of the Institute for Development of Human Resources, an interdepartmental research agency. His work focused on infant and early child stimulation through parent education and was carried out with disadvantaged mothers in the north central Florida area. Gordon believed that early intervention in babies' lives in the form of teaching mothers ways to stimulate their infants would help break the poverty cycle. This large-scale project was the basis for Gordon's work with the Follow Through program.

What was unique about Gordon's work was the link he forged between home and school, between parent and teacher. Home visits, close monitoring, and extensive in-service training made the program quite complex. Although the original project ended in the 1970s, Gordon's vision of the parent as educator continues in a wide variety of programs today. Gordon discusses some models of parent education in the following selection from his article "Parent Education and Parent Involvement: Retrospect and Prospect," *Childhood Education* (vol. 54, 1977).

After Gordon completed his work in Florida, he became the Kenan Professor and dean of the School of Education at the University of North Carolina. He is the author of a number of books, including *Baby Learning Through Baby Play: A Parent's Guide for the First Two Years* (St. Martins Press, 1970), *Child Learning Through Child Play: Learning Activities for Two- and Three-Year-Olds* (St. Martin's Press, 1972), and a textbook entitled *Human Development*.

Parent education probably began with the first grandmother in the cave telling her daughter how to rear a newly arrived infant. Of the many biblical references we can quote, my favorite is the injunction in Leviticus instructing the Hebrews "Thou shalt teach . . . diligently unto thy children."

Skipping several thousand years, we might place the beginning of the modern era of parent education at 1801, when Pestalozzi (1801) wrote *How Gertrude Teaches Her Children*. He states in a letter to a friend:

> From the moment that a mother takes a child upon her lap she teaches him. She brings nearer to his senses what nature has scattered afar over large areas and in confusion, and makes the action of receiving sense-impressions and the knowledge derived from them, easy, pleasant, and delightful to him (cited in Kessen 1965, p. 102).

During the next few decades, emerging concern for the early years of life and the role of the parent can be found in the beginnings of the kindergarten movement and (in the early 1840s) in Froebel's book, *Mother's Songs, Games, and Stories*. One of those illustrated games is "patche-kuchen," which you will recognize as "Pattycake"!

Before the turn of the twentieth century, the United States began to feel the effects of Pestalozzi and Froebel. Parent education and parent involvement in the U.S.A. have followed two main directions.

1. The first, stemming from the European influence, essentially involved middle-class and well-educated people. It was linked intimately in the 1920s with the Progressive Education movement and Deweyian thought. Examples can be found in the child study movement and in the development of the PTA [Parent-Teacher Association], mental health associations, and parent cooperative nursery schools, as they emerged in the 1930s. These efforts often used group approaches to both parent education and parent involvement. Parents generated activities which, in cooperation with professionals, led to lay organizational programs. The aims were not simply to learn about rearing one's own children but also, in keeping with Deweyian doctrine, to influence and shape the broader society. Schlossman (1976) has reviewed this direction in his study of the history of parent education from 1897 to 1928.

2. Paralleling this approach was one that in today's jargon we might call *mainstreaming*. This called for utilizing parent education and home visitations to integrate the flow of immigrants into the mainstream. The schools were obviously involved in stirring the mix in the melting pot. But some efforts transcended schools—examples were the visiting nurse programs, home visitors to people such as my grandparents on New York's lower side, the social work movement in the settlement houses, and the emergence of the adult education movement. In rural America these two approaches were linked through the work of the agricultural extension service and the home demonstration agent.

Establishment of the Children's Bureau in 1913 was originally designed to strike a blow at child labor. But the Bureau very soon found itself developing pamphlets and other materials on childrearing practices for parents. These pamphlets were disseminated through the home-demonstration system and also through hospitals and other means, including Congress, to the parents of newborn children. Because understanding the language of the pamphlets required a high degree of literacy, however, they did not really have an impact on the mainstreaming effort.

Most materials developed during this period reflected the middle-class pattern. The content stressed either descriptive norms of development or parent behavior to rear socially acceptable and academically successful children. Examples of such publications are the National Society for the Study of Education 1929 yearbook, *Preschool and Parental Education;* books by John B. Watson and Arnold Gesell; and the series of Iowa child welfare pamphlets of the 1930s and early '40s, including one by Ralph Ojemann (1941) on reading.

A lull occurred during or immediately after World War II, especially in the "mainstreaming" side of the picture. Massive immigration had long since ceased, and our energies were diverted to other things.

In the 1960s the two diverse approaches reemerged with some strength. The middle-class parent education approach changed from the progressive education type of emphasis to one more psychotherapeutic in nature, especially therapy as represented by the ideas of Carl Rogers and his associates (Baruch 1949; T. Gordon 1970; Ginott 1965). In the 1970s suggestions for parenting begin to reemerge from the conditioning orientation, this time not from the classical one of Watson but from the operant conditioning movement (Becker 1974).

Counterparts to the earlier organizational efforts are those of various groups of parents with special problems, the organizations stressing natural childbirth or breast feeding, and the informal groups of parents of infants and toddlers and the like. Of course, the PTA, the mental health associations, and parent cooperatives have continued since their founding.

Mainstreaming shifted from a concern for the integration of the immigrants from Europe to an awareness of groups in the American population *outside* the mainstream: our own indigent poor, the immigrant waves from the farm to the city represented by the movement of southern blacks, the immigration of Puerto Ricans to New York and other urban centers, the Chicano in the Southwestern United States, and the Appalachian poor in thirteen states on the Eastern Seaboard. The best single representation of all that effort, beginning about 1965, was the "War on Poverty." Of all of the influences in the American society since the turn of the century, this was the first large-scale federal government effort since the initial establishment of the Children's Bureau in 1913. Basic to the effort were longitudinal early intervention research projects (Weikart 1970; Gray 1970; Levenstein 1970; and Gordon 1967, 1969). Government programs are represented by Head Start, Parent and Child Centers, Home Start, Parent Child Development Centers, Title I, and Follow Through.

While these developments were going on here, similar developments occurred abroad. A parent education movement in the middle-class tradition, founded at the turn of the century in France, led by 1964 to the formation of the International Federation for Parent Education. This federation developed general policy statements that resembled those supporting government efforts and the variety of private efforts and publications in the United States.

Central themes common to these parallel lines of middle class and mainstreaming, in Europe and the United States, can be summed up in three statements: (1) the home is important and basic for human development; (2) parents need help in creating the most effective home environment for that development; and (3) the early years of life are important for lifelong development.

TODAY

Several reviews give us an updated picture of the state of the art of parent education, especially in the mainstreaming dimension: Gordon 1970; Goodson and Hess 1975; Gordon et al. 1975; and Honig 1975. It is no coincidence that the last three reviews have a 1975 date. Two ACEI [Association for Childhood Education International] pamphlets grew out of papers presented at the 1975 Texas Conference on Infancy directed by Joe Frost: *Understanding and Nurturing Infant Development* (1976) and *Developing Programs for Infants and Toddlers* (1977).

U.S. Secretary of Health, Education, and Welfare (HEW) Joseph Califano has indicated that strengthening the family rather than strengthening institutions to deal with the family will be a major thrust of his department in the days ahead. The Office of Child Development (OCD)—now called the Administration for Children, Youth and Families—continues, fortunately, to support Parent Child Development Centers, Child and Family Resource programs, Home Start efforts within Head Start, and Head Start itself. Unfortunately, however, most of these local programs are small-scale and non-longitudinal. The Office of Education (OE) through its regulations for Title I, Follow Through and PL94-142 requires parent involvement as distinct from parent education.

PROSPECT

Let us look at where we are in 1977. Are we climbing aboard a new educational bandwagon? Do we see parenting education and parent involvement as a new kind of panacea? We have to address certain critical questions:

1. What are the philosophical assumptions underlying programs? Do they still perpetuate the separate mainstreaming and middle-class movements?
2. What is the place of parent education outside of parent involvement in the school?
3. What is the role of the school (or agency) in parent education vis-a-vis the role of the family in parent involvement in the school? If there are parent-directed emergent group efforts, as we have seen in the middle-class tradition, and government-required parent involvement in the decision process in the mainstreaming, how do these roles of parents relate to those of parents as receivers of child development or educational information?

4. What are the evidences that various programs have been successful and what is meant by success?

Assuming answers can be found to the above, newcomers to the parent-movement typically face another set of questions:

- How do you select and train and supervise home visitors, if that is the model you plan to use?
- What should be the level of training of personnel who work with parents?
- What are the comparative advantages of home visitor or center or mixed type of programs?
- How should television and other media be used?
- How do you design multi-discipline approaches?
- How do you get parents to participate?
- How do you sustain their level of involvement?
- How do you build flexibility into a program?
- Crassly, where do you get the money? How do you convince legislators and educational bureaucrats that education dollars should be spent outside the classroom?
- How do you improve the pre- and inservice training of teachers and other professionals in reference to working with parents?

Some answers are found scattered in the literature. But generally the answers are not available in any comprehensive, organized fashion. This may not be possible. What, then, can one say?

For a long time I have been concerned about the American tendency to seek the short-term, easy, package-solution to problems and, within that context, to view the school as the remedial agent for society's ills. This single shot, "offer a course" approach often ignores the social context, assumes a power for formal education it most likely does not possess, and overlooks the fact that schools are but one subsystem within the society.

A useful analytic approach is the systems viewpoint. By placing the issue of parent involvement and parent education in a systems context (Brim 1975; Bronfenbrenner 1976), we can examine assumptions that underlie current programs and deal with our first question.

Three Models

Family Impact. At the heart of the mainstream tradition is the Family Impact Model, whereby parent education from local agency or school is designed to have an impact on the family so that the child will "fit" the school and the system's goals—to get those who are out of the system into it.

Underlying such efforts is a set of assumptions. Applied to parent education, these are: that specific answers exist; that the family wants to be "in" but doesn't know how; that changing the parent, in some way, without changing anything else, will enable entry; that knowledge and attitudes of parents are keys to entry. In the middle-class tradition, the assumptions are also that "the" right way to rear a child can be learned from books, peers or experts, and that the parents, using these, can be successful childrearers. To state these assumptions is not to deny their power or validity. This model is the basic one for all formal education. The larger core assumptions are that there is a body of information necessary for life and for a career, that a teacher knows and teaches it, and that individuals learn and apply it. This view, which holds sway from "basic skills" to postgraduate refresher courses in medicine or education, is a legitimate and respectable approach.

This model is the major thrust of most school-based efforts and of many state-supported child mental health and Appalachian Regional Commission projects.

With some justification, some people feel that this strategy treats symptoms (parent-child behaviors, family transactional patterns) without attacking root causes, without clearly understanding subcultural strengths, and/or without recognizing the varieties of positive ways of childrearing. Nevertheless, if we attend to these programs' goals, the data seem reasonably clear from both the longitudinal early intervention studies as summarized in Palmer (1977) and Goodson and Hess (1975), that lasting effects are evident on the intellectual and academic performance of children. The research efforts have been generally small-scale, with heavy university involvement.

For example, our Florida families—whose parents we home-visited beginning when the children were three months old and who were involved for at least two continuous years before they were three years old—have a significantly lower percentage of their children assigned to special education in third grade (six years later) and significantly higher percentage of their children who performed better on the MAT [Miller analogy test] than did children who had been randomly assigned to the control population. That is a long-term positive effect.

With emerging concern for cross-generational efforts and parenting education programs for high school youth, the parent-oriented early education programs offer possible models for the involvement of youth in efforts that not only are socially useful in the community but also provide them with understanding of families and of child development in ways that should impact upon their own roles as parents. It would be rather easy to incorporate the home-visit program, with suitable supervision, into a variety of high school efforts in which high school youths are trained as home visitors. Further, in many places in which infant centers are located on school grounds, the activities developed in programs lend themselves to use in infant and early childhood centers.

Adult-education and family-life education people are also drawing implications from the two strands of parent education work. In a recent position paper, they state such goals as:

1. Developing educational potentials of parents for social, mental, emotional and physical growth of children.
2. Improving parent-child communication throughout the life cycle.

3. Clarifying parental responsibilities and competencies in developing emotional stability of all family members young and old. . . .
4. Expanding and upgrading community resources supporting parents, including child care facilities (Cromwell and Bartz 1976, pp. 18–19).

Although the Family Impact Model is time-honored and seemingly successful, we still need to raise some issues concerning its prospects.

Both parent-education traditions use forms of the family-impact model. The middle-class tradition is voluntary, self-selective, often informal and group self-managed, and the content based upon the parents' perceptions of need. The "mainstreaming" tradition is usually programmatic, funded or connected to a government agency, run by professionals, and based upon "expert" perception of parents' needs.

Today we need ways to synthesize the strengths of both traditions. For example, new parents, regardless of social class, may need more specific help than in the past in the physical health and cognitive as well as the affective domains.

To accomplish this synthesis, if we see the school system as the major social agency, we need to answer such questions as:

1. Where do the schools acquire the wisdom to know what parents need? (Our evaluation of programs—Gordon et al. 1975—showed the nonexistence of need assessment.)
2. Do such programs run the risk of seeing parents as clients and lowering parent self-esteem and sense of potency vis-a-vis the system?
3. Where do school personnel get the training and develop the attitudes and skills necessary for working with parents from diverse backgrounds?
4. Is this a new version of the melting pot—like the home visitors of the 1890s who dealt with my grandparents? Is that necessarily bad? As a corollary,
5. Are there universal parent-child behaviors we wish to foster? What is the evidence?

I cannot answer the first four questions, but we have data on the fifth. If a common system goal is still "making it" in schools as they are, the data are clear.

We find many indications, across culture, of common family variables that influence scholastic achievement. The data from American studies (Coleman 1966; Mayeske 1975; Gordon 1969, 1977; Hess 1969), from the international educational achievement studies (Coleman 1975; Keeves 1972, 1975; Purves 1973; Thorndike 1973), and from British longitudinal studies (Pringle, Butler and Davie 1966; Davie, Butler and Goldstein 1972; Wedge and Prosser 1973) all show that the variables are not magical. They have to do with, among others, whether: (1) parents see themselves as teachers of their children; (2) they talk with them, not at them; (3) they take them to the libraries or the museums or the parks: (4) they sit around the dinner table and share and plan; (5) they listen; (6) they display a child's work on the refrigerator or the wall; (7) they themselves read and talk about what they read.

Further to be noted are such variables as communication processes, values, sense of family and family pride, self-concept and sense of potency of the family members, which also influence the child's development. Some of these may be functions of class and caste. The American intervention studies show, however, *within* social class and caste, that these variables are important (Gordon 1976; Carew 1977; and Elardo, Bradley and Caldwell 1975).

School Impact Model. Here the issues are the same as those Moynihan (1969) raised when he analyzed four views of community intervention in decision-making:

> The essential problem with community action was that one term concealed at least four quite distinct meanings. Organizing the power structure, as in the Fort Foundation Programs ... expanding the power structure, as in the delinquency program ... confronting the power structure as in the Industrial Areas Foundation program ... and finally, assisting the power structure as in the Peace Corps (Moynihan 1969, p. 168).

Another type of maximum feasible misunderstanding rises out of the fact that many programs incorporate both the Family Impact and the School Impact models in the same project. Head Start, Home Start and to some degree Follow Through and Title I are examples. What is the maximum feasible misunderstanding?

Try this logic tree: Your young child is not doing well in school. (1) This is because you need help—you are out of the system. (2) This is because you lack knowledge/skills in childrearing (or dominant culture childrearing). (3) Therefore, we will help you learn. (4) But, since this is your child, you should have something to say. (5) Therefore, even though you are either deficient or different, we will put you on a policy council to tell us what to do! But, as Moynihan said, "The exercise of power in an effective manner is an ability acquired through apprenticeship and seasoning" (p. 137). Parent involvement for this model requires a form of parent education different from learning to improve one's own home—such as education in budgeting, parliamentary procedure, knowledge of local agency and federal regulations, skill in communication with the power structure, group decision-making processes and the like.

In practice, despite a certain sense to this model, it can lead to conflict *unless* both parents and program people recognize their *mutual* needs to learn *from each other.* Parent involvement for this model also requires a new form of teacher education! Teachers and school administrators, or any other professional involved in working with this model, need to learn new attitudes toward parents, new skills in communication and group processes and sharing. Both groups need help in relating to each other when the task is common decision-making.

If we are serious about the second model, it may intrude very heavily on the first. Parents may not see any need for the parent education that school people design, or they may see needs to change *teacher* behavior, rather than their own.

Implementing this model calls forth another set of concerns:

1. How do we reconcile conflicting views about what is good for children?
2. How do we solve the possible struggle for power over programs?
3. How do we resolve the maximum feasible misunderstanding, in which school systems may want (or permit) parent involvement in decision-making if it enhances the school system *as is* (the Peace Corps meaning), and parents may want to make major modifications in the school system (the Industrial Areas Foundation meaning)?

Some say that *both* models are merely topical treatments—that what is needed to help the family is to change the larger systems in which it is embedded. For example, within our American framework, changes might be required in the systems of welfare, health care, work (flextime, mobility for promotion), media, etc.

Community Impact Model. As applied to parent education and parent intervention, this third model is usually represented by a so-called "comprehensive service" component. But, here again, we face the strategy issues of the previous two models. Many parent involvement/parent education programs adopt the strategy of helping parents learn about available services or find ways to get them *to* services—both within the Family Impact Model. Others try, through parent councils and parent advisory committees or child advisory committees, to give parents something to say about who should deliver services and where and how these should be delivered (School Impact Model).

Although both strategies are useful, they place the blame for obviously needed change upon one of the weaker agencies in the system—the family. The family has no lobby, local or national; the American Medical Association does. If the families in programs, as they usually were from mid-1960s to now, were the "outside the system" ones, this places perhaps an unattainable expectation on them. We, the "powerful"—the educators and social service and health bureaucracies—are *telling* them to change us!

If the families are middle class, they are usually primarily interested in getting the system to be more responsive to their individual needs and are not interested in fundamental change.

The community impact model may seem the weakest and most futile, requiring us to step back and view our society and its efforts as a whole. It may make us feel overwhelmed, like Sisyphus, rolling the rock up the hill. It may imply that the other models should be abandoned. Such an analysis may seem unduly cynical or pessimistic, giving aid and comfort to the enemy; but that is not my intent. Much that is good and useful can be found in the variety of Parent Education/Parent Involvement efforts in which many of us have engaged. Results *do* show that the Family Impact Model works. The School Impact Model, too, has led to changes in the way parents and professionals see each other and, in some situations, to legislation and local district change. The

Community Impact Model, as used in Head Start, clearly improved the health of many children, at least for the time they were in the program, and brought many formerly powerless people into the political mainstream.

Indeed, a national survey of the Impacts of Head Start Centers on Community Institutions reported that

> there does seem to be a relationship between the degree of parental participation in Head Start centers and the extent of centers' involvement in the institutional change process. . . . It would seem that Head Start involved the poor (the parents) in its organizational structure, this structure in turn had a tendency to become a vehicle through which Head Start contributed to the background for change (Kirschner, 1970).

We sometimes forget that Head Start was funded under the community action agency legislation and, in this area, made a significant impact.

Efforts in all three models need to continue to be enlarged. Today our prospects are so improved that we can develop and use a Community Impact Model as well as continue and strengthen the other two more micro models. Much will be required of us to move to this level. We will make errors, be faced with fragmentation of effort, and suffer territorial agency wars. The odds are high, but so are the stakes. My overriding concern is that our efforts not continue to be piecemeal, unsynthesized, small-scale and sporadic, but that they be placed in the broader social system context. We need to tie, where possible, parent education efforts to work, family income, and housing and zoning programs, medicare and medicaid, teacher education, professional education of social workers, psychologists, etc.

The American family, school and many elements of the system at all levels are in a state of flux. Change is not pleasant, and planned change is not always either possible or the outcome predictable. Further, change takes time. We need to ask ourselves not only the tactical questions, which relate to the state of the art and to what we have learned about the "how-to's," the retrospective questions; but also the strategic issues—why are we doing this? How does it fit into the larger social scheme? What do we hope to accomplish within the narrow confines of a specific program? What else ought to be done? What are our basic assumptions about people—what they need and want, how they learn and grow, what we desire for them? These prospective questions face us and the administration.

As you have seen, the issues and approaches have been with us for a long time. Although many of us *are* trying diligently to teach our children, the content has changed. Sharing Pestalozzi's dream, we must apply it to men and women, fathers as well as mothers. Many of us *are* working for change within the larger system, and our hopes are still high.

PART FIVE

Educational Systems for Young Children

Chapter 11 Employer-Sponsored 279

Chapter 12 Federal Involvement in Early Childhood 289

Chapter 13 Research 317

Chapter 14 Reform/Policy 350

CHAPTER **11**
Employer-Sponsored

11.1 ROBERT OWEN

The Life of Robert Owen

Employer-sponsored child care is not a twentieth-century innovation unique to the United States. Robert Owen (1771–1858), an industrialist in Scotland, devised the first "modern" on-site nursery school for the children of employees at his cotton mills. In 1816 living conditions of working-class families were dismal. Owen toured the New Lanark community and determined that parents were "ignorant of the right method of treating children." He devised a system for operating schools for all children over the age of one, designed the innovative curriculum, and employed the teachers. Of particular interest to Owen was his "infant school," which he personally observed and supervised until the right teacher could be found. He claimed that he founded the first infant school.

Some of Owen's methods were in direct contrast to common practice in Great Britain. He believed that corporal punishment and abusive language should not be used with young children, and he looked for teachers who had "inexhaustible" patience. He favored multiage groupings, pairing the four-, five-, and six-year-olds with two- and three-year-olds. Discovery learning, particularly through regular field trips, was promoted above book learning. Perhaps his most progressive idea was his insistence that no grades be given and that assessment be based on individual progress. These marks of what is now called developmentally appropriate practice were evident in the first employer-sponsored programs at Owen's New Lanark establishment. Owen provides a glimpse of his infant schools in the following selection from *The Life of Robert Owen* (1857).

I had ... acquired the most sincere affections of all the children. I say of all—because every child above one year old was daily sent to the schools. I had also the hearts of all their parents, who were highly delighted with the improved conduct, extraordinary progress, and continually increasing happiness of their children, and with the substantial improvements by which I gradually surrounded them. But the great attraction to myself and the numerous strangers who now continually visited the establishment, was the new infant school; the progress of which from its opening I daily watched and superintended, until I could prepare the mind of the master whom I had selected for this, in my estimation, most important charge,—knowing that if the foundation was not truly laid, it would be in vain to expect a satisfactory structure.

It was in vain to look to any old teachers upon the old system of instruction by books. In the previous old school room I had tried to induce the master to adopt my views; but he could not and would not attempt to adopt what he deemed to be such a fanciful "new-fangled" mode of teaching, and he was completely under the influence of the minister of the parish, who was himself also opposed to any change of system in teaching children, and who considered that the attempt to educate and teach infants was altogether a senseless and vain proceeding. I had therefore, although he was a good obstinate "dominie" of the old school, reluctantly to part with him, and I had to seek among the population for two persons who had a great love for and unlimited patience with infants, and who were thoroughly tractable and willing unreservedly to follow my instructions. The best to my mind in these respects that I could find in the population of the village, was a poor simple-hearted weaver, named James Buchanan, who had been previously trained by his wife to perfect submission to her will, and who could gain but a scanty living by his now oppressed trade of weaving common plain cotton goods by hand. But he loved children strongly by nature, and his patience with them was inexhaustible. These, with his willingness to be instructed, were the qualities which I required in the master for the first rational infant school that had ever been imagined by any party in any country; for it was the first practical step of a system new to the world;—and yet with all my teaching of all classes of the public, it is still little understood in principle, and not at all yet conceived in practice, although the high permanent happiness through futurity of our race depends upon the principle and practice in all their purity being correctly carried into execution by all nations and people.

Thus the simple-minded kind-hearted James Buchanan, who at first could scarcely read, write, or spell, became the first master in a rational infant school. But infants so young, also required a female nurse, to assist the master, and one also who possessed the same natural qualifications. Such an one I found among the numerous young females employed in the cotton mills, and I was fortunate in finding for this task a young woman, about seventeen years of age, known familiarly among the villagers as "Molly Young," who of the two, in natural powers of mind, had the advantage over her new companion in an office perfectly new to both.

The first instruction which I gave them was, that they were on no account ever to beat any one of the children, or to threaten them in any manner in word or action, or to use abusive terms; but were always to speak to them with a pleasant countenance, and in a kind manner and tone of voice. That they should tell the infants and children (for they had all from one to six years old under their charge,) that they must on all occasions do all they could to make their playfellows happy,—and that the older ones, from four to six years of age, should take especial care of younger ones, and should assist to teach them to make each other happy.

. . . [T]he plan which I pursued was a very simple one, and was obtained by a close and accurate study of human nature, not from books, (for these were very generally worse than useless,) but from the infant, child, youth, and man, as formed under a false fundamental principle, as was evident by the entire past history of the human race. To form the most superior character for the human race, the training and education should commence from the birth of the child; and to form a good character they must begin systematically when the child is one year old. But much has been done rightly or wrongly before that period. From that age no child should be brought up isolated. Every child should now be placed in the first division of a school for infants of from one to three years of age, and from thirty to fifty in number,—the latter number easily to be superintended by a properly chosen female,—instead of, as at present, one or two or three infants of such age being thoroughly spoiled by the attendance upon them of young persons wholly ignorant of human nature. In this first division the foundation of a good and rational character may be easily laid, by attending to the formation of every habit, to their manner, their disposition, and their conduct to each other; and in this respect I gave them but one rule or lesson for practice, and that was, from their entrance into the school, to endeavour to make each other very happy. And it is surprising how soon and how effectually this practice is acquired under a superintendent possessing the required unceasing love for children, and who has been properly instructed before commencing the task. These children, to be well trained and educated, should never hear from their teacher an angry word, or see a cross or threatening expression of countenance. The tone of voice and manner should be, impartially to them all, kind and affectionate. They should be out of doors in good air at play, as much as the weather and their strength will admit. When beginning to be tired of play in their play-ground, they should be taken within the school room, and amused by the teacher, by showing and explaining to them some useful object within their capacity to comprehend,— and a young active well taught teacher will easily find and provide something that they will be interested in seeing and in hearing it explained. While awake they should be actively occupied either at this amusement or at play; and thirty to fifty infants, when left to themselves, will always amuse each other without any useless childish toys. In our rational infant school in New Lanark, a mere child's toy was not seen for upwards of twenty years. When however any infant felt inclined to sleep, it should be quietly allowed to do so.

Punishment, in a rationally conducted infant school, will never be required, and should be avoided as much as giving poison in their food.

The second division, from three to six, should continue to be treated in the same manner, except that their walks into the country should be frequent, and the objects brought to them for examination and explanation should be advanced in interest in proportion to the previous acquirements of the children, and to their age for better understanding them.

Books in infant schools are worse than useless. But at six, so trained and educated, a solid foundation will have been formed for good habits, manners, disposition, and conduct to others, and, so far, a consistent and rational mind will be given, varying in many particulars in different individuals, but all good and natural, according to their respective organizations.

No marks of merit or demerit should be given to any; no partiality shown to any one. But attention to each should be increased in proportion to natural defects or deficiency of any kind, physical or mental. "I see by your school," I continued, "that it is after this age that you, like other masters of schools, receive your pupils. But to a great extent the character is made or marred before children enter the usual school room."

11.2 JAMES L. HYMES

Industrial Day Care's Roots in America

James L. Hymes (b. 1913), an educator and author, has dedicated his life to early childhood education. He is known for his books *Teaching the Child Under Six, Discipline, Effective Home-School Relations, Living History Interviews,* and *Year in Review (1971–1990),* among others. Hymes received degrees from Harvard University and Columbia University Teachers College. Hymes began his career in the Works Progress Administration (WPA) nursery schools of the 1930s. He then became the director of the Kaiser Day Care Centers of Portland, Oregon. This large child-care and education program was the first of its kind—employee child care financed by private industry. The Kaiser Company's Portland shipyards were part of wartime industry, and many mothers were employed there. Adjacent to the shipyards, centers were constructed to provide child care, take-home meals, and other family support services. With the shipyards operating around the clock, the centers were open 24 hours a day, 364 days a year. Hymes discusses the evolution of the Kaiser centers in the following selection from "Industrial Day Care's Roots in America," *Proceedings of the Conference on Industry and Day Care* (1970).

The Kaiser program was a bold and decisive demonstration of employer-sponsored child care. Wartime services for children, some supported by federal funding, were innovative and exciting, and they rallied the support of many communities. Unfortunately, such an expensive, comprehensive program as the Kaiser Company's was destined to be closed at the end of World War II. After the war, Hymes served two years as president of the National Association of Nursery Educators, during which he bemoaned the retrenchment he saw occurring in child care around the nation. Hymes was also a professor of early childhood education at the State University of New York at New Paltz. Later he was an influential member of the National Planning Committee for the Head Start compensatory education program.

Although the Kaiser program existed for a very short time, many of its innovations are seen today in programs with extended child-care services.

With your permission I will talk about the Kaiser centers, hoping that the experience . . . may prove of general interest, and talking in terms of those things that seem to me to have some relevance to our meetings of the last two days and the problems of today.

In the spring of 1943 in Portland, Oregon, in the middle of World War II, the Kaiser Company decided that the government-supported Lanham child care centers, located in residential areas throughout the city, were not convenient enough or numerous enough to meet its very pressing needs for women workers. It therefore decided to establish two centers, one at the Swan Island Shipyard and the other at the entrance to the Oregon Shipyard, specifically for the workers in those two yards.

I think I am being accurate in saying that their decision was based on a naive (as one looks at it at this point, but at that time, quite genuine) assumption that the care of children presented no major problems and that the company would have no difficulty in staffing the centers from the large numbers of women who were applying for jobs. But at that point the entire Portland social and educational community rose up in arms. I suspect in part because this was being done by industry; I suspect in part because it was being done by an industry which was disturbing and troubling the placid prewar life of Oregon, and in part because this was a service for workers. I am guessing.

In any event, in a very short time they educated Edgar Kaiser, who was the president of both companies, to what was a new awareness to him—that there was a profession that concerned itself with the care of young children, and that this care was not something that one undertook lightly, just using whomever happened to apply either for a welder's job or a teacher's job or what-have-you.

May I again remind you I am talking of 1943. . . . I am talking of a company which had had most of its experience in dam building and in rather isolated parts of the country where the questions of day care were of no pressing concern.

They proceeded with the construction of two buildings, one at the entrance to each of the yards. At that time, the notion of a building or service located at the place of work, as opposed to being located in the residential communities was quite unusual. The architect had never before designed a day care center; I suspect no architect had ever before designed one. He came through with two buildings of fifteen rooms each, built in a circular shape, with a central enclosed play area. Each room contained 1,500 square feet of usable space.

I think it is fair to say that once Kaiser realized there was a professional job to be done here, he then said—in what I would be inclined to call typical Kaiser fashion—"By golly, if we're going to do it, we're going to do it in the best possible way. If there are professional people in this field, find me the best in the country."

I wish I could stop at this point and say he turned to me, and that I solved all of his problems. But I welcome the chance to say that on the almost unanimous recommendation of people all over the country, he turned to Dr. Lois Meek Stolz, who had been director of the Child Development Institute at Columbia, and who has been on the staff of Stanford University. . . . She said she would be delighted to serve as the consultant, provided someone whom she knew well could be the person on the spot. So I, as a graduate of the Child Development Institute, came in under this special arrangement.

I am trying to report to you (I hope not too briefly) a decision that I think was consciously made by industry: "If we are going to do it, we are going to do it well. If we are going to do it, we are going to do it in a way that will redound to our everlasting credit, and make us proud and pleased that we ventured into this field."

I might say, jumping ahead to what I thought might make a good conclusion, that Edgar Kaiser received the medal awarded by *Parents Magazine* in 1944 for Outstanding Service to Children. I know—at least in 1944—he was completely proud and pleased to feel that he had done a job which could be so recognized.

Dr. Stolz, myself and the others who very quickly joined us approached our task with great hesitancy. Today we talk of day care as a commonplace. We talk of extending the ages downward. We think of day care as one of our pressing needs and something which is bound to grow in the future.

It may be that as you work in the field professionally you get cautious and scared. We were tremendously aware of several kinds of hazards. One was the potentially large numbers of children who might be involved. If you become responsible for large numbers of other peoples' children, it does something to scare you.

Second was the fact that these were young children. All of our training had said to us that if you want one good word to attach to the under-six age in general, it is "vulnerable." We are very apt today to talk of how significant these years are for gains and growth and learning and adventure. It is very important to recognize that these years are equally significant for potential hurts and damages. So to be responsible for large numbers of other peoples' children in these vulnerable years was something we approached with concern.

Day care had to mean for us, as it does for everyone, long hours. We had a very sharp awareness, since all of us had been involved in smaller day care programs before, that the long hours of day care open up a threat. No one has ever advocated the long hours of day care for the child's well-being. Day care is a recognition of a family's need and of a social need, but it involves a threat as far as the child goes. And our concern was whether or not we could do a job that would take into account these long hours, the young age of the children, the general problems involved in separation, and so on.

I say all this because our staffing, I think, may shock you. Within the limits of our ability to get staff, we had a totally professional staff. The director of each center was a specialist within the field. I served as the over-all director. Dr. Stolz was my boss.

Under the director of each center, who held at least a master's degree in the field, there were other supervisors responsible for groups of rooms. Each group teacher was trained; every assistant teacher was a trained professional in the field of early childhood education or child growth and development.

The nutritionist of the centers was a woman who is today still regarded as America's best child nutritionist, Dr. Miriam Lowenberg. She assembled a staff considered expert in her field. A pediatrician attached to the Kaiser medical program in the area was on the staff. There were 10 registered nurses and a staff of four, and then later two very highly trained social workers.

I am trying to imply two or three kinds of things in bundling up the notion of staff. One: we were scared even with a top-notch staff. We did not feel it was a snap to care for other peoples' kids over the long hours of a day, and that day care would always work out well and everybody was sure to benefit from it. I am trying also to imply what must be obvious—this was an expensive operation. When I say that at the end Kaiser could among other satisfactions hold a medal in his hand and know in his heart (and that is where you are supposed to know it, isn't it, in your heart?) that this was a good job, the satisfaction didn't come lightly and it didn't come cheaply and it didn't come without much effort.

The goal of our program was to help recruit people to the Kaiser yards which desperately needed womanpower for the war job of producing ships. The job of our centers was to help people stay on the job and help people feel content on the job. Our commitment was that no matter what happened, we would never turn anyone away. The company commitment was: Get anybody you need so you can do the job at the level of competence you feel is important. It was an interesting compact between what I will call the professional staff and the business organization.

There was another kind of compact that was made, unconsciously I am sure, and I don't know whether this was a compact that we made with ourselves as professionals or whether it was a compact which emerged out of the human relationships as we began working with parents and with children. It had to do with the idea of service.

My title, for example, was not as manager of the "day care department" of the Kaiser centers, or the "child care department," but as manager of the Child Service Centers. We hoped that the word "service" would denote a program that was never finished and never completed, one constantly emerging as we worked on more intimate terms with the people who were relying upon us to do a job.

If I say this in educational terms, I would say that each of us built a new and fresh commitment to meeting the needs of the people as they emerged, as we got to know each other. We tried to stay in tune with people. We tried to flow with people. I think I can perhaps make the point best if I quickly run down some of the services that emerged as our program developed.

The centers were open 364 days a year. We closed on Christmas Day. (There were no ships built on Christmas Day.) We had anticipated that our lowest age level would be age 2. As professional people we were troubled because we regarded age 3 as the safe cut-off point: we recognized as you get down below age 3 things do get a little bit tighter. It was very soon apparent, however, that the largest single age level at which there were available children was 18 months to 24 months; so we began programs for children 18 months of age.

I might quickly add that although we had never anticipated it, we were led into school-age programs on school holidays. . . . There seemed to be so many school holidays when the public schools were not caring for the children.

We had always known that we would have to operate on swing shifts and day shifts. It was soon apparent that there was a need on the graveyard shift as well, so for much of the year our centers were open 364 days of the year, 24 hours a day, although no one child was there for more than the shift his mother was working.

The facilities of the centers included an infirmary where children who were "mildly ill" (and I hope I will never be asked to define this) were cared for. These were the youngsters who were not quite well enough to be in the group of children and yet were not so ill as to necessitate their staying home. We were pleased with this service, because from the standpoint of the yard, the mother was needed and it was important that she be free to go to work.

The infirmary was staffed by nurses whose responsibility was the physical care of the children. Each also had a full complement of teachers, because even the seriously sick child (and we were not dealing with those) has needs other than just his physical needs.

The infirmary also gave physical examinations when these were requested (people were free to turn to their own doctors if they had them, of course), and stood ready to give all immunizations.

One service was Home Service Food. Our kitchens undertook to prepare the major part of the food for the family, which could then be picked up by day-shift mothers as they called for their children. I might say parenthetically that this was much appreciated by the secretaries and by the executives of the company, but was used relatively less by the yard-working women, who somehow seemed to feel it was their bounden responsibility to cook the meal for their husband and children themselves. Nevertheless, it was a useful service.

With fingers crossed we did what many people speak of today in an offhand kind of way as a drop-in service. We finally developed what we called our Special Service Group. The service began one day when a father came running in and said, "Her name is Eileen," and ran out. His wife was in labor in the car and he was leaving his youngster with us for the day. I might have said, "We only take children who come regularly, day after day," but I couldn't catch him! So Eileen pushed us further along the line of discovering that as you work closely and intimately and on friendly human relationships with people, you find there is more and more that you can do, more and more that people hope somebody will help them with.

We had bathtubs which we anticipated would be used for water play and which were, for the most part. Except, some youngsters had traveled across the county, coming by day coach, which took four days. I remember one instance when a family arrived; the mother knew only that her husband worked for Kaiser. There were 125,000 employees in three yards. We bathed her four kids, and "slept" them and fed them while other people tried to find her husband and reunite the family. I am trying to suggest a concept of meeting needs—a way of living with people, in which everyone who has something to give, gives it.

There isn't time to detail every development. Let me simply list a mending service we developed and an experiment with a shopping service. We were trying to help mothers who worked all day, to save them from having to stand in line.

I hope without my saying it that I am implying to you a comparable way of working with children in groups. I wish I could say that every teacher always felt that she fully succeeded in helping every child. No teacher ever quite feels this way. Because the teachers were trained, they sensed the many needs of the youngsters: emotional needs, social needs, intellectual needs. To serve them well is a challenging task, and a demanding one.

I still have the good fortune to see many of the teaching staff, now scattered in different parts of the country. I am always taken with how those who worked with children can to this day remember children's names. This is one of the unusual, startling qualities of the really good teacher, a sign of one who has lived with youngsters and feels intimately bound to them.

I find I cannot give you costs. I have uncovered one figure that shocked me. Our teachers were pleased to come for a whole wide variety of reasons—the excitement, the challenge, the opportunity to make a contribution to war service, *and* because we were paying excellent salaries. We paid $60 a week, which is $3,000 a year! . . . [T]hat was regarded by highly trained teachers as an excellent salary! . . . We had excellent staff, excellent salaries, excellent equipment.

How do you sum it up? A medal? I have a file of letters from parents who came to me saying, "This is the most wonderful thing in the world." Letters of gratitude and appreciation went to Kaiser. I once figured out at the end of the program that we cared for 3,811 different children. We began with a handful of children in each of the two centers. Our maximum attendance was 1,005 after a little more than a year in these two centers. We provided a total of 249,268 child care days. We freed 1,931,827 woman work hours, enough to build three Liberty ships, if you wanted to build three Liberty ships.

We did it all at tremendous expense. I have to end by saying this was wartime. This was a cost-plus contract. I thank all of you because you or your parents paid for it. I am taken with how costly good services to children and families have to be. I am taken with how costly bad services always are.

CHAPTER 12 Federal Involvement in Early Childhood

12.1 DOAK S. CAMPBELL, FREDERICK H. BAIR, AND OSWALD L. HARVEY

Educational Activities of the Works Progress Administration

During one of America's lowest economic periods, the Works Progress Administration (WPA) was created to operate massive federal work relief programs. The WPA programs supplemented the sparse state education and work opportunities caused by the Great Depression. The earliest relief programs were educational, intended to reemploy teachers who had worked in rural elementary schools before they were closed for lack of funds. Within several months, nursery schools for young children of "needy and unemployed" parents were established. For the first time, nursery schools and parent education programs in the United States were coordinated through a national advisory agency.

In 1936 President Franklin Roosevelt appointed the Advisory Committee on Education to study the relationship of federal and state aid to education and to make recommendations. Doak S. Campbell, dean of the Graduate School of Education at George Peabody College for Teachers, and Frederick H. Bair, superintendent of Bronxville Schools in New York City, prepared *Educational Activities of the Works Progress Administration* (U.S. Government Printing Office, 1939), one of several studies commissioned for the committee. Oswald L. Harvey, a member of the committee, finalized the report.

Although the WPA nursery schools were created to augment temporary relief programs and existed for only 10 years, their effect is still evident in early childhood education. These were not baby-sitting services but comprehensive programs of preschool education. With the support of federal funding and a commitment to high standards, teachers were able to experiment with new teaching techniques and methods. The following selection, which is from the committee's report, shows how the WPA nursery schools expanded the field of early childhood education.

*R*elief alone is not enough if the recipient feels that unless he gives work in return for assistance he loses his self-respect. But work relief alone is also not enough if the recipient feels that the payment made is not an acknowledged wage but charity still. Even work relief at an acknowledged wage is not enough, however, if, while in receipt of that relief, the recipient is engaged in work which does nothing to maintain the skill he has, or even helps to destroy it. To be most effective, relief should be rehabilitative; it should restore self-confidence, maintain occupational skills, and develop such added skills as may be necessary in keeping up to date, or in transferring from one occupation to another. And in very essence rehabilitative relief is an educative function.

The Works Progress Administration operates a work relief program, established on an acknowledged standard wage basis, and fundamentally rehabilitative in function. It represents, however, only a step in the evolution of a relief program which, from a policy of outright relief financed and administered by local agencies, has passed through a phase of indiscriminate work relief under first local and then national auspices to its present form of selective work relief under basically national auspices with State and local collaboration. . . .

ORIGIN AND DEVELOPMENT OF THE EDUCATIONAL PROGRAM

The initial approach to the relief of persons affected by the depression was both timid and exigent. Only gradually was the magnitude of the disaster appreciated, and accurate information concerning its incidence was not available. Local relief funds were soon exhausted, and supplementary loans made by the Federal Government proved to be inadequate. It soon became obvious that only through concerted effort under Federal auspices, supported by the wealth of the entire Nation, could the problem be faced with any anticipation of successful accomplishment. Obvious, too, was the fact that direct relief was in many cases wasteful of human resources. For the sake of morale alone, it was desirable that the idle be kept busy; it was still more important, however, that the unemployed worker should not be allowed through desuetude to lose his former skills. Work relief and education appeared to offer the most appropriate solution.

Federal Emergency Relief Administration

When the Federal Emergency Relief Administration was established in May 1933—about three years after the depression began—the general principles of administration, financing, and employment had already been fairly clearly outlined as the result of experience.

Immediate needs were met by direct relief and public works employment. Public works employment, however, could not provide an adequate solution to the problem of the rehabilitation and maintenance of the special skills peculiarly characteristic of professional and semiprofessional workers. The number of needy persons in this white-collar group was not known, but it was evident that many were teachers who, because of the financial straits of local governments, were unemployed.

Consequently, one of the first releases to the States from the Federal Emergency Relief Administration authorized the expenditure of relief funds in the employment of unemployed teachers in rural elementary schools closed for lack of funds. The release also authorized the employment of needy unemployed persons (not necessarily teachers) competent to teach adults to read and write English. The supervision of the program was delegated to the State educational authorities. Thus the initial step in the educational program of the relief administration expressed indirectly the principles of its future policy: The restoration of normal educational facilities; the rehabilitation of unemployed teachers; the development of an educational program for adults; the employment on that program of persons not necessarily previously trained as teachers; and State responsibility for the supervision of the program.

In September 1933 a member of the staff of the Office of Education, who was especially well qualified in the field of adult education, and a member of the staff of the Federal Board of Vocational Education were appointed to direct the educational program of the Emergency Relief Administration. The operating division thus established was designated the Division of Education Projects.

Within a month thereafter the educational program had been extended to include: The vocational training of unemployed adults, the vocational rehabilitation of handicapped adults, and the general educational training of unemployed and other adults in need of such training as "to fit them to take their part as self-supporting citizens." Shortly afterwards workers' education classes and nursery schools for "young children of pre-school age in the homes of needy and unemployed parents" were established. And before the end of the year the program was still further extended to include resident schools for unemployed women eligible for relief, the employment of college students on part-time jobs, and aid to small urban schools in financial distress. During the summer of 1934 a program of parent education was established.

Thus almost inadvertently the education program developed as an essential part of the relief program, and the way was prepared not only for the selective relief of a special group of unemployed persons—namely, the teachers—but also for the provision of economic, cultural, and social rehabilitation of unemployed workers in general. In December 1933 the quota for unemployed teachers was increased by 40,000 and additional funds for their employment were provided. . . .

Thus, by the time the Works Progress Administration was established in June 1935, the foundations of the education program had been substantially laid and the major fields of educational activity marked out. . . .

EDUCATION FOR FAMILY LIVING

That field of educational endeavor under the Works Progress Administration emergency program which includes nursery schools, parent education, and homemaking education may be designated broadly as education for family living. Although in the official regulations governing operating procedures the constituent activities are separately and specifically described, functionally they are considered as a whole and are combined under a single specialist on the staff of the national director of the Division of Education Projects.

Prior to the establishment of the Federal Emergency Relief Administration, nursery schools and parent education were already well known in the United States as educational functions promoted by highly effective private national agencies. Homemaking was included as part of the Federal vocational education program. When the Division of Education Projects was established as a constituent part of the relief program in 1933, specialists in nursery school and parent education were appointed to the staff of the national director of the emergency education program. . . .

Nursery Schools

To avoid duplication of existing educational services and to meet the most urgent needs, the Division of Education Projects of the Works Progress Administration has confined its activities to pre-school and post-school groups. Thus that group of children too young to be accommodated under existing public school provisions became one of its possible fields of service.

Prior to the establishment of the emergency education program various organizations of national repute had carried on experiments in the care and training of young children, and there was a growing conviction that more

comprehensive educational provision should be made for all children during
the earlier years. In the emergency program many educational leaders saw an
opportunity to conduct this experimentation in wider areas. They urged that
the program be carried on in such a way as to warrant the continuation of the
services on some sort of a permanent basis. Representatives of the major agencies concerned were invited as a committee to advise the Federal Emergency Relief Administration concerning the development of the nursery school
program.

During the first year of the program no funds were provided by the
Federal Emergency Relief Administration for purposes of State supervision.
The national advisory committee obtained the necessary funds from private
sources and employed persons whose services were offered to such States as
wished to avail themselves of their advice. Only the best available personnel
was employed. . . .

It was generally recognized that for this activity to be successful a program for the intensive training of teachers must be provided, and this became
the primary objective of supervision. Thus early in the development of the
program high standards of workmanship were established and the value of
supervision demonstrated. During the second year the costs of supervision
were paid from Federal sources, and the possibilities of improving standards
were thus assured.

With the establishment of the Works Progress Administration, earmarked
funds specifically for educational purposes were no longer available. Thus the
funds for the nursery school projects were derived from the same common
pool as were those for all other types of projects, such as construction, conducted in the States. Under the circumstances there was considerable doubt
that funds for nursery schools would be available. That the nursery school
program did not decline under these less assuring conditions is in major part
due to the fact that the public was convinced of its worth. By this time the
universities, colleges, and normal schools, which have been most effective in
the promotion of nursery school education, had begun to develop a more comprehensive program of pre-school education. The training of teachers and other
professional personnel was conducted in the major demonstration centers.

Although pre-service training is a great asset, events showed that in-service training to some extent can be substituted for it. Prospective teachers therefore were selected with the utmost care from the available relief rolls, and
employed on the State-wide nursery school projects. They received their initial
training while working at the best available demonstration centers, whence
they were assigned to schools established in other localities in the State. To a
large extent in-service training took the place of pre-service training on the
program. And it was found that relief personnel, though lacking many of the
usually required academic qualifications, frequently turned out to be excellent
teachers, provided they could be given expert supervision and expert training
while on the job. The enthusiasm of local public school officials, who helped to
select the best potential personnel, further insured the success of this selective
employment procedure. Many colleges and universities which heretofore had
not given training in this field now organized their work in order to provide
the necessary training facilities.

The emergency nursery school is not intended as a convenience for the relief of parents; it is not a crèche but an educational institution, including in its routine proper nutrition, health service, supervised play, and training in good habits of personal care and behavior. The nursery school program is intended for "children from two to four years of age inclusive, from homes of those eligible for any form of Federal or State relief or work relief, or from similar low-income families." Among those families the need is so great and the number of nursery schools relatively speaking so small that many children who would profit by nursery school attendance cannot be admitted. There are in addition large numbers of families just above the low-income groups who would gladly enroll their children if facilities were made available. In fact there is an increasing demand from groups able to pay some tuition that they be allowed the same privileges as are now allowed to the low-income groups. Since existing facilities are not sufficient to care for more than a small proportion of even those in the low-income group, it is obvious that some other provision will be necessary before nursery schools can be made available to the general public.

The maintenance of an educational program for the parents of the children attending the nursery schools is considered an integral part of the nursery school program. This aspect of the work is discussed later in the section on parent education.

Even though it is the policy of the emergency education program to set up a nursery school only after substantial request for the service has been made by the local community, the demand for nursery schools simply cannot be satisfied. . . . The Works Progress Administration nursery school program exists in every State, has been extended into rural as well as urban areas, and applies to non-white as well as to white persons. Financial support is as yet largely confined to local agencies, but there is every reason to think that as the States become financially better able to make provision for nursery school education the program will come to be looked upon as an essential part of the State school system.

. . . The program employs over 5,400 persons of whom more than 3,200 are teachers. During November 1937 it conducted nearly 1,500 full-day units and enrolled about 40,000 children. Regular enrollments constitute slightly more than 3 percent of all enrollments on the entire emergency education program.

Nursery schools under the emergency program are of four types, which, however, are not mutually exclusive. They are to be found (1) as an integral part of the public elementary school system, though conducted by the Works Progress Administration; (2) as observation and training centers attached to universities, colleges, and normal schools; (3) as high school laboratories in connection with courses on child care and training; and (4) as separate units established and conducted by local community agencies, but not housed in public school buildings. It is estimated that about two-thirds of the nursery schools are located in public school buildings; this is evidence of the interest of school authorities in the worth of the program.

At the State level there are very few advisory committees concerned with the nursery school program; in Oklahoma and Indiana are two that operate very effectively. At the local level a great many nursery schools have advisory committees; communities which lack committees are urged to develop them.

Although in no case has a community completely taken over a program in nursery school education, there is an increasing tendency to augment the sponsors' contribution to the program, particularly in the matter of food costs. Local sponsors have always provided rent, heat, light, and some medium for cooking, and have usually provided equipment.

Most active and effective cooperation in the nursery school program is provided by the local school systems, the local parent-teacher associations, and the various social and educational agencies interested in child welfare. Among the most valuable of these agencies are the State and local departments of public health, which supervise the health facilities and services essential to a successful nursery school program.

... The fact that competent teachers on the emergency nursery school program frequently obtain employment in the primary grade departments of the public schools tends to lower the average level of ability of those remaining. Only by careful selection of new candidates, followed by a vigorous program of in-service training and by skilled supervision, has it been possible to maintain satisfactory standards.

With these reservations in mind it may be noted that, in 1934–35,

> ... while only a limited number of the persons employed as teachers in the emergency nursery schools had had previous experience in that field yet many had had some experience which might be expected to contribute to their work in the nursery schools. Of [those] who had had no previous employment it is probable that many had graduated recently from teacher training institutions.

Of all teachers then employed on the nursery school program approximately one-fourth had a bachelor's degree or more, and almost two-thirds had from 2 to 4 years of normal school training. A number of assistants were obtained from students aided by the National Youth Administration and from public high school pupils interested in studying child development.

... [T]he children ... came "from all socio-economic levels in approximately the same proportions as the general population, with some tendency to come in greater proportions from the slightly skilled and laboring groups." The homes from which they came were smaller and more crowded, and the families larger and more mobile than were those of the general population; and in equipment and cultural possessions, in toys and books, the homes were less well supplied. In 1935 approximately 85 percent of the children were white, 11 percent Negro, and 4 percent of other races.

> On the average each nursery school had a little better than 2 teachers, a part time nurse, a part time dietitian-cook, and a part-time janitor, handy man, or maid. The two and a fraction teachers probably include a head teacher, an assistant teacher and some help from another person, sometimes a nurse or the dietitian-cook.

The median number of staff members per school unit was 4.4, and of children per staff member 9.2. The schools were distributed by type of community roughly as follows: About 54 percent were in "cities", 34 percent in "small towns", and 12 percent in "villages" and "rural areas." In rural areas the major problem was transportation; it has been suggested that the solution lies in the employment of itinerant teachers. Most of the schools were open all year, and from about 8 a.m. to 3 p.m. for five days a week. A unit consisted of approximately 30 children, under the care of from 3 to 4 staff members, and was required to maintain an average daily attendance of 20 children.

It is not possible to determine accurately the cost of operating the emergency nursery schools. Salaries vary according to the relief wage rates for the areas concerned, but on the average they approximate $60 a month for teachers. Food expenses vary even more markedly, depending on the extent to which the local community contributes to nonlabor costs; it is, however, generally agreed that $0.12 is about the lowest possible average daily cost per child sufficient to meet nutritional needs. Rent, heat, light, equipment, and health services are usually provided in large part by the local community.

The quality of the program appears to be uniformly good throughout the States, largely because of the excellent quality of supervision and the policy of careful selection of teachers. Standards have been maintained by abandoning the program in communities unable or unwilling to adhere to the required standards, and by a thoroughgoing system of in-service training of teachers.

It is regrettable that the excellent reporting system which obtained in this program during the first two years of its development no longer exists. On the basis of such reports not only was it possible to inform the public more accurately concerning the achievements and characteristics of the program, but also to plan future policy more intelligently.

12.2 KEITH OSBORN

Project Head Start: An Assessment

Keith Osborn was an early childhood educator and educational consultant who had a special interest in community action programs benefiting children of poverty. During his tenure as chairman of the Division of Community Services at the Merrill-Palmer Institute in Michigan, Osborn was asked to serve on the National Planning Committee for Head Start. This comprehensive program for four- and five-year-olds was designed to maximize children's total development prior to entering school. In his role as Head Start's chief educational consultant, Osborn championed intensive teacher training and full medical and nutritional services in all programs.

When the project began in the summer of 1965, children of the poor arrived en masse at child development centers across the nation. It was an auspicious beginning: 560,000 children, 256,000 volunteers, 41,000 teachers, and 2,500 centers. But the numbers are not the only story. In the following selection from "Project Head Start: An Assessment," *Educational Leadership* (November 1965), Osborn discusses the original summer project and chronicles "the largest program for young children ever sponsored by our government." He anticipates ways that Head Start will affect young children, families, teaching, and community programs.

*D*uring the past summer over 550,000 children in approximately 2,500 Child Development Centers throughout the country participated in a preschool program formally known as Project Head Start. Project Head Start is one of several Community Action Programs operated under the Office of Economic Opportunity. This project represented the largest program for young children ever sponsored by our government.

Geographically speaking, there were programs as far north as the Arctic Circle; as far south as American Samoa; as far east as the Virgin Islands; as far west as Guam. Children came from rural and urban areas, from Indian reservations and Eskimo villages, from migrant groups and "the Hollows" of West Virginia. In some counties one out of three children who entered kindergarten or first grade this fall were in Head Start programs during the summer.

The project also involved over 100,000 adults—parents, teachers, physicians, psychologists and other professional and volunteer workers. It is noteworthy that while the actual operation of the program could be administered by any local nonprofit organization, over 80 percent of the centers were sponsored by local school systems.

These general facts can give the reader some idea of the scope of the project.

The growth and time element of Head Start are rather remarkable. Implemented in June of 1965, the program was not conceived until November 1964. A Planning Committee was formed during that month composed of outstanding professional leaders, including George Brain, James L. Hymes, Jr. and Jack Neimeyer. A Project Director, Julius B. Richmond, M.D., was named in February.

During the early planning stages the project was referred to as the Kiddie Corps and it was felt that perhaps fifty to one hundred thousand children would be involved in an eight week summer program. By late February the response of local communities was so great (approximately 65 percent of all counties in the U.S. wanted programs) that the projected enrollment was estimated between five and six hundred thousand. While the basic outlines of the program were formulated between November–January, for all practical purposes the actual work of the project (community planning, funding, orientation of teachers) took place over a period of four months. At this writing plans are being considered to: (a) initiate programs to "follow-up" on Head Start children, (b) to begin year-around programs wherever possible, and (c) plan for the second Head Start program for the summer of 1966.

OBSERVATIONS

Since research data on the project are not available at this early date, the following statements are based on my observations of the program.

1. The concept of the child development center. One of the most significant aspects of the project is the general idea of a Child Development Center, since Head Start encompasses more than an educational program *per se.*

The Child Development Center is both a concept and a community facility. In concept it represents drawing together all the resources—family, community and professional—which can contribute to the child's total development. It draws heavily on the professional skills of persons in education, health, nutrition, and social services. It recognizes that professional and nonprofessional can make a meaningful contribution. It emphasizes the family as fundamental to the child's total development and the role of the parents in developing policies and participating in the program of the center.

As a community facility the Child Development Center is organized around the classroom and the play area. It provides a program for health services, parent interviews, feeding of children, and meetings of parents and other residents in the community. This concept recognizes that some children have been deprived in many areas—and that the lack of intellectual stimulation is only one of several gaps for the children of the poor. While the concept of nursery school is sound, the concept of a Child Development Center seems more appropriate for the children served by Head Start.

A Doctor—A Dentist—A Hot Meal

My observations of programs throughout the country reinforce this belief. Many children received early diagnosis of medical problems which were unknown to the parents. In some instances dental diagnosis showed that a "slow learning" problem was in reality a dental problem. In other cases a "discipline problem" turned out to be a medical one.

Most of the children in Head Start were provided with at least one hot meal each day. One teacher told me, "Head Start is providing several of the children in my group with the only substantial meal they receive."

2. Teachers and program. Approximately 40,000 teachers served in Head Start Centers during the summer. Many of these teachers had not had previous experience with children of this age and cultural milieu. As a result there were instances in which third and fourth grade teachers taught miniature versions of these grades and treated the children more like preadolescents than like preschoolers.

Some of the centers were more concerned with seating arrangements and school readiness *per se.* A number of centers concentrated on teaching of reading and numbers and failed to provide a program which would make up for earlier cultural losses in these children.

Program Problems

In some instances the children were highly regimented and programs were lacking in flexibility, thus many golden opportunities were missed for individualized instruction of children. It is unfortunate that more centers did not provide programs which could meet both individual and group needs. I would quickly add that this shortcoming was not due to lack of staff—the teacher to pupil ratio in Head Start was 1 to 13 and the adult to child ratio about 1 to 5. Rather it was usually a lack of imagination on the part of the teacher.

Fortunately, the majority of teachers did capitalize on the small group and did make the transition to preschool types of curriculum. Activities included art, stories, science activities, creative play and visits to various community facilities. These programs were designed to stimulate children's thinking—but, in contrast to situations mentioned earlier, the curriculum was geared to the interests and abilities appropriate to children of this age.

Small Groups a Success

I feel much of the success of the program was due to the factor of class size. For years educators have asked for small groups and Head Start has demonstrated the value of such class size. The most consistent comment from teachers was in terms of class size and their feeling that substantial gains were possible since they could provide each child with maximum individualized instruction. Whether or not communities will ultimately bear the high cost of small group instruction is another matter. However, this may be the price we must pay for earlier deprivation.

I also believe that the program will ultimately affect the entire educational field in another way. Everywhere I went, school administrators were discussing ways to extend school downward. I feel the most immediate change will be a rise in kindergarten programs in school districts where no program exists; in other districts, there will be a move to extend schooling to three and four year olds.

Parents-Teachers Alerted

Perhaps Head Start's biggest contribution has been its effect on the teacher himself. This could be seen in three ways: (a) alerting the teacher to the needs of the poor, (b) seeing the progress which could be made in eight weeks in a small group setting, and (c) a commitment on the part of the teacher to follow through with these children in the fall.

3. Parents and community. Just as the quality of teaching varied, so did the quality of work with parents and with the commitment of the community. In some centers parents participated fully in all aspects of the program. Parents served as committee members and, in several instances, as committee chairmen of the center. Parents also served as teacher aides, story tellers, cooks, carpenters and secretaries.

This type of participation is a basic part of the philosophy of the Community Action Program. I am convinced that this philosophy is sound and is justified. By and large parents of culturally deprived children are as concerned with the welfare of their young as any other parents. Perhaps even more so— since these parents know the long term effects of an inadequate education. At one center a Head Start father told me that his teen-age son had more respect for him since he had assumed a role of importance in his community. A number of parents talked of returning to school. Many parents went to the Public Library for the first time to obtain books for themselves and their children.

In some centers, however, there was little or no parent participation. Part of the lack of parent participation was doubtless due to the "crash" aspect of the program, since some communities were unable to mobilize their parents as quickly as others. However, we encountered many instances—often in programs run by the local school system—where no real effort was made to include parents in any way. If this program is to be more than first aid, we must bring parents into the center and include them in all aspects of the program.

4. The child. Research data and success in school this fall will ultimately provide the information as to how successful the Child Development Center was in providing children with a head start into life.

But for me—as well as many teachers, physicians, social workers and others who worked actively in the program—the day to day, here and now experience which the children received made the program a success.

New Thrills of Childhood

There were some dramatic instances of children who had never seen themselves in a mirror or children who used a telephone for the first time.

But for nearly all of the children there was a "first" at painting, crayons, child-oriented facilities, or visits to the zoo, supermarket and the fire station. Many situations which middle-class children take for granted, the Head Start child experienced for the first time. Many of these youngsters had never had a book read to them.

Certainly the Child Development Center cannot in eight weeks make up for four years of deprivation. It did not attempt to do so. Rather the program attempted to provide some of the medical, nutritional and educational advantages the children of more affluent parents enjoy. It attempted to give these children a better beginning—or as we at the Office of Economic Opportunity called it—a Head Start.

Editor's Note: Ordinarily a letter of transmittal is just that—it transmits. However, the letter that accompanied Keith Osborn's article did more than transmit. It gave a sense of the excitement and almost of exaltation felt by many of the persons responsible for initiating and carrying out the pioneering venture for young children that was called Project Head Start. The letter follows:

Saturday
Sept. 11, 1965

Dear Robert:

During Head Start, I was brought to Washington by the Office of Education as Educational Consultant (three days a week) and placed on temporary assignment to the Office for Economic Opportunity with Project Head Start. I went in February so I had the opportunity to see the project grow from infancy.

I must admit the past few months have been the moot exciting in my life. As one who taught as a nursery school and kindergarten teacher, it was gratifying to see others become equally interested in the education and welfare of young children.

There were some problems (at times we referred to the project jokingly as "Head Ache" and "Head Shrink") but many more satisfactions—I hope I have presented both fairly. However, I am really prejudiced and perhaps much too close to the Project. It was a huge success. In spite of some poor teaching—there were many more examples of great teaching—and of teachers and administrators who worked long hours on short notice to insure success of the program.

I wish I knew how to tell this part of the story—the many nonprofessionals (the secretaries at OEO and other personnel who worked 12–15 hours every day between February and June—because they wanted these children to have a Head Start in school—the bus driver in West Virginia who took time off from his regular job and went to the Center to have juice and crackers with "his" children because they asked him to. The Head Start Center in Mississippi that met in a church which was burned to the ground by some whites—and they opened the next day in a tent. The farmer who lived near an Indian Reservation and who each morning saddled his horse, forded a river and picked up an Indian child—who would not have attended a Center otherwise.

An ADC (Aid-to-Dependent-Children) mother who worked four hours daily in one center—without pay—she paid a baby-sitter to care for her other children—why? Because she wanted these children to get the schooling she never had. The Kentucky principal who worked at two jobs for four months so his county could have Head Start. The Negro principal in Georgia who will probably lose his position in the school system because of his stand in following the "spirit" that Head Start is for *all* children regardless of color. Numerous consultants who, on an hour's notice, dropped everything and flew all over the country to help communities plan for Head Start. I visited one cook (a volunteer) working in a "tenant farm" center—there were no fans and only one small window in the kitchen—the temperature was 97° outside—she was cooking fried chicken and baking rolls for the children. Or even the school superintendent who received funds for 30 migrant children and then returned the funds because the families moved before the Center opened.

I don't know how you tell these stories in an article—it is really unfortunate—since they represent the true flavor of Head Start.

Sincerely,
Keith (Osborn)

12.3 ROCHELLE BECK

The White House Conferences on Children: An Historical Perspective

"By the safeguard of health and the protection of childhood we further contribute to that equality of opportunity which is the unique basis of American civilization." The concepts in this statement are quite contemporary; however, it was President Herbert Hoover who uttered these words in 1929, in announcing the third White House Conference on Children. Beginning in 1909, when Theodore Roosevelt was president, White House conferences highlighting children's health and well-being have been convened each decade. These conferences have been a federal form of advocacy. With each decade, ever-increasing numbers of experts have brought the needs of children to the steps of the White House.

Although the vast majority of recommendations coming from the White House conferences have not been legislated, some outcomes are notable: As a result of the first conference on the care of dependent children, the Children's Bureau in the Department of Labor was organized. Although it took more than three decades, the federal aid to education recommendations of the 1930 conference were finally legislated in 1965. From these conferences have come important documents stressing the comprehensive rights and needs of children, particularly the Children's Charter of the 1930 conference and the Children's Bill of Rights of 1970. Although the conferences have been responsible for changes on both national and state levels, Rochelle Beck notes some consequential ironies of the conferences in the following selection from "The White House Conferences on Children: An Historical Perspective," *Harvard Educational Review* (November 1973). Beck makes comparisons among conferences across the decades and finds a vast distance between political rhetoric and reality in legislating for change.

When she undertook her analysis of the proceedings of the White House Conferences, Beck was a faculty member of the College of Education at Harvard University.

*T*his analysis is based on the proceedings of the seven White House Conferences: The Conference on the Care of Dependent Children (1909), the Conference on Child Welfare Standards (1919), the White House Conference on Child Health and Protection (1930), the White House Conference on Children in a Democracy (1940), the Midcentury White House Conference on Children and Youth (1950), the Golden Anniversary White House Conference on Children and Youth (1960), and the White House Conference on Children and Youth (1970). They are available from the U.S. Government Printing Office, Washington, D.C.

> Sometimes when I get home at night in Washington I feel as though I had been in a great traffic jam. The jam is moving toward the Hill where Congress sits in judgment on all the administrative agencies of the Government. In that traffic jam are all kinds of vehicles . . . There are all kinds of conveyances, for example, that the Army can put into the street—tanks, gun carriages, trucks . . . There are the hayricks and the binders and the ploughs and all the other things that the Department of Agriculture manages to put into the streets . . . the handsome limousines in which the Department of Commerce rides . . . the barouches in which the Department of State rides in such dignity. It seems to me as I stand on the sidewalk watching it become more congested and more difficult, and then because the responsibility is mine and I must, I take a very firm hold on the handles of the baby carriage and I wheel it into the traffic.
>
> —Grace Abbott, 1934

The responsibility Grace Abbott assumed for bringing the needs of children to the attention of the federal government reflected a shift in the way we view children and the appropriate role of government in providing for their care. Women had led humanitarian movements before. But where the goal had been to improve the unfortunate circumstances of society's neglected young, the notions for reform had been largely informal and nongovernmental, specific to local communities and run by people from them, and constrained in scope by the family's grip on children as private property. Twentieth century social reformers had different views. Children, they said, were this country's most precious natural resource—and in this metaphor the discussion of policy governing child welfare was shifted to the public domain. Once it was there, they reasoned, the federal government had to recognize the needs of children along with its other national interests. Formal governmental agencies and procedures were necessary. As Lillian Wald wrote, "The national sense of humor was aroused by the grim fact that whereas the federal government concerns itself with the conservation of hogs and lobsters and has long since established bureaus to supply information concerning them, citizens who desire instruction and guidance for the conservation and protection of children have no responsible governmental body to which to appeal."[1] The reformers prevailed upon President Theodore Roosevelt to hold a national conference to promote the establishment of such a governmental body.

Thus, the first White House Conference on Children was created to discuss and marshal support for governmental planning and protection of the nation's children. But the Conference was more than a political and practical event. It was a symbolic act of government, stating explicity that certain needs of children would come within its purview. Once every decade since 1909, the federal government has convened such a conference, reaffirming its commitment to monitor and report on children's status in society.

But what, exactly, does that commitment entail? How are those certain needs settled on? Have they shifted over time? Other than providing a symbol, what is the federal responsibility for the welfare of children, and how is it related to the family, the community, the experts, and the other agencies which share the job of childrearing? The Conferences have left behind a rich written record that illuminates these and other questions. The proceedings and recommendations, reverends' prayers and presidential addresses, experts' reports and concerned citizens' testimony provide a tapestry of information, weaving the needs of children with other dominant social, political, and economic themes. The style, tone, and content of the written documents vary greatly, as must have the Conferences themselves. In part, the differences can be explained by major historical events, changes in the characteristics of the participants, or leaps in knowledge or sophistication. But some of the distinctive features are due to the constantly evolving way in which this society sees and treats children. The proceedings of the White House Conferences on Children provide fascinating material for reflecting on this evolution.

The 1909 White House Conference on the Care of Dependent Children was organized by Jane Addams and Lillian Wald, leaders of the settlement house movement, along with the National Child Labor Committee, a group seeking to limit child labor, and other political and social leaders. These people were humanitarians, outraged by the abuses they saw dependent groups suffer in the growing cities and the depressed rural areas. Not only children, but immigrants, women, and those unable to compete in the fierce marketplace of industrialization were the objects of their concern. But they also were worshippers of industrialization and the precision, efficiency, and objectivity it introduced into the language and thinking of the country. Corporate management experts mapped out the flow of products and manpower to increase efficiency and production; planning and organization seemed to "pay off"; and gathering facts in order to direct the use of material resources was lauded as enlightened public policy. In an effort to apply this policy to human resources, 200 experts from the fields of medicine, education, data collection, and social work were invited to set an agenda for a Children's Bureau. The Bureau would gather statistics; compare rates of growth, mortality, dependency; make information available to states and individuals; and plan and support scientific research needed for the rational planning of programs for the nation's human resources. Jane Addams' address to the 1909 Conference sums up its motivation:

If my topic contemplated the devices for minimizing the labor in harvesting a field of wheat or producing a gross of buttons, if I were asked to name the world's famous inventions for minimizing mechanical friction or for saving human labor, there is no doubt that the inventions would all be American, and that if I were challenged I could quite simply invite you to take a walk through the neighboring patent building. But when we are asked to consider together the newest devices for minimizing dependency, those inventions to keep wage-earning parents alive and able to care for their own children, unfortunately for our pride we are obliged to enumerate the devices found in every other modern nation in greater abundance than they were found in America.[2]

The second Conference, the White House Conference on Standards of Child Welfare, was held in 1919. The mood of this Conference is best represented by the word "standards," reflecting the focus of the new Children's Bureau which had finally been approved by Congress in 1912. There had been doubt in both Senate and House about the appropriateness of a federal body to oversee child welfare. Some congressmen seriously questioned the constitutionality of federal regulations in an area which was formerly the province of the states. Voluntary groups such as the Society for the Prevention of Cruelty to Children were afraid that a federal agency would constrain their activities, and the Department of Education saw the recordkeeping and information functions of the Bureau as a threat to its sphere of influence. Amid much opposition, the Children's Bureau came into being with modest plans for action and modest funds to carry out those plans. In the 1912 debate one senator noted, "Congress has appropriated $25,000 to conduct the work of the Children's Bureau. This Congress is not wont to be so parsimonious in matters of property. Why become so economical in matters of human life? This body has already appropriated $600,000 for dealing with hog cholera. It has provided $375,000 for the study of the cotton-boll weevil. The most precious asset of the Nation is not its swine nor cotton crop. It is the army of children. With them rests the future of the Republic."[3] Careful not to threaten various interest groups, the Bureau focused its work narrowly on infant and maternal mortality and health. It gathered statistics and launched educational programs for mothers to reduce the incidence of deaths associated with childbirth. In a crash program to register all births and raise the consciousness of mothers regarding child health, May 1, 1918, was designated Child Health Day; it was followed by Baby Week; and the 1919 Conference was the culmination of Children's Year.[4] Thus, the 1919 conference was dominated by physicians with facts and figures reporting the state of maternal and child health. Emphasis on efficient use of human resources still prevailed, but the Conference delegates were careful not to overstep their perceived mandate, limiting recommendations to revising standards rather than advocating more active programs.

The 1930 Conference was on Child Health and Protection and it was a radical departure from the previous Conferences. Broad in scope, it said something about almost every aspect of childhood and adolescence. Education, mobility, labor, vocational training, the family, and recreation were included as well as concerns about health, the handicapped, and child growth and development. Each of the first two Conferences had 200 participants; the 1930 Conference assembled "3,000 men and women, leaders in the medical, educational, and social fields as they touch on the life of the child."[5] Although representatives of many local groups concerned with children were included, the reports of pediatricians and educators, and a growing number of presentations by child psychologists, dominated the proceedings.

As our mechanism has become more intricate the need for education and training of the expert . . . becomes more and more evident. If we compare the mother of the past who nursed her own child to the one who must now rely on prepared foods, we find that between the mother and the child we have a whole series of persons and forces upon which the safety of the child depends. . . . Beyond baby-hood we have substituted another whole series of organized services between the mother and her child and have replaced much of the home training of the child with these activities . . . kindergartens, playgrounds and schools under government or private auspices. . . . We face the absolute necessity of making good in all of this through expert service. It is probably true that it is beyond the capacity of the individual parent to train her child to fit into the intricate, interwoven and interdependent social and economic system we have developed. The gospel of instinct is obsolete.[6]

The tension between the role of experts and natural parents in caring for children was manifested in the Conference's ambiguous outlook toward the family as the primary childrearing institution. President Hoover summed it up in 1930 by saying:

. . . such responsibility as was assumed for children outside the home was in the beginning largely based on what we call charity. We have seen what was once charity change its nature under the broader term welfare and now those activities looked upon as welfare are coming to be viewed merely as good community housekeeping. In a word, parental responsibility is moving outward to include community responsibility.[7]

However, he went on, " . . . we must force the problem back to the spot where the child is. This primarily means, and should mean, the home. Our function should be to help parents, not replace them."[8]

President Hoover thus reaffirmed one of the most sacred institutions of America: the family. In 1909, the conferees stated unequivocally that "Home life is the highest and finest product of civilization," and that a child should not be deprived of it except for urgent and compelling reasons.[9] Each Conference echoed this sentiment. However, there were subtle differences in tone. The 1930 Conference was more casual about the family; it recognized its limitations and called for extra-familial institutions to supplement parental responsibility. In this period there is less gloomy talk about the demise of the traditional family:

Statistics on marriage, divorce, size of families have been interpreted to indicate disintegration of family life. . . . And all the conditions of production and consumption are tending to remove from the home certain functions formerly considered inherent in family life. On the other hand, evidence equally indicates that the family is not undergoing any fundamental changes. . . . The very fact that it has survived to the present time is an indication that it fulfills deep-seated needs of the human race.[10]

Rather than panic about family stability, the 1930 Conference urged family change through parent education. It said,

An interesting feature of all researches on the family is the resistance of the rural family to change. A recent study has shown them to be disinterested in money matters, antagonistic to change, and staunch in the maintenance of older ideals of family life. . . . The apparent discrepancy between the picture of the stable family presented by rural culture and the poorer adjustment of rural children seems to warrant conjecture that there are aspects of the older family pattern which should be changed.[11]

The Depression formed the backdrop for the 1930 Conference and shaped the tone of the recommendations. Individuals were urged to pitch in and work hard to prevent economic privations from permanently damaging the young. Sensitivity to the needs of children—all children rather than only dependents, the whole child rather than the child with particular handicaps—probably was enchanced by Dewey and the Progressives. Throughout the proceedings, caution was urged against the overuse or misuse of standardized intelligence tests or other statistical means to rank order and single out children.

In 1940, the nation knew that despite its reluctance, it would be drawn inexorably into World War II, and the Conference bore the stamp of that international burden. The proceedings of the White House Conference on Children in a Democracy reads like the kind of propaganda statement we later attributed to the Soviets. The word "democracy" appears so often it seems trite. Every aspect of the child development, health, education, welfare, or family life was tied to patriotism, freedom, democracy, and the American way of life. Infant and maternal mortality had to be eradicated so that a free nation would lead the way in scientific progress. Families should remain stable and the number of children increased so there would be more freedom-loving people on the earth to counterbalance the forces of oppression. Mobilization of war, and the resulting disruption of communities as wives and children moved to be near their men in military bases, became the impetus for remarkable strides in maternal health and community cooperation in planning health and education services. The ideal of cooperation, left over from the New Deal era and revitalized by the sacrifices for the war effort, was invoked in support of the welfare of children as well as the democratic way of life. The Conference's statement of purpose expressed these overriding considerations: "Can a free people by conscious effort rear their children so that their capacities will be developed for cooperative citizen action in exercising their responsibilities of citizenship in a democracy?"[12]

This Conference placed major responsibility for meeting children's needs on a centralized public school system. Rhetoric surrounding the functions of the family was strikingly demystified. The committee report entitled "The Family as the Threshold of Democracy" limits parental responsibilities to basics: "Giving the child food, shelter, and material security is the primary task of the family."[13]

Judging from the Midcentury Conference on Children and Youth, 1950 was a tense and threatening year for Americans. Midcentury was a time for pausing and assessing what had been accomplished, and reflecting on how the future might benefit from past experience. Although the Conference formally recognized this, the majority of its speakers, including the President, were preoccupied with the terrible fear of nuclear obliteration. They could not rouse themselves from their pessimism to plan constructively for the needs of children. Conference participants were transfixed by the atomic bomb and the realization that it could be used by others, the tense cold war, the fear which would soon allow McCarthy to exercise his repressiveness, and mobilization for yet another war, this time in Korea.

A surprising number of clergymen addressed the 1950 Conference. Most reports invoked the name of God to guide the wisdom of the recommendations, to enter into the home and preserve the family, to speak to youths and stop their wanderings, and to watch over the fate of the world. It is as if in a time of crisis the nation as a whole had turned to religion for psychological support. President Truman, in one of the most tentative and qualified opening addresses ever given at a White House Conference, said, "We cannot insulate our children from the uncertainties of the world in which we live or from the impact of the problems which confront us."[14] The threats to healthy growth and development were articulated in the 1950 Conference more clearly than ever before: the damage to individuals from industrialization ("We live in a machine civilization.... The machine may be a Frankenstein monster.... It threatens men's free spirits. It makes them uniform and conditions them to an automatic response—which is just as tyrants wish."[15]); the damage to communities by urbanization ("We live in an urban civilization with ... low standards of competitive success and the mass anonymity that dwarfs personality. Brick chasms echoing to a lonely tattoo of multitudinous feet."[16]); the multiple dangers of war, the bomb, and communism; and the dissolution of home life ("Our mechanistic, urban and worrying world has wreaked its worst havoc on the home...."[17]). A clergyman summed it up by saying, "In such a world it is strange that any child survives. There must be a special providence watching over fools and children."[18]

Whatever doubts paralyzed the thinking of the Conference, it did move ahead in two important areas: broadening participation generally, and increasing the power of professionals. The membership of previous White House Conferences had been drawn predominantly from professional groups with participation by some leading citizens. The 1950 Conference, however, sought to involve citizens' groups from the beginning. Labor union representatives particularly were asked to help design programs resulting from the Conference's recommendations. At the same time, the 1950 Conference document was the most sophisticated yet in language in recommendations relying on developmental psychology and social work. Although youth were included for the first time in planning and attending the Conference, the major theme was one of professional wisdom. Dr. Spock talked about the overriding importance of mother love, but recommendations overflowed calling for more research and pointing out the need for increased professional qualifications and expertise in relating to children. As the number of lay people invited to the Conferences increased, so did the impact of the professionals.

The 1960 White House Conference on Children and Youth reflected the growing alienation of youth which was incipient in 1950. Although a number of important advances had been made during the 1950's in health, psychological research, and education (most notably the formal end to racial segregation), the 1960 Conference was disproportionately concerned with adolescents or "teenagers" in trouble. In 1950, a disturbing number of youths had been showing signs of alienation and uprootedness. A list was presented of groups of adolescents found wandering the country. Called "Children on the Move," it estimated numbers of homeless or dislocated youths, including migrant agricultural workers' children, children in families who move to industrial or construction areas, immigrant children, children of military families, runaways, and transient youth.[19] In 1960, the Conference was set on finding ways to turn these youths' isolation and discontent away from destructiveness and delinquency and toward constructive citizenship. Increase in violent crimes committed by adolescents, the growing culture of gangs, lack of obedience or ambition, and social and political apathy were the foci for most of the presentations at the Conference. Some spokesmen argued that international aggression waged by adults was responsible for breeding interpersonal violence among youths. The tone of the Conference was one of desperate handwringing over juvenile delinquency. National emphasis on youth was also attacked as placing too much pressure on that age group.

In contrast to the 1930 Conference, changes in the family were no longer regarded calmly in 1960, but were seen as dangerous signs heralding the future breakdown of society. A large number of recommendations called for parent education beginning in high school to help young people understand the responsibilities of marriage and the privilege of parenthood. The 1950 Conference had pledged to "work to conserve and improve family life," and called for further study of the underlying causes of broken homes and divorce.[20] In a speech entitled "The Key Role of the Family," a 1960 participant said, "The family occupies a place of centrality in American society; its sovereignty is essential to the child's development which is its basic task. In the fulfillment of this goal, the family has been strengthened and protected by American law and tradition. The family should continue to occupy a key place in our planning for education and health." But, he continued, "The current American attitude toward the family is akin to what happens when a man is hit by a truck—no one dares to touch him for fear of hurting him more. Some pray—and all resolve not to get involved."[21] Involvement was what the Conference recommended, however, with specific motions urging uniform state laws to raise the marriage age to eighteen for females and twenty-one for males, "to strengthen divorce and separation laws, including a mandatory 'cooling off' period with counseling."[22]

The 1970 Conference marked another radical departure from the preceding ones. There were major differences in presentation, language, and emphasis. The report is almost slick in format compared with the routine, staid, research-like documents of the six earlier Conferences: it has modern streamlined printing, categorized and separated by three-color drawings of flowers simulating children's art. Children's essays, poetry, and literature were used along with other kinds of evidence to illustrate points or programs. Children's developmental, health, and educations "needs" were transformed into their "rights," the foundations of which were the same inalienable rights of life, liberty, and the pursuit of happiness guaranteed to every adult citizen. "We conceive of 'rights' as the intrinsic entitlements of every human born or residing in the United States. . . . We must recognize [children's] inherent rights which, although not exclusively those established by law and enforced by the courts, are nonetheless closely related to the law."[23]

The 1960 Conference had some 7,600 participants and in its concern with the problems of adolescents it overlooked concerns of young children. The planners of the 1970 Conference remedied this by proposing two separate conferences: one for children (ages 0–13) and one for youth (ages 14–24). Some 450 pages were devoted to the concerns of the former group. Thus, the care taken in presentation, the forcefulness of the language, and the attention paid to young children reflect the importance of providing for the early years of life.

The chairman of the Conference described the mood of the participants. "Many brought to Washington a deep unease . . . a strong sense of urgency—a feeling that we must act *now* if our society is to flourish."[24] Repeated over again in each of the forums and present in a majority of the recommendations is a demand for the federal government to reorder national priorities. Perhaps indicating the mood of the participants, standards and statistics were replaced by calls for action and advocacy. Several separate forums came up with the idea of a Federal Office of Child Advocacy to connect with advocates in local communities and ensure that the rights of children were being upheld.

In 1970, two different ways of looking at the family emerged. One, foreshadowed in 1960, assumed that women would seek activities outside the home and that this trend could not be legislated away. In 1960, a resolution "that except for the most urgent reasons, mothers refrain from work outside the home which interferes with the primary parental responsibility of childrearing" was defeated.[25] Instead, the group recommended the establishment of day care centers and other services to aid the working mother. This recommendation was extended in 1970 to emphasize universal comprehensive day care and allied services. On the other hand, income maintenance was seen as another alternative for contributing to family support: " . . . since family stability is essential to observance and demonstration of a healthy value system, we recommend a family assistance plan based upon a family income standard that will assure reasonable economic security."[26] With the conviction that programs for children could not circumvent the family, it was urged that developmental, cognitive, health programs have increasing participation of and concern for the whole family.

Several intriguing ironies emerged as one reads through the proceedings of all the Conferences. First, although each Conference was called specifically to gather information, plan programs, and set priorities for the next decade, every Conference turned out to be more a reflection of the preceding decade than a plan for the future. It is fascinating that no one at the Conferences seemed to realize this. Each opening address begins with a brief summation of the past Conferences and then goes on to say that the present one will digest all this information and lay out a map for the coming decade. Yet each Conference then devotes most of its rhetoric and recommendations to solving dilemmas of the decade before, which often are not the major concerns of the next decade.

A second irony is that each conference is nostalgic for the good old days. Later Conferences bemoan the complexity of their tasks and long for the "simpler" problems of the first few Conferences. Yet the problems of the first Conferences do not seem simple at all. The participants greatly feared that the old order was breaking down with a rapidity and callousness that threatened the fabric of society. The 1950's and 1960's saw that television and jet travel were shrinking the world and disrupting communities; yet in the 1940's radio and the automobile were reputed to have had the same effects; and even earlier there are chronicles of a time, before the 1890's, when " . . . neither the radio nor the phonograph brought the outer world into our precincts . . ." and before "bicycles came in and flocks of young people wheeled past their elders sitting on the porches. . . ."[27] It is true that later conferences perceived better the relationship between general social reform and child welfare and often were overwhelmed by the complexity of the task. They discussed helping children indirectly by eliminating racial discrimination or by improving their family's economic condition. But problems such as infant mortality were just as knotty in 1909 as they are today.

Related to this inflated nostalgia is the disparity between how Conference participants pictured rural life and what in fact it was. The story goes that America began as an agrarian culture, and the family and other institutions were comfortably matched to that lifestyle. Then wrenching demographic changes upset the ecological balance and caused problems for children's emotional, intellectual, and physical development. Yet Conference after Conference shocks itself with statistics that show farm or rural children in worse condition than city children. Despite the hazards of higher rates of divorce, illegitimacy, industrial accidents, and moral depredation of the cities, a 1930 study of 8,000 school children found that "urban children seem to be better adjusted than rural children."[28] As more people migrated to cities, services for them became more economical and the need for them was more clearly perceived. Services required equally urgently by scattered rural residents were overlooked. Rural life was idealized wistfully even as the poverty, illness, and deprivation there extended beyond that of cities.

Another irony is the distance between recommendation and implementation, between rhetoric and reality. The language which is most hopeful as one reads through Conference reports raises children above the materialistic concern with resources, labor, or specific illness and talks about their needs in comprehensive and developmental terms. The 1930 Children's Charter was such a statement, and it looks remarkably like the 1970 Children's Bill of Rights drawn up by Mary Kohler. These documents stress rights such as parental love and respect for children, a society free from discrimination, equality of educational opportunity, elimination of abject poverty, and the freedom to pursue different developmental paths based on individual choice or need. It would be reasonable to expect that these kinds of statements, uttered at a White House Conference by the nation's political and professional leaders, would shift the terms of discussion about children, making them people in their own right. If any such movement has occurred, it has been at a glacial pace. Over the sixty years of Conferences, any recommendations which frontally attack these issues have been tabled or defeated at the administrative or legislative level. For example, the 1930 Conference suggested that the federal government provide subsidies for some states to help them meet their educational expenditures in order to equalize educational opportunity among states. In 1940, this discussion was expanded and it is hard to distinguish it in sophistication and logic from *Private Wealth and Public Education*,[29] the book which in 1970 laid the conceptual groundwork for the *Serrano** case. With the Supreme Court's recent verdict in *Rodriguez*, federal aid to equalize school financing may well be an agenda item again at the 1980 Conference. Only the more prosaic recommendations have made a discernible legislative or bureaucratic impact. Myriad standards for affecting numbers of counselors in schools, student-teacher ratios, minimum physical education requirements, vocational education recommendations, and so on have been made and have found their way into many departments of education and schools.

The Conferences since 1930 have said they were interested in *all* the nation's children, yet in reality only special needs or special groups have been given adequate attention in proposed programs, appropriations, and research. The state has long had some responsibility for society's dependent children: orphans, illegitimates, handicapped, emotionally disturbed, mentally retarded, physically or morally abused or abandoned. Conference participants have told themselves and the nation that "what the best and wisest parent wants for his own child, that must the community want for all its children."[30] But, until the 1970 Conference, heavy emphasis was placed on providing for children "at risk" or children with special needs.

A final irony, which some would find wholly predictable, is that although discrimination against racial, ethnic, or religious groups has been deplored at all the Conferences, this injunction has had little effect on the differential quality of educational, health, and other social welfare services available to minority children. Every Conference has offered recommendations to end discrimination. The sociological and psychological studies reported in 1940 and 1950 on the adverse effects of poverty and segregation for the health, emotional well-being, and educational achievement of minority children contributed to the evidence used in the *Brown*** decision in 1954. However, again, movement in this area has been painfully slow despite the overwhelming consensus and proclamations of the White House Conferences.

Reading seven transcripts of White House conferences—each with more participants, more studies, more recommendations and more pages than the preceding one—could leave the impression that these meetings have had more than symbolic importance. The federal government has been exhorted to establish, to maintain, and to embellish its responsibility for the care of children over the years. And in some crude measure, they have been fruitful. Certainly more federal personnel, programs, and dollars are directed to children now than ever before. But the proceedings also give evidence of several significant barriers to federal intervention.

Ever since the first White House Conference, there have been deep-seated fears about the encroachment by government on the fundamental American

---

*[*Serrano v. Priest* (1971), in which the plaintiff challenged the constitutionality of California's policy of using local property taxes as a basis for school financing. The main contention was that this method of funding led to disparities in school quality between richer and poorer districts. A number of like cases were subsequently brought, including *San Antonio Independent School District v. Rodriguez* (1973).—Eds.]

**[*Brown v. Board of Education of Topeka, Kansas* (1954), in which the Court declared racial segregation of schools unconstitutional.—Eds.]

values of voluntarism, individualism, family autonomy, and localism. Although the trend has been toward more federal responsibility for greater numbers of children, this trend has not been unopposed. After all, there is a strong tradition of voluntarism in America. In colonial times few formal institutions were needed to cope with dependents or persons in need. The community and the church informally provided for these people. In the late nineteenth century and on into the twentieth, many of the humanitarian agencies established (e.g., the Societies for Prevention of Cruelty to Animals and Children, the settlement houses, foundations, etc.) were private, voluntary agencies which maintained staunch independence from local government in order to set their own standards and policies. Even in the 1930's and 1940's when federal intervention took a quantum leap, the Presidents prevailed upon the population voluntarily to sacrifice and cooperate with the policies which were invoked only because of the magnitude of the crises (and which, it was assumed, would disappear once the economy was healthy or the war was over). As the growth of federal responsibility continues, so the reflex toward voluntarism never entirely abates. When a new menace is encountered, the first response is for private rather than public regulation. As an example, the 1950 and 1960 Conferences acknowledged the potentially dangerous influence of the electronic media on children. But their major recommendations were for network maintenance of good taste, producers' thoughtfulness regarding programming, and, as a last resort, regulation by the Federal Communication Commission, not a particularly powerful influence on the content of the media.[31]

American pride of individualism exerts the same kind of countervailing influence. In 1930, President Hoover gave his views: "In democracy our progress is the sum of the progress of the individuals. . . . Their varied personalities and abilities must be brought fully to bloom; they must not be mentally regimented to a single mold."[32] Similarly, in 1940, in order to safeguard against the homogenizing implications of extensive public education, the Conference maintained, "The supreme educational and social importance of individual traits should be recognized throughout the educational system. An educational system that truly serves a democracy will find no place for the philosophy or the methods of mass production."[33] Federal intervention in the lives of children is to some extent equated with mass production methods. Interestingly, however, the federal government has increased its involvement in the lives of children by using this very romanticization of individualism. In the 1950's and 1960's, the slogan for education was "maximizing individual potential"; in the 1970's it is "individualized instruction." In order to implement these objectives, federal involvement and support has grown steadily.

Belief in the inviolacy of the family also has moderated Conference enthusiasm for federal intervention. The 1930 Conference, while urging unprecedented steps by various levels of government to help needy children, sought to soften the impact of these recommendations by warning, "We want a minimum of national legislation in this field. No one should get the idea that Uncle Sam is going to rock the baby to sleep."[34] In 1950, one participant observed that in America " 'Rugged individualism' is in fact 'rugged family-ism.' "[35]

Perhaps the strongest opposition to large federal provision for children comes from the political forces that protect states' rights and local government.

When the Children's Bureau was proposed in 1909, senators and congressmen who considered "general welfare" to be reserved to the states, argued it to be unconstitutional. Although subsequent Conferences have often urged far-reaching comprehensive services or coordination of services, the enabling legislation has usually been defeated (e.g., federal aid to education was first advised in 1930 but not legislated until 1965). It is interesting to note that the thrust for direct federal intervention may be diminishing. The failure of much of the social welfare legislation of the 1960's funded and managed by the federal government and often deliberately avoiding state authorities, seems to have persuaded some social reformers to try a different plan. The 1970 Conference, while the most comprehensive of all in terms of recommending services, federal expenditures, and potential target groups of children, made an overarching recommendation that the federal government should encourage and support the efforts of state groups involved in the White House Conference process. It urged every state to establish an effective and permanent "assessment of the status of children" commission, jointly funded by federal, state, and local resources, whose major functions would be: a) to develop an accountability mechanism which would enable local communities to measure their needs and progress; and b) to implement those programs and policies which would enhance the status of all children. Thus, along with an increase in federal expenditures, would come decentralization of decision-making to smaller units of government, working closely with the family.

It has been said that the voices of some groups are notoriously missing from their own histories. Obvious examples spring to mind such as blacks, working class people, and immigrants. Children are in an even worse position than other oppressed groups because they are disenfranchised—completely silent legally. Thus the documents dealing with children omit their voices almost entirely. The proceedings of the Conferences read like a history of ideas and programs, with problems seen through the eyes of adults, rather than reports dealing with flesh and blood children. Whatever the intentions of the writers (and most were good-hearted, well-meaning social reformers, child psychologists, pediatricians, and educators), and whatever their real contact with children, their prescriptions for programs, their definitions of needs, their causes for concerns somehow lose the child in the process. In the sweep of seven decades, the image conveyed is one of children, smaller than anyone else, lighter in physical weight and political clout, easily picked up and blown wherever the winds of economic, political, and social movements were heading.

NOTES

1. Robert H. Bremner, ed. *Children and Youth in America*, Vol. II. (Cambridge, Mass: Harvard University Press, 1971), pp. 257–258.
2. *White House Conference*, 1909, p. 99.
3. Bremner, pp. 776–777.

4. Dorothy E. Bradbury, *Five Decades of Action for Children: A History of the Children's Bureau* (Washington, D.C.: U.S. Department of Health, Education and Welfare, Social Security Administration, 1962), p. 12.
5. *White House Conference, 1930*, p. vii.
6. *White House Conference, 1930*, p. 17.
7. *White House Conference, 1930*, p. 16.
8. *White House Conference, 1930*, p. 23.
9. *White House Conference, 1909*, p. 5.
10. *White House Conference, 1930*, p. 134.
11. *White House Conference, 1930*, p. 137.
12. *White House Conference on Children in a Democracy,* 1940, p. 4.
13. Rochelle Kessler. Unpublished working paper of the Carnegie Council on Children, New Haven, May 2, 1972, p. 7.
14. *White House Conference, 1950*, p. 52.
15. *White House Conference, 1950*, p. 53.
16. *White House Conference, 1950*, p. 53.
17. *White House Conference, 1950*, p. 54.
18. *White House Conference, 1950*, p. 55.
19. *White House Conference, 1960*, p. 270.
20. *White House Conference, 1950*, p. 30.
21. *White House Conference, 1960*, p. 99.
22. *White House Conference, 1960*, p. 160.
23. *White House Conference, 1970*, p. 347.
24. *White House Conference, 1970*, p. 12.
25. *White House Conference, 1960*, p. 167.
26. *White House Conference, 1970*, p. 11.
27. Kessler, p. 11.
28. *White House Conference, 1930*, p. 178.
29. John E. Coons, Williams A. Clune III, and Stephen D. Sugarman, *Private Wealth and Public Education* (Cambridge, Mass: Harvard University Press, 1970).
30. Bremner, p. 751.
31. Kessler, p. 3.
32. *White House Conference, 1930*, p. 13.
33. *White House Conference, 1940*, p. 365.
34. *White House Conference, 1930*, p. 24–25.
35. *White House Conference, 1950*, p. 270.

CHAPTER 13 Research

13.1 G. STANLEY HALL

The Contents of Children's Minds on Entering School

G. Stanley Hall, one of the founders of modern American child psychology, was driven by a search for a "science of the soul of man." To find this, he believed it was necessary to conduct an exhaustive description of developmental stages from birth to death, so he embarked on systematic studies of large groups of children and adolescents. Prior to Hall's work, what was known of children's growth was from "baby biographies" by philosophers and biologists. The scope of Hall's work led him to devise a new research instrument, the questionnaire, to gain information about children's behavior, knowledge, and interests.

Hall felt that the development and education of the young child was the most important function of society. During his tenure at Johns Hopkins University, Hall passed this belief on to two of his students, John Dewey and Arnold Gesell, both of whom became pioneers in the field of child development. Hall envisioned kindergartens and nursery schools with interdisciplinary support teams of educators, psychologists, and doctors. Because of his strong interest in education and his work with educators, schools began raising their standards for sanitation, health, lighting, and ventilation.

Hall's paper "The Contents of Children's Minds on Entering School," published in Theodate L. Smith, ed., *Aspects of Child Life and Education by G. Stanley Hall and Some of His Pupils* (Ginn & Company, 1907) and from which the following selection is taken, enjoyed great popularity for over 30 years and was translated into several languages. The study described by

Hall, for which he utilized the then-innovative questionnaire, is frequently referred to as marking the introduction of the child study movement. It is written in the classic research style of the day, with little evidence of control or objectivity. Hall employed a simplistic method to draw relationships between personality and background experience.

*I*n October, 1869, the Berlin pedagogical *Verein* issued a circular inviting teachers to investigate the individuality of children on entering the city schools, so far as it was represented by ideas of their environment. Individuality in children, it was said, differed in Berlin not only from that of children in smaller cities or in the country, but surroundings caused marked differences in culture capacity in different wards. Although concepts from the environment were only one important cause of diversity of individuality, this cause once determined, inferences could be drawn to other causes. It was expected that although city children would have an experience of moving things much larger than country children, they would have noticed very little of things at rest; that to names like *forest*, e.g., they, with an experience only with parks, would attach a very different set of concepts from those of the country child. The fact that country children who entered city schools behind city children caught up with them so readily was due to the fact that early school methods as well as matter of instruction were better adapted to country children. Conversation with children in collecting the statistical materials would, it was predicted, tend to interesting and surprising results. . . .

It was with the advantages of many suggestions and not a few warnings from these attempts that the writer undertook, soon after the opening of the Boston schools in September, 1880, to make out a list of questions suitable for obtaining an inventory of the contents of the minds of children of average intelligence on entering the primary schools of that city. This was made possible by the liberality of Mrs. Quincy Shaw, who detailed four excellent teachers from her comprehensive system of kindergartens to act as special questioners under the writer's direction, and by the coöperation of Miss L. B. Pingree, their superintendent. All the local and many other of the German questions were not suitable to children here, and the task of selecting those that should be so, though perhaps not involving quite so many perplexing considerations as choosing an equally long list of "normal words," was by no means easy. They must not be too familiar nor too hard and remote, but must give free and easy play to thought and memory. But especially, to yield most practical results, they should lie within the range of what children are commonly supposed or at least desired or expected, by teachers and by those who write primary textbooks and prescribe courses of instruction, to know. Many preliminary half days of questioning small groups of children and receiving suggestions from many sources, and the use of many primers, object-lesson courses, etc., now in use in this country, were necessary before the first provisional list of one hundred and thirty-four questions was printed. The problem first considered was strictly practical, namely, what may Boston children be, by their teachers, assumed to know and have seen when they enter school; although other purposes more psychological shaped other questions used later.

The difficulties and sources of possible error in the use of such questions are many. Not only are children prone to imitate others in their answers without stopping to think and give independent answers of their own, but they often love to seem wise, and, to make themselves interesting, state what seems to interest us without reference to truth, divining the lines of our interest with a subtlety we do not suspect. If absurdities are doubted by the questioner, they are sometimes only the more protested by the children; the faculties of some are benumbed and perhaps their tongues tied by bashfulness, while others are careless, listless, inattentive, and answer at random. Again, many questioners are brusque, lacking in sympathy or tact, or real interest or patience in the work, or perhaps regard it as trivial or fruitless. These and many other difficulties seemed best minimized by the following method, which was finally settled upon and, with the coöperation of Mr. E. P. Seaver, then superintendent of the Boston schools, put into operation. The four trained and experienced kindergarten teachers were employed by the hour to question the children in groups of three at a time in the dressing room of the school, so as not to interrupt the school work. No constraint was used, and as several hours were necessary to finish each set, changes and rests were often needful, while by frequent correspondence and by meetings with the writer to discuss details and compare results, uniformity of method was sought. The most honest and unembarrassed child's first answer to a direct question, e.g, whether it has seen a cow, sheep, etc., must rarely or never be taken without careful cross questioning, a stated method of which was developed respecting many objects. If the child says it has seen a cow, but when asked its size points to its own finger nail or hand and says, *so big*, as not unfrequently occurs, the inference is that it has at most only seen a picture of a cow, and thinks its size reproduced therein, and accordingly he is set down as deficient on that question. If, however, he is correct as to size, but calls the color blue, does not know that the cow is the source of milk, or that it has horns or hoofs,—several errors of the latter order were generally allowed. A worm may be said to *swim* on the ground, butchers to kill only the bad animals, etc.; but when hams are said to grow on trees or in the ground, or a hill is described as a *lump* of dirt, wool as growing on hens, as sometimes occurs, deficiency is obvious. Thus many visual and other notions that seem to adults so simple that they must be present to the mind with some completeness or not at all, are in a process of gradual acquisition, element by element, in the mind of a child, so that there must sometimes be confessedly a certain degree of arbitrariness in saying, as, except in cases of peculiar uncertainty, the questioners attempted to do, that the child has the concept or does not have it. Men's first names seemed to have designated single striking qualities, but once applied they become general or specific names according to circumstances. Again, very few children knew that a tree had bark, leaves, trunk, and roots; but very few indeed had not noticed a tree enough for our "pass." Without specifying further details, it may suffice here to say that the child was given the benefit of every doubt and credited with knowledge wherever its ignorance was not so radical as to make a chaos of what instruction and most primary text-books are wont to assume. It is important also to add that the questioners were requested to report manifest gaps in the child's knowledge *in its own words*, reproducing its syntax, pronunciation, etc. . . .

[Table 1] shows the general results for a number of those questions which admit of categorical answers, only negative results being recorded; the italicized questions in the "miscellaneous" class being based on only from forty to seventy-five children, the rest on two hundred, or, in a few cases, on two hundred and fifty. . . .

In the . . . table, which is based on Boston children, only columns 2 and 3 are based upon larger numbers and upon less carefully restricted selections from the aggregate returns. In 34 representative questions out of 49, the boys surpass the girls. . . .

[O]n the whole, we seem to have here an illustration of the law that we really see not what is near or impresses the retina, but what the attention is called and held to, and what interests are awakened and words found for. Of nearly thirty primary teachers questioned as to the difference between children from kindergartens and others, four saw no difference, and all the rest thought them better fitted for school work, instancing superior use of language, skill with the hand and slate, quickness, power of observation, singing, number, love of work, neatness, politeness, freedom from the benumbing school bashfulness, or power to draw from dictation. Many thought them at first more restless and talkative.

There are many other details and more or less probable inferences, but the above are the chief. The work was laborious, involving about fifty thousand items in all. These results are, it is believed, to be in some degree the first opening of a field which should be specialized, and in which single concept groups should be subjected to more detailed study with larger numbers of children. One difficulty is to get essential points to test for. If these are not characteristic and typical, all such work is worthless. We believe that not only practical educational conclusions of great scope and importance may be based on or illustrated by such results, but, though many sources of inaccuracy may limit their value, that they are of great importance for anthropology and psychology. It is characteristic of an educated man, says Aristotle in substance, not to require a degree of scientific exactness on any subject greater than that which the subject admits. As scientific methods advance, not only are increasingly complex matters subjected to them, but probabilities (which guide nearly all our acts) more and more remote from mathematical certainty are valued.

From the . . . table it seems not too much also to infer: (1) That there is next to nothing of pedagogic value, the knowledge of which it is safe to assume at the outset of school life. Hence the need of objects and the danger of books and word cram. Hence many of the best primary teachers in Germany spend from two to four or even six months in talking of objects and drawing them before any beginning of what we till lately have regarded as primary-school work. (2) The best preparation parents can give their children for good school training is to make them acquainted with natural objects, especially with the sights and sounds of the country, and to send them to good and hygienic, as distinct from the most fashionable, kindergartens. (3) Every teacher on starting with a new class or in a new locality, to make sure that his efforts along some

TABLE 1

321

Name of the Object of Concept	Per cent. of Ignorance in 150 Girls	Per cent. of Ignorance in 150 Boys	Per cent. of Ignorance in 50 Irish Children	Per cent. of Ignorance in 50 American Children	Per cent. of Ignorance in 64 Kinder-garten Children
Beehive	81	75	86	70	61
Ant	59	60	74	38	26
Squirrel	69	50	66	42	43
Snail	69	73	92	72	62
Robin	69	44	64	36	29
Sheep	67	47	62	40	40
Bee	46	32	52	32	26
Frog	53	38	54	35	35
Pig	45	27	38	26	22
Chicken	35	21	32	16	22
Worm	21	17	26	16	9
Butterfly	14	16	26	8	9
Hen	15	14	18	2	14
Cow	18	12	20	6	10
Growing clover	59	68	84	42	29
Growing corn	58	50	60	68	32
Growing potatoes	55	54	62	44	34
Growing buttercup	50	51	66	40	31
Growing rose	48	48	60	42	33
Growing dandelion	44	42	62	34	31
Growing apples	16	16	18	12	5
Ribs	88	92	98	82	68
Ankles	58	52	62	40	38
Waist	53	52	64	32	36
Hips	50	47	72	31	24
Knuckles	27	27	34	12	23
Elbow	19	32	36	16	12
Right from left hand	20	8	14	20	4
Wrist	21	34	44	9	19
Cheek	10	12	14	14	4
Forehead	10	11	12	10	7
Throat	10	18	14	16	14
Knee	4	5	2	10	2
Dew	64	63	92	52	57
The seasons	59	50	68	48	41
Hail	75	61	84	52	53
Rainbow	59	61	70	38	38
Sunrise	71	53	70	36	53
Sunset	47	49	52	32	29
Star	15	10	12	4	7
Island	74	78	84	64	55
Beach	82	49	60	34	32
Woods	46	35	46	32	27
River	38	44	62	12	13
Pond	31	34	42	24	28
Hill	23	22	30	12	19

lines are not utterly lost, should undertake to explore carefully section by section children's minds with all the tact and ingenuity he can command and acquire, to determine exactly what is already shown; and every normal-school pupil should undertake work of the same kind as an essential part of his training. (4) The concepts which are most common in the children of a given locality are the earliest to be acquired, while the rarer ones are later. This order may in teaching generally be assumed as a natural one, e.g., apples (as appealing directly to the child without mediate process) first and wheat last. This order, however, varies very greatly with every change of environment, so that the results of explorations of children's minds in one place cannot be assumed to be valid for those of another save within comparatively few concept spheres.

The high rate of ignorance indicated in the table may surprise most persons who will be likely to read this report, because the childhood they know will be much above the average of intelligence here sought, and because the few memories of childhood which survive in adult life necessarily bear but slight traces of imperfections and are from many causes illusory. Skeins and spools of thread were said to grow on the sheep's back or on bushes, stockings on trees, butter to come from buttercups, flour to be made of beans, oats to grow on oaks, bread to be swelled yeast, trees to be stuck in the ground by God and to be rootless, meat to be dug from the ground, and potatoes to be picked from the trees. Cheese is squeezed butter, the cow says "bow wow," the pig purrs or burrows, worms are not distinguished from snakes, moss from the "toad's umbrella," bricks from stones, etc. An oak may be known only as an acorn tree or a button tree, a pine only as a needle tree, a bird's nest only as its bed, etc. So that while no one child has all these misconceptions, none are free from them, and thus the liabilities are great that, in this chaos of half-assimilated impressions, half right, half wrong, some lost link may make utter nonsense or mere verbal cram of the most careful instruction, as in the cases of children referred to above, who knew much by rote about a cow, its milk, horns, leather, meat, etc., but yet were sure from the picture book that it was no bigger than a small mouse.

For 86 per cent. of the above questions, the average intelligence of thirty-six country children who were tested ranks higher than that of the city children of the table, and in many items very greatly exceeds it. The subject-matter of primers for the latter is in great part still traditionally of country life; hence the danger of unwarranted presupposition is considerable. As our methods of teaching grow natural we realize that city life is unnatural, and that those who grow up without knowing the country are defrauded of that without which childhood can never be complete or normal. On the whole, the material of the city is no doubt inferior in pedagogic value to country experience. A few days in the country at the age of five or six has raised the level of many a city child's intelligence more than a term or two of school training without could do. It is there, too, that the foundations of a love of natural science are best laid. We cannot accept without many careful qualifications the evolutionary dictum that the child's mental development should repeat that of the race. Unlike primitive man, the child has a feeble body and is ever influenced by a higher culture about him. Yet from the primeval intimacy with the qualities and habits of plants, with the instincts of animals,—so like those of children,—with which hawking and trapping, the riding on instead of some distance behind horses, etc., made men familiar; from primitive industries and tools as first freshly suggested, if we believe Geiger, from the normal activities of the human organism, especially of the tool of tools, the hand; from primitive shelter, cooking, and clothing, with which anthropological researches make us familiar, it is certain that not a few educational elements of great value can be selected and systematized for children, an increasing number of them, in fact, being already in use for juvenile games and recreations and for the vacation pastimes of adults. A country barn, a forest with its gloom and awe, its vague fears and indefinite sounds, is a great school at this age. The making of butter, of which some teachers, after hearing so often that it grew inside eggs or on ice, or was made from buttermilk, think it worth while to make a thimbleful in a toy churn at school as an object lesson; more acquaintance with birds, which, as having the most perfect senses, and most constant motion in several elements, even Leopardi* could panegyrize [praise highly] as the only real things of joy in the universe, and which the strange power of flight makes ideal beings with children, and whose nests were sometimes said to *grow* on trees; more knowledge of kitchen chemistry, of foods, their preparation and origin; wide prospects for the eyes—these elements constitute a more pedagogic industrial training for *young* children, because [they are] more free and play-like, than sewing, or cooking, or whittling, or special trade schools can, and are besides more hygienic. Many children locate all that is good and imperfectly known in the country, and nearly a dozen volunteered the statement that good people when they die go to the country—even from Boston. It is things that live and, as it were, detach themselves from their background by moving that catch the eye and with it the attention, and the subjects which occupy and interest the city child are mainly in motion and therefore transient, while the country child comes to know objects at rest better. The country child has more solitude, is likely to develop more independence and is less likely to be prematurely caught up into the absorbing activities and throbbing passions of manhood, and becomes more familiar with the experiences of primitive man. The city child knows a little of many more things and so is more liable to superficiality and has a wider field of error. At the same time, it has two great advantages over the country child, in knowing more of human nature and in entering school with a much better developed sense of rhythm and all its important implications. On the whole, however, additional force seems thus given to the argument for excursions, by rail or otherwise, regularly provided for the poorer children whose life conditions are causing the race to degenerate in the great centers of population, unfavorable enough for those with good homes or even for adults.

Words, in connection with rhyme, rhythm, alliteration, cadence, etc., or even without these, simply as sound pictures, often absorb the attention of children and yield them a really aesthetic pleasure either quite independently of their meaning or to the utter bewilderment of it. They hear fancied words in noises and sounds of nature and animals, and are persistent punners. As but-

*[The poet and philosopher Giacomo Leopardi, whose work, inspired by a bitter and painful life, was marked by a sense of despair and hopelessness.—Eds.]

terflies make butter or eat it or give it by squeezing, so grasshoppers give grass, bees give beads and beans, kittens grow on the pussy willow, and all honey is from honeysuckles, and even a poplin dress is made of poplar trees. When the cow lows it somehow blows its own horn; crows and scarecrows are confounded; ant has some subtle relationship to aunt; angleworm suggests angle or triangle or ankle; Martie eats "tomarties"; a holiday is a day to "holler" on; Harry O'Neil is nicknamed Harry Oatmeal; isosceles is somehow related to sausages; October suggests knocked over; "I never saw a hawk, but I can hawk and spit too;" "I will not sing do re mi, but do re *you;*" "Miss Eaton will eat us"—these and many more from the questioners' notes; the story of the child who, puzzled by the unfamiliar reflexive use of the verb, came to associate "now I lay me," etc., with a lama; of the child who wondered what kind of a bear was the consecrated cross-eyed bear, as he understood the hymn "The consecrated cross I'd bear"; or of another, who was for years stultified as against a dead blank wall whenever the phrase "answer sought" occurred, suggest to us how, more or less consciously and more or less seriously, a child may be led, in the absence of corrective experience, to the most fantastic and otherwise unaccountable distortions of facts by shadowy word specters or husks.

In many of the expressions quoted the child seems playing with relations once seriously held, and its "fun" to be joy over but lately broken mental fetters. Some at least of the not infrequently quite unintelligible statements or answers may perhaps be thus accounted for. Again, the child more than the adult thinks in pictures, gestures, and inarticulate sounds. The distinction between real and verbal knowledge has been carefully and constantly kept in mind by the questioners. Yet of the objects in the above table, except a very few, like triangle and sparrow, a child may be said to know almost nothing, at least for school purposes, if he has no generally recognized name for them. The far greater danger is the converse, that only the name and not the thing itself will be known. To test for this danger was, with the exceptions presently to be noted, our constant aim, as it is that of true education to obviate it. The danger, however, is after all quite limited here, for the linguistic imperfections of children are far more often shown in combining words than in naming the concrete things they know or do not know. To name an object is a passion with them, for it is to put their own mark upon it, to appropriate it. From the talk, which most children hear and use, to book language is again an immense step. Words *live* only in the ear and mouth, and are pale and corpse-like when addressed to the eye. What we want, and indeed are likely soon to have, are carefully arranged child vocabularies and dictionaries of both verbal forms and meanings, to show teachers just the phonic elements and vocal combinations children have most trouble with, the words they most readily and surely acquire, their number and order in each thought sphere—and the attributes and connotations most liable to confuse them. To that work it is believed the method here employed has already furnished valuable material in protocol soon to be augmented and digested. . . .

If children are pressed to answer questions somewhat beyond their ken, they often reply confusedly and at random, while if others beside them are questioned they can answer well; some are bolder and invent things on the spot if they seem to interest the questioner, while others catch quick subtle suggestions from the form of the question, accent, gesture, feature, etc., so that what seems originality is really mind reading, giving back our very thought, and is sometimes only a direct reproduction, with but little distortion because little apprehension, of what parents or teachers have lately told them. But there are certain elements which every tactful and experienced friend of children learns to distinguish from each of these with considerable accuracy—elements which, from whatever source, spring from deep roots in the childish heart, as distinct from all these as are Grimm's tales from those of some of our weakly juvenile weeklies. These are generally not easily accessible. I could not persuade an old nurse to repeat to me a nonsensical song I half over-heard that delighted a two-year-old child, and the brothers Grimm experienced a similar difficulty in making their collections. As many workingmen nail a horseshoe over their door for luck, and many people really prefer to begin nothing important on Friday, who will not confess to a trace of super-stition in either case, so children cling to their "old credulities to nature dear," refusing every attempt to gain their full confidence or explore secret tracts in their minds, as a well-developed system of inane illusions may escape the scrutiny of the most skillful alienist. As a reasoning electric light might honestly doubt the existence of such things as shadows because, however near or numerous, they are always hidden from it, so the most intelligent adults quite commonly fail to recognize sides of their own chil-dren's souls which can be seen only by strategy. A boy and girl often play under my window as I write, and unconscious words often reveal what is passing in their minds when either is quite alone, and it is often very absurd or else meaningless, but they run away with shame and even blushes if they chance to look up suddenly and catch me listening. Yet who of us has not secret regions of soul to which no friend is ever admitted, and which we ourselves shrink from full consciousness of? Many children half believe the doll feels cold or blows, that it pains flowers to tear or burn them, or that in summer when the tree is alive it makes it ache to pound or chop it. Of 48 children questioned 20 believed sun, moon, or stars to live; 15 thought that a doll, and 16, that flowers, would suffer pain if burned. Children who are accounted dull in school work are more apt to be imaginative and animistic.

The chief field for such fond and often secret childish fancies is the sky. About three fourths of all questioned thought the world a plain, and many described it as round like a dollar, while the sky is like a flattened bowl turned over it. The sky is often *thin*, one might *easily break through;* half the moon may be seen through it, while the other half is this side; it may be *made of snow*, but is so large that there is *much floor sweeping* to be done in heaven. Some thought *the sun went down at night into the ground* or just behind certain houses, and went across, on, or under the ground to *go up, out of*, or *off the water* in the morning; but 48 per cent. of all thought that at night it *goes* or *rolls* or *flies*, is *blown* or *walks*, or *God pulls it up* higher out of sight. He *takes it into heaven*, and perhaps *puts it to bed*, and even *takes off its clothes* and puts them on in the morning, or again it *lies under the trees* where the angels *mind it*, or goes through and *shines on the upper side of the sky*, or goes *into* or *behind the moon*, as the moon is behind it in the day. It may *stay where it is*, only we *cannot see it, for it is dark*, or the *dark rains down so*, and it *comes out when it gets light so it can see*. . . . Only in a single case were any of the heavenly bodies conceived as openings in the sky to let light or glory through, or as eyes of supernatural beings,—a fancy so often ascribed to children and so often found in juvenile literature. Thunder, which, anthropologists tell us, is or represents the highest God to most savage races, was apperceived as God *groaning* or *kicking*, or *rolling barrels about*, or *turning a big handle*, or *grinding snow*, *walking loud*, *breaking something*, *throwing*, *logs*, *having coal run in*, *pounding about* with a *big hammer*, *rattling houses*, *hitting the clouds*, or clouds *bumping* or *clapping* together or *bursting*, or else it was merely *ice sliding off lots of houses*, or *cannon in the city* or sky, hard *rain down the chimney*, or *big rocks pounding*, or *piles of boards falling down*, or very hard rain, hail, or wind. Lightning is God *putting out his finger* or *opening a door*, or *turning a gas quick*, or (very common) *striking many matches at once*, throwing *stones and iron for sparks*, *setting paper afire*, or it is light going outside and inside the sky, or stars falling. God keeps rain in heaven in a *big sink*, *rows of buckets*, a *big tub* or *barrels*, and they *run over* or he *lets it down* with a *water hose* through a *sieve*, a *dipper with holes*, or *sprinkles* or *tips* it down or *turns a faucet*. God makes it in heaven out of nothing or out of water, or it gets up by *splashing up*, or he *dips it up off the roof*, or it *rains up off the ground when we don't see it*. The clouds are *close to the sky;* they move because the *earth moves and makes them*. They are *dirty, muddy things*, or blankets, or *doors of heaven*, and are made of fog, of *steam that makes the sun go*, of smoke, of *white wool* or *feathers and birds*, or *lace* or *cloth*. In their changing forms very many children, whose very life is fancy, think they see veritable men, or more commonly, because they have so many more forms, animals' faces; and very often God, Santa Claus, angels, etc., are also seen. Closely connected with the above are the religious concepts so common with children. God is a *big*, perhaps *blue man*, very often seen in the sky on or in the clouds, in the church, or even street. He *came in our gate, comes to see us sometimes*. He lives in a *big palace* or a big *brick* or *stone house on the sky*. He makes lamps, babies, dogs, trees, money, etc., and the angels *work for him*. He looks like the priest, Fröbel, papa, etc., and they like to look at him, and a few would like to be God. He *lights the stars so he can see to go on the sidewalk* or *into the church*. Birds, children, Santa Claus, live with him, and most but not all like him better than they do the latter. When people die they just *go*, or are *put in a hole*, or a box or a *black wagon that goes to heaven*, or they *fly up* or are *drawn* or *slung* up into the sky where God *catches* them. They *never can get out of the hole*, and yet all good people somehow get where God is. He *lifts* them up, they *go up on a ladder or rope*, or they carry them up, but *keep their eyes shut so they do not know the way*, or they are *shoved up through a hole*. When children get there they have candy, rocking-horses, guns, and everything in the toy-shop or picture book, play marbles, top, ball, cards, hockey, hear brass bands, have nice clothes, gold watches, and pets, ice cream and soda water, and no school. There are men who died in the war made into angels, and dolls with broken heads go there. Some think they must go through the church to get there, a few thought the horse cars run there, and one said that the *birds that grow on apple trees are drawn up there by the moon*. The bad place is like an *oven* or a *police station*, where it burns, yet is all dark, and folks want to get back, and God *kills* people or *beats them with a cane*. God makes babies in heaven, though the Holy Mother and even Santa Claus make some. He *lets them down or drops them,* and the women or doctors *catch* them, or he leaves them on the sidewalk, or *brings them down a wooden ladder backwards and pulls it up again,* or mamma or the doctor or the nurse *go up and fetch them,* sometimes *in a balloon,* or they *fly down and lose off their wings in some place or other and forget where they came from,* or *jump down to Jesus,* who *gives them around.* They were also often said to be found in flour barrels, and the *flour sticks ever so long you know,* or they *grow in cabbages,* or God *puts them in water,* perhaps *in the sewer,* and the doctor gets them out and *takes them to sick folks that want them,* or the milkman brings them early in the morning, they are dug out of the ground, or bought at the baby store. Sometimes God *puts on a few things* or else *sends them along if he don't forget it;* this shows that no one since Basedow believes in telling children the truth in all things.

Not many children have or can be made to disclose many such ideas as the above, and indeed they seem to be generally already on the ebb at this age, and are sometimes timidly introduced by, *as if, some say,* it is *like,* or *I used to think.* Clear and confident notions on the above topics are the exception and not the rule, yet children have some of them, while some are common to many, indeed to most, children. They represent a drift of consentient infantile philosophy about the universe not without systematic coherence, although intimidated and broken through at every point by fragmentary truths, often only verbal indeed, without insight or realization of a higher order, so that the most diametrical contradictions often subsist peacefully side by side, and yet they are ever forming again at lower levels of age and intelligence. In all that is remote, the real and ideal fade into each other like clouds and mountains in the horizon, or as poetry, which keeps alive the standpoints of an earlier culture, coexists with science. Children are often hardly conscious of these contradictions at all, and the very questions that bring them to mind and invite them to words at the same time often abash the child and produce the first disquieting self-consciousness of the absurdity of his fond fancies that have felt not only life but character in natural objects. Between the products of childish spontaneity, where the unmistakable child's mark is seen, and those of really *happy* suggestion by parents, etc., the distinction is as hard as anywhere along the line between heredity and tradition. It is enough that these fancies are like Galton's composite portraits, resultants in form and shading of the manifold deepest impressions which what is within and what is without have together made upon the child's soul in these spheres of ideas. Those indicated above represent many strata of intelligence up through which the mind is passing very rapidly and with quite radical transformations. Each stratum was once, with but a little elaboration, or is now somewhere, the highest culture, relegated to and arrested in an earlier stage as civilization and educational methods advance. In children belief in the false is as necessary as it is inevitable, for the proper balance of head and heart, and happy the child who has believed or loved only healthy, unaffected, platonic lies like the above, which will be shed with its milk teeth when more solid mental pabulum can be digested. It is possible that the present shall be so attractive and preoccupying that the child never once sends his thoughts to the remote in time and place, and these baby fancies— ever ready to form at a touch, which make the impartation of truth, however carefully put, on these themes impossible before its time; which, when long forgotten, yet often reverberate, if their old chords be struck in adults, to the intensity of fanaticism or even delusion—shall be quite repressed. If so, one of the best elements of education which comes from long experience in laying aside a lower for a higher phase of culture by doubting opportunely, judiciously, and temperately is lost.

13.2 GRETA G. FEIN AND
ALISON CLARKE-STEWART

Day Care: Opportunities and Dangers

Over the past two decades, Greta G. Fein and Alison Clarke-Stewart's survey of the complex issues surrounding the care of young children has become part of the knowledge base for professionals in social services and education.

Fein (b. 1929), currently at the University of Maryland, studied at the Bank Street College of Education prior to receiving her Ph.D. in child development from Yale University. She is familiar with child-care issues from her teaching experience in several children's centers. Clarke-Stewart, who also completed her Ph.D. at Yale, is affiliated with the University of California, Irvine.

According to Fein and Clarke-Stewart, research and development in the 1960s and 1970s brought much attention to child care. However, Fein and Clarke-Stewart believe there was a tendency to rely on mistaken assumptions and to use makeshift evaluations in reaching quick answers to simplistic questions regarding child care.

The following selection is from Fein and Clarke-Stewart's *Day Care in Context* (John Wiley, 1973), a notable book on the historical, social, and educational facets of child-care programs. In it, the authors outline the importance of considering the aims and consequences in evaluating program effectiveness. Notice the relationship between the research issues they raise and the current controversy over reliance on test scores for determining a child's ability.

*P*roperly, day care is not an arrangement, a program, a service, or an institution. Day care is what happens when the child, his family, and a community resource come together. It occurs in a philosophical, historical, social, and political context; it is defined by characteristics of the child, the family, and the resource, and it is comprehended through a web of presuppositions, expectations, and empirical observations. Day-care models consider how this interaction changes when the available resources change; how resources may vary with variations in children and families, and how changes and variations modify the way children, families, and communities function. Day-care models can become the basis of new institutions. Our conception of the function of models merely ensures that when new institutions do emerge they will be linked to the life experiences of parents and children.

With thoughtful planning day care can become an opportunity to advance our knowledge of children. It can realize the visions of its eighteenth-century founders of all the wonderful things that would enhance the well-being of children all over the nation. With narrow purposes and scant resources, day care is at its very least a passing fancy and at its worst a national disaster. . . .

Superordinate Programs

One observer of caregiving institutions abroad (Wolins, 1969a,b) has suggested that successful programs contain the following features:

1. Successful programs assume the inevitability of a good outcome because they see themselves as working with essentially normal children in need of help and guidance and not sick children in need of treatment.
2. They are strongly ideological, pressing in on their wards from all directions with clearly articulated and highly valued philosophical and ethical positions.
3. They assert the child's capability to make a contribution and require him to do so.
4. They provide clear examples of mature group membership.
5. They enjoy community support and esteem.
6. They provide an older child with a peer society that stands for adherence to adult values.

We suspect that these features apply not only to programs that are oriented to group child care but also to others that reach out to parents and to broader family groups. It is appropriate that we identify superordinate programs capable of articulating a point of view and of generating confidence and respect. The Education Professions Development Act created the foundations for one kind of superordinate program: a national network of opportunities to receive training in child care and development. Still another kind of superordinate program might be aimed at dealing more directly and quite broadly with the social and physical context of the child's life; for example, the notion of a "parent-child center" (misnamed in that the activities of such a center need not take place in a physical facility) was advanced in *A Bill of Rights for Children* (Hunt, 1967a). The purpose of a parent-child center is to forge relationships between families and community resources and to provide opportunities for members of the family to plan and participate in activities beneficial to young children and themselves. Such a program acknowledges the principle formulated by Robert Woods (1898)—that the resources of civilization are not available to people unless they are mediated by institutional provisions that are functional for the powers and limitations of the people they are intended to serve.

Yet a program label and a large domain does not constitute a superordinate program. Issues related to the care of children cover different dimensions along which alternatives can be ordered; for example, where should major program concentrations be located? One solution is obvious—in neighborhoods. Even here, however, there are options. If integration is a desired goal, the extent to which this goal can be satisfied by neighborhood programs that follow segregated residential patterns will be limited. Yet not all neighborhoods are segregated. Perhaps the greatest concentration of resources ought to be in "transitional" neighborhoods in which working class ethnic minorities live precariously side by side for often brief and unhappy periods. It may be that child-care programs of broad scope located in such areas might contribute to the stabilization of integrated communities in which the major issue is not poverty but rather the mutual adaptation of diverse life styles.

Child-care programs need not be circumscribed by established political or geographic boundaries. They can be affiliated with religious, educational, cultural, or social institutions as well as neighborhoods. Furthermore, the notion of a "center" can be redefined as a locus for analysis, research, program development, training, and dissemination. At least one model might consider a "center" charged with the task of developing practical extensions of child-care programs founded on theory and research. The undertaking would require talents that cross disciplinary and professional categories and concerns that range from the abstract to the particular.

Indeed, the form of superprogram most suited to a pluralistic society might be one that cultivates an array of possibilities, that systematically examines the relative merits of each, and has protection from political pressures for instant solutions. Such a program might take the form of a national child-development institute charged with the formulation and implementation of a long-term prospectus for the children of the nation. The types of program explored could span diverse child-care arrangements, in groups and in families, with parents, neighbors, or professionals. Programs might focus on economic, anthropological, medical, sociological, or child-development issues, yet still retain an interdisciplinary base. The point is that we know too little about how families, communities, or subcultures determine the environments of children, too little about how social institutions change, and too little about how new institutions influence the existing social and psychological scheme. We know too little about how environments present developmentally significant problems and too little about the kinds of solution parents and children will accept. The image of the child and the evolution of research and application might differ for each program. Surely one part of the common mission would be to consider shifts in national values, family-life styles, and working schedules and to project child-care programs relevant to alternative future national states. Institute programs, once formulated, implemented, and tested, would be available for large-scale replication when a national consensus regarding the desirability of such a program appeared. It may be that a national, application-oriented institute could not acquire the necessary immunity from political pressures under governmental auspices. The sponsorship of such a system might be undertaken by a consortium of private foundations concerned with child care.

We cannot solve the vast administrative and budgetary problems of expanded child-development programs before defining the central missions of these programs, before identifying the factors that determine program effectiveness, and before finding ways of assessing these. We need to define a process (much in the same way the founders of our country defined a process—the system of checks and balances) that would ensure the evolution of adaptive child-development services. We need to specify core institutions and the relations among them: development and research institutions, implementation institutions, and disinterested, critical review institutions.

The resources of private foundations might be most suited for the development of controversial innovations that pose disturbing questions and explore radical solutions, free from short-term shifts in national concerns. The vast resources of the federal government are needed to ensure the nationwide dissemination of child development services. In addition, a system of checks and balances would require a panel of independent, disinterested experts who would continuously monitor, advice, and criticize.

The seeds of a child-development institute have already been sown (Miller, 1970). Replication mechanisms may soon be available—the Community Coordinated Child Care Program (4-C), for example, was designed to encourage communities to coordinate existing day care, preschool, and other child or family services (Day Care and Child Development Council, 1969a; United States Department of Health, Education and Welfare, 1969a, b). Systems for facilitating the delivery of day-care services (Collins & Watson, 1969), improving services (Goldsmith, 1965; Host, 1960), and extending day-care concerns to health and medical care (Eisenstein, 1966; Peters, 1964) have been explored and proposed. What these possibilities need now is a set of well-defined relationships and responsibilities.

Ingenious Paradoxes

Although, as a nation, we may lack superordinate goals, we have a national viewpoint clearly expressed in the bookkeeping system used to index national prosperity. How we calculate the costs of day care is very much a function of the way we define goods and services and the values we assign to them. Clearly, the costs of day care cannot be determined without some estimate of the cost of mothering and fathering, and the benefits of day care cannot be determined without some specification of the benefits derived from competent mothering and fathering. It may be our greatest national shame that child care and child rearing as it occurs in American homes does not appear on the books as a "good" or a "service," that it has no occupational status, and that it is rarely considered relevant to the day-care issue, even though day-care costs are intimately related to child-care and child-rearing functions.

Suppose, for example, we computed the total cost of exemplary 24-hour institutional child care, education, health, and so on, during the first 18 years of life. Let us then separately calculate the ordinary cost of "schooling" (i.e., nursery school, preschool, elementary school), material things (food, clothing, housing), and other services incurred by parents during a child's lifetime and then subtract these two figures, that is, the family expenditures from the total institutional costs for a single child. The difference would represent the "cost" of parenting, a monetary estimate of the services parents render when they rear a child and maintain a home. We suspect that this figure would be impressively large and would approximate a respectable hourly pay rate.

At least this exercise would underscore the irony of our willingness to assign a monetary value to machine tending, cow tending, and institutionalized child care, to the provision of paid household, medical, educational, and office services, but our reluctance to do so for parental caregiving. Undoubtedly, there are good reasons for this reluctance (Good grief! Must everything be reduced to numbers and dollars?). Yet when we examine the balance sheet, which presumably reflects the work activity of American citizens, the failure to represent parenting as a "natural" national resource inexorably elevates work in the factory, the store, the office, or the classroom above work in the home.

With an accounting system so strongly rooted in the value of material goods and paid services, it is not surprising that the "working" mother has become a model for successful womanhood and that the job of "mothering" has become increasingly devalued (Collins & Watson, 1968). The logic of our accounting system subverts the *work* ethic for a *compensation* ethic, and work that does not carry a price goes unrewarded and unsung. The consequences of the compensation ethic become evident when we examine national subsidies to private institutions. Gans (1971) has whimsically suggested that the oil depletion allowance be named the Oil Producers Public Assistance Program, that we talk about the Tobacco Growers Dole, Aid to Dependent Airlines, or Supplementary Benefits to Purchasers of Tax-Exempt Bonds. The fact that giant industries cannot make it on their own seems to cause little embarrassment or discomfort, yet when support to families is an issue we assume that no services are being rendered, no work is being performed, and that the need for a subsidy reflects incompetence and failure. At the very least our accounting system is inconsistent, and the direction of the inconsistency leans toward punishing and belittling small and diverse social units while rewarding and respecting the large and monolithic for failures that do not seem to be qualitatively different. It seems appropriate to challenge a bias that permits us to supplement industrial enterprises more casually than it permits us to supplement caregiving enterprises.

DAY-CARE ISSUES FOR TODAY AND TOMORROW

The Child

... Day care that focuses on the child becomes unavoidably future-oriented, for within a developmental framework the present and the future are interlocked. Understanding the 5-year-old is, in a sense, understanding what the 3-year-old will become. . . . [T]he child [is] an extraordinary problem definer-solver, whose development hinges both on the nature of information available to him and on the kind of sense-making competence he has already acquired. The child and his human and material environment interact to determine his future development.

Problems and Environments

Environments are structured; physical, social, and institutional environments have internal rules and relationships. The same variables that influence the child's development are present in each—the family, the school, the neighborhood, the day-care center—but differ in distribution, salience, and patterning. Teachers may act like parents; school materials can be found in the home; and the child models peers as well as adults. We are struck by the common dimensions of environments, but we are also struck by the absence of comparative analyses that would describe points of overlap and elucidate uniquenesses.

Environments pose problems for the child and constrain his solutions. We need to know more about the range of problems generated by different environments, how they are defined by different children, and what solutions will be accepted by different caregivers.

Aims

An appropriate aim for day care in the past may have been to ensure the survival of children through "custodial care." Today, however, the aim of day care must be much more than that. It must offer opportunities for the development of competence, for children and their caregivers. Competence takes many forms, involves many domains (e.g., social, problem solving, and language) and can be attained in many environments (e.g., school, home, and day-care center). A broad concept of day care is surely necessary to accommodate such an aim. If a broad, educational-developmental approach to day care is taken, one may visualize a future aim of day care as going beyond promoting competence to fostering "optimization" or "self-actualization" for all people. . . .

Complexity

It would be foolish to underestimate the problems and complexities involved in developing day-care programs or in evaluating them. One cannot assume that programs will evolve naturally, that they will intuitively evaluate themselves, or that valid evaluations can be tacked on *post hoc*. To design effective programs and to evaluate them adequately we need to know a great deal more about children than we now know. In the end sensible programs and informative evaluations are contingent on adequate solutions to the mysteries, the "baffling and challenging facts," that appear whenever we look at the child.

Recommendations

Day care is returning to the United States—suddenly, precipitously, and massively. Its return was neither expected nor prepared for, its continuation is uncertain, and its impact on the nation is difficult to predict. Vast numbers of children will spend a great deal of time in day-care settings outside their own homes. Some of these settings will approximate the ideal of one or another segment of society, whereas others will fall short of anyone's notion of what day care ought to be. A great many lives will be influenced by the alternatives we define today and the priorities we assign to them. Some of our choices hopefully will be wise; others undoubtedly will be foolish.

It is all very well to dream of a tomorrow that is far better than today, to concoct rational schemes diffused with hope, love, and wonder. What is needed now is an adequate appreciation of options for today and tomorrow and practical guidelines for choosing among them. It is toward satisfying the first need that we have directed our efforts in this book. What recommendations we have offered have been posed in the form of problems for appreciation rather than prescriptions for action.

The second need is perhaps more difficult to satisfy. We propose three strategies. One is to be future-oriented in our programming, to think in terms of long-range aims and long-term plans rather than the need for immediate, quick-and-easy results. Another strategy is to encourage the fascination with childhood and the preoccupation with education that seems to be entering our national conscience. Now, when young people are likely to be severe critics of their own families and their own education, the time may be right to introduce more high school and college programs that deal with the sociology, psychology, and anthropology of educational systems, the family, and childhood. Now, when parents are being offered more choices in the education of their children, it may be valuable to make available to them courses in education and human development. A society concerned and informed about children can best plan for their care.

These first two strategies counterbalance each other. We need a future orientation for programs in order to distinguish between the 3-year-old of today and the 3-year-old of tomorrow, but we also need a present orientation that appreciates the child's capacities, joys, and sorrows, whatever they happen to be, whether he is 3 or 4, 13 or 14. Programs may grow best in the shadow of tomorrow; we suspect that children grow best in the sunlight of today.

A third strategy is to utilize fully the power of research and analysis in sorting the trivial from the crucial, in weighing the evidence, in amassing additional evidence where it is needed to fill gaps in our knowledge. As we experiment, analyze, and act on the best knowledge currently available, we will surely become a citizenry that can master knowledge and yet challenge and question it. What we now know is valuable but not sacred, temporally and culturally relative but not invalid, laced with truth, salted with fiction, and enormously important for today and tomorrow.

Finally, we submit a pessimistic projection prompted by the accelerating pressure for a quick expansion of day-care services and by the clear indication that these services are seen as an adjunct to programs primarily concerned with welfare reform. Indeed, there may be too many short-term aims and too much political profit behind today's day-care boom to permit child-oriented planning to prevail. The ghosts of the distant past are still with us, and there is little in the recent past to offer comfort. As day care emerges once again from neglect to prominence, it rapidly approaches the threshold of another major national gamble. For all practical purposes the gamble on Head Start was lost; there is little reason to suppose that a gamble on day care will be won. Perhaps the reality of current pressures means that the best we can hope for is a way of softening the disaster. Perhaps institutions with long-term perspectives will eventually emerge to provide the stability and direction now missing but so sorely needed.

If the pessimism of this projection clashes with the optimism of earlier pages, it is because what *is* so often clashes with what *could be*. Consider, then, that our pessimistic projection might accurately reflect a possible future state for day care in the United States and that to realize a happier alternative will require extraordinary dedication and determination.

13.3 LAWRENCE J. SCHWEINHART AND DAVID P. WEIKART

Changed Lives, Significant Benefits: The High/Scope Perry Preschool Project to Date

What is known about the benefits of high-quality preschool experiences today is largely a result of the longitudinal research conducted by David P. Weikart and the staff of the High/Scope Educational Research Foundation. From 1957 to 1970 Weikart served as director of special services and director of research for the Ypsilanti, Michigan, public schools. While working for the school district, he designed and implemented the High/Scope Perry Preschool Project, a preschool program involving active learning for economically disadvantaged, urban, African American children. The program was developed because many of these children were entering school unready to learn and unexcited about learning.

What makes the High/Scope Perry Preschool Project so unique and valuable is the continual follow-up of participants. The original 123 children in the experimental and comparison groups have been interviewed at specific intervals by the staff at High/Scope over the past 30 years. The following selection is from "Changed Lives, Significant Benefits: The High/Scope Perry Preschool Project to Date," *High/Scope Resource* (Summer 1993), which discusses the findings from the interviews that were conducted when the participants were 27 years old.

The most notable findings are ones that were never anticipated when the project began in the 1960s. At that time, the only goal was to better prepare children for success in school. Today, Weikart and his colleague Lawrence J. Schweinhart have found significant benefits for the adults who attended the preschool program as compared with those who did not. The key findings are higher monthly income, greater rate of home ownership, lower number of arrests, fewer recipients of social services, and higher school graduation rates.

Schweinhart received his doctorate in 1975 from Indiana University and has served as chair of the Research Division at High/Scope since 1976. He is the author of many studies and monographs detailing the benefits of a high-quality, active-learning preschool program.

Weikart earned his Ph.D. in 1966 from the University of Michigan and founded the High/Scope Educational Research Foundation, a private research foundation, in 1970. In 1995 the foundation celebrated 25 years of high-quality educational and research programs involving young people from all over the world.

*T*he results are in. High-quality, active learning preschool programs can help young children in poverty make a better transition from home to community and thus start them on paths to becoming economically self-sufficient, socially responsible adults.

This information was presented by the High/Scope Educational Research Foundation at the annual meeting of Education Writers of America in Boston, Massachusetts, on April 18. The presentation made public for the first time the age-27 findings of the High/Scope Perry Preschool Project—a longitudinal preschool-effectiveness study that has lasted over three decades.

This article, which reviews the study's cumulative findings and most-recent conclusions, considers why some early childhood programs have long-term effects. It also examines the generalizability of this study's findings to other young children and to other preschool programs. Finally, it discusses the policy implications of High/Scope's Perry study and similar studies.

THE STUDY'S DESIGN

The High/Scope Perry Preschool Project is a study assessing whether high-quality preschool programs can provide both short- and long-term benefits to children living in poverty and at high risk of failing in school. The study has followed into adulthood the lives of 123 such children from African-American families who lived in the neighborhood of the Perry Elementary School in Ypsilanti, Michigan, in the 1960s.

At the study's outset, the youngsters were randomly divided into a *program group*, who received a high-quality, active learning preschool program, and a *no-program group*, who received no preschool program. Researchers then assessed the status of the two groups annually from ages 3 to 11, at ages 14–15, at age 19, and most recently at age 27, on variables representing certain characteristics, abilities, attitudes, and types of performance. The median percentage of missing cases for these various assessments was only 4.9%, and only 5% of cases were missing for the age-27 interviews. The study's design characteristics give it a high degree of internal validity, providing scientific confidence that the postprogram group-differences in performance and attitudes are actually effects of the preschool program.

THE FINDINGS AT AGE 27

... [F]indings at age 27 indicate that in comparison with the no-program group, the program group had

- Significantly[1] higher monthly earnings at age 27 (with 29% vs. 7% earning $2,000 or more per month)
- Significantly higher percentages of home ownership (36% vs. 13%) and second car ownership (30% vs. 13%)
- A significantly higher level of schooling completed (with 71% vs. 54% completing 12th grade or higher)
- A significantly lower percentage receiving social services at some time in the previous 10 years (59% vs. 80%)
- Significantly fewer arrests by age 27 (7% vs. 35% with 5 or more arrests), including significantly fewer arrests for crimes of drug making or dealing (7% vs. 25%)

As a group, the program females had significantly higher monthly earnings at age 27 than the no-program females (with 48% vs. 18% earning over $1,000) because more of the program females (80% vs. 55%) had found jobs. The program males, as a group, had significantly higher monthly earnings at age 27 than the no-program males (with 42% vs. 6% earning over $2,000) because the program males had better paying jobs. (Of employed males in the two groups, 53% vs. 8%, respectively, were earning over $2,000, which is a significant difference.)

Certain other significant differences between the program group and the no-program group at age 27 were discovered to hold for males only or for females only. For example, compared with no-program females,

- Significantly fewer program females, during their years in school, spent time in programs for educable mental impairment (8% vs. 37%).
- Significantly more program females completed 12th grade or higher (84% vs. 35%).
- Significantly more program females were married at age 27 (40% vs. 8%).

As compared with no-program males,

- Significantly fewer program males received social services at some time between ages 18 and 27 (52% vs. 77%).
- Significantly fewer program males had 5 or more lifetime arrests (12% vs. 49%).

339

- Significantly more program males owned their own homes at age 27 (52% vs. 21%).

The findings listed here have economic values that prove to be benefits to society. Compared with the preschool program's cost, these benefits make the program indeed a worthwhile investment for taxpayers and for society in general:

OVER THE LIFETIMES OF THE PARTICIPANTS, THE PRESCHOOL PROGRAM RETURNS TO THE PUBLIC AN ESTIMATED $7.16 FOR EVERY DOLLAR INVESTED.

Furthermore, the positive implications of the study's findings for *improved quality of life* for participants, their families, and the community at large are of tremendous importance.

THE EARLIER EDUCATIONAL-PERFORMANCE FINDINGS

Throughout the course of the longitudinal study, preschool program effects were reflected in the educational performance of the preschool program participants. Over the years, the program group produced significantly higher scores than the no-program group on tests of

- Intellectual performance (IQ) from the end of the first year of the preschool program to the end of first grade at age 7
- School achievement at age 14
- General literacy at age 19

In addition, as compared with the no-program group, the program group

- Spent significantly fewer school years in programs for educable mental impairment (with 15% vs. 34% spending a year or more)
- Had a significantly higher percentage reporting at age 15 that their school work required preparation at home (68% vs. 40%)

CONCLUSIONS—AND QUALIFICATIONS

At the end of almost three decades of research, FIVE CONCLUSIONS seem warranted.

1. Children's participation in a high-quality, active learning preschool program at ages 3 and 4 created the framework for adult success, significantly alleviating the negative effects of childhood poverty on educational performance, social responsibility, adult economic status, and family formation.

2. The lives of both the program group and the no-program group have followed a predictable pattern of development since their early school years. Any subsequent intervention, such as school remediation, special education, or criminal justice measures, has not seemed to improve the life course of study participants. In particular, although grade retention and programs for educable mental impairment were intended to help youngsters, girls placed in these situations were nevertheless very likely to drop out before completing high school.

3. During the school years, the preschool program's effects on females were different from its effects on males. For females, the preschool program appeared to create the interest and capacity to remain in school and graduate, in spite of difficulties presented by such problems as teen pregnancy. For males, the preschool program appeared to affect not their likelihood of high school graduation, but their adjustment to society. The program seemed to create for them a chain of events that led to their assuming greater social responsibility; this included a distinct lessening of criminal and other antisocial behavior.

4. The essential process connecting early childhood experience to patterns of improved success in school and the community seemed to be the development of dispositions that allowed the child to interact positively with other people and with tasks. This process was based neither on permanently improved intellectual performance nor on academic knowledge.

5. The lifetime economic benefits to the preschool program participants, their families, and the community far outweigh the economic cost of their high-quality, active learning preschool program. If this program had not been offered, the direct costs to society in lost labor-force participation, increased criminal behavior, and additional welfare support would have far exceeded the program's costs.

Some QUALIFICATIONS must be added to the Perry study's conclusions. First of all, we must keep in mind that *the findings describe two groups, but not every individual in those groups.* While some young people rose above their backgrounds to reach new levels of opportunity and performance, the improvements for most were incremental rather than radical. Although the significant differences between the program group and the no-program group are of extraordinary personal and social importance, not every program participant succeeded, and not every member of the no-program group failed. Even though it can be said that the preschool program, by providing significant benefits, provided participants with a partial "inoculation" against the negative effects of poverty, it cannot be said that the preschool program in any sense offered a "cure" for the problems of poverty.

A second qualification is this. As much as the High/Scope Perry Preschool Project data support the extraordinary value of high-quality early education in breaking the cycle of poverty, *preschool programs are only one part of the solution.* If the nation is to really confront poverty and its related problems of unemployment, welfare dependence, crime, and drug abuse, much broader social-policy action is needed. Improved educational opportunities at *all* levels, access to medical care, affordable housing, effective job-training programs, elimination of institutional racism—all these must play a part as well. The significance of the role of high-quality, active learning preschool education should be neither overrated nor underrated.

A final qualification concerns the preschool program itself. Special note should be taken that the preschool program responsible for the effects talked about here had these four defining aspects of high quality:

- A developmentally appropriate, active learning curriculum
- An organized system of inservice training and systematic, ongoing curriculum supervision
- An efficient, workable method of parent inclusion and involvement
- Good administration, including a valid and reliable, developmentally appropriate assessment procedure; a monitoring system; and a reasonable adult-child ratio

High quality is essential if the promise of early childhood education is to be realized. While preservice staff training, adequate staff salaries and benefits, appropriate space and materials, and health and nutrition services all contribute to the quality of a program, full realization of high quality requires an effective curriculum for the participating children and their families. There is probably nothing inherently beneficial about a program in which a child interacts with an extrafamilial adult and a group of peers each day; *a curriculum must be involved, to define the program's organization and delivery.* It is long past time to insist that the delivery and organization of all early childhood programs meet these standards of quality.

WHY SOME PRESCHOOL PROGRAMS HAVE LONG-TERM EFFECTS

What makes a program experience at ages 3 and 4 so powerful that it can change the pattern of participants' lives, even when they reach adulthood? Why do the effects of some early childhood experiences last a lifetime?

What Is Crucial About the Age?

Early childhood, because of its timing in the child's physical, social, and mental development, is an opportune time to provide special experiences. Physically, preschool-aged children have matured enough to have a fair amount of both fine- and gross-motor coordination and to move about freely and easily; they are no longer toddlers. Socially, preschoolers have largely overcome any earlier fears of strangers or unfamiliar locations, and they usually welcome new settings and new interactions with peers and adults. Mentally, 3-

and 4-year-olds have developed extensive ability to speak and understand and can use objects in a purposeful way. Piaget saw preschool-aged children as being in the preoperational stage—needing to learn from actual objects—and on the threshold of the concrete-operational stage—being able to learn from symbols and signs (Piaget & Inhelder, 1969). When children are fully concrete-operational in thought processes, at age 6 or 7, schools begin instruction in the sign/symbol-based skills of reading, writing, and arithmetic.

Thus preschool-aged children are also on another kind of threshold—the threshold of participation in the formal school setting. Participating in any new setting entails forming new habits of interaction with persons and objects in the setting, and a person's initial behavior in the setting quite naturally creates expectations by others that affect this formation. Therefore preparation for a new setting should focus on influencing initial behavior so it leads to the formation of desirable patterns of interaction. If expectations in the new setting were based only on superficialities (knowing colors, knowing letters of the alphabet), desirable initial behavior could be easily achieved (by drilling on color names, memorizing the alphabet). However, because desirable behavior in the new setting also involves positive underlying dispositions, habits, and skills, the initial behavior must be rooted in these dispositions, habits, and skills. Therefore, an early childhood program in the year or two just prior to school entry is truly the "chance of a lifetime"—the optimal time to develop the child's capacity to respond effectively to the learning opportunities that the school setting will later provide.

What Is Crucial to the Program?

Our best appraisal of the High/Scope Perry Preschool Project results is this: *It was the development of specific personal and social dispositions that enabled a high-quality early childhood education program to significantly influence participants' adult performance.* Erikson (1950) pointed out that the typical psychological thrust of 3- to 5-year-olds is towards developing a sense of initiative, responsibility, and independence. Katz and Chard (1993), discussing the importance of children developing the dispositions of curiosity, friendliness, and cooperation, pointed out that good preschool programs support the development of such traits. These personal dispositions cannot be directly taught, but they can develop under appropriate circumstances as the by-products of children's engagement in appropriate, active learning experiences. This suggests looking at specific circumstances and program strategies that support the development of desirable traits and dispositions.

The preschool program that was developed in the course of the Perry Project employed what today is known as the High/Scope Curriculum. It is a curriculum that relies heavily on **active, child-initiated learning experiences** during which children plan, or express their intentions; carry out their intentions in play experiences; and then reflect on their accomplishments.

These three elements of an active learning curriculum—**children's expression of intent,** their **independently generated experiences,** and their **reflections**—are central to the definition of child-initiated learning activities.

Outcomes of such learning activities include the development of dispositions important to lifelong learning—initiative, curiosity, trust, confidence, independence, responsibility, and divergent thinking. These traits, valued by society, are the foundations of effective, socially responsible adulthood.

When children participate in an active learning curriculum, they develop self-control and self-discipline. This control is *real power*—not over other people or materials, but over themselves. Understanding what is happening in the surrounding environment, realizing that those around them are genuinely interested in what they say and do, and knowing that their work and effort have a chance of leading to success give children a sense of control that promotes personal satisfaction and motivates them to be productive. While no single factor assures success in life, the **sense of personal control** is certainly a major force. A high-quality, active learning preschool program should support and strengthen this way of thinking.

GENERALIZABILITY OF THE FINDINGS

We must carefully consider the generalizability of findings from the High/Scope Perry Preschool Project and of findings from similar studies if we are to make good use of the research. Some opponents of preschool programs *undergeneralize* the Perry findings, whereas some proponents *overgeneralize* them.

Undergeneralizers say that the preschool program that was involved had unique qualities that could not be duplicated elsewhere—that its cost was impractical, or that large-scale programs cannot duplicate its operating conditions, or that teachers similarly qualified cannot be found today.

Overgeneralizers claim that the Perry study established the long-term benefits of Head Start or state-funded preschool programs or child day care programs—without considering the quality of any of these programs. *Neither undergeneralizers nor overgeneralizers of the Perry study findings are contributing to the development of sound public policy.*

Defining Who Was Served and How

Generalizing the findings of the High/Scope Perry Preschool Project demands attention to two aspects of the project—its *participants* and its *program operation*. Replication of the characteristics of the participants *and* the characteristics of the program should lead to replication of the effects, within the study's intervals of statistical confidence. The question is, How broadly can we define the population and the program and still retain confidence that similar effects will result? Such definition requires careful judgment involving (1) selecting descriptive categories for the participants and for the program and (2) estimating what constitutes tolerable variation in these categories if replication of the original study is to be achieved.

For this purpose, **we define the study participants as children living in poverty.** We believe that within poverty, generalization can be made across specific socioeconomic conditions, across specific ethnic groups, across specific times, and across specific locations within developed countries. Cautious generalization might even be made to locations within less developed countries.

For purposes of generalization and replication, **we define the program as a high-quality, active learning program for 3- and 4-year-olds:** a program designed to contribute to their development, with daily 2½-hour sessions for children Monday through Friday and weekly 1½-hour home visits to parents, and with 4 adults trained in early childhood education serving 20–25 children. It is reasonable to generalize program effects to other programs with these features, but again, the question lies in the degree of tolerance permitted in the variability of the program's features. Three sets of features will be considered here.

Features That Bring About Results

One set of program features concerns the sessions held daily for 20 to 25 children, and the parent outreach:

ACTIVE LEARNING: The active learning approach used in the children's classroom sessions and in the home visits should **encourage children to initiate their own developmentally appropriate learning activities.**

PARENT INVOLVEMENT: The program should **include a substantial outreach effort to parents,** such as weekly home visits and parent group meetings, in which staff acknowledge and support parents as genuine partners in the education of their children and model active learning principles for them.

A second set of features has to do with the program's timing and duration:

AGE OF CHILDREN: The program should **serve children at ages 3 and 4,** the years just prior to school entry.

PROGRAM DURATION: Children should attend the program for **two school years;** the evidence from this study for limiting preschool programs to only one school year is weak, based on only 13 program participants.

TIME PER WEEK: The program should have **at least 12½ hours a week of classroom sessions for children**—2½ hours a day, 5 days a week. Variation of an hour or so more or less each week should not matter. A full, 9-hour-a-day program, if it meets all the other standards of quality, would probably produce similar if not greater effects.

A third set of features has to do with the program's staffing, training, and supervision:

STAFF-CHILD RATIO: The staff-child ratio should be **1 adult for no more than 10 children and preferably for no more than 8 children.** While the Perry program had 4 adults for 20 to 25 children, the High/Scope Curriculum has since been used with very positive results in classes having 2 adults for 16 young children (Schweinhart, Weikart, & Larner, 1986), and in classes having 2 adults for as many as 20 young children (Epstein, 1993).

INSERVICE TRAINING PROGRAMS: Staff need **systematic training in early childhood development and education.**

STAFF SUPERVISION: The Perry Project's teaching staff worked daily with supervisory staff in training and planning. Staff need **ongoing supervision by trained supervisors or consultants who know the curriculum** and can assist in its implementation by individual teachers and with individual children. Inservice training and curriculum supervision result in high-quality preschool programs with significantly better outcomes for children (Epstein, 1993).

Preschool programs that do not serve children living in poverty and that are not of high quality, within reasonable degrees of tolerance, cannot lay claim to replicating the program used in the High/Scope Perry Preschool Project and thus are not likely to achieve its long-term effects.

POLICY IMPLICATIONS

The issue of insuring program quality (see Willer, 1990) should be the focus of congressional and legislative debate on funding for Head Start and similar publicly sponsored preschool programs. This need for quality was recognized in the last (1991) program authorization of Head Start, called the Head Start Quality Improvement Act. Because present funding levels do not allow these programs to serve *all* young children living in poverty, there is a danger that the debate will be framed solely in terms of expanding enrollment. Findings of the High/Scope Perry Preschool Project and similar studies indicate that the congressional debate over increased funding for Head Start ought to be over how much to spend on quality improvement (especially training and assessment) versus program expansion. In light of the documented benefits of high-quality programs, it would be irresponsible to permit current programs to continue or expand without substantial efforts to improve and maintain their quality.

The Importance of Assessment

Fundamental to any effort to improve Head Start quality is widespread **formative assessment** of current Head Start program-implementation and outcomes for young children. This assessment must focus not only on the performance of teaching staff in implementing high-quality, active learning programs but also on the outcomes regarding young children's development. The assessment tools used should embody a vision of what such programs are about and what they can accomplish. For the assessment of teaching staff, two such tools are the Early Childhood Environment Rating Scale (Harms & Clifford, 1980) and the High/Scope Program Implementation Profile (High/Scope

Educational Research Foundation, 1989; Epstein, 1993). One such tool for the assessment of young children's development is the High/Scope Child Observation Record (COR) for Ages 2½–6 (High/Scope Educational Research Foundation, 1992; Schweinhart, McNair, Barnes, & Larner, 1993). Assessment of young children's development needs to be consistent with principles of active learning and the cognitive, social, and physical goals of preschool programs. Many evaluations, even by respected researchers, have been limited to narrow tests of intellectual and language performance, or worse, to brief screening tests noted mainly for their brevity and inexpensiveness. Such tests, unfortunately, are only marginally related to the proper goals of high-quality preschool programs.[2]

The Importance of Knowing the Limits

Existing research *has defined the potential effectiveness of Head Start and similar programs*, establishing that programs—if they are done well—can improve children's success in school, increase their high school graduation rates, reduce their involvement in crime, and increase their adult earnings. But because research findings fail to define the limits of program variation within which these extraordinary societal goals can be realized, it is too easy for policymakers to ignore these limits.

Some examples, from state-funded preschool programs, show how the process of ignoring the limits works. When, in Texas, it seemed politically feasible to establish a staff-child ratio of 1 to 22 in a program for at-risk 4-year-olds, state legislators did not challenge the adequacy of this ratio, fearing that any hesitation in supporting the program might have enabled the program's opponents to eliminate it altogether. When Michigan legislators planning to spend $1,000 per child on a new state preschool program received expert testimony that the minimum cost for high-quality preschool programs was $3,000 per child (a decade ago), they decided to increase Michigan's spending per preschool child—to $2,000.

Based on existing knowledge, the standards of quality for Head Start and other publicly funded preschool programs should be set high. But, because the nation has finite resources, research on the allowable limits of program variation should begin immediately. One important area for "limits research" would be staff-child ratios. This report recommends a staff-child ratio of 1 adult for no more than 10 children. Since existing research does not answer the question of whether one adult can deliver an effective program for more than this number of children, it would be unnecessarily risky at this time to operate large-scale programming with more than 10 children per adult—unless the programs were operated as part of experimental studies that provided new knowledge about the effectiveness of various staff-child ratios.

Similarly, we need to probe the lower limits of teacher qualifications for delivery of effective preschool programs. Surely, effective programs require staff trained in early childhood development and education, but what level of training is required? Must all teaching staff have the same level of training?

Many variations in staff training are possible. The important question is, What would a well-designed research study be able to determine about minimal qualifications?

Any of the other components of preschool program quality presented in this article could, and should, be subjected to like scrutiny. There is widespread acceptance of the importance of an active learning curriculum for young children, but what should it look like? There is widespread acceptance of the importance of a strong outreach to parents, but the outreach described in this article focuses on the parent-child relationship, whereas some other forms of outreach have focused on the provision of various educational and social services to parents. What is the proper balance?

The definition of preschool program quality presented in this article is a research-based summary of what is most likely to help young children living in poverty to achieve the striking benefits reported here. But *quality* should have a dynamic definition, constantly under development, constantly being refined by the results of new research studies.

A Place to Start

The most important public policy recommendation from this study and similar studies is a call for **full funding** for the national Head Start program and similar programs—enough to not only **serve all 3- and 4-year-olds living in poverty** but also **provide each of them with a high-quality, active learning preschool program.** The national Head Start program is the place to start, because it has a long history as well as experienced teachers and administrators. Congress has already authorized full funding for the program, but sufficient dollars for full funding have yet to be appropriated. Given the quality-of-life benefits as well as the economic return on investment found in this study and in similar preschool-effectiveness studies, the rationale for finding the dollars is compelling. The High/Scope Perry Preschool Project documents a very specific way that we can invest in our own future by investing in our children.

NOTES

1. A group difference identified as significant was found by the appropriate statistical test to be statistically significant with a two-tailed probability of less than .05.
2. Epstein (1993) found that high-quality programs using the High/Scope Curriculum developed in the High/Scope Perry Preschool Project helped participating young children to achieve significantly higher scores than young children in other high-quality programs on the High/Scope Child Observation Record in initiative, social relations, creative representation, and music and movement; but these same children did not achieve higher scores on a screening test—Developmental Indicators for the Assessment of Learning, Revised (DIAL-R, Mardell-Czudnowski & Goldenberg, 1990).

Epstein, A. S. (1993). *Training for quality: Improving early childhood programs through systematic inservice training* (Monographs of the High/Scope Educational Research Foundation, 9). Ypsilanti, MI: High/Scope Press.

Erikson, E. H. (1950). *Childhood and society.* New York: Norton.

Harms, T., & Clifford, R. M. (1980). *Early Childhood Environment Rating Scale.* New York: Teachers College Press.

High/Scope Educational Research Foundation. (1989). *Program Implementation Profile (PIP) manual.* Ypsilanti, MI: High/Scope Press.

High/Scope Educational Research Foundation. (1992). *High/Scope Child Observation Record (COR) for Ages 2½–6.* Ypsilanti, MI: High/Scope Press.

Katz, L. G., & Chard, S. C. (1993). The project approach. In J. L. Roopnarine & J. E. Johnson (Eds.), *Approaches to early childhood education* (2nd ed.). New York: Macmillan Publishing Company.

Mardell-Czudnowski, C., & Goldenberg, D. S. (1990). *Developmental Indicators for the Assessment of Learning—Revised.* Circle Pines, MN: American Guidance Services.

Piaget, J., & Inhelder, B. (1969). *The psychology of the child.* New York: Basic Books.

Schweinhart, L. J., McNair, S., Barnes, H., & Larner, M. B. (1993, summer). *Observing young children in action to assess their development: The High/Scope Child Observation Record.* Educational and Psychological Measurement, 53.

Schweinhart, L. J., Weikart, D. P., & Larner, M. B. (1986). Consequences of three preschool curriculum models through age 15. *Early Childhood Research Quarterly, 1,* 15–45.

Willer B. (Ed.). (1990). *Reaching the full cost of quality in early childhood programs.* Washington, DC: National Association for the Education of Young Children.

Lawrence J. Schweinhart and David P. Weikart

CHAPTER 14 Reform/Policy

14.1 DOROTHY W. BARUCH

When the Need for Wartime Services for Children Is Past—What of the Future?

In the early 1940s, when America was hoping for an end to the war, those involved in wartime projects began to assess what they had accomplished. One of the projects created by the war industry—child-care services—had been highly successful in assisting mothers to move from home to job. As a result, nursery schools and child-care centers in cities with war-related work were bursting at the seams by 1943. Their success was measured in terms of the contributions made to children's lives. Child care brought health protection, medical services, and better nutrition, not to mention a secure place to meet emotional and educational needs. In addition, wartime child-care centers made significant contributions to families, by increasing parenting skills, and to community cohesiveness, by mobilizing whole communities in a common endeavor.

In the following selection from "When the Need for Wartime Services for Children Is Past—What of the Future?" *Journal of Consulting Psychology* (1945), Dorothy W. Baruch anticipates the contributions of wartime child-care services in the years after the war. She acknowledges the expansion of services and the extension of facilities necessary to accommodate peacetime changes. It is interesting to compare Baruch's projection that mothers would continue to work after the war with the actual outcome in the 1950s.

Baruch (1899–1962) received degrees from the University of Southern California, Whittier College, and Claremont University. She developed the Department of Preschool and Parent Education at Whittier prior to establishing her practice as a psychologist in California. Due to her strong interest in child care nationwide, Baruch was instrumental in organizing the first public relations program for the National Association of Nursery Educators. Baruch is the author of several children's books, including *Dumbo, Four Airplanes,* and *Pitter Patter.* She also authored *Parents and Children Go to School,* one of the first early childhood books emphasizing parent involvement with education.

*A*ll over the country we are hearing a new note of hope—the prediction that war may be over far sooner than we have heretofore dared anticipate. As the end of hostilities appears not too dimmed by far-stretching distance, those who have worked on various war-long projects, are stopping at moments to wonder: What have we really accomplished? What must we still do if we are to help end the war as rapidly as possible? And what of the future, after war is past?

These same questions rise in the minds of many people who have worked in and for the child care services. Those who have watched and tended the first beginnings, those who have experienced the spread and the growth, those who have added their own strength to strengthening the program—all alike are trying now to evaluate: What have we accomplished? What must we still do? And where will we go later, at the close of the war? . . .

WHAT MUST . . . BE DONE?

The war is not yet over. To bring it to a successful end, vast manpower resources must be maintained. The child care centers have made it possible for many mothers to stay on the job. They must still do so. In certain areas their services must even be expanded.

Manpower Trends Call for Further Extension of Facilities

There are three specific facts related to manpower needs at the present time which bear influence on the child care situation. The first fact is that in many areas the labor pool has been drained to the dregs. Not only must the people who are at present on the job, stay on the job—still more people are needed. The child care centers, however, in most of the heavy war areas, serve only a very small portion of the women who must have care for their children.

The long waiting lists bring evidence that the demands far exceed the resources. This means that expansion of services is necessary.

The second manpower fact connected with the matter of child care is that many women and men alike now in essential war industries are, in the face of war's end, saying to themselves: "You'd better get yourself a more permanent job—one that won't end with the war but that will continue in peacetime." As a result, many are checking out of war industries and are moving into a more permanent type of employment. This does not mean, however, that they no longer need child care facilities. They still do.

The third manpower fact is closely related. As vacancies are created by this exodus from war industries, a new group of women are moving in. These are the young wives of servicemen. They are the girls with small babies who are finding that G.I. Joe's paycheck just isn't enough to live on. And, because the plants are desperate for labor, they are snapping them up. This means that children of a new age group are sorely in need of good care. It means that child care services must be extended downward, so that babies under two need not suffer neglect.

The Need for Infant Centers

In one locale, estimates on the basis of plant surveys and other data showed in the fall of 1944 that there were approximately 11,000 babies under two years whose mothers were working in war industries. Very conservatively these reports placed 2,500 babies as desperately in need of care.

The same adverse conditions that prevailed earlier for older children now prevailed for this younger group. They were being left in parked cars and in locked rooms, uncared for, unfed. Foster homes were not available. An exhaustive study of the community showed that about 475 new foster homes appeared on the horizon from month to month, but that about 471 homes closed down their foster-care facilities in the same periods. Apparently many women who had been willing to work by taking care of other peoples' children found that their time could be less strenuously and more profitably spent. Several other facts also pertained to the situation. Although there were over 150,000 Negroes in the area, with a large number working in war industries, there was not one foster home for Negro babies. Furthermore, the cost of foster care was prohibitive, especially on G.I. Joe's pay. Charges ran from $15 and $20 a week for day care up to $75 and $80 for twenty-four hour care.

It is self-evident that differences of opinion as to best policies and procedures would rise in relation to many aspects of infant care. However, in relation to the matter of twenty-four hour care, there can be no arguments among people who have acquired even a minimal insight into children's psychological needs. Contact between mother and child must be maintained. We had good proof of this in the early days of the Russian experiment when it was found that babies given twenty-four hour care out of their homes were lacking in initiative, independence and self-confidence, and were developing apprehensiveness and timidity. Children must be with their mothers for some part of each day. Moreover, they must have both good care and wise guidance in the hours of separation.

What is being done to provide such care and guidance?

In the early part of 1944, questionnaires were sent to the chief school officers in all the states. One question asked whether any programs for infant care had been set up for children of working mothers. It requested names and addresses of persons who could furnish details on such programs. Questionnaire returns indicated that infant care had been undertaken in fourteen states. Follow-up letters were then written for more detailed information. In all but one instance, the type of care mentioned was foster-home care. The only thing approaching group care was a large home run by two women and licensed by the State Department of Public Welfare to accommodate ten children under two. The Public Health Nursing Association contributed its services. In almost all instances where foster homes were described, two problems were reiterated, namely the difficulty of locating sufficient homes to take care of the need and the difficulty of furnishing adequate supervision.

Since the time these returns were received, at least one city has ventured forth into a larger scale infant care project. A brief review of its experience sheds light on one type of excellent solution to a most difficult problem.

In May, 1944, two infant centers were opened at the continued instigation of industry in an area where plant surveys were showing that fourteen and sixteen per cent of the children of working mothers were under two. The parent-teacher association incorporated. They then sponsored the project, sending in a request to the federal works agency for Lanham Funds. Meanwhile, because of the urgency of the matter, the industries in the area helped to finance the project. The cost per child per day was estimated at $2.80 of which the fee paid by the parent covered $1.00. The local child care committee helped to set up the project. The State Department of Social Welfare issued a license permitting the operation of the centers, and the fire department and local health department helped in the setting up of standards. The county welfare donated the clothing. The Navy gave the cribs. The Federal Public Housing Authority furnished the building where the centers were housed. In short—a total community mobilized in preventing damage to the physical and mental health of its youngest inhabitants.

Prior to the opening of the centers, a study revealed many types of haphazard and precarious care. Infants had been entrusted to several different people while a mother was at work: to a neighbor in the morning, to another at noon, to an eight- or ten-year-old brother or sister later in the day. Frequently infants were placed in unlicensed homes. Costs were prohibitive. One woman whose husband was missing in action in the South Pacific was paying $125 a month for the care of an eighteen-months-old baby and a child of four in a foster home.

After the opening of the two centers, a different picture prevailed for the all-too-few babies who could be accommodated. A registered nurse was in charge at each center. The staff included one attendant for every five or six babies. Rigid inspection and meticulous health conditions have prevented any epidemic from spreading. When babies arrive in the morning, they are immediately changed into sterilized clothing before joining the group. A visitor must be ascertained free from any communicable illness and must put on a sterilized gown before being admitted. The formula room is open only to the attendant who makes up the formulae. The most beautiful cleanliness is maintained. The daily program is adapted to the different age levels. It includes opportunity for rest and sleep; proper food and sunshine; and for play, attention and love. The progress made by the babies enrolled has been marked. One little undernourished, wizened baby—very low mentally—showed improvement in intellectual responses as well as in physical condition after a few month's care.

Due to the success of the two centers and to the increasing demand, eight more centers are being added.

Other Things Needed

In addition to the infant centers, various communities are clamoring for more *facilities to take care of children when they are ill; more buildings to house the centers; more teachers and more teacher training.*

Because of the teacher shortage, some communities have ventured forth courageously in the *utilization of volunteers.* More of this sort of thing needs to be developed. Reports of successful outcomes have been sent from several places. In one locale, volunteers have assisted with arts and crafts, dramatics, music and story telling in the school-age centers. In this manner, people with talent of one sort or another have been able to contribute regularly in ways that have enriched the program. In another place, volunteers have come in occasionally to give talks and to bring in various facets of community living. In still other places, volunteers have been used as part of the staff working with the children in the regular day-by-day activities. At both nursery-school and grade-school ages one community reports having one or two volunteer workers scheduled in each of its centers every day. In other communities students from teacher training institutions are being utilized; and also high school and junior high school students from classes in homemaking and family-life education. The variety of contributions that volunteers can bring to the centers is endless especially when they have undergone, as many have, the training courses set up for them.

There is little place left in the scheme of things for the traditional attitude of hands raised high at the idea of a lack in the dependency and effectiveness of voluntary effort. That volunteers are capable of as continuous and devoted a job as paid workers has been ably demonstrated. One center, in fact, at its outset, was staffed entirely by volunteers. The volunteers consisted of two professional nurses, school teachers, twelve trained child care aides, Red Cross canteen cooks, a public health nurse, a pediatrician and a director.

Today the center is in a small house in a public school. It is a Lanham-supported child care center caring for eighty children aged two to fourteen. The director says:

> We continue to work with many of the old volunteers and some new ones too. Three courses for the training of aides have made possible fresh recruits. We are one of the few centers that has been able to set up a five-day working week for

teachers from the very beginning. This was possible because a number of volunteers were well enough trained to take a teacher's place on her day off. One of the most important reasons for using volunteers is that it brings the community into the center. Every day the community works in the center in several capacities.[1]

The result of such endeavors in terms of increased community support is obvious. Obvious, too, should be the lesson to the public schools. If the use of volunteers could be adopted in kindergartens and upward, not only would the program for children be enriched. The school's place in the community would be strengthened. The support given the schools by the community would be advanced. . . .

WHY CONTINUE?

The value of nursery school was stressed in terms of its contribution to child development and to family life and parent education. One person said, "It seems reasonable to expect mothers to want this care after the war. They are more aware of the advantages for their children and the help that they, as mothers, are given. . . . These war years have educated parents to the importance of good nursery school guidance." Another adds that the facilities are needed as a "help for many mothers in getting back to normal life. . . ." Another person in an earlier communication stated,

> I see a need for the extension of child care centers for children of parents other than those employed, on account of the modern prevalence of families too small to provide in the home recreational facilities among brothers and sisters under parental guidance. I see a need for many small neighborhood recreation centers for children up to ten or twelve . . . also think that school buildings and playgrounds should be properly equipped and kept open under proper supervision the year round for children over twelve and for adults.

Still another person brings out the practical fact that both nursery schools and school-age centers "need to continue after the war because some of the young men who left high school for the war and who married will probably not be receiving wages large enough to take care of their families. Therefore, both man and wife will work."

Type of Support Anticipated

Another aspect which the questionnaire inquired into was the matter of support. It asked: According to existing state laws, could you operate and support the child care facilities as part of the regular school system? . . . Of the 44 states giving information on nursery schools, 12 states indicated that laws existed permitting operation and support; 32 states, that such laws did not exist. Of the 42 states furnishing information pertaining to extended day care,

TABLE 1

Types of Support Anticipated in States Indicating Continuance
of Child Care Services

	Nursery Schools No. States	Extended Care No. States
Public funds		
Federal funds	3	2
Federal and state funds	1	0
Federal, state, and district	1	0
State funds	2	3
State and district or local school funds	5	1
District or local school funds	1	3
Public combined with private funds		
Federal funds plus tuition	2	0
District or local school funds plus tuition	2	1
District or local school funds plus tuition or "other" unspecified private contributions	1	2
District or local school funds plus industrial,, commercial, service organizations, and "other" unspecified contributions	2	0
Private funds		
Private contributions (unspecified)	7	10
Tuitions plus private contributions (unspecified)	1	0
Tuitions plus contributions from service organizations and PTA	1	0
Private contributions plus community chest funds	1	1
Funds from industry	0	2
Total	30	25

19 indicated that there was permissive legislation; 23, that state laws permitting such operation and support did not exist. Several replies indicated that extended day-care centers could continue with recreation funds.

Still another part of the questionnaire inquired more fully into the various types of support that the person answering anticipated. Tabulation was made of the indications from those states in which either one or both persons answering the questionnaires had signified that the facilities would probably continue in the postwar period [Table 1]. From this tabulation it will be seen that various combinations of public and private funds were thought of, as well as the utlitization of either type of funds alone. Where federal funds were looked forward to, mention, in two or three instances, was made to the possibility of utilizing Federal Aid to Education allotments, should this Bill pass Congress.

Commenting on further legislation in the states, opinions appeared to concur on the advisability of permissive legislation that would make available either state or district funds and that would also allow for the collection of fees from the parents to defray a part of the cost. Provision for credentialing of teachers, licensing of nursery schools and setting of standards by the state departments of education were brought out as other phases of desirable legislation. Very clearly delineated was the universal accord that nursery schools should continue as an integral part of the public school system—as a helpful extension of the public schools downward—*not* as an endeavor separate or apart.

One further point should be mentioned in connection with legislation. It is the fact that funds must be provided without discrimination in the Southern states where segregation unfortunately still pertains. The equitable treatment provided under the Lanham Act must be continued. Some sort of federal provision for this will need to be made. Otherwise, we will go on expending a part of our useful potentially capable citizenry through educational deprivation and neglect.

CONCLUDING STATEMENT

We have engaged in a war these past years aimed at preserving democracy and at bringing into being a better world. If we are to succeed in our endeavor, we must not only win along the far-stretched battle fronts. We must win at home. One of our major battles is to bring up sturdy, courageous and healthy children. Only by such means will we remain free from further turmoil and hate.

The child care centers have taken their place on the war front. They have shown themselves worthy of continuing to serve children and parents in the postwar world, not as facilities set apart and outside of what is commonly done for children and parents, but as a well-integrated and cohesive part of what all the schools of the nation must eventually undertake.

NOTE

1. In a letter from Dorothy Robin, director (and volunteer), Hempstead Child Care Center, Hempstead, New York, March 17, 1944.

Social Reform and Early-Childhood Education: Some Historical Perspectives

Although preschool education was gaining credence in the 1960s, especially for urban and underprivileged children, Marvin Lazerson of Harvard University believed that it was incapable of living up to its mandates for educational reform. He felt that preschools were being asked to do too much and were receiving too little support.

The following selection is an excerpt from Lazerson's essay "Social Reform and Early-Childhood Education: Some Historical Perspectives," *Urban Education* (April 1970). In it, Lazerson harshly reprimands early childhood educators and social reformers for their tendency to confuse pedagogical reform with social change. This confusion created an apparent lack of any real commitment to solving the problems of urban areas and a narrowing of educational practice. According to Lazerson, reform activity and education became separate functions in society, dividing school from community. He projected that preschool programs, devoid of true community-based experiences and commitments, would not improve school achievement, much less lead to social reform.

*T*o a historian, today's discussion of preschooling for urban children are particularly mortifying. The debates seem to make slight inroads into previously formulated conceptions. Admittedly, we have established an elaborate rational for early-childhood education. Psychologists and social scientists tell us that children can learn at an early age and warn us about the dire consequences of "cultural deprivation." Phrases like "social intervention" on behalf of the urban child, forging a bridge between home and school, and "learning to learn" seem to have become permanent parts of the regular incantations of

American educators and their philanthropic and governmental colleagues. These gains may have led us to some educational breakthroughs. We seem to be committed to more and better schooling for the young and the quality of our pedagogy may improve as a result. If nothing else, Headstart has made us critically aware of how children are brought up and what they do or do not accomplish in school. We are becoming sympathetic to the plight of children taught by those who doubt the youngsters' ability to learn, and hopefully this will enhance teacher training.

Despite all this, however, I am terribly pessimistic about the possibilities of substantive social change through preschooling. Too often discussions of educational reform appear to be a means of avoiding more complex and politically dangerous issues. As many of us have come to recognize, education is a lot cheaper than new housing and new jobs, and a lot less controversial than active enforcement of civil rights and antidiscrimination legislation. Preschool programs which tell us that their participants will succeed in school and life during the next two decades cannot really be tested at the present time, and in the meanwhile, we wait out the social problems which plague us. We are thus left with what has become a fairly typical example of educational reform: even greater calls for school responsibility while the social problems which have the greatest effect on schooling are largely ignored. The schools—in this case, preschooling—are asked to do too much, and are given too little support to accomplish what they are asked. A variety of interest groups, however, are satisfied: educators because they get status and funds, social reformers because they believe in education, and government officials because they pass positive legislation without upsetting traditional social patterns. In this light, the movement for early-childhood education looks increasingly like a giant cop-out on the present, an elaborate ritual which focuses on the future as a way of avoiding meaningful action on today's pressing social needs.

All of this might seem unduly harsh. President Nixon, articulating proposals formulated during the Johnson administration, has called for "early intervention" to break the cycle of poverty. He has asked for a broadening of supportive services—preschooling before the ages of three and four now found in Headstart, more intensive year-round and follow-through programs, and expanded social services. Seeking expertise and efficiency, he has urged the transferral of Headstart from the experimental and frequently inefficient Office of Economic Opportunity to a newly proposed Office of Child Development in the Department of Health, Education and Welfare, the latter hardly a model of efficiency. Unfortunately, the President has simultaneously shown himself incapable of any real commitment to the problems of the urban areas. Adopting this attitude of "keep it cool," he shows little inclination to tell Americans that something is significantly wrong in our cities. His programs to counter poverty, discrimination, and unemployment are virtually nonexistent and where they appear are often retrogressive. We are thus confronted with a situation in which the President emphatically calls for broad governmental involvement in education while withdrawing the government from active participation in social change.

In itself, this discrepancy between commitment and rhetoric would be depressing. But the problem of educational reform goes beyond the failings of the current administration and encompasses the widespread and historical use of education as a surrogate for social reform. Our assumptions about education and society, even more than our practices, lead me to pessimism about the fate of the early-childhood education movement. In these terms, the particular policies offered by the Nixon administration are only part of an evolving tragedy. In the simplest terms, we confuse pedagogical reform with social change, and are satisfied with the former without realizing how little impact it has on the latter. While we discuss social issues, we so institutionalize our educational reforms that we narrow our practices, and in the process, divorce the schools from the communities they are supposed to serve. The results are tragic, for we continue to believe that an adequately functioning school is the basis for a society in which equality of opportunity is secured. That we risk such an occurence becomes apparent when today's early-childhood movement is compared to an earlier attempt at resolving ghetto problems through preschooling: the kindergarten of late nineteenth and early twentieth century America.

THE EVOLUTION OF KINDERGARTENS

Begun as an emancipatory institution for the cultured and affluent, designed to supplement the family, the home, and motherhood by recognizing the uniqueness of childhood, kindergartens were a major institutional adaptation to the needs of the young. Drawing upon new attitudes toward childhood—a sense of its special uniqueness and significance—early kindergartners tried to evolve a coherent view of the way in which a child grows. . . .

Stimulated by a rising tide of concern over immigrant life and urban poverty, settlement-house workers, philanthropists, and educators sought to make the kindergarten into a supplement for the children of poor, unstable families. This transition was dramatically portrayed by Kate Douglas Wiggin, author of *Rebecca of Sunnybrook Farm* and numerous other best-selling children's books. During the 1870s, Mrs. Wiggin ran a private kindergarten for the wealthy in Santa Barbara, California, when she suddenly has "a vision of how wonderful it would be to plant a child-garden in some dreary, poverty-stricken place in a large city, a place swarming with un-mothered, undefended, undernourished child-life." Within a matter of months, she was in San Francisco's crowded ghettos in charge of a settlement kindergarten.

The rationale for this commitment quickly became familiar. Parents who worked, were poor, spoke a foreign language, or seemed otherwise maladjusted to urban life should send their children to such classes because—as the editor of *Century Magazine* wrote—the kindergarten provides "our earliest opportunity to catch the little Russian, the little Italian, the little German, Pole, Syrian, and the rest and begin to make good American citizens of them." And when the kindergarten attained general acceptance, and was transferred from the settlement houses to the public schools, it was still thought of as having special uniqueness for children of the poor. . . .

The advocates of the urban kindergarten thus blended generalizations about all children with views about the particular needs of slum children. They emphasized the importance of getting the child early, while he was still suscep-tible to proper molding. They stressed the dangers of allowing the young to grow untutored. While they contended, for example, the children learned best through play, they rejected any notion that *unsupervised* play was properly educational—what the urban child learned on the street was harmful. City and family life outside the classroom appeared as hostile antagonists of the kinder-garten, and to counteract their influence, children learned about birds and flowers, streams, and clean white houses. Kindergartners harped on the inade-quacy of home and family for the urban poor, the threat of later social anarchy from youth and adults inadequately trained as children, and the difficulties of adult success for children not introduced to proper behavior patterns.

. . . Every teacher was asked to spend her afternoons visiting her pupils' homes, or inviting mothers into the classroom for special teas and talks on health and child care and discussions on the problems of their common exist-ence. What happened in the classroom was supposed to be transferred to the home and neighborhood. Children who were clean and thrifty taught cleanli-ness and thrift to their parents. Through the child, the family could be reached, and through that, the society. In this way, kindergarten advocates saw pre-schooling as one of the great instruments of urban reform. . . .

Conflicts within the kindergarten and between elementary school and kindergarten teachers profoundly affected the institutionalization of early childhood schooling. The early kindergarten had depended upon certain uni-versalities: all children grew in a particular way, they needed similar training. Whether applied to the affluent or the slum, a uniform kindergarten program provided the most effective means of socializing the child. After 1900, however, growing doubts about the ability of slum children to learn, buttressed by a new emphasis on educational testing and upon the categorization of children, led to a differentiation of program. What was proper depended upon the ethnic, class, and social status groupings of the children: the deficiencies of slum life meant that slum children needed special educational techniques. Whereas the kindergartens of the upper classes focused on free play and the removal of restraints and inhibitions, providing an atmosphere of independence, occa-sional creativity, and a general expansion of home activities, most kindergar-tens, and especially those for the urban poor, committed themselves to the inculcation of discipline and orderly behavior patterns believed absent in the child's environment, and thought so necessary for success in the first grade. . . .

Simultaneously, the professionalization of kindergarten education—its transfer from the social settlements and philanthropic-minded originators to elementary school educators concerned with establishing a secure identity and status—worked against the broader commitments to social change. Rather than seeking to reform life in the slum, kindergartens centered on the child's relationship to the school. Children were trained to enter the first grade; kin-dergarten teachers were responsible for that task, not for amelioration of slum problems. Reading readiness, not shared learning experiences between the gen-erations, dominated kindergarten education. The early desire that kindergart-ners teach only one-half the day, spending the remainder with children in their homes or with parents in the classroom, dissolved as teachers now taught double sessions. While this change implicitly recognized that the teachers hostile to the life of the poor were not going to undertake substantive social reform, the withdrawal of the kindergarten from its social reformist orientation helped to isolate the urban school from the community it served. Educators, applauding the introduction of kindergartens, could ignore the social problems which shaped their work.

THE PRESCHOOL COMPARED AND CONTRASTED

Historical analogies are at best tenuous and dangerous. Yet the issues in this case are important and the evidence compelling enough to allow us to draw parallels between the introduction of the kindergarten—the major innovation in early-childhood education in the late nineteeth and early twentieth centuries—and the thrust of our present debates over preschool programs. In an earlier period, great urban tension revolving around the influx of non-English speaking immigrants and exposure to slum life produced a host of reform measures. Better housing, public health facilities and legislation, municipal reorganization, and the wave of social agitation forming the progressive era made reform and revision the dominant ethic of a generation. Much of that reform activity involved education: pedagogical change, social services in the school, licensing and professionalization of teachers, new curricula. This thrust toward social amelioration, when combined with a new enthusiasm for childhood and the child study movement, gave impetus to the kindergarten as a preschool innovation. Today's early-childhood education movement derives from similar roots. The findings of cognitive pyschologists like Martin Deutsch for the Institute for Developmental Studies, J. McVicker Hunt of the University of Illinois, Benjamin Bloom of the University of Chicago have synthesized the importance of early-childhood experience with the possibilities that children can learn more than we have given them credit for. When joined to the social reform thrust of the Kennedy-Johnson administration—the war on poverty and its adjuncts—preschooling seemed a logical approach to social problems, combining the possibilities for school achievement by the individual, and for community reform through the involvement of parents and para-professionals in the classroom. The middle class saw in Headstart a reiteration of the day nursery, the poor were anxious for day-care centers, and politicians could satisfy everyone by voting support for "our children." Both the earlier kindergarten and Headstart derive from the theory of cultural deprivation, the notion that parents of the poor—earlier, immigrants, today, blacks—cannot provide a foundation for success in the larger society. Then and now, educational reformers begin with a fundamental hostility to the home and life styles of the poor, and seek to overcome the gap between social classes by creating a bridge between school and home. . . .

This is not to say that the kindergarten at the turn of the century and preschooling today are identical. We are considerably more sophisticated about education and psychological growth now then we were then. Federal involvement—financial and supervisory—has dramatically altered the arena of political debate and decision-making. Schools are more important now than ever before, if only because our use of them as certifying agencies has become more extreme. Decisions about them, therefore, are more crucial. The present preschool movement is explicitly aimed at the poor; kindergartens have always possessed a middle- and upper-class clientele, the nursery schools even more so. Headstart's strongest public justification is the argument that it will improve school achievement, while the kindergartens drew on other themes. Yet taking into account these differences, the parallels remain incredibly striking, and, I am afraid, present developments will too likely resemble those of the past. Innovation is being put to work in the interests of traditional goals. Like the incorporation of kindergarten techniques into the lower elementary grades and the loss of distinctiveness in kindergarten education, the findings of cognitive psychologists will probably find their way into preschool programs under conditions and assumptions which may well mystify their originators. . . .

All of this is rather depressing, but it hardly touches the most distressing facet of the analogy: the continuing belief among the educational policy makers and teachers that educational problems are going to be resolved in the schools. The kindergartners, at first, recognized the fallacy of this position. They recognized that learning problems were social problems and that they were not simply going to be resolved in the classroom no matter how innovative the programs were. Though they were naive in believing that home visits and mother's clubs would influence social behavior, they at least recommended that teachers get out of the classroom and into the community. For a variety of reasons—economic, hostility from public school authorities, the ideology of discipline, and a declining faith in the ability of the poor to succeed— the commitment to social reform, limited as it was, foundered, and kindergartners soon accepted the notion that the problems of learning could best and, in practice, only be solved in the classroom. They thus turned their programs into preparatory exercises for the first grade. That is, kindergartners began by raising the bold notion that educational questions were at the root of social questions, but ended by substituting pedagogical reforms for social reform. In effect, they had unwittingly participated in a process which made educational change synonymous with pedagogical change.

This seems to me the most striking feature of the contemporary preschool movement. Today's educators and laymen alike readily agree that the problems of the schools go beyond the classroom. Every policy statement on compensatory education begins by asserting that poverty, discrimination, and unemployment are the key determinants of school achievement, and that revised teaching methods, class size, physical facilities, and curriculum may provide satisfaction for the policy makers and teachers, and in some cases for the community involved, but they are not going to resolve the educational problems of the ghetto. The overwhelming impression gleaned from the studies like the United States Civil Rights Commission's *Racial Isolation in the Public Schools* is that our problems are, at heart, social problems. This is crucial. We have got to see the broader issues involved in any educational reform. The schools cannot resolve our social problems, and conversely, if we want improved school achievement among the poor, we had better commit ourselves to substantial economic and community reform. School problems are thus not going to be resolved as long as the social conditions of the poor take second place to educational methodology, and American educators had better face up to that proposition.

But while this cautions against undue exaltation of school reforms, it is only a first step. This same argument has been used to justify poor achievement and inadequate teaching for some time, i.e., the schools cannot compensate for inadequate home life, or poor kids cannot learn. Nor does a recognition that educational and social reform are not the same thing mean that pedagogy is unimportant or irrelevant. The kindergartens of the turn of the century did represent improved childhood schooling, and in numerous ways the idea of happy children influenced our elementary schools to their benefit. Certainly better trained teachers, new approaches to learning, greater knowledge of children, and more realistic, relevant, and stimulating subject matter will improve the quality of our school systems. But educators are fooling themselves if they believe these are sufficient or even most important. They are deluding themselves if they think pedagogical adjustments are going to alter in any significant way the achievement patterns of the young, especially if they are carried out in isolation from the community involved.

It is here that I think our current preschool program is being misdirected. I am terribly afraid that two trends are emerging, with deleterious consequences to social reform. The first lies in the use of early-childhood education as a panacea. Without a concomitant commitment to vast changes in our urban environment—a commitment we still lack—preschooling will not significantly improve school achievement. We will soon become frustrated by the descrepancy between expectations and fulfillment, and will withdraw from any further commitments to education. The second trend lies in the growing professionalization of early-childhood education, and the related withdrawal from community activism. In its early stages, Headstart was closely connected to a host of local antipoverty projects. As part of the Office of Economic Opportunity, its participants saw themselves involved in communitywide reform. In Mississippi, for example, Headstart was intimately related to voter registration and civil rights. In a number of projects, mothers and neighborhood workers were brought into the classroom and participated in shared educational experiences with their children. Some of this continues, but increasingly professional educators are taking control of the preschooling movement. Those who have been hostile to the poor and have helped to give us static and deadening educational structures in the ghetto are now likely to turn early childhood education into a dull and barren learning experience. Demands are being made that parents be licensed if they are to aid in teaching, thereby once again setting up the dichotomy between the "good" education of the teacher and the "bad" education of the nonprofessional mother. What began in many areas as a community-based learning experience—and more important had the potential to become such a program—threatens instead to become another hostile intruder into the life of the poor. When attached to educators' unwillingness to fight for broad social reform, preschooling cannot be expected to be very meaningful to those it ostensibly serves.

I began this essay on a note of pessimism. Perhaps I am being unfair to the preschool movement, in many ways the most promising of the current activities on the educational scene since it continues to see itself in broad social terms and occasionally draws upon new insights in learning theory. Yet it is precisely for these reasons that I dread seeing all its energy, time, and money fall by the wayside, largely because the movement has failed to reflect upon what it is doing. Americans, as we are acutely aware, have tended to see their commitment to the schooling of the young as a reaffirmation of their faith in the future, an optimistic belief that in the child lies the well-being of society. Both the kindergarten movement at the turn of the century and the preschool programs of today assert that faith. There is, as I suggested, an alternative hypothesis. Early schooling for the child of poverty may represent an abdication of the present, an implicit statement that society is unwilling to grapple with the immediate issues of discrimination and poverty, but would rather postpone confrontation to a later date, naively expecting not to have to face the issues at all. Placing the child in school is an excellent means for achieving that postponement. In this sense, the preschoolers may once again settle for pedagogical rather than social reform, find that nothing has really changed, and give up hope in trying. Recognition of that possibility will, I hope, place our concern for early-childhood schooling in a different light. Our policies in the past, however, provide little cause for optimism.

The New Advocacy in Early Childhood Education

Sharon Lynn Kagan is a senior associate at the Bush Center in Child Development and Social Policy at Yale University. Her research focuses on reform and policy issues of early child care and education. She tackles serious questions of how America deals with young children and their families in the face of competing demands for scarce resources. One of her interests is seeking better outcomes for children by creating a collaborative, integrated early care and education system.

In the following selection from "The New Advocacy in Early Childhood Education," *Teachers College Record* (Spring 1989), Kagan analyzes advocacy and discusses four conditions for systematizing efforts to ensure success of a "children's agenda." She lists the reasons why the early childhood community seems ambivalent toward advocacy, and she identifies the consequences for the field of early care and education. One of the major reasons for the "advocacy hesitancy," according to Kagan, is the belief that curriculum planning and classroom teaching are considered the chief responsibilities of early childhood professionals. She contends that the belief is so prevalent in caregiver and teacher preparation that advocacy activities are almost nonexistent in preprofessional training. Another reason for hesitancy is that each decade brings different attitudes toward the use of political forces for child advocacy. As social action surges and wanes in America, attempts at advocacy vary in their effectiveness.

To prevent this from occurring in the future, Kagan suggests that the functions of advocacy for young children be congruent at the community, state, and national levels. She provides one model of community-based integrated collaboration that emphasizes assessment and comprehensive action plans to accomplish together what is impossible alone. Kagan contends that the key to solving the "advocacy hesitancy" problem is personal, intentional, and active involvement.

WHY ADVOCATE?

Advocacy in the child care and early education field has four main rationales, all of which are critically important to practitioners: (1) to preserve programs and safeguard slots for youngsters; (2) to increase service capacity, to enhance program quality, or to demonstrate that a new idea or program type can work, as in funding for demonstration programs; (3) to change the systemic infrastructure of the field, thereby making child care and early education more accessible, affordable, and equitable; and (4) to generate public awareness of the issues facing the field and facing children and parents. . . .

ADVOCACY IN ACTION

Given the urgent need for advocacy for young children and their families, just how does one go about this? Theorists suggest that the appropriateness of method depends on the issue, the forum, and the individuals involved. . . . Pelosi proposes a model community-based advocacy system that utilizes existing organizations and specifies relationships between the system's components, and between the system and the community. Adaptive to meet a community's changing needs, modifiable depending on neighborhood resources, and capable of individual and class advocacy, this model includes: (1) monitoring and assessing to identify advocacy needs; (2) management to set goals and distribute resources; and (3) action to design alternative projects or interventions and to obtain resources and implement designated plans. Perlman offers another alternative delineating three types of grass-roots groups: those that use direct action to pressure existing institutions to be more accountable, those that use the electoral system to replace existing institutions, and those that form alternative institutions to bypass existing powers. While complementary, these approaches may even be most successful when combined in an advocacy initiative, according to Perlman.

Building on Pelosi's list of advocacy functions, others cite educating the community and political decision makers through speaking engagements and the media, developing proposals based on the consensus of a majority of the organizations participating in the advocacy effort, forming additional and more representative alliances, and working in the court system.

In addition to advocacy at the community, state, and national levels, there is an educative component to advocacy. Advocacy not only involves political mobilization on behalf of specific programs and services, but embraces the generation and dissemination of knowledge. Educating parents regarding quality and the issues affecting quality is one form of public education, the fourth reason to advocate. Providing information and support to parents so that they can be effective advocates for their children and their children's programs is a linchpin of quality early education. Goffin even suggests that personal advocacy be part of each practitioner's job description, and that the parent-provider relationship be actively, extensively, and intentionally viewed as a forum for advocacy.

CONDITIONS FOR ADVOCACY IN EARLY CHILDHOOD

Given the particular history that pervades advocacy in child care and early childhood education, I suggest that four conditions are necessary before the field orchestrates large-scale efforts. *First, all early childhood professionals must stop regarding advocacy as aberrant leftist behavior and start treasuring it as a national resource.* Advocacy is the fuel that drives programs; without it, programs cease to exist. To ensure robust advocacy efforts, the nation must make advocacy an enduring part of its social system. Specifically, incoming professionals must be socialized to roles not only as future educators and caregivers, but as future advocates. To legitimate advocacy, practitioners need to understand the importance of the advocacy process and their critical role in it. Given their understanding of children and families, they are particularly well situated to be effective advocates. By understanding the legislative process and policy implications, they can increase their potency.

Second, advocacy must be greased. In Congress, when the term *greased* is used it means the wheels have been well oiled, the planning has been carefully done, and action is ready to begin. Advocates need to be well greased not just on strategy, but on substance. Their work must be thorough and not based on superficial assumptions about children. All too often, advocates reduce their own potency because they see reality through one side of a prism. Only when advocates are scrupulously objective in gathering and using data will they be regarded with credibility by policymakers. Being well prepared also means building constituencies across traditional interest groups and across professional disciplines. Unfortunately, advocacy organizations all too often lose their potency by falling prey to exactly the same syndrome they charge bureaucracies with: turf guarding. Weisner describes situations in which legislators are bombarded with a disorganized collection of special interests as the "competitive model" of coalitions. He explains that this approach is generally poorly received and will not benefit these interests. No matter how well greased the wheels, if advocacy organizations are fractured they cannot go far.

Third, the advocacy community must work with early childhood practitioners to carve out realistic, appropriate, and differentiated roles for advocates and practitioners. Professional advocates need to spend time courting practitioners, not only policy-makers. It is exciting and chic to solicit support in state capitols and Washington, D. C., but this must not be done at the expense of soliciting support in local neighborhoods and communities. Practitioners offer perspectives and connections that will aid advocacy efforts. In return, professional advocates must assist practitioners in understanding the consequences of various policy initiatives in terms of their own programs. How would the addition of a school-based initiative impact my program? Which pieces of legislation would enable my community to augment its services mostappropriately?Whether such analyses are done on a program basis or in concert with other community providers, the first lens must focus on impact at the program and local level.

The fourth condition is that advocates must ground their positions in principles of child development. By doing so, advocates will automatically be required to place priority on quality and continuity in children's services. A "more slots" approach to policy is not sufficient. The field must craft a long-haul vision that simultaneously increases services and addresses the following problems, which are endemic to the field: (1), compensation and benefits; (2) the dichotomy between care and education; and (3) the social stratification of children.

Clearly the issue of insufficient compensation, including working conditions and benefits, must be addressed if the profession is to advance. The difficulty of attracting early childhood staff will foster "staff-stealing" and continue to put programs against each other. An overall strategy, devised to attract and recruit qualified people into child care and early education and to pay them adequately, is a necessary precondition for program expansion. No matter how many slots are funded, unless there are enough providers to teach children in these slots, programs will be precluded from opening. States simply, program expansion will be capped without adequate personnel. Program quality will also be diminished because, without adequate compensation, caregivers will leave the field, causing discontinuity for children and programs.

While the field is acknowledging that the dichotomy between care and education is a rhetorical rather than a reality-based issue, proposed legislation, with only a few exceptions, perpetuates the care-versus-education debate. As individuals and as a field, the early childhood community must stem the public perception that care is not educational and that education is not caring. The field must encourage people to acknowledge that quality exists in all sectors. All early childhood professionals need to guard against legislation that will fragment the field and work to ensure collaboration across sectors and programs. The field must stop stressing differences between care and education, and realize that legislative and programmatic success are contingent on a common vision.

Finally, for decades federal and state child care and early education policies have perpetuated intense social and economic stratification of children. Many programs have been established with stringent guidelines, making them accessible only to special-needs or low-income youngsters. Middle- and higher-income families must seek programs elsewhere. In effect, early childhood policies segregate preschool-age children by income when integration is the law for school-age youngsters who are merely one year older. While on the brink of exciting new efforts on behalf of children, the field of early childhood care and education must look beyond "more slots" and use these opportunities to alter policy stances that stratify children.

This is a new era, an era in which each member of the early childhood community has the chance to redress inequities in the field that have been troubling for so long. Now there is a chance to make some fundamental improvements that will improve child care and early education in this country for years to come. We must put ambivalence aside, muster our energy, and stay informed and active. The profession needs all its members, practitioners and advocates, now as never before.

1.2 From Jean-Claude Bringuier, *Conversations With Jean Piaget* (University of Chicago Press, 1980). Translated by Basia Miller Gulati. Copyright © 1980 by The University of Chicago. Reprinted by permission of University of Chicago Press. All rights reserved.

1.3 From David Elkind, "The Hurried Child: Is Our Impatient Society Depriving Kids of Their Right to Be Children?" *Instructor & Teacher*, vol. 91, no. 5 (May 1982). Copyright © 1982 by Scholastic, Inc. Reprinted by permission.

2.1 From Anna Freud and Dorothy T. Burlingham, *War and Children* (Medical War Books, 1943). Originally copyrighted by Foster Parents Plan for War Children, Inc., now known in the United States as Childreach. For information, contact Childreach, 155 Plan Way, Warwick, RI 02886-1099, 800-556-7918.

2.2 From Robert Coles, *The South Goes North: Volume III of Children of Crisis* (Little, Brown, 1971). Copyright © 1967, 1968, 1969, 1970, 1971 by Little, Brown & Company, Inc. Reprinted by permission.

2.3 From Marian Wright Edelman, *The Measure of Our Success: A Letter to My Children and Yours* (Beacon Press, 1992). Copyright © 1992 by Marian Wright Edelman. Reprinted by permission of Beacon Press.

3.1 From Abigail Adams Eliot, "Report of the Ruggles Street Nursery School and Training Center," in Samuel J. Braun and Esther P. Edwards, eds., *History and Theory of Early Childhood Education* (Wadsworth, 1972). Copyright © 1972 by Wadsworth Publishing Company. Reprinted by permission.

3.2 From Katherine H. Read, *The Nursery School: A Human Relationships Laboratory* (W. B. Saunders, 1950). Copyright © 1950 by W. B. Saunders, Inc. Copyright © 1955 and renewed 1983 by Holt, Rinehart & Winston, Inc. Reprinted by permission.

3.3 From Alice Sterling Honig, "Quality Infant/Toddler Caregiving: Are There Magic Recipes?" *Young Children*, vol. 44, no. 4 (May 1989), pp. 4–10. Copyright © 1989 by The National Association for the Education of Young Children. Reprinted by permission.

4.1 From Elizabeth P. Peabody, *Guide to the Kindergarten and Intermediate Class*, rev. ed. (E. Steiger, 1877).

4.2 From Patty Smith Hill, "Kindergarten," in *The American Educator Encyclopedia* (American Educator, 1941). Copyright © 1941 by The Association for Childhood Education International, 11501 Georgia Avenue, Suite 315, Wheaton, MD. Reprinted by permission.

4.3 From Bernard Spodek, "The Kindergarten: A Retrospective and Contemporary View," in Lilian G. Katz, ed., *Current Topics in Early Childhood Education*, vol. 4 (Ablex, 1982). Copyright © 1982 by Ablex Publishing Corporation. Reprinted by permission.

5.1 From Friedrich Froebel, *The Education of Man* (D. Appleton, 1897). Translated by W. N. Hailmann.

5.2 From Mildred B. Parten, "Social Participation Among Pre-School Children," *The Journal of Abnormal and Social Psychology*, vol. 27 (1932–1933).

5.3 From Lucy Sprague Mitchell, *Our Children and Our Schools: A Picture and Analysis of How Today's Public School Teachers Are Meeting the Challenge of New Knowledge and New Cultural Needs* (Simon & Schuster, 1951). Copyright © 1951 by Simon & Schuster, Inc. Reprinted by permission. Notes omitted.

372

Acknowledgments

6.1 From Maria Montessori, *The Montessori Method: Scientific Pedagogy as Applied to Child Education in "The Children's Houses"* (Robert Bentley, 1965). Translated by Ann E. George. Copyright © 1965 by Robert Bentley, Inc. Reprinted by permission.

6.2 From Harriet M. Johnson, *Children in the Nursery School* (John Day, 1928). Notes omitted.

6.3 From Sybil Kritchevsky, Elizabeth Prescott, and Lee Walling, *Planning Environments for Young Children: Physical Space* (National Association for the Education of Young Children, 1969). Copyright © 1969 by The National Association for the Education of Young Children. Reprinted by permission.

7.1 From John Dewey, "Three Years of the University Elementary School," Stenographic Report of a Speech Prepared for a Meeting of the Parents' Association of the University Elementary School (February 1899).

7.2 From Samuel Chester Parker and Alice Temple, *Unified Kindergarten and First-Grade Teaching* (Ginn & Company, 1925). References and some notes omitted.

7.3 From Elizabeth Jones and Louise Derman-Sparks, "Meeting the Challenge of Diversity," *Young Children*, vol. 47, no. 2 (January 1992), pp. 12–18. Copyright © 1992 by The National Association for the Education of Young Children. Reprinted by permission.

7.4 From *Developmentally Appropriate Practice in Early Childhood Programs Serving Children From Birth Through Age 8* (National Association for the Education of Young Children, 1987). Copyright © 1987 by The National Association for the Education of Young Children. Reprinted by permission. References omitted.

8.1 From Susan E. Blow, "Kindergarten Education," in Nicholas Murray Butler, ed., *Education in the United States* (J. B. Lyon, 1900). Notes omitted.

8.2 From Margaret McMillan, *The Nursery School* (E. P. Dutton, 1919).

8.3 From Robert Rosenthal and Lenore Jacobson, *Pygmalion in the Classroom: Teacher Expectation and Pupils' Intellectual Development* (Holt, Rinehart & Winston, 1968). Copyright © 1968 by Holt, Rinehart & Winston, Inc. Reprinted by permission. References omitted.

8.4 From Lilian G. Katz, "Developmental Stages of Preschool Teachers," *The Elementary School Journal*, vol. 23, no. 1 (1972), pp. 50–54. Copyright © 1972 by The University of Chicago. Reprinted by permission of University of Chicago Press.

9.1 From Dorothy H. Cohen and Virginia Stern, *Observing and Recording the Behavior of Young Children* (Teachers College Press, 1958). Copyright © 1958 by Teachers College, Columbia University. Reprinted by permission of Teachers College Press.

9.2 From Arnold Gesell, "Early Mental Growth," in Arnold Gesell et al., *The First Five Years of Life: A Guide to the Study of the Preschool Child* (Harper & Row, 1940). Copyright © 1940 by Pogoda Books, London, England. Reprinted by permission.

9.3 From Samuel J. Meisels, "Uses and Abuses of Developmental Screening and School Readiness Testing," *Young Children*, vol. 42, no. 2 (January 1987), pp. 4–9, 68–73. Copyright © 1987 by The National Association for the Education of Young Children. Reprinted by permission. References omitted.

10.1 From Bettye M. Caldwell, "What Is the Optimal Learning Environment for the Young Child?" *American Journal of Orthopsychiatry*, vol. 37, no. 1 (January 1967), pp. 8–21. Copyright © 1967 by The American Orthopsychiatric Association, Inc. Reprinted by permission.

10.2 From Margaret O'Brien Steinfels, *Who's Minding the Children? The History and Politics of Day Care in America* (Simon & Schuster, 1973). Copyright © 1973 by Margaret O'Brien Steinfels. Reprinted by permission of Simon & Schuster, Inc. Notes omitted.

10.3   From Ira J. Gordon, "Parent Education and Parent Involvement: Retrospect and Prospect," *Childhood Education*, vol. 54 (1977), pp. 71–79. Copyright © 1977 by The Association for Childhood Education. Reprinted by permission. References omitted.

11.1   From Robert Owen, *The Life of Robert Owen* (1857).

11.2   From James L. Hymes, "Industrial Day Care's Roots in America," *Proceedings of the Conference on Industry and Day Care* (1970). Copyright © 1970 by James L. Hymes. Reprinted by permission.

12.1   From Doak S. Campbell, Frederick H. Bair, and Oswald L. Harvey, *Educational Activities of the Works Progress Administration* (U.S. Government Printing Office, 1939). Notes omitted.

12.2   From Keith Osborn, "Project Head Start: An Assessment," *Educational Leadership* (November 1965). Copyright © 1965 by The Association for Supervision and Curriculum Development. Reprinted by permission.

12.3   From Rochelle Beck, "The White House Conferences on Children: An Historical Perspective," *Harvard Educational Review*, vol. 43, no. 4 (November 1973), pp. 653–668. Copyright © 1973 by the President and Fellows of Harvard College. Reprinted by permission. All rights reserved.

13.1   From G. Stanley Hall, "The Contents of Children's Minds on Entering School," in Theodate L. Smith, ed., *Aspects of Child Life and Education by G. Stanley Hall and Some of His Pupils* (Ginn & Company, 1907). Notes omitted.

13.2   From Greta G. Fein and Alison Clarke-Stewart, *Day Care in Context* (John Wiley, 1973). Copyright © 1973 by Greta G. Fein and Alison Clarke-Stewart. Reprinted by permission. References omitted.

13.3   From Lawrence J. Schweinhart and David P. Weikart, "Changed Lives, Significant Benefits: The High/Scope Perry Preschool Project to Date," *High/Scope Resource* (Summer 1993). Copyright © 1993 by The High/Scope Educational Research Foundation. Reprinted by permission.

14.1   From Dorothy W. Baruch, "When the Need for Wartime Services for Children Is Past—What of the Future?" *Journal of Consulting Psychology* (1945). References and some notes omitted.

14.2   From Marvin Lazerson, "Social Reform and Early-Childhood Education: Some Historical Perspectives," *Urban Education* (April 1970), pp. 84–87, 89–91, 93–101. Copyright © 1970 by Sage Publications, Inc. Reprinted by permission. References omitted.

14.3   From Sharon Lynn Kagan, "The New Advocacy in Early Childhood Education," *Teachers College Record*, vol. 90, no. 3 (Spring 1989). Copyright © 1989 by Teachers College, Columbia University. Reprinted by permission of Teachers College Press. Notes omitted.

Index

a priori thought, 21
abandonment, fear of, in children living through wars, 29–36
Abbot, Grace, 304
ability grouping, 204
Abrams, Eliot, 46
academic achievement, hurried children and, 24, 25
achievement training, for disadvantaged children, 198–199
active learning, 120, 343, 345
activities, physical environment and, 135–143
adaptive behavior, mental growth and, 231–232
adaptivity, intelligence as, 251
ADC (Aid to Dependent Children), 302
Addams, Jane, 305
adoption, 43
advocacy, early childhood education and, 366–370
after-school care, 181
aggression: in children living through wars, 33, 35; toddlers and, 74
air raid anxiety, in children living through wars, 34–36
altruism, infants and toddlers and, 74–75
American Dream, collapse of, 43
American Froebel Union, 78
Ames, Louise Bates, 239, 241, 243
Anderson, J. E., 251
antibias curriculum, 160–168
arithmetic. See mathematics
art, 87, 97, 125–126, 152, 172, 175, 299; in nursery school, 58, 64–65
Arunta people, of Australia, 22
Asbell, Bernard, 201
assessment: observation and, 211–245; preschool programs and, 346–347
Association of Childhood Education International, 82, 90, 156, 269
associative group play, in nursery school, 114–119
Australia, Arunta people of, 22
authoritative parenting, 74–75
authority, fear of, conscience and, 35–36
autoeducation, 130–131
autonomy vs. shame and doubt, Erikson's theory of, 3–13

"back to basics" movement, 170
Bagdikian, Ben, 263, 264
Bair, Frederick H., on educational activities of the Works Progress Administration 289–296
Bakker, Jim, 46
balls, as toys, 110–111
Bank Street School, 120–129, 329
Barr Scale for Occupational Intelligence, 115
Baruch, Dorothy W., on post–World War I child-care services, 350–357
basal reader, 173, 174
Baumrind, Diana, 74
Bayley, Nancy, 252
Beck, Alice, 96
Beck, Rochelle, on the White House Conferences on Children, 303–316
before-school care, 181
Binet, Alfred, 251
biology, personality and, 4–5
blocks, 97, 137–138; Froebel and, 109–110, 111–112; recording children's use of, 211, 223
Bloom, Benjamin, 95, 253, 362
Blow, Susan E., on kindergarten education 185–190
body movements, child's use of material and, 216–217
Boesky, Ivan, 46
Brain, George, 298
Braun, Samuel J., 53
Bringuier, Jean-Claude, interview with Jean Piaget by, 14–22
Bronfenbrenner, Urie, 265
Brown v. Board of Education of Topeka, Kansas, 313
Bryan, Anna, E., 156
Buchanan, James, 280
Burlingham, Dorothy T., on children in crisis, 29–36
Butler, Nicholas Murray, 186

Cahen, Leonard, 202
Caldwell, Bettye M., on the optimal learning environment for the young child, 246–25
Califano, Joseph, 269

375

*Notable
Selections in
Early
Childhood
Education*

Campbell, Doak S., on educational activities of the Works Progress Administration, 289–296

Carter, Jimmy, 47

catastrophes, understanding of, in children living through wars, 29–36

Child Development Center, Head Start and, 298–299, 301

child-centered education, 96

Children's Bill of Rights (1970), 303, 312

Children's Bureau, 267–268

Children's Defense Fund, 42

choices, nursery school children and, 58, 60

Churchill, Winston, 42

Clark, Burton, 201

Clark, Kenneth, 202

Clarke-Stewart, Alison, on day care, 329–336

classical conditioning, 268

clay, recording children's use of, 211–223

Cleveland, Grover, 78

closed system model, of human development, 251

cognitive facilitation, in infant/toddler programs, 75

cognitive growth, day care and, 251–252

Cohen, Dorothy H., on recording a child's use of materials, 211–223

Coles, Robert, on vitality in ghetto children, 37–41

colic, 7

"colorblind," teachers as, 162

Commissioner of Education's Annual Report of 1870, 78–79

Community Coordinated Child Care Program, 332

Community Impact Model, of parent education, 274–275

community work, kindergartens and, 82–84

comparisons, children and, 58, 61–62

compensatory education, 363

competence, children's: day care and, 334; personality development and, 252

competition, children and, 58, 61–62

competitive model, of coalitions, 368

complex play units, 144–149

Comprehensive Child Development Act, 260

compulsory schooling laws, 259

conciseness, in lessons, 131–134

concrete operations, 16, 343

conscience, 11, 177; fear of authority and, 35–36

consolidation, as developmental stage of preschool teachers, 205–210

constructive aggregations, 109

continuity of care, in infant/toddler programs, 75

copying, use of, in art, 125

crisis, children in, 29–49

cultural deprivation, 358, 362

cultural diversity, in the classroom, 160–168

curriculum: antibias, 160–168; developmentally appropriate, 169–181; unified, for nursery school, kindergarten, and primary grades, 90–91

dame school, 78

dancing, 125

Dann, Sophie, 250

Dante, 131, 188

day care, 246–258, 259–265, 311, 329–336; employer-sponsored, 279–288

day nurseries, 53–77

death, understanding of, in children living through wars, 29–36

Deaver, Michael, 46

Demos, John, 262–263

Derman-Sparks, Louise, on cultural diversity in the classroom, 160–168

destruction, reaction to, in children living through wars, 32–34, 35

developmental screening tests, 233–245

developmental stages, of preschool teachers, 205–210

developmental theories, kindergarten and, 95–96

developmentally appropriate practice, 164, 169–181, 242, 342, 345; in employer-sponsored day care, 279–282

Dewey, Emily, 120

Dewey, John, 120–121, 156, 157–158, 267, 308, 317; on three years of the university elementary school, 150–155

diagnostically oriented kindergarten, 98

discipline, 131, 363; nursery school children and, 67–68

discovery learning, 279

divergent thinking, 344

diversity, cultural, in the classroom, 160–168

divorce, 307

double development, 185

double sessions, in kindergarten, 84, 361

dramatic play, 122–123, 128, 139, 221

drug abuse, 43, 45

Edelman, Marian Wright, on children in America, 42–49

educare, 246

Education Professions Development Act, 330

Edwards, Esther P., 53

Elementary and Secondary Education Act of 1965, 198, 199–200

Eliot, Abigail Adams, on nursery schools, 53–55

Elkind, David, on the hurried child, 23–28

Ellison, Ralph, 38

employer-sponsored day care, 279–288

environmental issues, 43

376

*Notable
Selections in
Early
Childhood
Education*

Erikson, Erik, 29, 72, 343; on a healthy personality for every child, 3–13
ethnic issues, in the classroom, 160–168
evaluation: developmentally appropriate practice and, 178–179; of disadvantaged children, 202–213; importance of, to nursery school teachers, 56–70
experiments, science and, 175
exploration needs of infants and toddlers, 72–73
extensity, social participation and, 116

factory system, schools as, 25–26
family, effect of day care on, 259–265
Family Impact Model, of parent education, 270–272, 274
family preservation services, 48
fear, anxiety and, 35
federal government, early childhood education and, 289–316
feeding, of infants, sense of trust and, 6, 7, 73, 74
Fein, Greta G., on day care, 329–336
Follow Through, 96, 98, 266, 268, 269, 273
formative aggregations, 109
foster care, 48, 352, 353
Freedman's Bureau, 47
Freud, Anna, on children in crisis, 29–36, 250
Freud, Sigmund, 3, 29
Froebel, Friedrich, 78, 82–91, 94, 96, 158, 185–190, 192, 267; on the school and the family, 107–129
Frost, Joe, 269

Gesell, Arnold, 268, 317; on early mental growth, 224–232
Gesell School Readiness Screening Test, controversy over, 233–245
ghetto children, vitality in, 37–41
gifted children, 198
gifts, Froebel's theory of, 107–113, 187, 189
Goethe, 188
Gordon, Ira J., on parent education and parent involvement, 266–275
grades, developmentally appropriate practice and, 178–179
Great Depression, and educational activities of the Works Progress Administration, 289–296
grouping, developmentally appropriate practice and, 179–180
growth, and learning, 3–28
guidance, in kindergarten, 85, 87–89
gun control, 43, 45

Haines, Jacqueline, 239
Hall, G. Stanley, 82, 224; on the contents of children's minds on entering school, 317–328
halo effect, disadvantaged children and, 202
handicapped children, 226
hand-work, in school, 153–154, 157
handwriting, 158–159
Harding, Warren, 47
Harvey, Oswald L., on educational activities of the Works Progress Administration, 289–296
Head Start, 40, 46, 47, 48, 96, 100, 268, 269, 273, 283, 297–302, 336, 346, 347, 359, 362, 363, 364
health care, for infants and toddlers, 74, 175
Herodotus, 188
hidden assumptions, day care and, 249–255
High/Scope Perry Preschool Project, 337–349
Hill, Patty Smith, on kindergarten, 82–91
history, 152, 154
home experiences, dramatic play and, 122
Home Start, 268, 269, 273
homelessness, 45–46
Homer, 188
Honig, Alice Sterling, on quality infant/toddler caregiving, 71–77
Hoover, Herbert, 303, 307, 314
human right, childhood as, 28
Hunt, M. McVicker, 95, 362
hurried child, Elkind's theory of, 23–28
Hussein, Saddam, 46
Hymes, James L., 298; on industrial day care's roots in America, 283–288
hyperactivity, 25
hypotheses, science and, 175

Ilg, Frances, 243
imagination, 11–12
immigration, parent education and, 267, 268, 360, 362
income, and school success, 198
independence, growth of, in nursery school children, 58, 65–66, 177
independently generated experiences, child-initiated learning and, 343–344
individual attention, infant/toddler caregiving and, 71–77
individuality, as one of Froebel's gifts, 111
indoor play equipment, for nursery schools, 142–143
initiative vs. guilt, Erikson's theory of, 3–13, 343, 344
institutions, infants raised in, trust and, 6–7, 10, 248–251, 252
intelligence, as adaptivity, 251
intensity, social participation and, 116
intent, child-initiated learning and, 343–344

International Federation for Parent Education, 268
International Kindergarten Union, 82, 90, 156
interpretation, importance of, to teachers of nursery school children, 56–70, 220
interview technique, Piaget and, 14–22
invented spelling, 173–174

Jackson, Shamal, 44
Jacobson, Lenore, on disadvantaged children, 196–204
Johnson, Harriet M., 120; on the physical environment for learning, 135–143
Johnson, Lyndon, 47, 199, 359, 362
Jones, Elizabeth, on cultural diversity in the classroom, 160–168

Kagan, Sharon Lynn, on the new advocacy in early childhood education, 366–370
Kaiser Day Care Centers (Portland, OR), during World War II, 283–288
Kant, Immanuel, 21
Katz, Lillian G., 92, 202, 343; on developmental stages of preschool teachers, 205–210
Kennedy, John F., 47, 362
kindergarten, 24, 78–103, 107–113, 150, 317–328; curriculum for, 120–129; evolution of, 360–362; mental growth in, 224–231; screening tests for, 233–245; training teachers for, 185–190; unification of curriculum of, with first grade, 156–159
Kinderseminar, Freud's, 29
Kluckhohn, Florence, 199
Kritchevsky, Sybil, on how to analyze play space, 144–149

Lally, J. Ronald, 71
language, 16; mental growth and, 231–232
language arts, 139, 173–174; in kindergarten, 126–127. See also reading
language mastery experiences, for infants and toddlers, 73
Lanham Act, 353, 354, 357
late bloomers, 24
laws of learning, 85, 87
Lazerson, Marvin, on social reform and early childhood education, 358–365
learning, and growth, 3–28
"learning by doing," Dewey's theory of, 150
learning centers, 172
learning disabilities, 25
learning environments, 130–149
learning to learn, 358
Leopardi, Giacomo, 323
Leviticus, 267
Lincoln, Abraham, 46–47, 78

lines, as one of Froebel's gifts, 112
Lipton, Rose, 248
local government, rights of, federal child-care programs and, 314–315
love: ability to, healthy personality and, 4; infant/toddler caregiving and, 71–77
Lowenberg, Miriam, 285

Madison, James, 47
mainstreaming, 180, 267–268
manipulatives, math, 174
Mann, Horace, 78
Mann, Mary, 79. See also Peabody, Mary
materials, recording a child's use of, 211–223; for use in the school's physical environment, 135–143
mathematics, 97, 98, 110, 133, 158, 172, 174
matter, conservation of, 20–21
maturationist view, of child development, 237–238
maturity, as developmental stage of preschool teachers, 205–210
McClure, Jessica, 43–44
McMillan, Margaret, 54, 55; on the training of nursery school teachers, 191–195
media, 24, 43
Meisels, Samuel J., on the uses and abuses of developmental screening and school readiness testing, 233–245
memory, picturesque, 80
mental growth, early, 228–232
Miller Analogy Test, 271
minimal brain damage, 25
Mitchell, Lucy Sprague, 135; on learning through play and experience, 120–129
models, use of, in art, 58, 64–65, 125
Montessori, Maria, 55, 96, 142; on how lessons should be given, 130–149
morally lost, America as, 45
Morgan, G. Campbell, 42
morning talk, in kindergarten, 87
Morrill Land-Grant Act, 46–47
Mother Play, 187, 188
mothers, day care and, 249–250
motivation, 177–178
motor characteristics, mental growth and, 231–232
Moynihan, Daniel Patrick, 273
multicultural education, 160–168, 175–176
Murphy, Lois B., 252
music, 54, 97, 125–126, 143, 157, 172, 175

NAEYC (National Association for the Education of Young Children), 161, 92–103, 205, 242, 246; on developmentally appropriate curriculum, 169–181
National Association of Nursery Educators, 283, 351

378

*Notable
Selections in
Early
Childhood
Education*

National Council of Primary Education, 156
neighborhood, as part of kindergarten curriculum, 123–125, 152
Neimeyer, Jack, 298
New Deal, 47
Nixon, Richard M., 260, 359, 360
nuclear family, 261
nuclear weapons, 308–309
nursery schools, 53–77, 317, 362–365; and the High/Scope Perry Preschool Project, 337–349; mental growth in, 225–231; modern improvements in theory and curriculum of, 85–91; physical environment of, 135–143; social participation in, 114–119; teachers of, 191–195, 205–210; Works Progress Administration and, 289–296

obedience, as one of Froebel's gifts, 111
object lessons, in kindergarten, 78–81
object permanence, 16
objectivity, in lessons, 131–134
observation: and assessment, 211–245; importance of, to nursery school teachers, 56–70; science and, 175
occupations, Freobel's theory of, 107–113, 187
Ojemann, Ralph, 268
onlooker behavior, in nursery school children, 117
operant conditioning, 268
organized, cooperative group play, in nursery school, 114–119
Osborn, Keith, on Head Start, 297–302
outdoor play equipment, for nursery schools, 140–141
Owen, Robert, on employer-sponsored day care, 279–282

paint, recording child's use of, 211–223
Paley, Vivian, 166
parallel play, in nursery school, 114–119
parent education, 307–308; and Works Progress Administration, 289–296
parents, 246–275, 342, 345; kindergarten and, 85, 89–90
Parker, Samuel Chester, on the history of the unifying of kindergarten and first-grade education, 156–159
Parten, Mildred B., on social participation among preschool children, 114–119
patterns, use of, in art, 58, 64–65
Peabody, Elizabeth P., on object lessons in kindergarten, 78–81
Peabody, Mary, 78. *See also* Mann, Mary
peek-a-boo, 6
permanent use, of play equipment in nursery school, 139–140
perseverence, 177
personal control, sense of, 344

personality, as one of Froebel's gifts, 111
personality development, in children, Erikson's theory of, 3–13
personal-social behavior, mental growth and, 231–232
Pestalozzi, Johann, 89, 267, 275
philanthropy, kindergartens and, 82–84, 360, 361
phonics, 174
physical education, 154, 172, 175, 176
physical environment, activities and materials for, 135–143
Piaget, Jean, 14–22, 23, 95, 164, 238, 251, 343
picturesque memory, 80
play, 107–129; hurried children and, 27–28; for infants and toddlers, 73–74; in nursery schools, 54–55; symbolic, 16
play materials, in kindergarten, 85–87
play space, how to analyze, 144–149
points, as one of Froebel's gifts, 112
policy, early childhood education, 350–370
positive form, use of, for suggestions, 58–60
post-traumatic stress syndrome, 45
potential units, of play space, 145
poverty, effect of, on children, 37–41, 42–48, 196–204; preschool programs and, 337–349, 358–365
Pratt, Caroline, 120, 141
prejudice, cultural diversity and, 161–162
premature birth, 44
preoperational thought, 16, 343
Prescott, Elizabeth, on how to analyze play space, 144–149
prescriptive programs, in kindergarten, 93
pressure, hurried children and, 23–28
Primary Council, 82, 90
primary grades: curriculum for, 120–129; modern improvements in theory and curriculum of, 85–91; unification of curriculum of, with kindergarten, 156–159
productive activities, in kindergarten, 185
progressive education, 94, 267, 308, 362
progressive use, of play equipment in nursery school, 139–140
project learning, 96, 150, 171, 172, 205
prosocial behaviors, in infants and toddlers, 74–75, 176
Provence, Sally, 248
psychonanalysis, 29
psychopathic personality, mistrust and, 6
psychosocial development, Erikson's theory of, 3–13
Public Law 94–142, 269
public schools, 46–47

quality infant/toddler caregiving, 71–77
quality of life, improved, for participants in High/Scope Perry Preschool Project, 337–349

379

*Notable
Selections in
Early
Childhood
Education*

quiet play, in nursery school, 54–55

racism, cultural diversity and, 160–168
Read, Katherine H., on the teacher's role in nursery school, 56–70
readiness, kindergarten, 94–95; standardized tests to assess, 233–245
reading, 73, 97, 98, 159, 187, 268, 361; hurried children and, 25
reconstruction, as one of Froebel's gifts, 112
redirection, motivation and, 58, 63–64, 177
reflections, child-initiated learning and, 343–344
reflective activities in kindergarten, 185
reform, early childhood education and, 350–370
rejection, children's perception of hurrying as, 27
reliability, of school readiness tests, 233–245
renewal, as developmental stage of preschool teachers, 205–210
research, 317–349
resignation, in ghetto children, 40, 41
resourcefulness, of ghetto children, 38
retention, 24, 179, 341
reversibility, 20
Rheingold, Harriet, 252
Richmond, Julius B., 298
Rogers, Carl, 268
Roosevelt, Franklin, 290
Roosevelt, Theodore, 303, 304
Rosenthal, Robert, on disadvantaged children, 196–204
Rousseau, Jean-Jacques, 252

San Antonio Independent School District v. Rodriguez, 313
School Impact Model, of parent education, 273–274
schools, as factory system, 25–26
Schweinhart, Lawrence, J., on the High/Scope Perry Preschool Project, 337–349
science, 97, 152, 153–154, 172, 174–175, 187, 299
self-fulfilling prophecy, disadvantaged children and, 196–204
semi-structured play materials, 213
sense experiences, play and, 138
sensory-motor intelligence, 16, 73
Serrano v. Priest, 313
setting, child's use of materials and, 214
settlement houses, 360
shared activities, for infants and toddlers, 73–74
Shaw, Quincy, 318
short-sighted, America as, 46–47
simple play units, 144–149
simplicity, in lessons, 131–134

single-parent families, 44, 46
sky, children's ideas about, 325–327
Smith, Theodate L., 317
social and emotional growth, day care and, 251–252
social reform, and early childhood education, 358–365
Social Security Act, 45
social studies, 172, 174–175
social value, of reading, 159
social welfare, kindergartens and, 82–84
social-emotional development, 176–177; day care and, 251–252
Society for the Prevention of Cruelty to Children, 306, 314
solitary play, in nursery school, 114–119
Sophocles, 188
sound practice, 150–181
space requirements, for nursery school, 137, 144–149
spelling, invented, 173–174
Spencer, Herbert, 191, 192
spiritually impoverished, America as, 45
Spock, Benjamin, 8, 260, 309
Spodek, Bernard, on kindergarten, 92–103
staffing, developmentally appropriate practice and, 179–180
standardized testing of disadvantaged children, 203–204; in kindergarten, 97–99; for school readiness, 233–245
states' rights, federal child-care programs and, 314–315
Steinberg, Lisa, 43
Steinfels, Margaret O'Brien, on the history of day care in America, 259–265
Stern, Virginia, on recording a child's use of materials, 211–223
stimulus, child's use of materials and, 214
Stolz, Lois Meek, 284
strategic positions, for supervision, nursery school teachers and, 58, 68–69
structured play materials, 213
suggestions, effective, to nursery school children, 58, 66–67
super play units, 144–149
supervision, strategic positions for, in nursery school, 58, 68–69
Supreme Court, 313
surfaces, as one of Froebel's gifts, 111–112
survival, as developmental stage of preschool teachers, 205–210
symbolic play, 16
Synoptical Table of Gifts and Occupations, 111–112

Taussig Industrial Classification, 115
teachers: cultural diversity in the classroom and, 160–168; inadequate preparation of kindergarten, 99–100; preparation and

380

*Notable
Selections in
Early
Childhood
Education*

development of, 185–210; role of, in nursery school, 56–70
television, children and, 263–264
temperament, infant/toddler caregiving and, 72–73
Temple, Alice, on the history of the unifying of kindergarten and first-grade education, 156–159
testing, standardized: of disadvantaged children, 203–204; in kindergarten, 97–99; for school readiness, 233–245
theme approach, to curriculum, 121–122, 174–175, 187
3Rs curriculum, in kindergarten, 94–95, 96
time, hurried child and, 26–27
Title I program, 198, 199–200, 268, 269, 273
toilet training, 9
tracking, 204
transition grade, between kindergarten and first grade, 179
transitions, between activities, 181
Truman, Harry, 309
trust vs. mistrust, Erikson's theory of, 3–13, 344

unity, as one of Froebel's gifts, 111
unoccupied behavior, social participation and, 116–117
unstructured play materials, 213

validity, of school readiness tests, 233–245
variety, play spaces and, 146, 147

verification, science and, 175
violence: in America, 42–48; effect of television, on children, 263–264
vitality, in ghetto children, 37–41
voice, tone of, used with nursery school children, 58, 61, 62–63
volume, conservation of, 20–21
volunteers, in child-care centers, 354–355

Wald, Lillian, 304, 305
Walling, Lee, on how to analyze play space, 144–149
war, effect of, on children, 29–36
War on Poverty, 47, 268, 362
Watson, John B., 255, 268
webbing, curriculum, 150
weight, conservation of, 20–21
Weikart, David P., on the High/Scope Perry Preschool Project, 337–349
welfare, 40, 41, 47
White, R. W., 252
White House Conferences on Children, historical perspective on, 226, 265, 303–316
Wiggin, Kate Douglas, 360
Wilson, Woodrow, 47
work, ability to, healthy personality and, 4
Works Progress Administration, educational activities of, 289–296
World War II, effects of, on English children, 29–36; employer-sponsored day care during, 283–288; need for child-care services following, 350–357